I0795632

# DISTANT STAGE

Rethinking Canada in the World
Series editors: Ian McKay and Sean Mills

Supported by the Wilson Institute for Canadian History at McMaster University, this series is committed to books that rethink Canadian history from transnational and global perspectives. It enlarges approaches to the study of Canada in the world by exploring how Canadian history has long been a dynamic product of global currents and forces. The series will also reinvigorate understanding of Canada's role as an international actor and how Canadians have contributed to intellectual, political, cultural, social, and material exchanges around the world.

Volumes included in the series explore the ideas, movements, people, and institutions that have transcended political boundaries and territories to shape Canadian society and the state. These include both state and non-state actors, and phenomena such as international migration, diaspora politics, religious movements, evolving conceptions of human rights and civil society, popular culture, technology, epidemics, wars, and global finance and trade.

The series charts a new direction by exploring networks of transmission and exchange from a standpoint that is not solely national or international, expanding the history of Canada's engagement with the world.

http://wilson.humanities.mcmaster.ca

1 Canada and the United Nations
Legacies, Limits, Prospects
*Edited by Colin McCullough and Robert Teigrob*

2 Undiplomatic History
The New Study of Canada and the World
*Edited by Asa McKercher and Philip Van Huizen*

3 Revolutions across Borders
Jacksonian America and the Canadian Rebellion
*Edited by Maxime Dagenais and Julien Mauduit*

4 Left Transnationalism
The Communist International and the National, Colonial, and Racial Questions
*Edited by Oleksa Drachewych and Ian McKay*

5 Landscapes of Injustice
A New Perspective on the Internment and Dispossession of Japanese Canadians
*Edited by Jordan Stanger-Ross*

6 Canada's Other Red Scare
Indigenous Protest and Colonial Encounters during the Global Sixties
*Scott Rutherford*

7 The Global Politics of Poverty in Canada
Development Programs and Democracy, 1964–1979
*Will Langford*

8 Schooling the System
A History of Black Women Teachers
*Funké Aladejebi*

9 Constant Struggle
Histories of Canadian Democratizatin
*Edited by Julien Mauduit and Jennifer Tunnicliffe*

10 The Racial Mosaic
A Pre-history of Canadian Multiculturalism
*Daniel R. Meister*

11 Dominion over Palm and Pine
A History of Canadian Aspirations in the British Caribbean
*Paula Hastings*

12 Harvesting Labour
Tobacco and the Global Making of Canada's Agricultural Workforce
*Edward Dunsworth*

13 Distant Stage
Quebec, Brazil, and the Making of Canada's Cultural Diplomacy
*Eric Fillion*

# Distant Stage

## *Quebec, Brazil, and the Making of Canada's Cultural Diplomacy*

ERIC FILLION

McGill-Queen's University Press
Montreal & Kingston • London • Chicago

© McGill-Queen's University Press 2022

ISBN 978-0-2280-1414-0 (cloth)
ISBN 978-0-2280-1415-7 (paper)
ISBN 978-0-2280-1512-3 (ePDF)
ISBN 978-0-2280-1513-0 (ePUB)

Legal deposit fourth quarter 2022
Bibliothèque nationale du Québec

Printed in Canada on acid-free paper that is 100% ancient forest free (100% post-consumer recycled), processed chlorine free

This book has been published with the help of a grant from the Canadian Federation for the Humanities and Social Sciences, through the Awards to Scholarly Publications Program, using funds provided by the Social Sciences and Humanities Research Council of Canada.

Financé par le gouvernement du Canada | Funded by the Government of Canada | Canada | Conseil des arts du Canada | Canada Council for the Arts

We acknowledge the support of the Canada Council for the Arts.

Nous remercions le Conseil des arts du Canada de son soutien.

---

**Library and Archives Canada Cataloguing in Publication**

Title: Distant stage: Quebec, Brazil, and the making of Canada's cultural diplomacy / Eric Fillion.

Names: Fillion, Eric, author.

Series: Rethinking Canada in the world; 13.

Description: Series statement: Rethinking Canada in the world; 13 | Includes bibliographical references and index.

Identifiers: Canadiana (print) 2022026600X | Canadiana (ebook) 20220266212 | ISBN 9780228014140 (cloth) | ISBN 9780228014157 (paper) | ISBN 9780228015123 (ePDF) | ISBN 9780228015130 (ePUB)

Subjects: LCSH: Cultural diplomacy—Canada—History—20th century. | LCSH: Cultural diplomacy—Brazil—History—20th century. | LCSH: Canada—Foreign relations—Brazil. | LCSH: Brazil—Foreign relations—Canada. | LCSH: Canada—Cultural policy. | LCSH: Brazil—Cultural policy.

Classification: LCC FC251.B72 F55 2022 | DDC 303.48/271081—DC23

---

This book was typeset by Marquis Interscript in 10.5/13 Sabon.

# Contents

# Acknowledgments

Putting pen to paper to draft the opening sentences of this section of *Distant Stage* should not be difficult, but it is. I wrestle with words and turns of phrases, even clichés, when all that I really want to express are deep-felt thanks. I am indebted to too many people for joining me in thinking about the questions that inspired this project; for offering insightful comments on earlier iterations of the book or some of its parts; for helping me find the time and focus to research, write, revisit, and rewrite this history of Quebec-Brazil-Canada cultural relations.

Graham Carr deserves my deepest gratitude for having urged me to pursue my interest in the topic of cultural diplomacy. He brought to this project his enthusiasm, positivity, and immense knowledge, not to mention his patient advice and unwavering support. There are, of course, other Concordians whom I wish to thank: Peter Gossage, Ronald Rudin, Barbara Lorenzkowski, Nora Jaffary, Mary Vipond, Elena Razlogova, Eric Reiter, Donna Whittaker, Jean François Mayer, and Jean-Philippe Warren. On the other side of Mount Royal, at Université de Montréal, David Meren was unsparing in his help and efforts to initiate fascinating discussions, many of which left an imprint on the pages of this book: *merci*!

Sean Mills was just extraordinary during my two-year tenure as a post-doctoral fellow at the University of Toronto. *Distant Stage*, in its current form, would not exist without his constant encouragement and the generosity with which he shared his expertise and passion. In Toronto, I was privileged to be able to workshop some of the book's chapters with faculty members, post-doctoral fellows, and graduate students. A special shout-out to Luis van Isschot, Tamara Walker, Yvon Wang, Lucia Dacome, Timo Schaefer, Matthieu Caron,

Ed Dunsworth, Simon Vickers, Thomas Blampied, Kate Bauer, and Cathleen Clark. My sincere thanks also to Brendan Kelly, who is now at Global Affairs Canada.

I also want to acknowledge Karen Dubinsky, Lisa Pasolli, Steven Maynard, Rebecca Manley, and Matthew Colby for welcoming me at Queen's University, where I managed to put the finishing touches on this monograph. Also in Kingston, Lynda Jessup, Jeffrey Brison, and their North American Cultural Diplomacy Initiative colleagues provided much in the way of intellectual stimulation, preparing me – even if they did not know it – for my move to the city while providing me with opportunities to think more broadly about the significance of my research.

To my Brazilian friends and colleagues (and Portuguese-language instructors) at both ends of the hemisphere (in Montreal and Toronto as well as in Rio de Janeiro, São Paulo, and Brasília): *muito obrigado!* Special and wholehearted thanks go out to Mônica Leite Lessa, Pedro Henrique Belchior Rodrigues, Ariana Pedrosa, and Glauber Biazo.

I am also much obliged to my dear comrade John Gilmore, who was always an email away when I struggled to decipher the poor handwriting of some of the impromptu ambassadors discussed in this book. "Lacka daisical," really? There are many other brilliant people (most of them strangers) who prompted me to approach the topic of cultural diplomacy from angles I had not considered, providing timely, pertinent suggestions in classrooms or at conferences where I presented portions of what would become *Distant Stage*. They are important, even if unnamed.

The Social Sciences and Humanities Research Council of Canada, Concordia University, Fonds de recherche du Québec – Société et culture, University of Toronto, and Queen's University helped fund various stages of the research and writing of this book. I thank them for their generous support.

My gratitude extends to the archivists, librarians, and analysts who helped me find my way through their holdings, providing on-site or remote access to the thousands of pages (not to mention the countless photographs and recordings) on which this research is based. Many provided images for the book. I appreciate their willingness to photograph or digitize material amid difficult pandemic times.

Working with McGill-Queen's University Press has been but a pleasure. Jonathan Crago has been exceptional, believing in *Distant Stage* from its inception and guiding me with his colleagues – Elli Stylianou,

Kathleen Fraser, Jacqueline Davis, Jennifer Roberts, Alyssa Favreau, Filomena Falocco, and Ryan Perks, among others – through the many steps of the publication process. I wish to express additional thanks to Sean Mills and Ian McKay, editors of the Rethinking Canada in the World series, as well as the anonymous readers who reviewed my manuscript and offered valuable insights to help me tell a better, more compelling and complex story.

Valérie, I dedicate *Distant Stage* to you. Not only did you learn Portuguese with me, but you are also the best person in the world. I cannot imagine these last nine years (and more) without your cheerfulness and optimistic disposition. I am beyond fortunate to have you in my life.

# Abbreviations

| | |
|---|---|
| ACI | Arquivo Central do Itamaraty |
| AFEUL | Archives de folklore et d'ethnologie, Université Laval |
| AHI | Arquivo Histórico do Itamaraty |
| AN | Arquivo Nacional |
| BAnQ | Bibliothèque et Archives nationales du Québec |
| BANUFRJ | Biblioteca Alberto Nepomuceno, Universidade Federal do Rio de Janeiro |
| BBC-OS | British Broadcasting Corporation Overseas Service |
| CBC | Canadian Broadcasting Corporation |
| CBC-IS | International Service of the Canadian Broadcasting Corporation |
| CGEC | Canadian Government Exhibition Commission |
| CMQM | Conservatoire de musique du Québec à Montréal |
| CPR | Canadian Pacific Railway |
| CRCCFUO | Centre de recherche en civilisation canadienne-française, Université d'Ottawa |
| DCI | Divisão de Cooperação Intelectual |
| DGDAUDM | Division de la gestion de documents et des archives, Université de Montréal |
| DIP | Departamento de Imprensa e Propaganda |
| ESMO | École supérieure de musique d'Outremont |
| FB | Fundação Bienal |
| FGV-CPDOC | Fundação Getúlio Vargas, Centro de Pesquisa e Documentação de História Contemporânea do Brasil |
| KLSCDU | Killam Library Special Collections, Dalhousie University |
| LAC | Library and Archives Canada |

| | |
|---|---|
| LON | League of Nations |
| MC | Musée de la civilisation |
| MES | Ministério da Educação e Saúde |
| MVL | Museu Villa-Lobos |
| NA | National Archives |
| NFB | National Film Board of Canada |
| NGC | National Gallery of Canada |
| NGCLA | National Gallery of Canada Library and Archives |
| OCIAA | Office of the Coordinator of Inter-American Affairs |
| OCSM | Orchestre des concerts symphoniques de Montréal |
| OSB | Orquestra Sinfônica Brasileira |
| OSM | Orchestre symphonique de Montréal |
| PAU | Pan-American Union |
| PQ | Parti Québécois |
| SAGDUQÀM | Service des archives et de gestion des documents, Université du Québec à Montréal |
| SEMA | Superintendência de Educação Musical e Artística |
| TSO | Toronto Symphony Orchestra |
| UCLA | Union culturelle des Latins d'Amérique |

Jean Désy (centre) surrounded by President Getúlio Vargas (left) and Oswaldo Aranha (right) at a meeting of South American foreign affairs ministers, 1942 (FGV-CPDOC, OA-foto-256/10).

Corinne de Boucherville and her two children, Mariel and Jean Louis, playing the piano that Jean Désy acquired for the official residence, in *La Revue moderne* 25, no. 9 (January 1944): 18.

Newspaper ad featuring Jean Dansereau and Muriel Tannehill on the Light's *Ondas Musicais* radio show, 1943, in *O Radical*, 13 July 1943, 6.

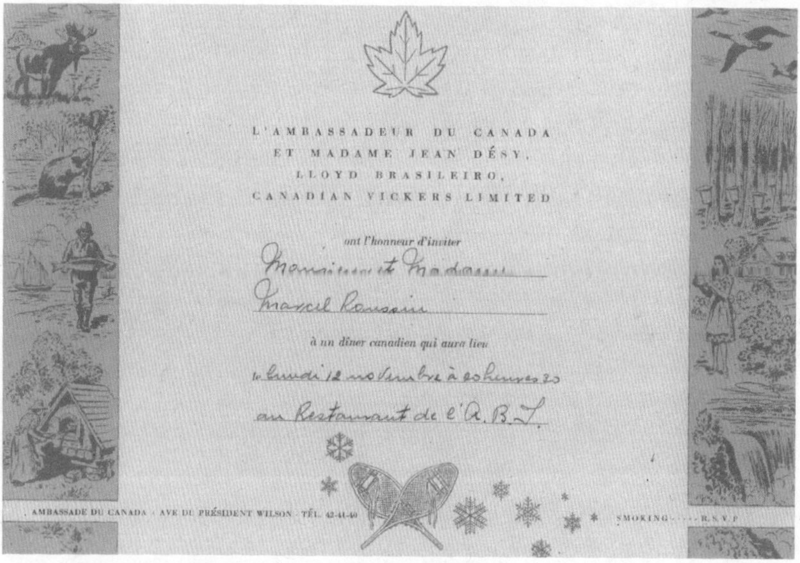


Marcel Roussin's invitation to the *Dîner canadien*, 1945 (CRCCFUO, P232/4/10).

Quatuor alouette with Father Marcel-Marie Desmarais (third from left) and his colleagues from the Dominican Order in São Paulo, 1945 (AFEUL, F454/6/6).

Canada's official and impromptu ambassadors, 1946 (LAC, RG25, vol. 3799). From left to right: Claude Champagne, "Lady MacMillan," Jean Désy, "Madame Champagne," Émile Gaudissard, Ernest MacMillan, and Benjamin Rogers.

EXPOSIÇÃO

DE

JACQUES DE TONNANCOUR

PATROCINADA PELA

EMBAIXADA DO CANADÁ

E PELO

INSTITUTO BRASIL-CANADÁ

DE 7 A 19 DE AGOSTO DE 1946

MINISTÉRIO DA EDUCAÇÃO E SAÚDE

Exhibition catalogue and illustration of Botafogo Bay
by Jacques de Tonnancour, 1946 (SAGDUQÀM, 170P-660/6).
© Estate of Jacques de Tonnancour/SOCAN (2021).

José Siqueira in Montreal for a session with Radio-Canada, 1946 (BAnQ, P48, S1/P23229). From left to right: Jean Beaudet, Alice Ribeiro, Siqueira, Léopol Houlé, Jean Lefebvre, and Yvonne Rivet-Gagnon.

Heitor Villa-Lobos in the Montreal studios of the Canadian Broadcasting Corporation, 1952 (MVL, Fotográfico – 77-16-101).

DEPARTMENT OF EXTERNAL AFFAIRS

MEMORANDUM

TO: Mr. Toyall

Security: UNCLASSIFIED

Date: February 9, 1960

FROM: M. E. Grant

File No. 2216-V-2-40

REFERENCE:

SUBJECT: Pictures at Rio de Janeiro. - Reference letters No. 44 of January 26, 1960 and No. 53 of January 27, 1960 from Rio de Janeiro.

On the attached file you will find the two letters under reference concerning the large pictures by Pellan. You will note that they are 6.4' x 10.1' respectively and therefore too large for our residences abroad. In my view, these two canvasses are not suitable for the Ambassador's office and are wasted in this location.

2. Mr. Chapdelaine has provided very complete details about these pictures and we have nothing to add from our own records. I am not at all sure whether these murals could be rolled up and packed for inclusion in Mr. Roger's effects. It would however seem desirable to have them returned to Canada for consideration by the National Gallery, following which decision could be taken regarding their disposition.

3. Attached for your information are two slides of the Ambassador's office at our Chancery in Rio de Janeiro, showing the pictures referred to. The one of the Totem poles and mountains could perhaps be used as a mural in the Waiting Room of the reception area, ninth floor, Canada House, New York.

4. Please be kind enough to review the correspondence and let me have the recommendations of the Selection Committee. Decision will have to be taken fairly promptly if the pictures are to be returned with Mr. Roger's shipment.

Head of Supplies and Properties Division

External Affairs correspondence to determine the fate of Alfred Pellan's *Canada West* and *Canada East* in Rio de Janeiro, 1960. "In my view, these two canvasses are not suitable for the Ambassador's office and are wasted in that location," wrote M.E. Grant, head of the Supplies and Properties Division of External Affairs. "It would … seem desirable to have them returned to Canada for consideration by the National Gallery, following which decision could be taken regarding their disposition" (LAC, RG25, vol. 2885).

Ellen Ballon performing in Rio de Janeiro, with Heitor Villa-Lobos conducting, 1946 (KLSCDU, MS-52-2/5.22).

# DISTANT STAGE

# Introduction

The staff at the newly established Canadian legation in Rio de Janeiro was busy looking for a piano (a French Pleyel, preferably) in the classified sections of various Brazilian newspapers in the fall of 1942.[1] The Department of External Affairs had approved the purchase of the instrument after thoughtful consideration of the arguments presented by its man in Brazil, the Montreal-born diplomat Jean Désy. On 14 September, he had marked his first year as minister plenipotentiary with a musical evening at his residence, borrowing a piano from a neighbour and inviting the French-Canadian tenor Raoul Jobin for the occasion. The event had taught Désy that the shared experience of music was conducive to social interactions and harmonious conversations. "Concerts of that sort," he remarked, are a "most convenient way of gathering in a friendly atmosphere many categories of people who may eventually become of great assistance to our cause."[2] His superiors in Ottawa were not in the business of investing in culture, but $600 was reasonable considering that a piano could also be considered legation furniture.

The opening of the legation in 1941, and its subsequent upgrade to an embassy, a little over two years later, were responses to profound changes brought about by the outbreak of war in Europe. With the conflict disrupting their respective transatlantic trade networks, Canada and Brazil hoped to consolidate their economic ties in the shadow of the United States' increasing political and cultural dominance of the hemisphere. The two aspiring middle powers intended to get to know each other better in an attempt to find common ground and to position themselves favourably in anticipation of a new postwar world order. Both saw themselves playing a leadership role in the hemisphere or in the broader Atlantic region. At the same time, Canada hoped to convince the South American giant to abandon neutrality and join the war effort on the side of the Allies. Désy was referring to the pursuit of these objectives when he made the argument that a piano would help him advance the national interest. Cultural relations, he believed, could nurture mutual understanding in addition to providing opportunities to develop a compelling image of Canada for the world to see.

That said, Désy was also set on elevating the status of French Canadians – himself included – on the domestic and international stages when he ventured into the realm of cultural diplomacy. While his staff was shopping for a piano, he commissioned his friend Claude Champagne to prepare a musical homage to Brazilians. The composer obliged by writing "Quadrilha brasileira," a piece inspired by an Indigenous folk melody from northern Brazil. Francisco Mignone promptly responded with his own musical homage: "Três prelúdios (sobre temas canadenses)," a short composition based on three French-Canadian folk songs. This exchange of musical gifts was showcased during Dominion Day celebrations held in Rio de Janeiro on 1 July 1943. At the invitation of the Canadian legation in Brazil, the Montreal pianist Jean Dansereau performed Mignone's work live on national radio, while Arnaldo Estrella, his Brazilian counterpart, premiered Champagne's "Quadrilha brasileira."[3] This elaborate series of musical events struck a resounding chord among Brazil's Francophile elites by situating Quebec, with Montreal as a noteworthy cultural centre in its own right, at the heart of Canada's emerging international identity in South America. Encores were in order.

## TAKING THE STAGE

This book delves into two neglected histories: that of Canada-Brazil relations, and the role played by culture in Canada's pursuit of an international identity, both of which saw French-Canadian diplomats, artists, and intellectuals take advantage of their country's hemispheric moment to adopt a posture of being-in-the-world.[4] Désy pioneered Canadian diplomatic relations in Brazil, first as minister plenipotentiary (1941–43) and then as ambassador (1943–47). His unorthodox approach to diplomacy was perhaps most apparent in the ways he used culture to project an engaging image of Canada in order to make it better known. He also wore many other hats as he held court at his home atop Rio de Janeiro's Santa Teresa hill: impresario, patron of the arts, and cultural mediator, among others. Like the artists with whom he worked, many of them friends or family, he pursued several agendas simultaneously while working across the boundaries between state and civil society, at the service of both French-speaking Quebec and the broader Canadian nation-state. His was a multifarious and multidirectional affair.

Removed as it was from the Pacific and European theatres of war, Brazil was arguably never a pressing issue for External Affairs, which also displayed a lukewarm interest in cultural matters. Rio de Janeiro must have felt like an oasis compared to war-torn Brussels, where Désy had previously been posted. Largely unsupervised, he had free rein to experiment. He had been in South America for barely more than a year when he reached out to Jobin, Champagne, and Dansereau. At around the same time, he commissioned Alfred Pellan, one of Quebec's champions of modernist art, to prepare two large paintings for the legation's waiting room. Soon after, he convinced the editors of the Brazilian magazine *A Vida* to publish an article that the Montreal-based art historian Maurice Gagnon had written about the works. Désy was learning how to mobilize his network back home. These initiatives laid the ground for a bilateral cultural agreement – the first of its kind for Canada – aimed at facilitating "the organisation and presentation of artistic exhibitions, concerts, lectures, radio programmes, films, and other activities."[5] Presented to External Affairs as something of a *fait accompli* by Désy, the agreement, formally known as the Exchange of Notes between Canada and Brazil Constituting an Agreement for the Promotion of Cultural Relations between the Two Countries, was signed on 24 May 1944.

This latest development was about projecting Canada abroad as much as it was about furthering Désy's vision of a bicultural federal state as the best approach to protecting, enriching, and broadening the reach of French-Canadian culture. Following in Dansereau's footsteps, the folkloric vocal ensemble Quatuor alouette spent two months performing on Brazilian stages and radio airwaves in 1945. Its tour overlapped with the artist residency of Jacques de Tonnancour, a young painter whose reputation was on the rise thanks to a series of well-attended exhibits organized through the embassy with the help of the National Gallery of Canada (NGC). Champagne himself travelled to Brazil the following year to give lectures and conduct the Orquestra Sinfônica Brasileira (OSB, or Brazilian Symphony Orchestra in

English).[6] Wilfrid Pelletier, founding artistic director of the Orchestre des concerts symphoniques de Montréal (OCSM), was in Rio de Janeiro at the time. Upon his return to Montreal, he helped introduce his compatriots to the music of the renowned Brazilian composer Heitor Villa-Lobos. This first decade of Canada-Brazil cultural relations culminated in 1952 with Villa-Lobos travelling north for an elaborate live performance destined for broadcast in South America. The invitation came from Désy, who had by then become, through a surprising turn of events, director general of the International Service of the Canadian Broadcasting Corporation (CBC-IS).[7]

If Désy occupies centre stage in this story, it is because of his pioneering role in the history of Canadian cultural diplomacy and the anomalous, if timely, moment of his tenure at the head of the CBC-IS during a period when many observers doubted that the former diplomat had the credentials to reinvent himself as a broadcast administrator.[8] His overshadowing presence provides a unique longitudinal window into the deployment of bilateral cultural relations over a period of roughly ten years when External Affairs had yet to equip itself in the sphere of cultural diplomacy. It was a decade of intense activity that centred mostly around Montreal and put French- and English-speaking Canadian know-how, economic power, and cultural sophistication on display for Brazilians and Canadians alike.

Désy, however, was far from alone in playing an active role in the making and positioning of Canada's – but also Quebec's and Montreal's – international image in South America. Serving the role of impromptu ambassadors, the artists mentioned above were equally resourceful and opportunistic when it came to using newly established diplomatic channels, operating across borders as well as within the power apparatus and parallel to it, to brand Canada in ways that could bolster their personal and professional ambitions. Not all of them were men or French-speakers. For example, the Montreal-born pianist Ellen Ballon commissioned Villa-Lobos to write his first piano concerto, which she premiered in Rio de Janeiro on 11 October 1946. That she did so on her own initiative, with next to no support from Désy or his staff, was a testament to her agency as a cultural ambassadress in a male-dominated world.[9]

Not only were the efforts deployed by these artists marked by competing nationalisms and divergent understandings of Montreal's place in the world, but they were also intertwined with a broad range of both individual and collective agendas that exposed various combinations of political, business, professional, religious, ethnic, linguistic, and even family ties. This book, then, also taps into the dynamic, relational messiness of Canada's first official foray into the realm of cultural diplomacy.

## MAKING ART MATTER

The practice of activating culture for both political and economic ends was neither new nor limited to the North Atlantic community of nation-states to which Canada belonged.[10] Yet in the context of the hemispheric relations of the 1940s, the United States' institutionalized approach to cultural diplomacy had a particular influence over other international actors. The Division of Cultural Relations and the Office for Coordination of Commercial and Cultural Relations between the American Republics (created in 1938 and 1940, respectively) aimed to shape elite or mass public opinion in other countries to counter anti-US-American sentiments and to assert, "through attraction rather than coercion," the hegemony of liberal developmentalism over communist and fascist ideologies in South America.[11] Through mediated cultural events, the two agencies sought to foster conversations and promote people-to-people interactions, both of which were seen as necessary first steps toward a firmer handshake between the United States and various South American nations.[12]

There were, and still are, considerable debates over what can be accomplished by mobilizing artists and trying to instrumentalize their work. On the one hand, there are those who champion utilitarian approaches whereby culture is periodically activated to secure consent or support for high-priority policies, such as sealing a trade agreement or establishing alternate channels of communication when a diplomatic impasse occurs. Others focus on building the national brand through broad, long-term strokes that tend to privilege projection over engagement. Still others see cultural diplomacy as a world-changing "global practice of promoting common understanding between peoples of all nations."[13] This third approach has the merit of moving beyond an essentialized conception of culture as nationally bounded and integrated.

A key component of a state's arsenal in the international game of influence, cultural diplomacy ultimately amounts to an "international actor's engagement of a foreign public through intervention of some kind in the cultural field."[14] It is an attempt to "manage the international environment" using culture.[15] The concept of culture is, of course, an elusive one. Understood in the abstract, it stands for "*both* the meanings and values which arise amongst distinctive groups and classes, on the basis of their given historical conditions and relationships, through which they … respond to the conditions of existence," writes Stuart Hall. It thus also includes "the lived traditions and practices through which these 'understandings' are expressed and in which they are embodied."[16] In other words, culture encompasses the range of competing mental maps, as well as the affective and aesthetic modes of communication, that individuals and groups rely on to make sense of the world and to situate themselves in it. It is, as a result, always fluid, relational, syncretic, and diffuse, even if it appears nationally bounded and integrated when looked at through a state-centric lens.

Canadians were late bloomers in this international game of influence if we consider the fact that it took the Royal Commission on National Development in the Arts, Letters, and Sciences (otherwise known as the Massey Commission) to elicit a sustained interest in cultural diplomacy. Even then, the commission's recommendations regarding the projection of Canada abroad constituted, at best, "an afterthought" in the early 1950s.[17] It was not until 1966 that External Affairs felt compelled to establish a Cultural Affairs Division, and it did so mostly as a response to Quebec's own advances in the realm of international cultural relations. The 1961 opening of the Maison du Québec in Paris, with the explicit support of the French government, constituted a direct challenge to Ottawa's prerogatives. It was founded on the notion that a province's domestic areas of jurisdiction (specifically education and, to a certain extent, culture) should extend to the global arena.[18] It is ironic that Désy's efforts neither spurred to action nor inspired decision-makers in External Affairs, most of whom promptly forgot about the 1944 agreement with Brazil, thus missing an opportunity to critically examine and gain insights from it on the eve of the challenge from Quebec. Until the 1960s, Ottawa's approach to international cultural affairs was limited to ad hoc, discontinuous, uncoordinated, and short-sighted initiatives by decentralized agencies often working at cross-purposes.[19]

Canada's postwar cultural rapprochement with Brazil constituted a blind spot on the radar of policy-makers and scholars, who have exhibited a sustained lack of interest in culture and South American affairs in the making and writing of Canadian diplomatic history. In fact, until only recently, the historical and contemporary literature deemed both to be largely irrelevant to Canada's international priorities.[20] This state of affairs also sprung from an inclination to focus on top-down, government-sanctioned initiatives that aligned with liberal nationalist narratives and spoke to the country's middle power aspirations in the North Atlantic world.[21] Combined insights from the fields of cultural studies, communications, and Canadian international history are now complicating this state-centric approach and its narrow geographical scope by attending to the elaborate international partnerships into which both state and non-state actors entered from the 1950s onward.[22]

In this book, I shift the focus even further by going beyond the Massey Commission and the Cold War, decentering the North Atlantic triangle while paying attention to the interplay between internationalism and nationalism in the context of Canada's contested federalism. Coincidentally, I also trace the entangled history of Quebec's cultural diplomacy to the transitional decade of the 1940s. I argue that French Canadians' self-conscious efforts to project their image overseas and develop an international identity were rooted in the politico-cultural changes engendered by the Second World War. Artists played a preponderant role in this process by making the most of Canada's hemispheric moment, working through or alongside official diplomatic channels to pursue their multi-faceted agendas, not all of which were complementary or easily reconcilable. In the eyes and ears of this story's protagonists, Brazil was a distant stage where internal Canadian identity politics and aspirations could be played out.[23]

## PERFORMING THE NATION

Quebec experienced dramatic changes at the turn of the 1940s as the clouds of war rolled across Europe. France's capitulation in the face of the invasion by Nazi Germany was unsettling to French Canadians. With ties to Paris cut off, many worried about the survival of a francophone cultural world in North America. Yet others saw this as a chance to rethink Quebec's and Montreal's place in the western hemisphere. Not only did the severance of ties with the former imperial metropole create an immediate and broader need for domestic French-language cultural productions, but it also generated opportunities within Francophile elite circles in South America. There was optimism in the air following the 1939 electoral victory of Adélard Godbout's provincial Liberal Party. The new premier's policies were in sharp contrast with those of his arch-conservative predecessor, Maurice Duplessis. His initiatives allowed liberal modernity to make some headway in Quebec, notably by enfranchising women and enacting legislative reforms in the areas of labour relations and education. However, the apparent ease with which Godbout made concessions to Ottawa on questions of provincial jurisdiction concerned staunch nationalists, some of whom displayed fascist inclinations in their support for Vichy France. French-English tensions over conscription, the fear of enemy aliens, and labour militancy also dampened the mood somewhat.[24]

Be that as it may, Quebec society continued to undergo profound transformations during the war, with Montreal setting the pace. As the site of a small but thriving movement of artistic modernism, the booming city benefited greatly from both Godbout's brand of liberalism and the influx of exiled artists. Taking music as an example, the 1943 opening of the government-funded Conservatoire de musique du Québec à Montréal (CMQM), under the leadership of Pelletier and Champagne, elevated the province's profile while preparing future generations for successful careers at home and abroad. The arrival of musicians fleeing Europe – the German-born cellist Lotte Brott and the pianist Helmut Blume, among others – further enriched the city's cultural life, in addition to fostering an openness to the world and a greater embrace of diversity.[25] The visual arts scene was equally transformed by this wind of change. As founding members of the Contemporary Arts Society, the painters John Lyman, Paul-Émile Borduas, and Fritz Brandtner (who was born in Germany) emerged as fierce crusaders for modern art. Erudite cultural critics such as Gagnon supported their cause. Pellan, who had just returned from the "City of Light" after more than a decade of immersion in cubist and surrealist milieus, also entered the fold.[26]

Like them, Désy adopted an internationalist posture, positing that French Canadians' distinctive cultural attributes (namely, their Catholicism and *latinité*, which they shared with many South Americans), rooted as they were in both the Old World and the New World, conveyed the sort of universal values that Canada and the international community needed more of in these turbulent times. Désy's politico-cultural views derived in part from his observation of the changes taking place in Montreal. They were also a function of his sense of fellowship vis-à-vis the intellectual elites of Europe, particularly in France, where he had studied and worked during the interwar years. This experience was a source of legitimacy and prestige to him. In fact, he saw himself as embodying the figure of the elite intellectual, which emerged during this period as "the flagship of a rational humanism opposed to the threat of political totalitarianism."[27] Désy adhered to that ideal, because of its potential as an antidote to defensive forms of nationalism and to various radical ideologies, which were making headway among certain pockets of Quebec society at the time.

At this conjuncture, people like Désy, Pellan, and Champagne exuded confidence at the prospect of new possibilities, not just *survivance*.[28] Cultural diplomacy appealed to them because it could validate their self-image and sense of place in the world, in addition to providing opportunities to enact leadership. It could help transform Montreal into a formidable centre of attraction, a cultural metropolis in its own right – perhaps even a surrogate Paris. Désy thus felt emboldened to emphasize the *fait français* and its contributions – past, present, and future – to Canada's national and international identities. His perception of the importance of Quebec's intellectual and cultural elites, combined with his belief in the possibility of *bonne entente* between French Canadians and their English-speaking counterparts, were in fortuitous alignment with External Affairs' autonomist impulse and desire to position Canada as a stalwart of inclusiveness and liberal democracy that other countries might emulate.

Established in 1909, the Department of External Affairs took several decades to blossom into a full-fledged agency. At its head was Joseph Pope, a competent public servant whose imperialist leanings prevented the articulation of a coherent, forward-thinking vision for Canada's foreign policy.[29] The Liberals' return to power in 1921 provided the context for a rethinking of the department's direction. The newly elected prime minister, William Lyon Mackenzie King, understood the importance of managing the interplay between domestic and international policies, especially with respect to core issues such as economic development and national unity. Oscar Douglas Skelton (commonly referred to as O.D. Skelton), a Queen's University scholar with a PhD from the University of Chicago, was brought in to inject life into the department's operation. Among other things, this meant championing the twin goals of expanding its diplomatic corps and developing Canada's international identity through overseas posts.[30]

As undersecretary of state for external affairs, Skelton worked to establish new posts so that Canada's voice could be heard on the international stage. By the end of the 1920s, the country had legations in

Washington, Paris, and Tokyo, but more were needed to project and consolidate Canada's sense of nationhood vis-à-vis Great Britain and the United States. The 1938 opening of a joint legation for Belgium and the Netherlands, with Désy at the helm, proved encouraging. In the following year's budget, Skelton allocated funds for diplomatic representation in both Argentina and Brazil, likely with the rationale that the establishment of legations in Catholic and Francophile South American countries would help counterbalance the high commissions planned for various Commonwealth countries.[31] Developments in war-torn Europe finally motivated King to accede to External Affairs' recommendations in light of "problems of markets for Canadian products, Pan-American developments in the economic and political spheres, and the added emphasis which both Great Britain and the United States were according to South American countries."[32] Skelton now had to find a suitable diplomat who would agree to relocate to Rio de Janeiro. Having abandoned his post in Europe after Germany's invasion of Belgium, Désy was all too eager to resume his diplomatic career, even if that meant heading south to a country about which he knew little.

Canadians were not completely ignorant of the South American giant, of course. The first significant breakthrough between the two countries occurred in 1931 when a Canadian trade mission visited Brazil and successfully advocated for close economic relations. Signed on 4 December of that year, the Exchange of Notes Regarding Commercial Relations between Canada and Brazil had minimal impact amid a severe worldwide economic depression, not to mention the fact that it maintained preferential treatment for the Commonwealth. Another agreement, signed in 1937, removed some of the restrictions on the circulation of goods, but Brazilian and Canadian businesses did not rush to reorient the flow of their activities since no direct merchant route linked the two groups, who were still reeling from the stock market crash of 1929. In fact, trade actually declined throughout the 1930s, until the war disrupted both Canada's and Brazil's economic ties to Europe, at which point Brazilian exports to Canada increased ninefold.[33] Seizing the moment, Minister of Trade and Commerce James MacKinnon headed south in 1941 to seal a new agreement that extended "unconditional and unrestricted most-favoured-nation treatment" to Brazil.[34]

This latest agreement and the opening of a legation in Rio de Janeiro were welcomed by Canadian businesses already established there, above all the Royal Bank of Canada and Brazilian Traction, Light, and Power Company. The latter was poised to benefit the most from this rapprochement. Established in 1912 through the merger of two similar enterprises in São Paulo and Rio de Janeiro (founded in 1899 and 1904, respectively), the company was known simply as "the Light" – or, less affectionately, as the "Canadian Octopus" – by Brazilians who used its public transit, electricity, and telephone services.[35] Its virtual monopoly in these areas made it "Canada's largest overseas corporation."[36] With its financial and intellectual power coming from various parts of the English-speaking world, the company's leadership did not fail to note that Canada's image as a friendly country could be an asset, especially considering the fact that Brazil had taken a dictatorial turn and was showing growing discontent in its relations with Great Britain and the United States in the late 1930s.

Protecting and advancing Canadian business interests in Brazil was consistent with the former country's economic and military imperatives during the war. It also provided a convenient opportunity to perform "middlepowerhood," which essentially amounted to a "subtle process of nationalist self-promotion" for the purpose of improving economic and political prospects.[37] More myth than reality, Canada's claim to middle power status conveyed Canadians' desire to occupy an advantageous position within the postwar international order then being envisioned at the 1944 Dumbarton Oaks Conference, where Great Britain, the United States, and the Soviet Union met to discuss the creation of the United Nations. It did not matter that Brazil was engaged in a similar pursuit of middlepowerhood.[38] The South American giant was a potential stage on which Canada could project itself as an autonomous middle power, as a linchpin in global affairs, even as a helpful fixer for its partners in the North Atlantic triangle.[39]

Officials in Ottawa may have been only marginally interested in Brazil, but they still understood that Canada had much to gain by consolidating its presence there. Brazilians had become suspicious of what they perceived as the United States' imperialist aims in the region. They also resented Great Britain's efforts to disrupt Brazilian-German maritime trade routes in the early years of the war. Developing closer relations with a hemispheric neighbour to the north could help them achieve some balance vis-à-vis the two major powers. In contrast, Canadians' own "perennial search" for a counterweight did not extend to Brazil, since the country did not have sufficient clout to impact dynamics within the North Atlantic triangle, and it was not yet clear what roles it could play in a multilateral setting such as the United Nations.[40] The issues that Canadians needed to address were more immediate, and they were contingent on the maintenance of robust triangular relations. Prior to joining the war on the side of the Allies in 1942, Brazil had sought to extract the greatest possible benefits from the growing ideological rivalry between belligerents in South America. It had, in the process, grown considerably close to European fascist regimes.[41] Canada, some thought, could steer Brazilians further toward the side of the Allies, in addition to helping restore their faith in liberal democracy. Not only that, it could also help smooth relations between Brazilians and the English-speaking world more broadly while acting as an intermediary between Great Britain and the United States in South America.[42]

Of the aforementioned objectives, promoting democracy was never an urgent matter, especially once Brazil declared war on Germany. This relative indifference vis-à-vis the illiberal practices of a wartime ally was due in great part to Brazilian president Getúlio Vargas's pervasive control and adroit use of the modern mass media to depict his dictatorship as a benevolent one. Created on 27 December 1939, his Departamento de Imprensa e Propaganda (DIP, or Department of Press and Propaganda in English) had as its mandate the shaping of public opinion around the "regime's doctrinal guidelines, in defence of culture, spiritual unity, and Brazilian civilization."[43] This meant, among other things, abating regional discontent and neutralizing the various factionalisms that undermined political and economic stability. The fifth-largest country in the world, this former Portuguese colony was built on the sweat and blood of nearly five million slaves, a jarring number that surpassed by ten times the number of enslaved persons brough to the United States.[44] Following the abolition of slavery in 1888, the country was rocked by tensions among various ethnic groups and social classes, including between landed and urban elites, who grappled with each other for several decades over the shifting power dynamics that accompanied the country's industrialization and urbanization. Vargas became president in 1930 following a bloodless coup staged by the military amid this volatile environment, a precedent that paved the way for his assumption of dictatorial powers seven years later.[45] Deposed in October of 1945 during another coup – this one staged in the name of a restoration of democracy – Vargas would return as a duly elected leader in 1951.

Through propaganda and censorship, the DIP disseminated Vargas's message of "paternalistic competency" and harmonious corporatism in an effort to instill in the populace a commitment to social harmony and moral responsibility.[46] It also championed the idea that *miscigenação*, or fluid race relations, preserved and enriched, rather than weeded out and sublimated, the traits and qualities of the population's three key groups: Indigenous peoples, Afro-Brazilians, and the descendants of white settlers.[47] The concept of *Brasilidade*, which loosely translates to "Brazilianness," conveyed the ideal of a strong and all-encompassing national identity. Domestically, this essentialized image helped promote social cohesion, even if the regime's approach to governance privileged urban, white middle-class Brazilians.[48] On the international stage, it served as a positive marker of differentiation since Brazil's image as a racial democracy compared favourably at the turn of the 1940s with those of Nazi Germany and the Jim Crow–era United States.[49]

Not everyone believed the images that the Vargas regime circulated, but most conceded that deviation from democratic principles by perceived partner countries was of secondary importance in the fight against the Axis powers. Perhaps unsurprisingly, this indifference was especially pronounced in terms of the attitudes toward South American regimes, like Brazil, which existed largely on the periphery of the world as Canadians knew it.[50] More striking was the way in which Canada's ambassadors, both official and impromptu, unscrupulously used the dictatorship's cultural infrastructure, and especially its publishing and broadcasting capabilities, to advance their own projects. Whereas the "danger of admitting undesirable propaganda into Canada virtually under government sponsorship" was a concern when debating whether or not to sign the 1944 cultural agreement, the idea of Canadians exploiting Vargas's propaganda machine for the purpose of national projection seemed to pose no such problem.[51] That the targeted audience was composed not just of Brazilians, but also of compatriots on the ground and those who followed the news back home, made this circular experiment in cultural diplomacy an especially paradoxical one.

## TUNING IN

Brazil was manifestly a distant stage in the minds of both state and non-state actors, who saw in Canada's rapprochement with the South American giant the opportunity to perform, and thus potentially actualize, their individual and collective aspirations, whether it was seeking recognition or asserting leadership. Their use of music and the visual arts as instruments of diplomacy in Brazil was about projection and self-representation, not engagement. It spoke first and foremost to their sense of place in the world and their relationship to the past. Through affective and aesthetic modes of communication, these Canadians interacted with their Brazilian interlocutors to mediate new connections to the idea of the nation. This process, however, was fraught with tension, because culture is always enmeshed with power and resistance to it.[52] Transnational cultural relations of the type seen in Brazil during this period were accordingly about inspiring new imagined communities as much as they were about navigating asymmetrical power relations. They facilitated the crossing of national and cultural boundaries while bringing about new margins and zones of exclusion.[53]

The French-Canadian diplomats, intellectuals, and artists who sought to place Quebec at the heart of Canada's international identity in Brazil had much to reckon with. For a start, they had to position themselves vis-à-vis Brazilians' cultural and racial difference, particularly the importance accorded to Indigenous folklore and Afro-Brazilian expressive cultures in the national imaginary. Although they interacted primarily with members of Brazil's predominantly white elite, this story's protagonists still had to respond to their hosts' discourse regarding *Brasilidade*. They also had to grapple with the realization that Canada was perceived in Brazil as existing squarely within the boundaries of the English-speaking world. This was the image that executives at the Light conveyed as Canada sought to find its place within the North Atlantic triangle. This configuration of nation-states, an "Anglosphere" of sorts, had racial underpinnings in that it was rooted, in part, in a discourse that foregrounded both whiteness and the idea of Anglo-Saxon exceptionalism.[54]

The belief that English Canadians' Britishness and French Canadians' *latinité* constituted valid racialized group identities, as well as the claim that racism was largely non-existent in Canada, provided a fitting framework through which to deal with this conundrum.[55] Indeed, the use of music and the visual arts to depict Canada as the product of a harmonious compact between "two founding races" allowed the predominantly male actors who participated in this cultural rapprochement with Brazil to define "Canadianness," so to speak, as a form of *métissage*, albeit one centred on whiteness.[56] Their elitist art of diplomacy was evidently anything but universal and apolitical. It was, rather, a means for them to develop and validate a self-image in relation to and against a Brazilian "Other" without undermining their privileges as members of a white settler society.

A literal translation of *miscigenação*, the term *métissage* may not figure in the written records, but the idea it signified in the context of Canada-Brazil relations (i.e., a cultural understanding of racial mixture) was a recurring undertone throughout Désy's decade-long cultural diplomacy.[57] Folded into it was the trope of *latinité*, which served to underscore a sense of affinity among peoples who traced their heritage to Mediterranean antiquity and spoke one of the Romance languages, preferably with a manifest love of French (i.e., Francophilia). If *latinité* helped convey the image of the two countries as "sister nations," it was also laden with normative assumptions about progress and civilization.[58] Likewise for the tropes of Catholicism and the family. Canada's involvement in Brazil, for all its nods to *métissage* and the notion of shared cultural values, neither challenged nor fundamentally unsettled the structuring weight of race (or class and gender for that matter) in Canadian international relations.[59] Yet it did provide a means of thinking creatively about ways of partaking in the transformation of the world, including one's own.

Canada's national performance in Brazil was as much about agreeing on a common language, or a set of cultural values, as it was about telling credible and compelling stories. Désy and his many impromptu ambassadors, like their Brazilian colleagues and interlocutors, were aware of the performative nature of the multi-faceted work that they were accomplishing as part of their two countries' rapprochement. They placed a greater premium on performance as a form of relationship building than they did on the search for authenticity. Yet when thinking about spectatorship and the need to actualize their country's self-image, Canada's envoys were concerned above all with convincing themselves and their compatriots in Brazil and back home rather than their hosts.[60]

*Distant Stage* examines how this process played out in the press, on stages, on radio airwaves, and in galleries, from Pellan and Champagne participating in Désy's first experiments in cultural diplomacy (chapter 1) to Dansereau's stay in Rio de Janeiro (chapter 2); from the signing of the 1944 cultural agreement (chapter 3) to Quatuor alouette's two-month tour of Brazil (chapter 4); from de Tonnancour's year-long artistic residency in the wake of the *Pintura Canadense Contemporânea* exhibition (chapter 5) to Champagne's collaboration with the OSB, an experience that he shared with his Toronto colleague Ernest MacMillan (chapter 6); and finally, with Villa-Lobos's 1952 concert at Montreal's Plateau Hall (chapter 7). By focusing on the founding years of Canada's official cultural diplomacy, these chapters shed a new light on the country's hemispheric moment and Quebec's place in it.[61] They follow a cast of French-Canadian protagonists as they moved centre stage, tentatively at first, and then with an assurance that betrayed an urgent need to consolidate gains and build momentum in the face of disputatious arguments about the merits of Désy's vision and the inadequacy of *métissage* as a rallying trope. *Distant Stage* is a story of origins and experimentation, of intricate manoeuvres and missed connections, of cultural awakening and the need for self-reckoning.

This book is based on the premise that music and the visual arts are, as affective and aesthetic modes of communication, rooted in historically specific, diverse, and complex cultural terrains, be they national or transnational. It examines culture as a dynamic and relational process that can either validate or fashion new identities and configurations of both power and resistance. It approaches cultural undertakings such as those staged in Brazil as "total social event[s]," to borrow an expression used by Georgina Born.[62] Building on Gilles Deleuze's theory of the *assemblage*, she approaches the act of producing culture as a constellation of mediations that engender relationships between and among artists, audiences, producers, and media. This means recognizing the historical specificity of creative acts, unearthing the discursive traces they leave behind, and attending to their multifarious forms of mediation: sonic and visual, corporeal and technological, spatial and temporal, and so on.[63] It means seeing cultural objects as neither autonomous nor immutable.

Furthermore, it is important to note that those who participate in an *assemblage*, or find themselves pulled into a constellation of mediations, possess agency even if they are often forced to cope with generally asymmetrical power dynamics. Positionality matters in cultural production. This is clearly the case when Western art appropriates, sublimates, erases, or engages (in one way or another) its non-Western counterparts.[64] Although this book focuses on the Canadian side of the story, it also argues that all parties concerned, including those who, at one time or another, found themselves on the receiving end of a particular initiative, had the prerogative to embrace, interpret, debate, or resist the messages and representations conveyed. Brazilians, in other words, were never passive interlocutors.

The analytics of mediation deployed in this book applies to both music and the visual arts. These modes of communication overlapped and intertwined, and sometimes clashed and worked at cross-purposes. For example, de Tonnancour created visuals for Quatuor alouette's concerts while preparing his solo exhibition, which took place following the group's series of concerts in Rio de Janeiro, São Paulo, and Petrópolis. Whereas the folk singers were delighted to associate with him, MacMillan did not think much of the young artist's work when he discovered it as a guest of the OSB in 1946: "I wish I could be more enthusiastic about de Tonnancour's paintings, because he is a nice fellow, but much of it is bland to me."[65] Sharing the stage was not always easy in Brazil. If music still predominates in these pages, it is not to stress its distinctiveness, but rather to use it as a means of illustrating the ways in which culture functioned more broadly as an instrument of diplomacy.

The sources examined here range from audio to textual and iconographic materials. They include, among others, the tour diaries of MacMillan and Quatuor alouette's Roger Filiatrault (as well as the personal papers of Villa-Lobos and José Siqueira, the director of the OSB); CBC-IS broadcasts, transcripts, programming schedules, and listeners' letters (Rio de Janeiro's Rádio Nacional performed a somewhat similar role in the southern hemisphere); internal correspondence, meeting minutes, and exhibition catalogues held at the NGC (the Fundação Bienal de São Paulo holds some records pertaining to Canada's cultural campaigns in Brazil); concert and art exhibition ads as well as reviews in Canadian newspapers and magazines (notable Brazilian publications include *Brasil Musical* and *O Jornal*); as well as External Affairs dispatches, correspondence, and reports (the archives of the Itamaraty, Brazil's Ministry of Foreign Affairs, are comparable in terms of scope). Examined together, the above categories of sources (in French, English, and Portuguese) provide multiple entry points into the constellation of mediations at the heart of this book, thus providing opportunities for new insights about the making of Canadian cultural diplomacy, seen both from above and below.

---

Rather than approaching culture as a benign and static object that can be instrumentalized in international relations, *Distant Stage* attends to the ways in which the production, dissemination, and reception of culture reflected and shaped people's values and their understanding of the world, including their biases and cultural assumptions. As such, it does not limit itself to writing the entangled history of French Canadians' self-conscious efforts to activate culture in their pursuit of an international identity in South America. Rather, it examines their discourses and practices, in addition to the social and symbolic meanings that they assigned to their art as active participants in their country's hemispheric moment. And if the broader international context appears as a backdrop to the actions of individuals on the ground, it is because it rarely (if ever) directly dictated the choices that state and non-state actors made when taking part in Canada's projection abroad. "In my opinion, it is culture that pulls people apart or brings them together," Désy reflected in an essay written shortly after his short tenure at the head of the CBC-IS.[66] The impromptu ambassadors who participated in his decade-long series of experiments in cultural diplomacy thought so too, even if they did not all agree on how best to render the particular tones and colours of the world as they saw and experienced it.

# 1

# Diplomatic Encounter

Jean Désy had been in Rio de Janeiro for a little more than two weeks when he finally had the chance to meet with President Getúlio Vargas. In the meantime, he had learned to navigate the capital, finding his way through its disorienting, yet stunning, topography, while contemplating with awe the extent to which racial harmony seemed to pervade the city's cultural and social life. Désy was likely caught off guard when Vargas remarked that Canada's "heterogeneous national components" somewhat resembled Brazil's own diverse ethnic makeup.[1] Was the president referring strictly to those Canadians who traced their lineage to France and Great Britain? Or was he also including Indigenous peoples and the various national and ethnic diasporas found in Montreal and Toronto, among other cities? He did not specify. Substantiated or not, the belief that Canada and Brazil shared the distinguishing attribute of being racial democracies would come to hold much appeal as a means for the two countries to demarcate themselves within the hemisphere.

This was not the only perplexing statement that Vargas made during his meeting with Désy. He was evidently aware that Canadians had embarked on a quest for autonomy in international affairs when he explained, "using French with great accuracy," that their two countries needed "to do something *new* together: something outside of the usual practice."[2] Désy listened attentively, unsure what to make of this cryptic message. Reporting to Prime Minister (and Secretary of State for External Affairs) William Lyon Mackenzie King, he hypothesized that Vargas wanted Canadians to take a creative path, one that would be distinct from those championed by the United States and Great Britain. "Both of these latter Powers had created a certain degree of irritation in Brazil; whereas Canada came with clean hands and a pure heart," Désy noted prosaically, clearly thinking that here was an opportunity for him and his staff to chart their own course through Rio de Janeiro's diplomatic landscape.[3]

Arriving in the Brazilian capital at a time when the United States' influence in the country was on the rise, Désy promptly set about trying to meet his host's expectations of a more imaginative Canadian presence. Inexorably, he found himself trying to decode and contend with the cultural tenets of Vargas's national project, notably *Brasilidade* and what he understood to be the elites' apparent Francophilia. Responding to the cues offered to him, he fashioned Canada's international image in terms that he believed were comprehensible to Brazilians, but also not likely to cause contention among his English-speaking colleagues or to undermine Canadians' (both French- and English-speakers) claims of privilege as white settlers who had maintained deep cultural ties to their former imperial metropoles of London and Paris. Accordingly, he foregrounded Canada's *fait français* and harnessed both culture and history to depict the country as a harmonious compact between two founding races, the English and the French.

The high point of Désy's first year and a half in Brazil – the initial phase of the two countries' nascent friendship – was arguably his decision to activate the visual and musical arts as metaphors for the nation. The works that he commissioned from Alfred Pellan (two large paintings titled *Canada East* and *Canada West*) and Claude Champagne (the musical composition "Quadrilha brasileira") were splendid, albeit unusual, instruments of diplomacy that conveyed Canadians' proficiency in the art of self-representation and dialogue. In foregrounding whiteness through these works, Désy offered his own take on the discourse of racial democracy, simultaneously engaging with and denying the Other, to delimit the terms by which to interpret Canada amid its rapprochement with Brazil.

## WARTIME RAPPROCHEMENT

Brazilians' favourable response to the opening of the Canadian legation was hardly surprising. After all, they had been the ones to push tenaciously for reciprocal diplomatic exchanges as a means of accumulating goodwill and leverage on the world stage. Not only was Brazil asserting itself as a regional power, but it was also striving toward middlepowerhood in an effort to secure a place of prominence in the postwar world order. Although the Vargas regime adopted a policy of pragmatic equilibrium in its dealings with the United States and the major European powers, trying to preserve "autonomy in dependency," it also understood that assertively raising Brazil's international profile through bilateral relations would enhance the dictatorship's credibility. It would also improve its ability to confront what it saw as a hostile neighbour in the form of Argentina and pursue certain national objectives: among others, more evenly distributed economic growth through industrialization and modernization, national unity, sovereignty, and territorial integrity.[4]

Brazil's passage from colony to nation, in 1822, and its transition from empire to republic, in 1889, may have been relatively peaceful, but its population remained starkly divided along ethnic, class, regional, and political lines up to and beyond the coup that brought Vargas to power in 1930. Segments of the country's elites had come to doubt the merit of liberal democracy after witnessing the destruction brought about by the First World War and the collapse of Western economies caused by the crash of 1929. The industrializing cities of the southeast had been shaken by the economic crisis, although not as much as the coffee-exporting regions of the Brazilian hinterland, which saw international prices for their products collapse. The 1930 coup promised a new beginning by ending the four-decade old hegemony of the increasingly ailing landed oligarchies from the states of São Paulo and Minas Gerais. A native of Rio Grande do Sul, Vargas succeeded in winning legitimate election on a populist and corporatist reform program in 1933. A failed communist-sponsored coup, however, ultimately provided him with the excuse to take his fascist-inspired national reconstruction project to its logical conclusion. Indeed, he assumed full dictatorial powers in 1937 with the establishment of the Estado Novo (or New State).[5]

Brazil's authoritarian proclivities were an inevitable source of anxiety as far as Great Britain and the United States were concerned. This was especially true of the British, who had kept a firm grip on the Brazilian economy up to the First World War, at which point their empire began to decline while the United States and Germany stepped up their efforts to pull the South American giant into their respective spheres of interest. The country's vast resources (coffee, cotton, cacao, but also iron ore, rubber, and quartz), not to mention its nearly eight thousand kilometres of Atlantic coastline, made it a valued partner as another European war became an increasingly likely prospect. In this context, Vargas sought to align his domestic and foreign policies by entering a game of seduction and negotiation with both the United States and Germany.[6]

The latter was somewhat advantaged since Brazil was home to a growing number of colonies of German migrants, most of whom had settled in the urbanized south, where their economic and cultural impact was felt most strongly. The two countries were tied to each other through an uncommon agreement whereby goods were exchanged by way of a special currency that could only be redeemed through bilateral trade. The agreement worked well for the Brazilians, who traded agricultural and mineral resources for industrial products and arms without having to empty their already depleted foreign exchange and gold reserves.[7] By 1938, German exports to Brazil surpassed those of the United States. Brazilians, especially military officers, many of whom had received training in Germany, were amazed by the rate at which the Nazi economy was growing. Pro-German sentiments thus ran deep in some pockets of Brazilian society. Fascism represented an appealing alternative to those who were distrustful of the United States' intentions in South America.[8]

Brazil's economic arrangement with Germany and its slide toward dictatorship were causes for concern, but President Franklin Delano Roosevelt, not wanting to encourage a further tightening of relations between the two countries, maintained a friendly disposition toward Vargas. Visiting Rio de Janeiro in 1936, he praised the Brazilian leader for his industrialization program, even crediting him as one of the "two people who invented" the New Deal.[9] Such posturing was consistent with the United States' Good Neighbor policy, which called for the nurturing of friendly relations, by opposition to economic sanctions and military interventions, as a means of asserting the hegemony of liberal developmentalism over other ideologies in the hemisphere.[10]

Both parties had much to gain by maintaining communication channels. The 1934 nomination of Oswaldo Aranha as ambassador to the United States was indicative of how important that relationship was. A loyal friend, confidant, and associate of Vargas, he was an earnest advocate for closer ties with the Roosevelt administration, although he also kept a critical eye on its policies vis-à-vis South America.[11] The outbreak of war in 1939 did not initially impede Vargas's game of seduction, because he knew how crucial his support would be in the event that the hemisphere needed to be defended against military attack. In 1940, he finally obtained arms and financial support from Roosevelt in exchange for raw materials and access to both naval and air bases. He then secured millions in Lend-Lease aid and got a confidence boost with the establishment of the Joint Brazil–United States Defense Commission. However, Japan's attack on Pearl Harbor and the subsequent entry of the United States into the conflict ultimately forced Brazilians to abandon their neutral stance. In the summer of 1942, Brazil declared war against Germany. The South American giant now found itself uncomfortably dependent on the North American hegemon.[12]

Early on in his presidency, Vargas recognized that Brazil would need another partner that could help it fulfill its domestic and international aspirations while offsetting the United States' preponderant power in the hemisphere. That is why he contemplated the possibility of developing strategic economic ties with Canada. From his position in Washington, Aranha followed Canadian politics closely, noting that the return to power of King's Liberals, in 1935, presented an opportunity to diversify hemispheric trade. Vargas, he insisted, had to seize the moment and replace the two countries' "idiotic treaty" of 1931, which maintained preferential treatment for Commonwealth nations at the expense of Brazil, with a more favourable agreement.[13] The 1937 Exchange of Notes Constituting a Commercial Agreement between Canada and Brazil fulfilled that objective by levelling the trading field for Brazilian businesses.

From that moment onward, the Vargas regime considered Canada a promising counterweight to the United States. The 1937 exchange of notes laid the groundwork for a more aggressive push to engage Canadians on the topic of diplomatic representation. That year, Brazilian authorities repeatedly approached Canada's trade commissioner in Rio de Janeiro to let him know that their government wished to exchange ministers. Lester S. Glass's encounter with Silvio Rangel de Castro, a member of the Ministry of Foreign Affairs (commonly referred to as the Itamaraty), had left him hugely perplexed. He confided to his superiors in the Department of Trade and Commerce that he had not realized that "the question was so important to Brazil." His interlocutors, he wrote, "would accept no refusal." "Personally, I am at a loss to know what steps to take, because actually it is none of my business," he added.[14] Glass was in Brazil to handle economic matters and he was not going to burden himself with diplomatic affairs. That he failed to see how the two were related, or that he was one of only a few official Canadian envoys in Brazil, was indicative of his lack of imagination.

Unhappy with Canada's silence, Aranha, who had just returned from the United States to head the Itamaraty, reached out to the British ambassador in Rio de Janeiro.[15] When this proved fruitless, he went through the Brazilian ambassador in London in an attempt to convince Vincent Massey, Canadian high commissioner in Great Britain, to bring up the issue with the Department of External Affairs. The message conveyed was that "Brazil is most desirous of establishing diplomatic relations with Canada, and hope[s] that such a proposal made by a leading South American country would commend itself to the Canadian government."[16] Aranha even contacted Kenneth H. McCrimmon, who managed Brazilian Traction, Light, and Power Company (popularly known as "the Light") from Rio de Janeiro, to deliver a message to decision-makers in Ottawa: "Pan America in general did not recognize the importance of Canada's continental position either politically or economically and ... a more intimate association of Canada in Latin American affairs would be of political value not only to Canada itself but to the United States in its endeavour to hold the South American countries more or less in line with democratic institutions."[17] Aside from the irony that a dictatorship was claiming as one of its priorities the flourishing of liberal democracy, it is revealing that Aranha thought it pertinent to reassure Ottawa that Washington would welcome Canadians' growing involvement in South America as model international citizens.

The Vargas regime was manifestly aware that hemispheric relations, including the question of membership in the Pan-American Union (PAU), was a contentious topic in Canada. On more than one occasion, Brazilians advocated for Canadian participation in the activities of the continental organization despite knowing that the United States' adherence to the Monroe Doctrine precluded it. Founded at the turn of 1890, the PAU promoted mutual understanding and unity of purpose among the hemisphere's republics, primarily with respect to economic and juridical matters, while also serving as the channel through which the United States promoted its liberal developmentalist agenda. From Washington's perspective, Canada had yet to demonstrate its autonomy from Great Britain in international affairs. It was also not a republic.[18] This did not prevent Aranha from alluding to Canada's middle power aspirations in his efforts to make Pan-Americanism more enticing.

Most Canadians, however, were arguably less concerned with taking part in Pan-American activities than they were with the spread of fascism on their side of the Atlantic. The *Montreal Gazette*, for example, reacted with incredulity to Vargas's claim that he had designed a "special brand of democracy" in 1940.[19] The newspaper criticized the president's disposition toward fascism and questioned his dubious ties to the Italian dictator Benito Mussolini. The Itamaraty promptly voiced its opposition to this unfavourable coverage in a letter to Undersecretary of State for External Affairs O.D. Skelton.[20] With Brazil's international image at stake, Consul General Aluisio Martins Torres assured the Canadian government that Vargas was committed to continental solidarity in spite of the country's non-aligned status at the time.

Skelton nurtured no illusions about the Estado Novo, but he was somewhat sympathetic to Brazilians and needed no convincing about the pertinence of establishing diplomatic relations with them. He had been to Rio de Janeiro in 1922, the year the country celebrated the first centenary of its independence. He had been struck by the similarities, in terms of both economic potential and political evolution, between Canada and Brazil. More importantly, Skelton had gained a further appreciation of the "practical advantages" that would result from Canadians exerting control over their "own international existence" after having witnessed Great Britain and the United States at work in Brazil.[21] Whereas the latter could not entirely be trusted, the former could hardly be expected to prioritize Ottawa when its interests conflicted with those of London.

At the time, Skelton was working his way from Queen's University to External Affairs with a firm belief that "Canada's material and political self-interests" lay in its ability to assert its autonomy on the international stage.[22] In 1930, he made the case for opening legations in countries such as Brazil as a way of helping Canadians to get noticed. The passing of the Statute of Westminster in December of the following year, an act of the Parliament of the United Kingdom that recognized the Dominions as self-governing entities capable of conducting their own foreign policy, put a good deal of wind in his sails. Still, it took another ten years for Prime Minister King to sign off on the proposal. It was clear by then that strengthening hemispheric relations was imperative if Canada was to achieve its national objectives, which included developing and consolidating trade relations, protecting overseas Canadian business interests, and promoting liberal democracy to ensure hemispheric stability.[23]

The question of national unity also came into play. Indeed, French Canadians who worried that their country's international identity was too closely connected with the English-speaking world were relieved to learn that the high commissions planned for South Africa, Australia, and New Zealand would be counterbalanced with legations in predominantly Catholic and somewhat Francophile countries. That said, membership in the Anglosphere still informed the decision to establish diplomatic relations with Brazil, since a stronger presence there could enhance Canadians' international profile by positioning their country as a mediator between Brazil and the anglophone world, as well as between Great Britain and the United States in South America.[24]

## SOUTHBOUND CANADIANS

The dominant Canadian presence in Brazil at the time was that of the Light, a company whose operations predated the opening of a trade office in Rio de Janeiro in the early 1910s. It is not that Canada's trade commissioners were ineffective, merely that their work was generally overshadowed because official matters pertaining to Canada were generally handled through the British embassy. Under these circumstances, the Canadians who ran the Light, and who therefore held a near monopoly on tramway systems, hydroelectric infrastructure, and telephone services in cities like Rio de Janeiro and São Paulo – to name just two of the company's centres of operation – wielded more influence than the government representatives whom Ottawa sent to either city. From 1916 to 1936, the company's electricity output climbed from 2.6 million to more than 1.2 billion kilowatts, the number of its telephones in use increased from 31,000 to 166,000, and the number of passengers boarding its trams more than tripled, from 2.5 million to roughly 9 million. It was a crucial fixture of the economic landscape and could thus be considered "one of the most important factors in the growth of Brazil's industrial development."[25]

With its head office in Toronto, the Light came to stand in for the Dominion of Canada in the eyes of many Brazilians during the Vargas era. This, along with its sheer size in Brazil, raise the question: Was the company the financial incarnation of Canadian imperialism? It was not, argue Christopher Armstrong and H.V. Nelles, who note that its "initial Canadianness was a function of a highly developed and concentrated capital market that could readily mobilize savings for domestic or foreign investment." Yet, emphasizing the "*international* character"[26] of the Light does not refute the fact that the metropolitan finance capitalism to which it owed its existence derived from imperial practices and marked the company as clearly belonging to the English-speaking world.[27] Its Canadianness, no less than its Britishness and connection to the British Empire, was inherent and arguably hard to miss.

Kenneth H. McCrimmon, a nationalist in the Canadian imperialist tradition, was the company's de facto official voice in Brazil during the 1940s. Born in 1890 on the shores of Lake Huron, in the Scottish Presbyterian town of Kincardine, Ontario, he studied law and then served in the 18th Battalion of the Canadian Expeditionary Force during the First World War, earning a Distinguished Service Order and ascending to the rank of major before an injury forced him to return home. His uncle, Sir Alexander Mackenzie, railway magnate and president of the Light, invited him to relocate to Brazil in 1920. McCrimmon's "knack for conviviality," his abilities as a "social convener," and the ease with which he established "intimate contacts" with people of influence, including Aranha, served him well, particularly when it came to using Canada's image as a trustworthy friend to advance the company's interests.[28] Not one to strive for Canadian autonomy from Great Britain in the international sphere, he could still appreciate the practical advantages of Pan-Americanism and bilateral diplomatic relations, particularly once Vargas raised the spectre of nationalization as a possible component of the Estado Novo.

McCrimmon thus willingly served as a facilitator between Canada and Brazil.[29] In the summer of 1937, he contacted Aranha to encourage him to take a break from his ambassadorial post in Washington to visit Toronto. The invitation to travel north came from him and the "Canadian Octopus," McCrimmon wrote in a friendly and humorous way.[30] The diplomat could not free himself before his recall to Brazil, where he accepted the offer to lead the Itamaraty. The news of Aranha's return to Rio de Janeiro and his nomination as minister was welcomed favourably at the Light since he had made clear to Vargas that he was "very much against the policy of extreme nationalization," a threat that hovered over the company and caused heightened uncertainty about economic prospects.[31] McCrimmon could therefore hardly refuse Aranha's verbal request, in 1940, to communicate to External Affairs Brazil's wish for reciprocal diplomatic representation, since his "personal relations with him" were of a "somewhat intimate nature."[32]

It is unclear how much of what was conveyed actually came from Aranha, but officials in Ottawa did take note that McCrimmon, who was known as a "very strong imperialist," now advocated for "direct Canadian representation in Brazil," which he saw as necessary for Canada to take its place "in the future commercial and political relations of this hemisphere."[33] What appeared as an about-face was in fact an effort to find a place and a role for the Dominion within the Americas without the need for Canadians on the ground to shed their Britishness. McCrimmon sought to accomplish this by using the tropes of Pan-Americanism and Good Neighborism. In an interview with *O Jornal*, he underlined Canada's "spirit of Americanism" and discussed his fellow compatriots' desire "to live in the happy and harmonious communion which is one of the bases of tranquility and of progress" in the hemisphere. Seeking to clarify his point, he added: "Canada, although belonging, with pride, to the British Commonwealth, is an American nation, sensitive to the influence and spirit of Panamericanism and which tends … to become part of the same fellowship and to reciprocate the same affection which binds all the nations of this continent."[34] The Canada he described was resolutely British in its origins and its destiny, even if it was realigning itself with the ideals put forth by the PAU.

McCrimmon's endorsement of Pan-Americanism and Good Neighborism was part opportunism and part public relations since his sense of Britishness continued to shape his reactions to events unfolding on the ground. The United States' unbending efforts to monopolize the stage and dictate the course of events in South America were especially troublesome to him. For example, he was profoundly upset to learn that Washington had refused to allow Ottawa to send observers to a PAU conference scheduled to take place in Rio de Janeiro in January of 1942. In a letter to the Light's president, Sir Herbert Couzens, McCrimmon decried the fact that Canada's efforts to attend the conference had been "torpedoed by the United States," whose objectionable policy vis-à-vis South America he described as "Great Britain and the British Empire – hands off!" He denounced the "sweeping anti-British remarks" of Import-Export Bank president Warren Lee Pierson and reserved his most severe criticism for Jefferson Caffery, the United States ambassador to Brazil, who considered "himself a sort of emperor" and acted dismissively toward both Canadian and British officials. Yet he concluded on a positive note by remarking that the North American hegemon's self-serving policies were bound to enhance "Brazilian sympathy for Great Britain."[35]

McCrimmon's public persona and the Light's deep connections to the English-speaking world informed Brazilians' perception of Canada in the opening years of the 1940s. It was an essentialized image that centred on the country's Britishness and its so-called exceptionalism as a settler colony turned Dominion. The "English race," a reporter noted, was responsible for the moral and material progress of the "great Canadian nation." More specifically, "Canadians perfectly portray all the British beauties and virtues, and in their blood predominates, substantially, that imperishable principle of love of freedom, human dignity, distinctiveness of manners and clothing that make the 'homo britannicus' a unique being."[36] If Canada was deserving of such admiration and trust, so was the Light, with its "friendly and vigorous tentacles."[37]

Such generous and flattering comments were intended for Canadian expatriates and their associates in Canada and Great Britain. It is likely that Brazilians knew either very little about the Dominion and its diverse population or that their knowledge of Canada centred mostly on the country's connections to the Commonwealth and to London. Or else, it was an indication that they were willing to indulge Canadians by appearing to validate and amplify whatever image the Light and its spokespersons projected. In fact, this third option is closer to the truth since more than a handful of Brazilian officials, including Vargas and his closest advisers, knew that Canada was a composite of provinces, each with their own complicated histories, rooted in both the British and the French Empires.

As minister plenipotentiary to Brazil, Jean Désy offered a compelling counterpoint to the image of Canadians as largely defined by their Britishness. Born in 1893, and growing up in a medical family in Montreal, he attended the Jesuits Collège Sainte-Marie before earning a degree in law at the Université Laval's satellite campus in Montreal. He then studied economics at the École libre des sciences politiques in Paris, returning home to practise law from 1915 to 1917. Shortly after, he joined the faculty of his alma mater, which had, in the meantime, obtained its autonomy as the Université de Montréal. A founding member of the institution's Faculté des sciences sociales, he taught political history as well as institutional and constitutional law. A student – and later a colleague – of economist Édouard Montpetit, Désy participated in the making of the modern university in Quebec. Like his mentor, he believed in the possibility of a *bonne entente* between French and English Canadians, placing emphasis on the *fait français* as one of the country's strengths.[38] As such, he straddled the fence between tradition and modernity, following the lead of Montpetit, who "formed part of a French-speaking Catholic elite that was looking for ways of living with feet in both the older and the newer worlds."[39]

A short, indefatigable man with an air of nobility about him, Désy was also a lover of literature, painting, and especially music, which he discovered at a young age through his cousin, Sister Marie-Stéphane, a member of the Sisters of the Holy Names of Jesus and Mary, who later became director of the École supérieure de musique d'Outremont (ESMO). His connections to the Quebec cultural milieu were numerous, and he carefully nurtured them whether he worked from Ottawa or overseas. In the words of A.-J. Sarrazin, journalist at Radio-Canada, the French-language side of the Canadian Broadcasting Corporation (CBC), Désy was "genteel, elegant, with the manners of a great seigneur, not one to be pompous, he knows how to set the necessary boundaries, all the while remaining approachable. He is not very tall … with a keen eye and the most beautiful hands. One can easily imagine him at the court of Louis XIV."[40] Désy's wife, Corinne de Boucherville, a descendant of ennobled aristocrat Pierre Boucher, founder and seigneur of Boucherville, a settlement south of Montreal, provided additional substance to his grand aura.

Désy's participation in the international networks that emerged through Quebec-France intellectual exchanges was crucial from a career standpoint. Of particular importance was the Comité France-Amérique, an organization of which he was a member before joining External Affairs in 1925. Founded in Paris in 1909, it had as its mandate the strengthening of ties between France and Quebec, but also Francophile South America. Membership in the Montreal chapter came with a subscription to *Revue de l'Amérique latine*, a publication that foregrounded *latinité* as a shared cultural attribute through which French intellectuals and their counterparts in the Americas could foster dialogue and collaboration.[41] Désy did not seem to have been much inspired by that publication. Having spent time in Paris as a student and later as a professor teaching history at the Université de Sorbonne, he was primarily concerned with acting as an agent of cultural transfer between Montreal and the former imperial metropole. This was a privileged position for a French-Canadian intellectual in the early to mid-1920s.

The kind of networked internationalism that the Comité France-Amérique promoted appealed to people like Désy because it elevated them to the status of role models for others seeking to resist the hegemony of the English-speaking world. The French Canadians who travelled back and forth across the Atlantic had assumed a sense of duty and importance, prestige and legitimacy, as champions of both France's cultural heritage and Canada's *fait français*. The image of Quebec they put forward was that of a nation that had moved beyond *survivance* to find its place within Canada and in the world. They came to embody what Michel Lacroix calls the *figure du retour d'Europe* (which roughly translates to "the figure who returns from Europe"), a type of intellectual that embodied, and thus performed (in writing, speeches, dress, and cultural taste), the privileged relationship that connected Montreal to Paris.[42]

Theirs was a paradoxical mission in that they had to acknowledge a gap between the two cities – between Paris as a metropolis of art and culture and Montreal as a modernizing city slowly transcending its status as a former colonial city – in order to assert their authority as agents of cultural transfer. To deal with this quandary, it was necessary for the *figure du retour d'Europe* to rethink the France-Quebec relationship within a broader international framework. Lacroix explains: "This gap between the two cultures, which constitutes the basis of [the figure's] journey, is also what causes him to experience a double shock, both on the way there and back." This transatlantic voyage, Lacroix adds, "brings into play a complex dialectic, which leads him to deepen his *américanité* in France and his *européanité* in Quebec, but also to transcend the duality of this relationship through triangular connections (Quebec-France-Latin America; Quebec-France-Europe) or various other forms of cosmopolitanism."[43] Brazil would provide Désy with the opportunity to resolve this quandary, but he had yet to figure out how to reorient himself within his position at the Université de Montréal in the mid-1920s.

This might explain why he joined External Affairs. King had given Skelton the go-ahead to hire a counsellor, a post that required a "law degree or membership in a professional bar association, two years of post-graduate studies in international affairs, practical experience in legal work, and good knowledge of both English and French."[44] Although he apparently was the sole applicant, Désy got the job because he was evidently qualified to handle the tasks that the undersecretary of state for external affairs had reserved for him, namely, "legal matters, protocol, treaties, the League [of Nations (or LON)], and, when time permitted, commercial subjects."[45] He subsequently held the posts of counsellor to the delegate at the LON, assistant to the permanent delegate at the LON, and counsellor at the Paris legation. He was also part of the department's delegation at the 1929 Conference on the Operation of Dominion Legislation and Merchant Shipping Legislation in London, and he represented Canada at the Conference for the Codification of International Law held in The Hague the following year. This experience equipped him to assume the title of minister plenipotentiary at the joint Belgium-Netherlands legation when it opened in 1938.

It would have been out of character for Désy to stay in Ottawa. Incorporated in 1855 and designated the capital of the Province of Canada two years later, the city experienced an initial period of growth in the decades following Confederation, but it was a distant contender for the title of cultural centre, and could not possibly rival Montreal, let alone Paris or other European metropolises. Skelton himself knew that his protegé "would be much happier and do a much better job of representation abroad than office work at home."[46] To some degree, this was a function of the French language's marginal status within External Affairs.[47] Furthermore, travelling overseas was a means to demarcate oneself within an ever-growing department. Skelton hired forty-three men between 1926 and 1941 (twelve of them were French Canadians). They were "young officers that resembled him – academically trained, versatile professional men ... who could write fluently and reason critically; and rock hard nationalists who were skeptical of hegemonic outreach, whether it emanated from London or Washington."[48]

Désy may have chaired the committee responsible for evaluating some of these recruits, but his relative seniority did not shelter him from the underhanded criticism of bitter colleagues seeking promotions. His nomination to the post of counsellor at the Paris legation was an especially sore point among some of the "civil servants" who tended to be "uncivil" to him.[49] That the attacks came from fellow French Canadians was not surprising; opportunities in France were few and competition was fierce. Under these circumstances, Skelton proved to be a perceptive and supportive mentor.

The aspiring diplomat did find French-speaking allies in the corridors of power. Some were from his time with the Comité France-Amérique. Raoul Dandurand, president of the organization and Canada's representative to the LON in the mid-1920s, encouraged King and Skelton to send him to Paris, where his expertise was most needed.[50] Désy also learned from Ernest Lapointe, King's Quebec lieutenant, about the intricacies of domestic politics and their potential impact on foreign policy. The two had travelled together as part of the delegation attending the 1926 Imperial Conference, which culminated with the Balfour Declaration on Dominion autonomy. Not only did Lapointe contribute to Canada's efforts to find its place on the international stage, he also helped add a French-Canadian voice to the management of foreign affairs by offering King sound and persistent advice about Quebec. "Your teaching and example made their mark on my training," Désy confided to him upon the opening of the joint Belgium-Netherlands legation.[51]

Désy's first stint as minister plenipotentiary was abruptly cut short by the outbreak of war. On 10 May 1940, German forces invaded Belgium. Eighteen days later, the country capitulated. At the sound of the first bombs, his wife and two children, Mariel and Jean Louis, fled through France to Portugal, where they safely boarded a ship headed to North America. Désy stayed behind with his staff, relocating first to the Belgian city of Ostend before fleeing to Paris and then Lisbon. From there, they travelled to London, where they split their time between the Park Lane Hotel and bomb shelters. Exhausted after a long journey, all suffered sleepless nights while the Battle of Britain raged on.[52]

A crushing feeling of despair overtook Désy, who saw no end to the calamity he faced, despite knowing that his mission was likely over. Writing to Skelton and King, he inquired about the future of the legation. Told to stay put, he replied that a home leave ought to be considered if relocation to a new post was impractical. Désy added: "I beg respectfully to submit that I consider myself as responsible for the life of my personnel and that responsibility for mine rests with you."[53] The tone and content of the letter displeased the prime minister. The young diplomat apologized profusely. In a separate letter to Skelton, he wrote in a "confidential and private manner," not to his "chief," but to the man who had "honoured" him with his "friendly confidence." He emphasized the hardship he had experienced since arriving in Europe, his wife's difficult pregnancy, the pain of being separated from family, and a recent illness: "I did suffer very deeply and I do continue to suffer from the separation both as a father and as a husband." He continued: "So much the more because day after day I have the acute and persistent sensation that my presence here is worthless ... and that I can render no service of any value either to my country or to my own family."[54] Whether External Affairs sent

Désy to Brazil to give him a much-needed break or to keep him away from Ottawa is difficult to say. The opening of a legation in an exotic city located practically at the Tropic of Capricorn was certainly a fortuitous turn of events.

## CULTURAL CROSSROADS

It was not initially clear to Désy what Rio de Janeiro's ties to the French-language world were in 1941. The city was neither Paris nor Montreal, that much he knew. He was therefore hesitant to express interest for the post. Argentina, where External Affairs also intended to send a minister plenipotentiary, was apparently on his radar, but he was told that the department was more interested in a candidate with a background in economics who could pioneer diplomatic relations there. He could not let the opportunity for career advancement pass; Brazil would have to do. Skelton had died in January of that year, so Dandurand stepped in to petition on Désy's behalf. He explained to King that the former minister to the Belgium-Netherlands legation would now "gladly go to Brazil," and that he would "advance his knowledge of Portuguese" if given an "inkling" of the department's intentions.[55]

That cue came shortly after, along with the official announcement of Désy's appointment. There was urgency in the air since Nazi propaganda threatened to create a rift between Brazil and the Allies. It was also imperative that diplomatic relations be established sooner than later to facilitate communication on questions of trade amid the uncertainties of war. Not only that, the oppressive heat and humidity of the Brazilian summer, which peaked around November and December, would make the work of establishing the legation difficult. There was little time to provide clear instructions to Désy; he arrived in Rio de Janeiro on 10 September 1941 with little more than an approximate idea of his mission there. This left him with plenty of time to get a sense for the pulse of the city. What he might not have realized is that he would be well-received in Brazil as a French-speaking envoy who had spent many years studying and working in France. Considering Brazilians' long-standing ties to Paris, he might even feel at home.

Since the heyday of the turn-of-the-century tropical *belle époque*, the country's cultural and political elites had developed their Anglo- and Francophilia at the expense of the Portuguese metropole.[56] It was France that made the most indelible mark on Rio de Janeiro, the capital of the First Republic and, since 1937, of Vargas's Estado Novo. Its central avenue evoked Paris with its architectural marvels, many of which – the Theatro Municipal (Municipal Theatre) and the Museu Nacional de Belas Artes (National Museum of Fine Arts), among other – were inspired by French landmarks (the Opéra de Paris and the Musée du Louvre, respectively). "The Avenida, like the *belle époque* for which it stood, pulsed between ... colonial realities and metropolitan dynamism, in a constant counterpoint," writes Jeffrey D. Needell. "Civilization and Progress were generally rendered in French," he adds.[57] The Quai d'Orsay, France's Ministry of Foreign Affairs, actively nurtured this inclination by strengthening Brazilian-French cultural relations through initiatives such as the 1922 foundation of the Institut franco-brésilien de haute culture. Wealthy Brazilians learned French as a second language or attended classes in *lycées*. Many travelled to Paris to advance their education or, for the more artistically inclined, to find inspiration.[58]

Brazilians' Francophilia was motivated partly by genuine cultural admiration and partly by political savvy. France's inability to fulfill its imperial designs on the region in the sixteenth century ironically positioned it to later exert great influence, argue Robert Stam and Ella Shohat. It was "precisely the lack of a strong political/economic relationship, and the lack of a major French demographic presence in Brazil, that opened the way for phantasmatic projections on both sides."[59] It began with the importation of Enlightenment ideals, some fuelling anti-colonial revolts, and the transformation of the capital, which gave the *belle époque* tropical city its peculiar skyline, not to mention the transatlantic circulation of peoples and ideas that propelled the country's passage to modernity. Brazilians heartily borrowed from France to advance their own intricate agendas. They were neither naive nor blind to the Brazilophile exoticism with which their interlocutors often greeted them. French visitors and expats, just like their French-Canadian cousins, did not necessarily pay any heed to Brazilians' agency, concerned as they were with finding evidence of Francophilia to validate their self-image.[60]

Throughout much of the nineteenth century, Brazil's growing bourgeoisie sought immersion in European "high" culture to define itself in relation to and against its continental neighbours. This process found its initial momentum in 1807 when the invasion of Napoléon Bonaparte's troops forced João VI, regent and heir to the Portuguese Crown, to temporarily relocate to Brazil. The royal family's presence in Rio de Janeiro transformed the city's sense of its place in the world. Returning home in 1821 to reassert his leadership as king, João VI left behind his eldest son to act as prince regent of the colony. Pedro led Brazilians to their independence a year later by declaring himself emperor of Brazil. His son, Pedro II, eventually took over and headed the constitutional monarchy until he was deposed in 1889. Through marriage, João VI's son and grandson both maintained ties with Europe's main cultural centres, particularly in Germany, Italy, and France. The passage from empire to republic did not dramatically alter the cultural preferences of the Brazilian elites. They continued to look toward Europe even though a landed oligarchy, whose fortunes were based on dairy farming and coffee, now governed their country.

Salons, cultural hallmarks of Pedro II's reign, carried over into the tropical *belle époque* and beyond. Originating in Italy, these cultural gatherings were an integral part of the Parisian landscape in the seventeenth and eighteenth centuries. In the early years of the republic, Brazilians embraced them as opportunities to affirm their elite status. Salons were "cultural oases" where people of influence articulated their vision of Brazil as a nation on par with Europe.[61] As informal stages, they served as emerging centres of power, with hosts and guests, patrons and artists exchanging ideas on how to best steer their country on the path of modernity and progress. Cultivating a taste for "high" art was a marker of intellectual sophistication and a liberal mindset. These were key attributes in the eyes of those who believed they were destined to lead their country into the twentieth century. By constituting themselves as a "high" society, urban elites "adopted practices in their homes that identified them not just with aristocratic status, but, *ipso facto*, with Europe," explains Needell. It was a process of national self-definition characterized by "metropolitan identification within a neo-colonial context."[62]

Brazil's intellectual and cultural elites, however, could not settle for a culture of imitation in their search for a distinctive voice that would resonate both at home and abroad. In their contact with Europe, they were constantly reminded of their difference, whether it was the essentializing depiction of the Amazon as the site of cannibalistic rituals, or the exoticist gaze directed at the *favelas* where Afro-Brazilians were forging a new music of the street – namely, samba. Out of salons and informal gatherings emerged a cohort of artists who responded to the need for a self-affirming culture by creating original, hybrid works that evoked Brazil's multi-layered histories and modernist inclinations:

among others, Emiliano Augusto Cavalcanti, Graça Aranha, Mário de Andrade, Oswald de Andrade, Víctor Brecheret, Anita Malfatti, and Heitor Villa-Lobos, all of whom helped organized the seminal 1922 São Paulo *Semana de Arte Moderna* (Modern Art Week).[63]

That landmark event – with its combination of poetry, music, theatre, and painting – launched a nationalist cultural revolution that centred on the quest for a distinctive Brazilian essence. Going beyond opposition to academicism in the arts, it both engaged with European art forms and spoke affirmatively of the country's rich cultural fabric. In doing so, it rejected the racial thinking that denigrated and sought to silence Indigenous and Afro-Brazilian expressive cultures. From abolition to the end of the First Republic in 1930, proponents of scientific racism in Brazil shared with their North American and European counterparts the belief that Caucasians possessed superior qualities, as evidenced especially by the size and scope of their imperial ventures. Unlike them, however, Brazilians did not object to interracial mixing, because they claimed that white genes would eventually prevail over those of the so-called inferior races. Be that as it may, the theory of racial whitening was no less sinister in calling for the erasure of the Afro-Brazilian and Indigenous Other through miscegenation. The artists who participated in the *Semana de Arte Moderna* played a fundamental role in rebutting that theory through works that championed *Brasilidade*, a form of exceptionalism otherwise known as the "fable of three races."[64]

The renowned composer Heitor Villa-Lobos was a key figure in this. Born in Rio de Janeiro on 5 March 1887, he developed an appreciation for music at an early age. His father, a writer and civil servant at the Biblioteca Nacional (National Library), was an amateur musician who enjoyed attending salons and operas. Villa-Lobos resisted the formal training that music schools offered. Primarily self-taught, he picked up the guitar as well as the cello and began performing with various ensembles (from street bands to orchestras) to widen his musical horizons. The young artist developed a deep appreciation for both classical music and popular sounds rooted in Afro-Brazilian culture. He also sought out recordings of Indigenous music in addition to undertaking research trips to Brazil's interior; through the Northeast as well as to the states of Mato Grosso, Goiás, and Minas Gerais.[65] His early works – for instance, "Danças africanas" and "Choros 1" – revealed a keen disposition for hybrid musical languages. His enlarged sound palette, inventive use of traditional instruments, and innovative rhythmic patterns aimed to make audible a cross-section of Brazilian geography and cultural life.[66] By 1930, Villa-Lobos had established his reputation as the upholder of Brazil's "musical mosaic."[67]

The composer became a staunch supporter of the Vargas regime because of the opportunities it afforded him and the ways in which its national project aligned with that of the modernist artists of his generation. During his fifteen years in power, the president astutely solicited the assistance of members of the country's cultural and intellectual elites in order to harness their "confidence in their ability to articulate their *own* vision of Brazil's identity and future."[68] They were apt candidates for Vargas's own revolution, and many accepted positions on various committees or in federal institutions and ministries due to their "unequivocal faith in Brazilian nationhood coupled with a sense of duty."[69] In their capacity as cultural producers, policy-makers, and administrators, they found a niche for themselves in the state apparatus. Villa-Lobos himself handled the "musical fitness" of Brazilian children, instilling in them nationalism and patriotism, discipline and civic pride, in his capacity as director of the Superintendência de Educação Musical e Artística (SEMA, a government body created to oversee education in music and art).[70] The work that artists and intellectuals undertook for the regime served the dual purpose of promoting national unity and projecting an engaging image of Brazil abroad, both of which ultimately helped lend credibility to the Estado Novo. It did not matter that *Brasilidade* was a construct that masked deep inequalities: the belief that a "Brazilian essence" existed was both reassuring and empowering in the Brazil of the 1930s and '40s.[71]

It was a persuasive image with which to greet foreign visitors, who for the most part circulated within white elite circles and had little to no contact with less privileged Brazilians. Skelton himself had noted, after visiting Rio de Janeiro in 1922, that Canada's "great southern counterpart" could teach "the exploitative 'white man' to the north" a thing or two about "racial tolerance."[72] Désy felt the same way upon arriving there. No doubt, his interaction with Vargas and Villa-Lobos, whom he met at a salon-type musical event, informed his admiration of the country. It led him to report uncritically of Rio de Janeiro's pre-Lenten Carnival as a "friendly, kind hearted, and genuinely tolerant" form of "communal rejoicing." "The crowd," he added, "is also truly representative in that white, black, brown, mulatos, mestiços, and every conceivable combination mix freely together without the slightest trace of race prejudice."[73] Désy seemed unaware that Carnival was under state sponsorship by then and that it served Vargas's national project by promoting and eliciting pride in the idea of *Brasilidade*.[74] He did, however, note that the United States' envoys regarded the event "patronizingly as the rather mad manifestation of a semi-negroid race, or else disapprove thoroughly as a complete waste of time and money."[75] He was prompt to associate with his hosts as a means of setting himself apart from US-American diplomats.

Brazilians engaged Canadians using the trope of racial democracy to elicit feelings of friendship and reciprocal esteem. By depicting their two societies as racially progressive, they sought to distinguish themselves within the hemisphere and create a sense of affinity that would be the basis for closer cultural, political, and economic relations. At the turn of the 1940s, Brazilian newspapers were replete with references to Canada's two founding races, the French and the English, who lived harmoniously and displayed exceptional benevolence toward immigrants and Indigenous peoples. This was what Vargas had in mind when he spoke to Désy about their two countries' "heterogenous national components."[76] Reporters had praised the Canadian "homo-britannicus" in the past.[77] They now celebrated its Latin counterpart using the minister plenipotentiary as a model of amicability and progressiveness. "He arrived speaking our language," wrote a journalist from *A Noite* before highlighting the important role played by French Canadians in the cultural and political evolution of Canada.[78] *O Radical* joined the chorus by noting that the "union of the two races" in Canada offered an "example for Humanity."[79] The assumption, or course, was that the same was true of Brazil.

An astute propagandist, Vargas was under no illusion that the national unity question had been resolved in either country. His regime was actively involved in shaping perceptions at home and abroad. As for the situation to the north, Lourival Fontes, former director of the DIP, painted an especially dismal picture of the relations between French and English Canadians. He described the former as a "conservative and reactionary race." According to him, they found purpose in their opposition to the latter, a non-cohesive group that lacked national consciousness due to their conflicting allegiances to the British Empire and the United States.[80]

Despite that knowledge, Vargas and his associates in government and the public sector proved surprisingly adept at staying on message and tailoring the trope of racial democracy to fit Canada. When mobilizing the fable of three races in international contexts, they tended to emphasize Afro-Brazilians rather than Indigenous peoples. The latter, however, predominated in the Vargas regime's interactions with Canadians, because of the prevalence of whiteness in representations of the North. Approaching Canada via the same logic that informed the concept of *Brasilidade*, Raul Leitão da Cunha, rector of the Universidade do Brasil (University of Brazil), could thus assert, during a public forum on Canada-Brazil cultural relations, that "Canadian history reveals the beneficent efforts of the coinciding influences of the energies and virtues of the aborigenes, Indians and Esquimoes, and of the Europeans, English and French, in the formation of the superior qualities of the Canadian people."[81] With this hyperbole, Leitão intended to underscore the exceptionalism of the Canadian and Brazilian settler experience. In doing so, however, he ascribed to Indigenous peoples a more important role (even if only in the past) than the one Désy had reserved for them in his narrative about Canada.

## CANADA'S IMAGE

Having taken the initiative, the Vargas regime found an eager interlocutor in Désy. "I want to live the Brazilian way," he told reporters, as if Canada's rapprochement with Brazil could be embodied.[82] In Rio de Janeiro, he felt a sense of purpose that he arguably had not felt since his days with the Comité France-Amérique. Here was an opportunity to act, once again, as an agent of cultural transfer – only this time culture would flow out of Montreal. He hoped to elevate the city's status to that of a cultural metropolis, a centre of French culture, perhaps even a surrogate Paris. His first meeting with the president alerted him to the potential benefits of foregrounding the image of Canada as a racially diverse nation. The musical evenings that he attended subsequently introduced him to the city's Francophile elite. Désy thus felt inspired to mobilize French-Canadian artists to speak of diversity and nationhood in terms that Brazilians could understand. He was, of course, bound to benefit from this on all fronts, even if it was only by accumulating cultural capital in his capacities as a diplomat and patron of the arts.

It was easy for him to embrace the image of Canada as a racial democracy: it aligned with his ideal of a bicultural federal state. It was also consistent with the country's efforts to present itself as a model in its pursuit of autonomy and middlepowerhood on the world stage.

It sent a potent message of tolerance and co-operation amid war with an optimistic eye to the peace that would follow. That said, it was evident to him that the only protagonists who mattered in the story of Canada were the descendants of white settlers. There were, accordingly, limits to transposing the concept of *Brasilidade* to the Canadian context. Désy tried to make that adamantly clear in the many speeches he gave in front of predominantly white elite Brazilian audiences.

A former professor of history, the Canadian diplomat excelled at weaving compelling narratives that would engage his audience. Canada and Brazil shared a past and a destiny, he remarked. Aside from their resource-rich and idyllic landscapes, the two countries were each penetrated by majestic rivers that carried the names of canonized Catholic figures: São Francisco and Saint Lawrence. Désy liked to populate his stories with "great men" like *bandeirante* (pioneer) Pascoal Moreira Cabral and explorer Pierre Gaultier de Varennes, or Jesuit missionaries Antonio Vieira and Jean de Brébeuf, whose lives left a deep imprint on the "community of influences" as well as the "community of habits and thoughts" that bound Canadians and Brazilians.[83] Our two nations "have slowly discovered, cleared, and fashioned the land which our ancestors had chosen for us," Désy explained. "We have humanised it in our image. We have peopled it with men, sacrifices, words, and thoughts. Our works have given it their impress. We can say ... that in the barbarous force of a new country an old root has found once more its adolescence." Désy marvelled here at the so-called exceptionalism of the two settler colonies, their warm and resilient community-oriented peoples, and the importance of culture in preserving "the essential features which differentiate us, while bringing us together."[84]

Although most of his protagonists were French Canadians, Désy noted that industrious and enlightened English-speaking Canadians played no small part in the nation's development. The two "founding races" had learned to live harmoniously with each other in ways that set them apart from less tolerant societies, he implicitly argued. The essentializing and dehumanizing depiction of Indigenous peoples, subsumed here within the "barbarous force of a new country," was intentional; Désy did not see them as active participants in his contemporary setting.[85] Neither did he assign any role to members of the many ethnic and national diasporas that helped build Canada and whose members were fighting valiantly on the battlefields of Europe and the Pacific.

In other words, white normativity had to prevail if Canadians and Brazilians were to revel in the belief that they were intimately connected. "Whiteness," Marilyn Lake and Henry Reynolds contend, "provided a mode of subjective identification that crossed national borders and shaped global politics."[86] It functioned as a "gate-keeping mechanism" that served to "justify claims of privilege" and sustain – both globally and domestically – the subjugating and excluding practices of settler societies, including Canada and Brazil.[87] The imagined community that Désy alluded to when he spoke of living the "Brazilian way" contained marked boundaries and zones of exclusion, even if it was informed by the discourse of *Brasilidade*. It upheld a "transnational form of racial identification" that emerged at imperial crossroads and "shaped white men's sense of collective belonging" as active agents in the West's so-called civilizing mission.[88]

Désy's view of history centred on white settler colonists at the expense of other groups deemed to be outside the nation. In this way, it adhered to a "logic of elimination" whereby the Indigenous Other had to be silenced, made invisible, and buried in the past for the idea of Canadian exceptionalism to hold sway.[89] Whereas *Brasilidade* called for an engagement with Indigenous cultures, the idea of "Canadianness," as a compact between two founding races, required relegating these same cultures to the distant past in the 1940s. The French, English, Scots, and Irish were those who cultivated and imbued with their spirited presence the "national terrain," Désy wrote.[90] By not writing Indigenous peoples or diasporic communities into his narrative, he could avoid discussing Canada's colonial legacy, and thus depict the country as having been forever white and free of racism.

The diplomat's first cultural initiatives in Brazil served to substantiate this particular reading of Canada's past. Cases in point are the two large paintings that he commissioned from Alfred Pellan, a towering figure of the Quebec fine arts world who had spent the greater part of the 1920s and '30s rubbing shoulders with the likes of Pablo Picasso, Henri Matisse, and Salvador Dalí. Having just returned from Paris, the artist brought to Montreal the "spirit of liberty and of acceptance," helping to transform the city in the early 1940s.[91] "A Fauve, a cubist, a surrealist, Pellan is much more than all that; he is the synthesis and the moving image of the modern era," wrote one of his contemporaries. Conscious that the gallery-going public was not entirely versed in these art movements, Pellan sought to facilitate its passage toward experimental forms of expression by revisiting the more familiar language of landscape painting made popular by the iconic Group of Seven. The "transitional style" that he championed upon his return to Canada appealed to Désy.[92] Not only did it speak to the legacy of Canada's first national art movement, but it also emerged out of the Paris-Montreal axis, thereby creatively easing the tension between tradition and modernity.

Titled *Canada East* and *Canada West*, the paintings arrived in Rio de Janeiro in March of 1943. "Murals received in perfect order. Enthusiastic. Very grateful," telegrammed Désy, who promptly hung the works in the waiting room of the legation.[93] They were large, colourful depictions of the country's landscape: from lively towns dotting the shores of a Laurentian Mountain river to majestic totem poles standing next to a densely built city, both against the backdrop of the Rocky Mountains. Pellan populated his paintings with men and women serenely engaged in working the land or admiring its spectacular beauty. They communicated both a connection to the past and a sense of optimism for the future. The sole Indigenous presence, a man stereotypically shown smoking a pipe and wearing a feathered headdress, appeared to be fixed in time as if on display for Pellan's tourists and urban dwellers. Side by side, the two works spoke of the settlers' westward march and the passage of time.

The act of mobilizing Indigenous expressive cultures, either through pictorial representations or state-sponsored displays and exhibits, constituted an assertion of authority over peoples deemed to be outside of the national project in the early decades of the 1900s. It served the state's efforts to dispossess Indigenous communities of their land and culture by making them invisible and denying them agency. The interwar landscape paintings of the Group of Seven, and that of other artists who followed in their footsteps, reinforced the "evolutionary narrative" of the Canadian settler society through barren sceneries or the depiction of totem poles as vestiges of the past left there for the taking.[94] A.Y. Jackson, co-founder of the group, could thus write of "Our Tottering Totems" as a "monument to a vanishing race."[95] Relegating the Indigenous Other to the distant past allowed him and his colleagues to present themselves as being solely responsible for fashioning a truly living, homegrown art for Canada. They were, ipso facto, echoing the "discourse of disappearance" that folklorists such as Marius Barbeau were advancing. As Leslie Dawn explains, this "discursive framework … included the proposition that the diverse native populations in Canada … had long been absent from the contemporary scene, and that they had left a vacant site to be filled by … artists who could produce the image of a nation based on their absence."[96]

Whether he intended it or not, Pellan helped put forward a similar view of the past with the paintings that he sent to Brazil. Ever resourceful, Désy managed to place two articles in Brazilian publications to convey that message. The Montreal-based art historian Maurice Gagnon explained in *A Vida* that the works were fashioned in the image of the Canadian people, a young, peaceful, blessed nation that believes in the fellowship of man. Gagnon continued: "The artist reveals the charm of a chosen land, loved by God. In authentic tones, he articulated the profound honesty of our race and the generous hospitality with which we … welcome the friend who falls under the charm of our landscape."[97] The totem poles, according to Gagnon, were part of the landscape that Pellan vividly juxtaposed against flourishing modern cities. They were artifacts of a time that came before the so-called discovery and cultivation of the land by the French. Robert Ford, one of External Affairs' promising new recruits and a member of Désy's diplomatic staff, offered a similar reading in a separate article published in *Sombra*.[98] These articles ensured that *Canada East* and *Canada West* were also seen and understood by those who may not have had a chance to actually visit the legation. They also positioned French Canadians as active, even leading, participants in the national terrain.

Désy deployed music toward similar ends. At around the same time that he commissioned the two paintings, he asked the composer Claude Champagne to prepare a cultural gift for Brazilians: a musical homage that would display French Canadians' sophistication and their cultural sensibility to *Brasilidade*. Like Pellan, Champagne studied in Paris, where he made a name for himself with the orchestral works "Hercule et Omphale" and "Suite canadienne." Back in Canada in 1929, he focused his energies on administrative and teaching duties while helping reform music education in Quebec. He was instrumental in setting the foundation for the provincial law to which the CMQM owed its existence. In his capacity as assistant director of the new institution, he busied himself trying to elevate the city's musical life by preparing future generations for successful careers within the province and beyond.[99]

Seeking inspiration in the works of Villa-Lobos and other Brazilian composers who were pushing the aesthetic boundaries of musical nationalism, Champagne wrote "Quadrilha brasileira," a composition for piano based on an Indigenous folk melody from Marajó Island.

Located in the north of Brazil, at the mouth of the Amazon River, the island had been home to a rich pre-Columbian culture that came to have potent symbolic meaning through the discourse of *Brasilidade*. Champagne most likely learned of the melody through one of his Brazilian counterparts, with Désy acting as an intermediary and translator. The composer was known and celebrated for his award-winning, folk-infused "Suite canadienne," a work based on French-Canadian songs from the days of New France. He was not, however, in the habit of appropriating Indigenous material. "Noël Huron," a carol that spoke of the Jesuits' civilizing mission, was a notable exception, though it was hardly a celebration of Indigenous culture. As an exercise in composition, "Quadrilha brasileira" was different, because it was for and about Brazilians.

Yet the piece revealed something about Canadians' position vis-à-vis Brazil. Encounters with the musical Other is rarely unproblematic in that asymmetrical relations are nearly always at play when Western music ventures into unfamiliar territory. The resulting power dynamics are often audible. As Timothy D. Taylor explains, such tensions have a noticeable impact on composition: "Political and geographical margins are peculiarly energetic sites where meanings are made, remade, altered, transformed, altered again," he writes. "It becomes clear that marginality – either as positionality or in representation – plays a pivotal role in forming and altering worldviews and thus … aesthetic processes."[100] Whereas Villa-Lobos enlarged his sonic palette and orchestration to engage with Indigenous expressive cultures, Champagne did not significantly modify his compositional practice. His musical homage was clearly indebted to the French school, notably the Romantic composers Ernest Chausson and Charles-Camille Saint-Saëns. The melody that inspired "Quadrilha brasileira" thus appeared sublimated, even subsumed, within the Western classical music tradition. Moreover, the piano piece appeared to move through time, evolving from Romanticism to Impressionism, with a major seventh chord ending that doubled as a "kind of wink" to Maurice Ravel.[101] In this way, it set the musical mood for Canada-Brazil relations by making audible the normative mindset that informed Champagne's – and by extension, French Canadians' – sense of place in the world.

Brazil's musical response to "Quadrilha brasileira" suggests that Désy's message about the disappearance of the Indigenous Other in Canada and the importance of French-Canadian culture was well understood. It came from Francisco Mignone, a celebrated pianist and composer-educator who studied in Italy with Vincenzo Ferroni prior to joining the faculty of Rio de Janeiro's Instituto Nacional de Música (National Institute of Music) in 1934. Like Villa-Lobos, he belonged to a school of artists who embraced the nation's cultural diversity by using complex harmonies and rhythms. In the winter of 1943, he wrote "Três prelúdios (sobre temas canadenses)," a short piano piece based on three French-Canadian folk songs. Mignone most likely composed it at the request of Désy, who planned to have it premiered, along with "Quadrilha brasileira," during the Dominion Day celebrations scheduled for 1 July 1943.[102] Instead of Indigenous melodies, "Três prelúdios (sobre temas canadenses)" featured vignettes from "Marianne s'en va-t-au moulin," "Sainte Marguerite veillez ma petite," and "À la claire fontaine," which spoke of French Canadians' connections to France and their deep roots in North America. Mignone had evidently assimilated Désy's and Champagne's language.

This exchange of musical gifts helped establish the terms – and delimit the boundaries – within which to think about Canada-Brazil relations. If the initiative for establishing reciprocal relations originated with the Vargas regime, its deployment owed a lot to Désy's willingness to reinvent himself as a new kind of diplomat and an eminent ambassador for French-Canadian culture. The speeches that he gave and the works that he commissioned during his first year and a half in Rio de Janeiro revealed the extent to which Canada's international image could be shaped by individual actors eager to conflate their personal and national identities. In Brazil, Désy seized the opportunity to resume the role of agent of cultural transfer, with the difference that Montreal now appeared to him as a cultural centre in its own right. He could therefore mobilize its artists and foreground their art to both elevate his status and project an image of Canada that he hoped would resonate at home and abroad. Championing the country's *fait français* in this way was judicious considering the Brazilian elites' perceived Francophilia. Moreover, it was easy to reconcile with Canadians' search for a distinctive voice on the international stage. His cultural diplomacy also underscored the usefulness of music and the visual arts in negotiating the boundaries of whiteness in Canada-Brazil relations. The two nations were getting to know each other. The stage, so to speak, was set for the next chapter in their cultural rapprochement.

# 2

# Musically Imagined Communities

Dominion Day celebrations in Canada were, for all intents and purposes, over by 11:00 p.m. on 1 July 1943. Or so it must have seemed to the shortwave radio enthusiasts synchronizing their equipment to northbound transmissions originating from Rio de Janeiro. Their reaction must therefore have been one of surprise when they realized that, not only were festivities taking place and continuing there, but one of their own, Jean Désy, wished them well on the airwaves. Then, there was music: "Três prelúdios (sobre temas canadenses)," performed by the French-Canadian pianist Jean Dansereau, followed by "Quadrilha brasileira," with Brazil's Arnaldo Estrella at the piano.[1] Sponsored by Rádio Nacional (National Radio), one of Getúlio Vargas's key instruments of domestic and foreign propaganda, this homage to Canada was unlikely to be heard by many of Désy's compatriots. But that did not matter since they were arguably never the primary target audience for the broadcast, whose real purpose was to generate press and interest for cultural diplomacy initiatives unfolding on the ground in Brazil. In other words, its aim was to amplify, even if only in appearance, a sense of proximity and a feeling of mutual esteem between Brazilians and Canadians.

Dansereau's presence in the Brazilian capital marked a pivotal moment in this cultural rapprochement. He and his wife, soprano Muriel Tannehill, arrived in June of 1943 for a series of concerts organized under the auspices of the Canadian legation. This official visit by an artistic couple, in the aftermath of Brazil's entry into the war, had no precedent in the history of the two countries' relations, which led the journalist H. Coutinho to highlight the significance of this "art offer" in the pages of *Jornal do Brasil*. "The Dansereau couple … is one more link in the strong chain of friendship that unites the two sister nations," he wrote enthusiastically.[2] They are "ambassadors" of "cultural harmony" from a country to which we are bound by "fraternal feelings," added a colleague from *Correio da Manhã*.[3] The trope of family deployed here underscored music's potential to affirm Canadians' and Brazilians' spiritual affinity and shared cultural values, attributes that appeared to substantiate the idea that the two nations had more in common with each other than with the United States.

The tour promised to call into existence a musically imagined community. Dansereau and Tannehill, just like their Brazilian counterparts – and with Désy's encouragement – displayed their differences in subtle ways, using music to come together under the shadow of the North American hegemon. Benedict Anderson's work on nationalism, which theorizes the concept of an imagined community, does not say much about music, despite making the argument that media and expressive cultures are integral to the constitution and endurance, across time and space, of collective identities. It does, however, point to the singing of national anthems as an "experience of simultaneity" that can bring up the image of "unisonance" and thus inform how people think about themselves and others. Imagined communities also emerge through "imagined sounds," Anderson concedes.[4] They tend to be nationally bounded, but not always. Indeed, "sonorous coexistence" often occurs in transnational contexts, thereby fostering new kinds of musically imagined communities that can "generate new identities" and help "imagine new configurations of international relations."[5]

By inviting Dansereau and Tannehill to perform in Rio de Janeiro, Désy set in motion a cultural campaign that reflected his astute reading of Brazil's politico-cultural landscape. First, the initiative was in keeping with the spirit of friendliness expressed through Claude Champagne's and Francisco Mignone's compositions. The Dominion Day event added a crucial embodied and affective dimension to this exchange of musical gifts. Second, the Dansereau and Tannehill tour clearly positioned "serious music" as the chosen language through which the two countries would pursue their rapprochement, which was consistent with Brazilians' preference as evidenced by the Vargas regime's own musical diplomacy. A cultural marker of sophistication and vitality, it was the language that one needed to master to take part in the concert of nations. The artistic couple proved to be adroit impromptu ambassadors in the way they helped project an exciting image of Canada. Moreover, and no less important, they were personable envoys whose art fostered heartfelt people-to-people interactions.

This latest exercise in musical diplomacy may have seemed superfluous, if not wasteful, with the conflict in Europe and the Pacific raging in the background, but it still served the purpose of advancing the legation's goals. Désy had a broad mandate that ranged from promoting trade, encouraging Brazilians in their war effort, and restoring their faith in liberal democracy. What is more, he brought to his job a particular understanding of how culture – French-Canadian culture, more specifically – could enhance Canada's image overseas. A skillful actor in the influence game in Brazil, Désy availed himself of the avenues presented to him. His opportunistic use of the dictatorship's cultural infrastructure helped ensure that Dansereau and Tannehill's tour was a productive one. The couple's stage and radio performances straddled the fence between tradition and modernity, as well as between difference and sameness, while conveying normative ideals about modernity and progress. They displayed cultural competence and leadership, which reflected well on Canada, but also on Quebec and Montreal. Most significantly, it inspired a musically imagined community that could perhaps chart its own path as a sort of counterpoint to the United States' cultural agenda in South America.

## LEGATION AFFAIRS

Désy found himself in uncharted territories when he arrived in Rio de Janeiro to pioneer diplomatic relations with Brazil. He was very much aware that Ottawa was more likely to support his cultural initiatives if they could be tied to the legation's overall objectives. That is how he got External Affairs to purchase a piano, a "highly desirable instrument of high class propaganda."[6] Likewise for Alfred Pellan's paintings, which were paid for by the Department of Trade and Commerce.[7] Désy's job, after all, was to depict Canada in the best light possible so as to build trust and increase trade prospects while getting Brazilians to side with the Allies in the war. There was a sense of urgency to this project since Nazi propaganda and covert agents were undermining the United States' efforts there by stirring up anti-US-American sentiments. Yet Désy was optimistic, even after just a few weeks in his post. Developments in Brazil are "drawing much nearer to our interests," and they will ultimately work in "our favour," he told his colleagues back home.[8]

Chief among these developments was the sealing of a new trade agreement in October of 1941. It was the high point of Minister of Trade and Commerce James MacKinnon's visit to Brazil. With a group of colleagues from Ottawa, he had travelled from Peru to Argentina, stopping in Chile and Uruguay along the way, to explore opportunities in South America. In Rio de Janeiro and São Paulo, the delegation met with Brazilian industrialists and financiers, connected with representatives from the Light as well as members of the British community, and lunched with Minister of Foreign Affairs Oswaldo Aranha, a "mark of rare goodwill." Vargas himself hosted an event for MacKinnon, "a singular honour which, by itself, would be sufficient to demonstrate the desire of the Brazilian government to make the Mission's trip successful," remarked Désy.[9] An improvement on the 1931 and 1937 agreements, the new deal extended unconditional and unrestricted most-favoured nation status to the South American giant. By the end of 1942, wartime trade with Brazil totalled nearly $15 million, a 30 per cent increase from two years earlier. That number paled compared to trade with the United States ($2.2 billion) and the United Kingdom ($909 million), but the growth was nonetheless an encouraging sign that Brazilians valued their relationship to Canadians.[10]

The Vargas regime's investment in this rapprochement was apparent in the efforts it deployed to have Canadians take part, even if only as observers, in the PAU conference scheduled to take place in Rio de Janeiro at the end of January 1942. President Franklin Delano Roosevelt, still dealing with the shock of Pearl Harbor, was hoping to bring the hemisphere's republics to his side and have them cut diplomatic ties to the Axis powers. MacKinnon and his colleagues from the trade mission argued that Canadians ought to participate in the organization's activities since they were best positioned to play the roles of "interpreter and mediator between the United States and Latin America."[11] Désy agreed and was inclined to encourage Aranha to lobby on behalf of Canada.

Brazil's support of Canada on the PAU question was evidently self-serving. The United States opposed extending membership, or even granting observer status, to the Dominion, because it was a constitutional monarchy and a member of the Commonwealth. The Vargas regime interpreted the State Department's firm position as a "further manifestation of United States Imperialism and desire of exclusive influence in South America."[12] Having Canada join could help change the balance of power in the organization. This could benefit Brazil, which was seeking to consolidate its status as a regional power. In the same way that MacKinnon thought Canada could mediate between the United States and the republics, Brazil thought it could mediate between the two North American neighbours on its own quest for middlepowerhood.[13]

There was an abundance of wishful thinking in the Vargas regime's expectation that Canada would consider further implicating itself in South American affairs. Granted, it was easy to misread recent developments as indications that the country was striving toward membership in the PAU. Expansion in trade and investments had been a major factor motivating Canadians to travel and set up operations in the region. Toronto- and Montreal-based capitalists were early pioneers of bilateral relations there. They laid much of the groundwork for the political and diplomatic ties that would be established in the 1940s. These non-state actors were among the first to advocate for greater autonomy from Great Britain in the making of external affairs. The experience of war gave additional momentum to Canada's passage from colony to nation, and it provided incentives to look south to both consolidate markets and search for opportunities to perform middlepowerhood. On the one hand, Canada could step in on behalf of Great Britain in South America, keeping a watchful eye on Commonwealth interests while London focused its energies and resources on winning the war in Europe. On the other hand, Canada's postwar self-interests were likely to be better served through close collaboration with the United States on hemispheric questions.[14] Ottawa needed to tread lightly if it was to avoid antagonizing either of its North Atlantic partners while it assessed whether the PAU was a viable avenue for pursuing such a conflicting agenda.

Opinions varied on the question of membership in the organization. Those who approached the topic from the perspective of economics, such as MacKinnon and the Light's Kenneth H. McCrimmon, were inclined to favour membership. Support also came from Quebec, where nationalists saw the PAU as either a vehicle to halt US-American imperialism or as a venue for amplifying the voices of those countries with a shared culture of Catholicism and *latinité*. Even London's Foreign Office thought – though without saying so publicly – that Canadian membership would have its benefits, notably by helping ensure "the retention of British imperial extensions," from the West Indies to the Falkland Islands.[15] Yet many in Ottawa perceptively feared that the South American republics would try to use Canada as a "counterweight to the United States," thus impeding its ability to adopt a carefully calibrated position in accordance with its priorities within the North Atlantic triangle.[16] In any case, there was insufficient public interest in the question, not to mention a general lack of knowledge about the specifics of hemispheric affairs, to warrant aggressively pushing for a seat at the PAU table. Not wishing to complicate relations with the Roosevelt administration, officials in Ottawa did not think it worthwhile to challenge the "technical difficulties" invoked to deny Canada an observer status. Although they were appreciative of the attention, they had little choice but to ask Désy to tell Aranha that he should "not, repeat not," propose that Canada be invited.[17]

President Vargas had plenty of reasons to be wary about the direction in which things were headed with the United States. His bargaining strategies created opportunities that looked promising at first. They made possible substantive financial (millions in Lend-Lease aid and direct investments in steel production) and material (weapons and munitions as well as various industrial goods) assistance, which allowed Brazil to modernize its economy and assert itself as a regional power vis-à-vis a perceived hostile neighbour like Argentina, a country engaged in its own quest for influence. However, much of this help was conditional on the United States getting access to air and naval bases in the Brazilian Northeast. The region was of interest due to its relative proximity to West Africa, some three thousand kilometres across the Atlantic Ocean. Like an exposed flank, the coast was vulnerable to attacks in the early years of the war. The United States constructed new airfields and naval stations there, and modernized existing ones, effectively transforming the area into a strategic base from which to partake in anti-submarine warfare or launch potential missions. Thousands of military and civilian personnel soon flooded the region, most of whom had little to no knowledge of Brazil and its diverse population. As Joseph Smith explains, they treated the country as a "satellite of the United States throughout the war."[18]

Increased racial tension was an unforeseen consequence of this wartime activity. Brazil eventually entered the conflict on the side of the United States, in part to cement its reputation as a capable and trustworthy ally. Participation could also help enhance the dictatorship's image. Its message of racial harmony was highly relevant in the context of the renewed internationalism embodied by the planned United Nations and in light of the atrocities perpetrated by Nazi Germany. Yet developments in the country's agricultural North undermined this. In an article published by *Correio da Manhã*, the widely respected writer Dinah Silveira de Queiroz decried the importation of white supremacist views to a region where Afro-Brazilians constituted most of the population. Not only did it jeopardize hemispheric solidarity, but it also undermined the principles of tolerance and freedom for which Brazilians were fighting in the war, she wrote. In a clever show of argumentative skills, she offered the following advice: "Let us remind ... our dear American neighbours of the *good neighbour* example that we are setting between whites and blacks."[19] The writer and politician Mauricio de Medeiros also spoke out on the issue. Referring to the United States' cultural penetration of Brazil as "Coca-Cola-lisation," he warned *Diario Carioca* readers that perverse capitalism, unfettered individualism, and racial prejudice were a threat to the moral and social fabric of their society.[20] Especially worrying to him were those Brazilians who, following examples set in the North, started promoting Jim Crow–like regulations in the predominantly white industrial South.

Désy reported on these matters as he learned about them in the press. They compelled him to think more critically about the myth of racial democracy and the class-based obstacles that limited the social and economic mobility of racialized peoples. Yet for all its shortcomings, he thought, Brazilians' approach to race relations was admirable. He therefore concurred with the two writers regarding the danger posed by the "gradual shift towards the American view-point in the 'whiter' parts of the country, which are also the most industrialised, that is São Paulo, and the states of the South, where, incidentally, the German element is strongest."[21] The idea that Canadians could claim the moral high ground was validated in the eyes of Désy when he received, on 13 May 1944, a "curious invitation" to be a guest of honour at a ceremony organized by the "coloured people of Brazil" who, seeking to commemorate the abolition of slavery in the country, wished to also "pay special homage to glorious Canada."[22] At the very least, it was an indication that the image of the country as the product of a harmonious compact between two tolerant peoples, the French and the English, resonated positively in 1940s Rio de Janeiro.

Watching from a distance, Canadian and British observers realized early on that the United States' image problem could work to their advantage. Some Brazilians voiced their frustration publicly in the press. Many others did so behind closed doors. They denounced the patronizing attitude, tactlessness, and arrogance of US-American envoys. They decried their self-serving ambitions and "lack of a spirit of genuine collaboration."[23] At first glance, Brazil appeared to enrich itself through this relationship, but the increased wealth resulting from the United States' economic penetration of the country also caused inflation and deepened social inequalities. British ambassador Noel Charles shared his thoughts on the matter with Désy: "The lavishness with which Americans are paid and the ways in which they live, especially the personnel at air and naval bases in the north, arouses envy and leads to unpleasantness."[24] Canada's minister plenipotentiary reached the same conclusion after discussing the issue with industrialists, reporters, and government officials in Rio de Janeiro. There is a "general dislike on the part of Brazilians of United States control of their country," he told Prime Minister William Lyon Mackenzie King in March of 1943.[25] In a separate, secret dispatch, Désy noted their "continuing suspicion … of American imperialist designs within the framework of Panamericanism."[26] The rhetoric of Good Neighborism, he argued, could only accomplish so much.

## MUSICAL PAN-AMERICANISM

For the greater part of the previous decade, President Roosevelt worked hard to improve his country's international image. In his 1933 inaugural address, he sought to reassure his South American counterparts that he desired to build bridges through trust and understanding, not coercion, and that bilateral and multilateral relations would henceforth take place in a spirit of true friendship. His Good Neighbor policy encouraged investment in cultural productions and artistic exchanges to promote mutual understanding and awareness between and among the hemisphere's republics.[27] The rise of fascism and the threat of communism rendered more urgent this cultural outreach. In 1938, the Roosevelt administration created the Division of Cultural Relations in the State Department. Two years later, it established an agency that became known as the Office of the Coordinator of Inter-American Affairs (OCIAA) under the leadership of the businessman and philanthropist Nelson Rockefeller. Good Neighbor activities were wide-ranging (from musical tours to film screenings, book exchange programs, and carefully curated exhibitions), and they rested on bold partnerships with cultural giants, such as Walt Disney Productions and the Museum of Modern Art, to give a positive spin on the United States' relations with South America. But however well-intentioned, this "cultural offensive" often doubled as "economic and psychological warfare," which tended to aggravate, rather than alleviate, uneasiness.[28]

Music was one of the preferred instruments to advance Good Neighborism. Departmental Order 768, to which the Division of Cultural Relations owed its existence, considered musical diplomacy to be a potent means of promoting the national interest.[29] The State Department thus equipped itself with a Music Sub-Committee that provided policy recommendations. In 1939, the United States hosted the first Inter-American Music Conference to encourage dialogue among musicians, producers, and agencies while also accumulating knowledge about cultural networks and infrastructure in South America. Rockefeller's OCIAA had its own Cultural Relations Division. Operating independently from the State Department, its Music Committee offered both advisory and operational expertise. As a component of an innovative propaganda machine, it had as its mandate to improve the United States' image, part of the larger effort to facilitate acceptance of – and support for – the country's goals in the southern hemisphere. It accomplished that by helping state agents and their non-state associates move into positions of influence as producers and critics as well as patrons and officiators. It sent prominent music scholars on lecture tours. It also sponsored concerts in cultural capitals, organized competitions with generous prizes, and invited foreign artists north. These initiatives served the dual purpose of bringing people together around the shared experience of music while putting on display the United States' resources and expertise.[30]

That Good Neighborism championed "serious music" so as to "bolster American cultural prestige" was, of course, purposeful.[31] In referring to classical or symphonic works as "serious music," State Department officials and their colleagues in Rockefeller's committee favoured an art form that appeared to them as superior, structurally and aesthetically, to less formalized and less complex vernacular musical sounds. As a value-laden synonym for "art music" or "erudite music," "serious music" conveyed a clear sense of elitism. Yet it also betrayed anxiety on the part of many of its champions, who often juxtaposed it against categories of "popular music" to reinforce cultural hierarchies in the search for legitimacy and power.[32] As an ideology, "serious music" was a response to the status anxiety felt by intellectual and cultural elites who grappled with the social and structural changes that accompanied modernity and nation building in Europe during the late eighteenth and early nineteenth centuries. By making "serious music" one of the pillars of their "high" cultural nationalism, these elites claimed that only they had the "technical, intellectual, and emotional resources" to consolidate the nation and give it both shape and direction.[33] A similar process was at work in the turn-of-the-century United States.[34]

As an ostensibly universal language, "serious music" seemed to require no translation. It was therefore portable.[35] This was particularly convenient for US-American musicians and producers who initially lacked a noteworthy repertoire of homegrown works to pull from.[36] To master this art was to demonstrate maturity and erudition, which were qualities expected of those in leadership positions. By the 1940s, the United States branded itself as "the global center of music, highbrow included."[37] It did so in part by placing emphasis on performance rather than repertory. In other words, it sought to dominate stages at home and abroad by mastering canons and setting standards for how they were to be performed. Working together, state and non-state actors shaped audience tastes through investments in musical education, the expansion of orchestras, the development of sound-reproduction technologies, and the construction of concert halls.

Performance served the United States well in that it offered a means of displaying its resources, expertise, leadership, and authority, with the stage offering a *mise en scène* in front of which the nation and its relationship to the rest of the world could be staged: the leader conducted, the orchestra performed, and the audience listened. Jessica C.E. Gienow-Hecht, in her study of sound diplomacy in the United States, further explains that

> the prolonged conservation of the nineteenth-century canon, the simultaneous expansion of the symphony scene, and the increasing cult of the performer during the interwar period dampened artistic visions of cultural internationalism. It also gave a decisive native twist to the production and dissemination of symphony music in the United States: works and artists migh be international, but the setting, the sponsorship, and the culture of performance was not. As such, symphony concerts became increasingly American affairs, celebrating the stage and its actors more so than the works performed. Rather than highlighting the United States' openness to outside imports, symphony orchestras were now supposed to export a specific segment of U.S.

> culture – highbrow performance – unknown to foreign audiences. Instead of reflecting the internationalism of the U.S. culture, they reflected U.S. ambitions to score points in the international arena by highlighting American cosmopolitanism and, hence, its qualification for world leadership.[38]

This "trial of cultural strength," to borrow David Caute's expression, was also a test of economic strength.[39]

Using "serious music" as an instrument of diplomacy, the State Department and Rockefeller's OCIAA sought to project power and rally the republics around the belief that they shared with the United States a common "high" art language – and accordingly, a common political outlook and set of values – despite variations in their national cultures. This musical Pan-Americanism purported to substitute an ostensibly universal approach to composition and performance for the nationalist undertones (be they folkloric motifs or themes) that permeated many South American works. It foregrounded what Carol A. Hess calls "sameness-embracing."[40] The resulting musically imagined community provided the framework within which state and non-state actors discussed culture as well as its intersection with politics and economics. The fact that critics, but also composers and promoters, north and south of the Rio Grande, appeared to forego nationalism for the sake of participating in the United States' initiatives did not mean that they were deaf or blind to the fact that Washington's musical Pan-Americanism was heavily politicized. They understood that it was both timed and tuned to the interests of the North American hegemon.[41]

## MUSICAL NATIONALISM

Brazilians were not novices when it came to modulating the tension between nationalism and universalism in the arts. Throughout much of the nineteenth century, Rio de Janeiro's elites immersed themselves in the "high" culture of Germany, Italy, and France to challenge the notion that they existed on the periphery of the world. They turned to classical and operatic music to elevate their society and place it on the path of progress. They leveraged their city's historical ties to the so-called Old World to claim for it the status of cultural metropolis in the New World. "By attending an opera or a concert in which European music prevailed, or by composing or performing homemade

European-style music, Rio de Janeiro residents could share with those in European centres … the ownership of something that for them represented 'civilization' and 'modernity,'" Cristina Magaldi explains. They could avoid "the general feeling of being left out on the periphery … in their attempt to disguise the sharp, local distinctions between 'here' and 'there.'" More than a "culture of imitation," their musical life expressed a desire to reimagine imperial Brazil as a dynamic centre of culture in its own right rather than a settler colony with no artistic voice of its own.[42]

Brazil's most accomplished composer at the time was Antônio Carlos Gomes. Born in 1836 in the town of Campinas, in the state of São Paulo, the aspiring artist moved to Rio de Janeiro in his early twenties. In the imperial capital, he discovered the great works of French and Italian composers, participating himself in the efforts to enrich the city's cultural life by blending European operatic music with Portuguese-language librettos dealing with Brazilian subjects. Adept at mixing musical and spoken languages, he achieved consecration with the premiere of his *Il Guarany* in Milan, Italy, on 19 March 1870. Based on a Brazilian novel, the opera employs the Italian language to tell the story of an interracial relationship between the daughter of a Portuguese colonist and an Indigenous man from Brazil's interior. Through *Il Guarany*, Gomes negotiated the tension between the "here" and "there" that preoccupied Brazilian elites. In evoking interracial intimacies in positive, romantic terms within the framework of European "high" culture, he helped them situate themselves vis-à-vis Europe. Supported by Emperor Pedro II, the composer gained international recognition during the "golden age" of opera, serving as a sort of "music ambassador" for the Empire of Brazil in the late nineteenth century.[43] Although not a nationalistic work per se, *Il Guarany* reflected "Brazil's early attempt to define itself as a nation, exactly by aligning its culture with that of Europe."[44]

Heitor Villa-Lobos came to play an important role in the "gradual process of decolonization" that characterized Brazilian music in the first half of the twentieth century.[45] Gomes's oeuvre, which belonged to the distant – not to mention foreign – Romantic era, was somewhat of an embarrassment to Brazilian modernists. In the spirit of *Brasilidade*, Villa-Lobos sought to find his own musical language by looking for inspiration in the musical innovations of Impressionist and avant-garde European composers.[46] The artists that he chose to feature during the *Semana de Arte Moderna*, the week-long event that provided impetus for a national cultural revival, included Erik Satie, Achille-Claude Debussy, and Francis Poulenc. They provided templates for his own inward explorations. "Polytonality, unstable tonal centers, new timbers, unconventional use of instrument combinations, and varied orchestral colors were among the 'new' characteristics of the works presented during the week," Magaldi explains, but it was Villa-Lobos's "attentive use of native materials to achieve those results that allowed him to creatively renew the exhausted European tonal system." Magaldi continues: "In his 'Danças africanas,' Villa-Lobos used stylized rhythmic patterns derived from Afro-Brazilian music as a means to explore new harmonies, and thus he achieved the most coveted goals of Brazilian modernists: the conciliation of the local, native tradition with the European model of modernity."[47] Whereas European modernists emphasized rupture and invention, Villa-Lobos and his contemporaries in Brazil championed (re)discovery and memory as a path forward.[48]

Villa-Lobos's two trips to France, in 1923 and 1927, helped consolidate his status at home. Partially funded by the Brazilian government, his overseas excursions were greeted with acclaim in Paris. The concerts fulfilled French desires for a musical Other while advancing the young maestro's own career.[49] At the same time, Villa-Lobos developed and tested new compositional ideas in addition to helping disseminate *Brasilidade* through the use of traditional folk material and syncretic forms of urban music.[50] The professional connections that he made in France and the press he received there won him celebrity status, which gave added legitimacy and urgency to the project of a Brazilian *modernismo musical* (musical modernism), of which he was now a pre-eminent ambassador. Villa-Lobos was essentially helping his contemporaries resolve the tension between the "here" and "there" that so preoccupied their predecessors. His approach demonstrated that "liberation comes from facing and matching, not from retreating."[51]

Such a posture inevitably shaped the composer's works and their reception in the United States. The 1939–40 New York World's Fair provided an exceptional venue to feature Brazil's contributions to the recent history of "serious music." The country's musical program included compositions by Villa-Lobos, Gomes, Mignone, and Burle Marx, who acted as musical director of the Brazilian pavilion. This was Villa-Lobos's first real opportunity to have his compositions heard and written about in the United States. And they made a dramatic impact because of their hybrid nature, more so than other Brazilian works. With its "density of texture, sheer volume, and array of primitive percussion instruments," his "Choros 8" proved especially destabilizing. It evaded sublimation and foregrounded *Brasilidade* in ways that were difficult to reconcile with musical Pan-Americanism. It was a "poor vehicle for sameness-embracing," writes Hess. She adds: "Acknowledging difference so blatantly had little place in the Pan Americanist project." Villa-Lobos's works were once again played in New York the following year as part of a Brazilian music festival held at the Museum of Modern Art. The critics who attended that event were no less perplexed.[52]

Such deployment of an eclectic sound palette, of vernacular elements and unusual rhythmic structures, by means of a compositional voice that evoked Brazil's rich cultural tapestry, could only be heard as a form of musical nationalism during the Vargas era. The use of music to mediate a connection to the idea of the nation was "a common objective" of the hemisphere's republics.[53] It reflected a desire for internal cohesion and stability, combined with the hope for some recognition amid the restructuring of the international order. "Musical nationalism," Thomas Turino explains, "is the conscious use of any pre-existing or newly created music in the service of a political nationalist movement, be it in the initial nation-building stage ... or during and after the moment of arrival to build and buttress the relationship between the general population and the state." An important distinction is that this "purely functional-processual definition precludes the possibility of deducing instances of musical nationalism from style alone."[54] Whereas some republics would tone things down to minimize discordance with US-led Pan-Americanist efforts, others – like Brazil – did not hesitate to turn it up a notch, using state resources and the full power of radio to proudly promote their distinctive sounds.

Villa-Lobos's name would become synonymous with the idea of musical patriotism, if not musical nationalism, through his association with the Vargas regime.[55] Upon his return from Paris in 1930, the composer met João Alberto Lins de Barros, the provisional governor of São Paulo and an amateur musician, with whom he discussed his idea that music held potential as an instrument for teaching citizenship and patriotism to the youth. Enthused, the Brazilian politician encouraged him to tour the state to test his idea and to "proclaim the power of Brazilian artistic will ... a thunder burst, formidable, unisonous and frightening BRAZILIAN ARTISTIC INDEPENDENCE." The venture caught the attention of Vargas, who named Villa-Lobos director of the SEMA.[56] The president understood the importance of art in unifying the country around a shared sense of identity. His political vision converging with the maestro's cultural project, music moved centre stage during the Estado Novo.[57]

Mario de Andrade, another central figure of the *Semana de Arte Moderna*, had a term for the kind of composer that Villa-Lobos embodied: "artist-worker."[58] The artists who fell within that category demonstrated a commitment to reconciling aesthetic concerns with a utilitarian and moralizing conception of art. Their artistic mission was also a social mission in that its value lay in how it contributed to the national project. Although Andrade and Villa-Lobos did not always see eye to eye, both men "stressed the social value and educational usefulness of music, but primarily art music nationalized through the invigoration of rural folk music."[59] They disliked exoticism and rejected the idea that the only acceptable approach to using folkloric elements was through sublimation into Western European artistic languages. Their preferred musical forms were those that travelled horizontally (throughout Brazil's diverse cultural geographies) and transcended vertical barriers (across class lines). Andrade referred to this type of music as "engaged art."[60] Villa-Lobos was one of its chief evangelists, even if it was at times difficult to dissociate the composer's career-building undertakings from his search for Brazil's musical soul.[61]

## CANADIAN MUSICAL DIPLOMACY

Désy familiarized himself with Rio de Janeiro's soundscape as soon as he arrived in Brazil. One of his first musical experiences came courtesy of the Banda do Batalhão de Guardas, the military band that performed Canada's national anthem on the day he presented his credentials to Vargas. His first Brazilian summer was coloured by the sound of Carnival and the voices of young singers performing "O Canada," presumably those same children that Villa-Lobos trained in his capacity as the director of the SEMA. Before long, Désy met the composer at one of the many salons frequented by the who's who of the city's elites. He likely went to one of the many concerts given by the OSB at the Teatro Municipal. He certainly attended at least one of the operas presented there – *Carmen* or *Manon*, if not *Werther* or *Faust*, all of which featured the French-Canadian tenor Raoul Jobin, who was on tour with the New York Metropolitan Opera in 1941 and 1942.

Désy's immersion in the city's cultural life and his chance encounter with Jobin inspired him to venture into the realm of musical diplomacy. The tenor had landed a prestigious job with the New York–based company after years in Paris with the Opéra Comique. French expatriate Solange Petit-Renaux had followed him across the Atlantic when the war broke out in Europe. The two shared the stage during representations of *Manon* at the Teatro Municipal.[62] They were Désy's first recruits for the musical evenings that he began organizing at his residence in September of 1942. From there, he purchased a piano and coordinated an exchange of musical gifts by commissioning Champagne and Mignone to compose original works in celebration of Canada's cultural rapprochement with Brazil: "Quadrilha brasileira" and "Três prelúdios (sobre temas canadenses)," two works that also helped bridge the distance between Montreal and Rio de Janeiro.

One of the factors driving Désy's nascent musical diplomacy in Brazil was the need to be seen and heard amid a flurry of cultural offerings and events. Reports coming out of the legation point to persistent concerns about the pervasive penetration of the country by the United States and the ways in which it overshadowed the presence that both Canada and Great Britain were trying to assert there. Désy and his British counterparts were both dissatisfied with the attitude of Ambassador Jefferson Caffery. They concurred with McCrimmon, describing the US-American diplomat as "constitutionally predisposed to dislike everything British, and this, combined with an inflated idea of the importance of his mission, has made him a most difficult man to get along with." Relations between and among diplomatic missions improved somewhat with the need for wartime coordination. Joint efforts to organize "British-American dinners and cocktail parties" helped. So did Rockefeller's visit in September of 1942, which generated an abundance of good press. Yet the "excessive play upon the sentiments of Pan-Americanism and Continental brotherhood" proved tiring to Brazilians, according to Désy.[63] It also sounded hollow in light of the challenges that accompanied the United States' presence in Brazil.

Another factor that motivated Désy was the realization that Good Neighborism threatened to undermine the "dominant position" of French culture in the capital.[64] To make matters worse, the Vargas regime cut its ties to France in November of 1942 after learning that Nazi officers, with the apparent complicity of the collaborationist regime of Marshal Philippe Pétain, had searched the Brazilian embassy in Vichy.[65] Relations did resume in the fall of the following year, but with Charles de Gaulle's government-in-exile, Forces françaises libres, not Pétain's Vichy regime. Jules Blondel, the new de facto ambassador, was given a warm reception in the capital, a sign that "France continues to hold a paramount place in the heart and mind of Brazilians."[66] Yet Blondel's resources were limited in the context of the war. He was hardly in a position to compete with the United States on the cultural front. If Désy felt angst in the face of France's decreasing influence in Brazil, he was also hopeful that the Canadian legation could help fill the space left open with regard to French-language culture.

Désy had plenty of arguments to justify his cultural campaign, and he knew just the right person to help him seize the moment: the pianist Jean Dansereau. Born on the outskirts of Montreal in 1891, Hector changed his name to Jean in the wake of the First World War, possibly to make himself more marketable or presumably in honour of Jean de Reszke, a Polish tenor with whom he worked as a *répétiteur*. Dansereau acquired a taste for music through his mother, who was a cousin of Calixa Lavallée, the accomplished composer who had written the music to "Ô Canada," a work which allegedly became, albeit unofficially, the country's national anthem with the visit of King George VI in 1939.[67] He studied at McGill University's conservatory before earning the 1914 Prix d'Europe, a prestigious annual competition sponsored by the provincial government and administered by the Académie de musique du Québec. In France, he studied with harmonist Charles-Marie Widor as well as pianists Isidore Philipp and Édouard Risler. Dansereau subsequently accompanied RCA recording artists in the United States (Mary Garden, among others), worked alongside Reszke, and performed throughout Europe until his return to Canada in 1938.[68]

After close to two decades overseas, the accomplished pianist was not quite ready to settle back in Quebec, especially with Désy calling for him to take on the role of cultural ambassador in Brazil. The Montreal that he rediscovered in October of 1938 was not the booming and culturally dynamic city it would become a few years into the war. His return was underwhelming, to say the least. Wilfrid Pelletier, then artistic director of the OCSM, invited reporters to join him in greeting Dansereau at the station. None came. Pelletier felt hurt and made it his mission to help the pianist re-establish his reputation at home.[69] By 1943, he was teaching at the ESMO and the CMQM, institutions where Désy had personal connections.[70] In addition to being an exotic destination, Brazil was most likely an opportunity for Dansereau to network with renowned composers such as Villa-Lobos and Mignone, thereby enhancing his image as a great cosmopolitan artist while familiarizing himself with his counterparts' approach to musical nationalism and music education.

In Quebec, the state had yet to instrumentalize music for nationalistic purposes, and the province's artists were not sufficiently organized to lobby for developments in that direction. The situation was no different in the rest of Canada.[71] Composers such as Champagne were indebted to early folklorists, notably Marius Barbeau and Ernest Gagnon, who provided both source material and inspiration for a deeper engagement with Quebec's musical past. They were also influenced by the canons of the Romantic era, the likes of Frédéric Chopin, who freely borrowed from folk songs and dances, thus revealing music's ability to elicit national sentiment.[72] They could no doubt learn from their South American contemporaries to help further transform Montreal into a vibrant cultural hub.

Accompanying Dansereau to Brazil was his wife, Muriel Tannehill, a native of New Jersey who was mistaken as Canadian-born in the Brazilian press.[73] The confusion was understandable considering her husband and the fact that she had spent the greater part of her formative years training in France under the mentorship of Reszke and Widor. She particularly liked singing works by French composers such as Maurice Ravel and Debussy, the latter being a favourite of Dansereau. Although the spotlight was on her husband, Tannehill's presence in Brazil did not go unnoticed, partly because she had rubbed shoulders with acclaimed Brazilian soprano Balduína de Oliveira Sayão (alias Bidu Sayão) who also studied with Reszke in the 1920s. More importantly, the image of an artistic couple made for great headlines, thereby bolstering the effort to promote more intimate cultural relations between Brazilians and Canadians.

Conscious of the fact that Brazilians consumed their share of propaganda every day (the Vargas regime's and that of the United States), Désy softened his musical diplomacy by presenting Dansereau and Tannehill primarily as his personal guests rather than as Canadian envoys. "Jean Dansereau is my compatriot and my friend," he wrote in the program notes for the pianist's first solo recital at the Teatro Municipal.[74] His promotional efforts spoke of closeness and intimacy, but also family, which Dansereau and Tannehill both embodied and projected on stage, in the press, and during outings with the Désys. Although Tannehill did not perform as often as her husband did, she helped set the musical mood for bilateral relations, even if only by her presence. As an artistic couple, they symbolized the interplay between tradition and modernity, between family and nation.[75]

Désy's reliance on the trope of family was deliberate. Following the example set by his Brazilian hosts, including Vargas, who emphasized his paternalistic side to depict his dictatorship as a benevolent one, Canada's minister plenipotentiary carefully crafted his fatherly image to draw attention to his leadership qualities and caring abilities.[76] Pictures of him with de Boucherville and their two children revealed paternal attributes that presumably qualified him for diplomatic work, especially since it involved managing relations between two sister nations.[77] Not only did these photographs convey the idea that he was both personable and dependable, they also suggested that serving one's country was analogous to serving one's family. Prior to leaving wartime London in 1940, Désy had confided to O.D. Skelton that he felt powerless, disoriented, and without a sense of purpose since the evacuation of the joint Belgium-Netherlands legation and the return of his family to Canada.[78] Now that they were reunited in Brazil, he was more inclined than ever before to emphasize the parallels between fatherhood and diplomacy. Désy's masculine sense of self thus increasingly became a composite of his domestic and civic identities, both of which derived from his relationship to his wife.

De Boucherville played a variety of crucial roles in Brazil, starting with helping her husband mould his public image. A descendant of ennobled aristocrat Pierre Boucher, founder and seigneur of Boucherville, she added substance to the notion that Désy's intimate connections to elite cultural and social circles reached deep into the past. The ambassadress herself projected a friendly image through charitable projects and at various social events, one of which involved facing off against other ambassadorial wives in an amicable horse-riding competition.[79] Participation in such initiatives was a means of nurturing harmonious relations and generating both goodwill and gratitude among the city's diplomatic community. However, the bulk of de Boucherville's work consisted of hosting and entertaining at the official residence to facilitate conversations and people-to-people interactions. Like other ambassadresses, she was the "true power behind the official hospitality scene" and an "invaluable asset" to her husband's official endeavours.[80] Her efforts did not just complement his work – they were essential for the overall success of the diplomatic mission. This domestication of diplomacy revealed the importance of "feminized domestic settings" for the "manly sort of trust-building" that diplomatic activity entailed.[81]

Reunited after trying times in war-torn Europe, the Désys worked together in Rio de Janeiro, finding anchors in an environment that appeared somewhat familiar to them. Photos of them with their two children waving tiny Brazilian flags circulated in the press when they arrived in September of 1941.[82] On Dominion Day the following year, the daily *Correio da Manhã* published an interview with the minister plenipotentiary. Pictured with his daughter, Désy spoke of his family and of how much they felt at home in Brazil. He confided that they had been seduced by the country's rich history, folklore, literature, and music, which reminded them of Canada. The two nations were similar, Désy suggested, in that they were resilient and both carried forward into the New World traditional Catholic values as well as the belief in the sanctity of family and nation.[83] If Désy's description of Brazil was reductive, it was because it had to be made to correspond to his self-image. Hence his confidence that he could channel the "feeling of family" that he found in Rio de Janeiro toward more intimate Canada-Brazil relations.[84]

In his capacity as minister plenipotentiary, Désy skillfully mobilized and consolidated his network of friends and contacts to reinvent himself as a cultural promoter; a status that helped him fulfill, both at home and abroad, his personal and professional ambitions. He had planned to get Dansereau and Tannehill to Brazil in the spring of 1943, but delays in the issuing of visas resulted in the visit being postponed by a few months.[85] This was all for the better, since the couple could then participate in Dominion Day celebrations. With the approval of his pianist friend, Désy wore the hat of an impresario, coordinating with the DIP and the Itamaraty to book concerts and arrange performances on Brazilian radio airwaves. He also reached out to the press, whose support proved essential to the success of this new experiment in cultural diplomacy. From early June to late August, Dansereau and Tannehill offered the gift of music to their Brazilian hosts, accompanying Désy on a round of social functions that put the artistic couple in contact with the city's political and cultural elites. Their multiple appearances on radio and in the press also made it possible for their music to reach into people's homes.

The Light lent a helping hand as well. The company had made an incursion in the realm of broadcasting in the spring of 1940. Its *Ondas Musicais* show aired on six radio frequencies for an hour every Tuesday, and the last two Fridays of each month. Brazilians were treated to fifty-five minutes of music with a short break in the middle during which the host offered advice on how to best take advantage of electricity's potential. The inaugural show featured the Ferdinand Strack Orchestra performing works by a variety of composers, including Pyotr Ilyich Tchaikovsky, Henry K. Hadley, and Brazil's own Gomes. Subsequent broadcasts followed a similar normative "sameness-embracing" orientation by seeking to appeal to "all the radio listeners who prefer the works of classical and modern composers who have already been consecrated by good musical taste."[86] *Ondas Musicais* was as much about marketing the Light to middle-class audiences most likely to require the company's services as it was about serving as a conduit for liberal developmentalism. Attuned to the United States' growing interest in the potency of music, the company espoused Pan-Americanism apparently unaware that Canada's musical output could be deployed to advance alternate propositions.

Désy outlined his views on the matter in the program notes for Dansereau's debut concert. The text established the terms by which to experience the performance, but its reproduction in *A Manhã*, the following day, indicated that it also served to delimit the frame within which to think about Canada-Brazil relations more broadly. Dansereau's debut featured a series of preludes by Debussy and Chopin, pieces that formed part of a canonical repertoire shared by many of the nations that partook in musical Pan-Americanism. Yet Dansereau was different by virtue of his French-Canadian roots and his *latinité*, Désy indicated. He emphasized his friend's cultural background in the program notes, remarking that this made him a particularly effective translator of both Old and New World sensibilities. Dansereau's virtuosity was about technique as much as it was about emotional depth. His mastery of Debussy's impressionist sonic palette was about capturing majestic landscapes with nearly scientific precision, whereas his heartfelt rendition of Chopin's romantic preludes was a testament to his humanity. Désy's insistence on this duality, as well as his discussion of Dansereau's background, indicated that one needed to engage with not only the repertoire and the performance, but also the man, his world view, and the values for which he stood. In some ways, Dansereau was Désy's musical alter ego.[87]

Promoters and critics took their cues from Désy in discussing Dansereau, "ambassador of Canada's musical art" and "French of old stock."[88] In Brazil, the pianist performed works by Debussy and Chopin, but also Franz Liszt and Ludwig van Beethoven, among others. One writer described the concert that he attended as a triumph.

Dansereau was a musical genius who combined virtuosity with sensitivity, he wrote.[89] The artist's personalized touch either denatured the works he played, or it augmented their resonance. The latter was generally truer according to a *Fon Fon* review, which noted how skillfully the French-Canadian envoy engaged with the great European masters without ever losing his personality.[90] His soulfulness and ability to turn the concert stage into an intimate space were qualities that made him different. Alda Caminha, writing for *Diario Carioca*, expected nothing less after having read Désy's program notes. She stressed Dansereau's difference, particularly with respect to his musically inquisitive mind and enchanting personality, which demonstrated a rare predisposition for the polyphony of the world.[91] Different indeed, concurred Caminha's colleague from *Correio da Manhã*.[92] Echoing Désy, a reporter from that same paper marvelled at Dansereau's ability to marry technique with emotion in a distinctively original style.[93] The widely respected musicologist and critic Ayres de Andrade also fell under the charm of Dansereau, although he thought that the pianist's personality shone best through the works of the great French composer Debussy.[94]

The emphasis on difference made it possible to think beyond the frame of musical Pan-Americanism even if Dansereau's repertoire centred on certain aspects of the Western classical canon. One critic, writing for *Diário de Noticias*, did describe the tour as a "good neighbor mission" serving continental ideals and values, but such a reading was the exception rather than the rule.[95] When music's potential to foster continental harmony was evoked, it was to better delineate the qualities that supposedly differentiated Canadians and Brazilians from peoples from elsewhere in the hemisphere. The image that emerged was that of two nations attached to tradition yet progressively-minded, industrious, non-imperialistic, peace-driven, sincere in their dealing with the world, and – most of all – both freedom-loving and spiritually inclined. According to music critics, Dansereau's goodwill cultural mission conveyed all these qualities. It rendered audible and corporeal the sororal ties that existed between the two "sister nations."[96]

These metaphors, although expressed in gendered terms, did not necessarily effeminize Dansereau and his performance of the nation. Like Désy, his composite masculine identity (as a husband and as an agile musician) tied in nicely with his newfound calling as an impromptu ambassador. Although the figure of the sensitive pianist deviated somewhat from normative gender models, Dansereau embodied emotional experiences in ways that were coded male in 1940s Brazil.[97] The press portrayed him as a grounded and sensible erudite performer whose skills commanded admiration and respect. Pictures showed him seated at a piano looking intent, with full mastery of the instrument. Dansereau played with so much vigour that one of Chopin's waltzes became something entirely different.[98] His repertoire's "manly lineage" lent credence to his stature as an authoritative performer.[99] In Rio de Janeiro, he rubbed shoulders with many of the greats, including Villa-Lobos and Mignone, to make a name for himself in the city's male-dominated cultural milieu. If there were any doubts about Dansereau's manliness, Tannehill's presence tended to assuage them.

Musical diplomacy thus offered multiple opportunities to fabricate, even amplify, fraternal feelings between Canada and Brazil. Dansereau's presence in the capital helped augment the Champagne and Mignone musical exchange with a performative component. On 1 July 1943, Rádio Nacional celebrated Dominion Day with a special program that featured Estrella and Dansereau premiering "Quadrilha brasileira" and "Três prelúdios (sobre temas canadenses)." Brazilians heard the performance live on radio at 5:00 p.m., while North American audiences listened to it via shortwave transmission at 11:00 p.m.[100] That evening, Dansereau entertained members of the Rio de Janeiro elite in the main hall of the Associação Brasileira de Imprensa (Brazilian Press Association). In addition to Mignone's and Champagne's works, he played folk-infused compositions by Canada's Ernest MacMillan ("Les jeunes filles à marier") and Achile Fortier ("Lève ton pied, bergère"). Tannehill then joined her husband and sang a few French-Canadian folk songs, to the great pleasure of the audience. As an additional friendly gesture, they dedicated their performance to Mignone and Villa-Lobos.[101]

Dansereau had the honour of being the first Canadian pianist to play in Brazil. He was also the first French-Canadian artist to embrace and execute the mandate of cultural ambassador given to him by Désy. In an interview with Sheila Ivert, published in the magazine *Carioca*, he attributed to Brazilians the same qualities that they had attributed to him. He complimented them for their generosity as well as for their distinctive personality and character. He may have stretched the truth when he claimed that their culture was well-known in Canada, but his intent was to remind Brazilians that, as a "creative civilization," they shared with Canadians a need for "a continuously renewed spiritual source."[102] Dansereau's fondness for his hosts was due in great part to the fact that he found traces – and heard echoes – of Paris in Rio de Janeiro, a city suffused with "the atmosphere of the old artistic and enlightened Europe." The connections that he made there and the praise that he received thus took on added significance in the eyes of colleagues back home. Jean Vallerand, secretary-general of the CMQM, spoke for many when he commended Dansereau for his role in disseminating a radiant image of French Canada overseas. "He accomplished this task artfully and with mastery," he wrote enthusiastically.[103] The pianist's short tenure as an impromptu ambassador in Brazil was a form of consecration. It placed a spotlight on the city's cultural milieu – to the great pleasure of its artists, critics, and administrators, many of whom proved eager to share in his success.

Not only did this series of musical events elevate Désy's status within Rio de Janeiro's and Montreal's elite circles, but it also further complicated the idea that Canada was defined first and foremost by its Britishness. Although the trope of *métissage* did not figure prominently in this particular initiative, it nonetheless informed perceptions. It also made it possible to think about this elaborate cultural offering as constitutive of an emerging musically imagined Canadian-Brazilian community. A piece published in *A Noite* shortly after the Dansereau and Tannehill's Dominion Day performance is a case in point. It presents Canada as a "romantic northern country, where spirit and 'finesse' miraculously fuse Latin grace with British solemnity, in the happiest and most perfect of alliances." Describing a room filled with Canadian and Brazilian flags, a symbol of harmony that spoke of the closeness between the two nations, the author noted approvingly that it is "now hearts that intertwine in a common affection, a feeling made more refined and more harmonious through the art of Jean and Muriel Dansereau."[104] As an exercise in cultural diplomacy and musical nation branding, the artistic couple's visit to Brazil was a tour de force.

However successful it may have seemed, Désy's musical experiment did not translate into concrete, actionable policy outcomes, whether political or economic. This was expected, as cultural diplomacy normally works its magic over the long term; a multifarious and diffuse object in international relations, its payoffs are rarely readily apparent. That said, it does set the mood and conveys information while creating forums for interaction through which to achieve dialogue and mutual understanding. The Dansereau and Tannehill tour placed French

Canadians centre stage in the projection of Canada's autonomous voice overseas. It mobilized the tropes of *latinité* and family to evoke the idea of a musically imagined Canadian-Brazilian community. In other words, it juxtaposed difference against the "sameness-embracing" hegemony of a Washington-driven musical Pan-Americanism. Désy was able to carry on with this experiment, unsupervised by his superiors in Ottawa and unperturbed by the urgencies of war, because of how far removed Brazil was from the issues that preoccupied Canadians in 1943. Yet he was also able, using music, to provide an experience of proximity that served as a backdrop to behind-the-scenes conversations taking place about a possible cultural agreement between the two nations.

# 3

# An Exchange of Notes

In February of 1946, External Affairs received a letter from Elizabeth Wood, an established sculptor and the chair of the Canadian Arts Council's Foreign Relations Committee, inquiring about the cultural agreement that Canada and Brazil had signed on 24 May 1944. She did not specify how she knew about it, but it is likely that she had stumbled upon one of a handful of newspaper articles reporting on the agreement at the time of its ratification. Since the reference and legislative libraries in the national capital had no copies on hand that she could consult, she wondered, "Does this mean that the document is still confidential and may not be circulated?"[1] It was not, but few people in Ottawa were willing to give it the type of publicity that Jean Désy and Brazilian officials thought it deserved.

Canada's minister plenipotentiary had presented the agreement almost as a *fait accompli* to his superiors in Ottawa, who agreed to it reluctantly after much debate. Not only did they have their doubts regarding culture's effectiveness as an instrument of diplomacy, they also did not want to alienate a province like Quebec, which was likely to construe the agreement, which included references to education, as an encroachment on its areas of jurisdiction. Moreover, they wanted to avoid other South American countries seeking similar concessions. Given Wood's position on the Canadian Arts Council, External Affairs could not entirely ignore her request, so the department did send copies of the document. The Information Division's Terence MacDermot, responding for the undersecretary of state for external affairs, noted, however, that the department had purposely given it "limited distribution" and that consultation should be "restricted to those ... having a direct interest in the subject."[2]

Such prudence ensured that successful implementation would lie not with External Affairs, but rather with individuals on the ground who were eager to capitalize on Canada's rapprochement with Brazil in their pursuit of opportunities. There was, of course, Désy, who orchestrated the agreement with Temístocles da Graça Aranha, head of the Divisão de Cooperação Intelectual (DCI, or Intellectual Co-operation Division), to provide additional legitimacy, at both ends of the hemisphere, to his cultural undertakings. This important development facilitated his fundraising efforts in the absence of financial support from Ottawa. He was thus able to establish the Instituto Brasil-Canadá (Brazil-Canada Institute), a sort of headquarters for all things cultural, in the summer of 1944. Marcel Roussin, a young scholar seeking to bolster his expert status as a South Americanist, closely followed the news coming out of Brazil; he had his eyes set on a research trip there. And indeed, in May of 1945, he left Canada as the recipient of a twelve-month scholarship offered by the institute. He, too, believed that a strong French-Canadian presence in the hemisphere was bound to enhance the country's international image.

Cultural diplomacy is, among other things, a means for states to assert some control over their image and messaging overseas. It is an opportunity to exert influence on the discursive and symbolic connections that culture activates at home and abroad. External Affairs' laissez-faire approach was consequential, even if only in the ways it allowed others, including its own official envoys in Brazil, to usurp narrative authority in the making of bilateral cultural relations. Désy was a skillful diplomat who got things done despite being something of a loose cannon who pursued his own agenda with the belief that it aligned with Canada's foreign policy objectives. His ability to proceed unencumbered was neither a sign of implicit support from his colleagues in Ottawa nor an indication that they were ideologically disposed to accommodate diverse, even competing, practices. Serious discussions about culture, diplomacy, and the emergence of a distinctive French-Canadian voice in foreign affairs, particularly in South America, had yet to take place in the East Block headquarters of External Affairs. Like Désy, Roussin operated in these blind spots, seizing Canada's hemispheric moment to champion the country's *fait français* and to conveniently position himself as an emerging expert.

## EXPERIMENTS IN CULTURAL DIPLOMACY

Brazil was no novice in matters of cultural diplomacy. The country had for decades been a sustained target of the Quai d'Orsay. Migrants, missionaries, scholars, industrialists, and members of organizations such as Action française, travelling with or without government support, also participated in the efforts to extend French hegemony across the Atlantic. From the later years of Pedro II's empire through the First Republic and the Getúlio Vargas era, state and non-state actors worked jointly to tout French culture – or more specifically, the French language – for its assumed universalism.[3] The objective was to gain the trust and admiration of Brazilians in order to exert greater economic and political influence on their society.[4] Although Brazil was home to the second-biggest community of French migrants in South America, they were easily outnumbered by groups arriving from Germany and Italy.[5] Nonetheless, they held considerable clout due to France's long-term, multi-pronged cultural offensive, which ranged from information campaigns in the press to the creation of the Institut franco-brésilien de haute culture and government-funded trips by professors called upon to help shape university life in Rio de Janeiro and São Paulo.[6]

The United States was also competing for influence in Brazil. Unlike in France, the relationship between government and the private sector in the United States was an uneasy one, with the latter anxious at the prospect of potential overreach by the former. Yet both parties occasionally managed to mobilize considerable resources and work jointly on information and cultural campaigns, particularly in times of crisis when cultural, economic, and political forces interlocked to create opportunities. This was especially true during the Good Neighbor era, which saw governments, businesses, broadcasters, film studios, and philanthropic organizations channel the mediating potential of art to promote liberal developmentalism and to counter anti-US-American sentiments in South America. The OCIAA and the State Department's Division of Cultural Relations worked hard to seduce and nudge Brazilian decision-makers into aligning their country's domestic and international policies with those of the United States in the early 1940s. Cultural diplomacy provided state and non-state actors in the United States with the means to conceal their broader strategic and hegemonic agenda behind innocuous "universal rhetoric."[7]

Brazilians, for their part, were neither credulous nor passive interlocutors. They engaged France and the United States willingly in order to reap benefits from the two countries' cultural offerings, whether it was the modernization of the university sector or the expansion of Rio de Janeiro's broadcasting capabilities, for example. They were also active beyond their country's borders, as evidenced by their participation in the Committee on Intellectual Cooperation, a cultural relations–focused advisory body attached to the LON, and the Inter-American Institute of High Culture, an initiative that failed to take off since it was promptly subsumed within Good Neighbor Pan-American initiatives.[8]

Vargas was especially proactive in deploying culture as an instrument of diplomacy to consolidate and legitimize his regime at home and abroad. He did so through bilateral channels, not just multilateral ones. Following the establishment of the Estado Novo, the dictatorship signed cultural agreements with Bolivia (1939), Cuba (1940), Chile (1941), Paraguay (1941), and the Dominican Republic (1943), while laying the foundation for similar arrangements with Ecuador, Peru, Argentina, Panama, and Mexico. On the eve of signing the agreement with Canada, Vargas and the Itamaraty could proudly state that they were successfully engaged in disseminating a positive and distinctive image of Brazil beyond its borders.[9] In short, Brazilians were successfully elevating their country's status in South America to offset the United States' and France's influence, all while positioning themselves as self-assured mediators between the two countries in the region.

Brazil had a cultural diplomacy apparatus that matched its aspirations to middlepowerhood. Its Serviço de Expansão Intelectual (Intellectual Expansion Service), created in 1934, and the Serviço de Cooperação Intelectual (Intellectual Co-operation Service), established in 1937 and renamed as the DCI a year later, were both engaged in projecting the country's image abroad. Their work often overlapped with that of the Itamaraty and the Ministério da Educação e Saúde (MES, or Ministry of Education and Health), both of which also sponsored cultural activities. Although it was marred by "lack of coordination" and "institutional disorder," this apparatus was still an impressive one.[10] Determined to win hearts and minds among elite circles in neighbouring republics, the Vargas regime sent books, films, and records to diplomatic posts throughout the region. Brazil's national broadcaster, Rádio Nacional, beamed its weekly *A Hora do Brasil* outward into the world. State-sponsored cultural missions by the likes of writer Alceu Amoroso Lima (alias Tristão de Ataíde), poet and neurologist Aloysio de Castro, and composer Heitor Villa-Lobos helped make Brazil shine on the hemisphere's stages. These efforts attested to Brazilians' "cultural leadership" in the face of formidable competition by more powerful and richer nations.[11]

It was logical for Brazil to seek closer relations with Canada, a distant neighbour that was engaged in a similar pursuit of middle-powerhood in the shadow of the North Atlantic's major powers: the United States, France, and Great Britain. Unlike the Itamaraty, External Affairs had no urgent desire to take the cultural diplomacy turn. Canadians' experience on that front was limited due to their long-standing and privileged relationships with Paris and London. However worried they may have been about the United States' economic and cultural penetration of their country, they were at least sparred their neighbour's propaganda in the 1930s. No surprise there, since President Franklin Delano Roosevelt, in a 1936 speech intended, in part, to promote the State Department's Good Neighbor policy in the southern hemisphere, had alluded to the border between Canada and the United States as the "noblest monument to peace and to neighborly economic and social friendship."[12]

In the early 1940s, Ottawa's experience on the cultural front was mostly limited to disseminating information about its war effort to counter Axis propaganda and rally support for the Allies. It accomplished that through the Bureau of Public Information and its more effective successor, the Wartime Information Board, established, respectively, in 1939 and 1942, which brought all "information policy under one roof" to reach as wide an audience as possible at home and abroad.[13] Much of the bureau's and the board's activities were focused inward in an effort to stir up patriotism and educate people about the sacrifices that the war required of them. A portion of this work was aimed at the United States. It spelled out Canadians' views of the conflict and called attention to their moral and material contributions with the intent of strengthening resolve south of the border.

The Wartime Information Board owed much of its success to its association with the National Film Board of Canada (NFB). One of its general managers, the pioneering Scottish documentary filmmaker John Grierson, was also commissioner of the film-producing government agency. Established through an act of Parliament in 1939, the NFB pursued the mandate of interpreting "Canada to Canadians and to other nations." From its inception, it served both nation building and nation branding purposes using the medium of cinema, most notably animation and documentary films, two cinematic languages in which Canadian artists excelled. Rather than impeding the growth of the NFB, the war provided the incentive and the means to build a catalogue of "progressive film propaganda of education, inspiration, and promise of a better tomorrow."[14] Its impressive wartime output elevated the status of Canadian filmmakers, both domestically and internationally.[15] The Wartime Information Board facilitated the distribution of these works, many of which – including *The War for Men's Minds* (Stuart Legg, 1943) and *Look to the North* (James Beveridge, 1944) – dealt directly with the war effort. The success of these NFB films and newsreels would eventually make the agency one of the most prized instruments for the projection of Canada abroad.[16]

Whatever success Canadians were having with the Wartime Information Board or the NFB on the propaganda front, it was confined to the North Atlantic. Established in 1942, the International Service of the Canadian Broadcasting Corporation (or CBC-IS) initially aimed to reach a broader audience so as to make Canada better known and to generate admiration for its achievements in the realms of culture, economics, and politics. However, wartime imperatives soon monopolized the broadcaster's energies and resources. Concerns with self-image and the search for an international identity capable of fostering national unity thus suddenly took on secondary importance. The CBC-IS found itself focusing almost exclusively on countering Axis disinformation and relaying news about the war effort to Canadian troops as well as allied and resistance factions throughout Europe.[17]

As for the Department of Trade and Commerce, it was in no position to take the lead on matters of cultural relations, although it did free up funds to pay for the Alfred Pellan paintings that Désy commissioned in 1942. The department had some experience with publicity and nation branding, having handled the promotion of Canada in the United States and in Europe to generate tourism and attract settlers. It had also collaborated with the National Gallery of Canada (NGC) to depict the country in the best light at international exhibitions. Yet the department's presence at these events had been underwhelming, to say the least, in that the image of Canada it had put forward was too conservative and not sufficiently oriented toward the future.[18] Created in 1918, its Motion Picture Bureau represented an attempt to improve the situation, but it, too, had struggled to keep up with the times, as evidenced by the fact that it was subsumed by the NFB in 1941.[19] Like External Affairs, the Department of Trade and

Commerce could not see itself coordinating and taking the initiative on cultural matters in South America, despite the promising wartime and postwar economic prospects there. The region seemed just too peripheral to Canada's international priorities to merit sustained attention.

## AGREEMENT FOR THE PROMOTION OF CULTURAL RELATIONS

Canada nonetheless entered into a bilateral cultural agreement with Brazil on 24 May 1944, a few months after elevating its legation in Rio de Janeiro to embassy status. Neither development was an indication that External Affairs wished to prioritize its relationship to the South American giant. The first of the two events was consistent with efforts to assert autonomy on the international stage. The change from legation to embassy occurred more or less simultaneously across diplomatic missions. As for the cultural agreement, External Affairs agreed to go ahead with it due to factors that were, for the most part, internal and thus unconnected to Brazil. The department may have lacked experience in the realm of cultural diplomacy, but it understood that domestic politics could, at times, be at odds with foreign policy objectives. Signing such an agreement could set an important precedent for delimiting provincial and federal areas of competence in international cultural relations. It was a compelling argument for generating enthusiasm among Désy's otherwise unimaginative colleagues in Ottawa.

It is not clear who, between Désy and his Brazilian hosts, initiated discussions regarding bilateral cultural relations, but the project most likely followed from Vargas's suggestion, on his first meeting with the Canadian envoy, that they "do something *new* together."[20] The DCI had been busy displaying to other peoples a compelling, "total image of Brazil" to cultivate in them a favourable predisposition toward Brazilian aspirations.[21] While the Vargas regime intensified its cultural offensive throughout South America, signing agreements with Argentina and Ecuador, among others, it saw Canada as a credible and promising ally in its quest for both influence in the region and a future role in the United Nations. Whether or not the two countries' economic and political relations would continue to grow at a steady rate after the war was difficult to predict, but there was optimism in the air, with Désy appearing equally committed to helping Brazilians and Canadians get to know each other better.

Désy demonstrated early on that he was willing and able to assume leadership on matters of cultural diplomacy. Beginning with the *soirée musicale* that featured the tenor Raoul Jobin, he then commissioned original compositions from Claude Champagne and presumably Francisco Mignone. Wearing the hat of an impresario, he organized a successful tour for the pianist Jean Dansereau and his wife, the soprano Muriel Tannehill, using his contacts at the Itamaraty and in Rio de Janeiro's broadcasting milieu. In addition to ordering sound recordings from Canada to play on the airwaves in Brazil, he arranged for local stations to relay programs by the recently established CBC-IS. He also decorated the walls of his residence and the legation with paintings from Canadian artists, Pellan being a favourite of his. The NFB lent a helping hand by sending a series of photographs for an exhibition on life in Canada planned for late 1944. The fact that photographs, not films, were considered was intentional. Désy believed that it was "obviously impossible" to compete against Hollywood-backed initiatives such as those of Nelson Rockefeller's OCIAA.[22]

Having a bilateral cultural agreement in place would no doubt make Désy's work easier and give it added legitimacy. Temístocles da Graça Aranha, director of the DCI, was his primary associate on this project. On 17 May 1942, they met to strategize. As a gesture of goodwill, and presumably to provide Désy with a taste of opportunities to come, T. da G. Aranha arranged for him to give a Dominion Day public lecture on the history of Canada. He also coordinated the translation and the publication of an article by the minister plenipotentiary in *Revista do Brasil*, a magazine popular among Rio de Janeiro's liberal elites. The two resumed discussions shortly after, meeting frequently and making plans to bring Canadian art to Brazil. In early December, they agreed on a draft for a five-point plan that covered a variety of topics: from promoting cultural manifestations to translating books and encouraging the exchange of students as well as professors.[23] T. da G. Aranha had been consulting with his Itamaraty colleagues since the first week of June, if not earlier. Désy, on the other hand, did not broach the topic with his superiors in Ottawa until 17 December 1942.

The fact that Désy brought up the question of a cultural agreement with Brazil the week before Christmas suggests that he was perhaps hoping that External Affairs, rather than dwelling on the details, would give him the authority to proceed with negotiations. He was acting intrepidly, knowing very well that his proposal was going to face indifference – or worse, resistance – in Ottawa. By presenting the agreement as something of a *fait accompli*, he likely thought that he was increasing his chances that it would be rubber-stamped. The five-point plan that he had designed with T. da G. Aranha appeared here relatively unchanged in the form of a three-point agreement: "(a) The Governments of the two countries will consider favourably the exchange of students, technicians, professors and lecturers; (b) The two Governments will favour the exchange of books, and the translation of works representative of cultural and technical progress in each country; [and] (c) The two Governments will encourage better acquaintance with the artistic and cultural productions of each other country." Anxious to seal the deal, Désy concluded his correspondence with a forceful call for action: "I need ... scarcely mention to you the importance ... of establishing our cultural propaganda on a definite and official basis, and I trust the Government will shortly authorise me to go ahead with negotiations, especially in view of the desire expressed by the Brazilian Government to conclude an agreement as soon as possible."[24] His reputation, of course, was on the line since failure to conclude the agreement after months of effort would tarnish his image, if not Canada's, in Brazil.

External Affairs could not, however, be expected to move too promptly on the issue, especially since this could be misconstrued by the United States as a form of British interference in South America. From Washington's perspective, Canada had yet to demonstrate its autonomy in international affairs. This was the rationale for the State Department's opposition to Canada attending the PAU meeting held in Rio de Janeiro in 1942.[25] On 8 January 1943, External Affairs sent a teletype message to Lester B. Pearson, then Canadian minister in Washington, informing him of Désy's project and asking if the United States had concluded similar bilateral agreements with South American countries in the past.[26] It seems likely that the strategy was to take the Roosevelt administration's pulse on the issue without asking directly whether or not it approved of Canada proceeding with the agreement. The response came a few days later: Washington had concluded no such agreements. "I understand they were afraid that if the agreements were not identical, it would immediately be a cause for complaint on the part of the Latin-American Republics themselves," Pearson added.[27] Norman A. Robertson, then the undersecretary of state for external affairs, promptly wrote to Désy to tell him not to proceed. His explanation was hardly original; he simply appropriated the language used in Pearson's message to describe the "general feeling" of the "Canadian authorities."[28]

Désy refused to take no for an answer. Assuming that his colleagues were primarily concerned with not hurting relations with their counterparts south of the border, he wrote back as follows: "I do not think that the United States might take offence at our concluding a more or less platonic cultural agreement with a friendly country."[29] Having downplayed the significance of the agreement, he urged Ottawa to reconsider. External Affairs contacted Pearson, once again, asking for additional information on Washington's views regarding cultural diplomacy.[30] His response was a repeat of his previous message, although he added that Charles A. Thompson, chief of the State Department's Division of Cultural Relations, had informed him, "off the record," that comprehensive agreements such as the one proposed by Brazil "seldom work" and that Canada "might think it expedient to resort to a practical arrangement" such as a less binding exchange of notes.[31] T. da G. Aranha and Désy were seemingly prepared to proceed in that way since they had been using the terms "agreement," "accord," and "exchange of notes" interchangeably throughout their discussions. If Ottawa had stalled on the issue for fear of antagonizing its neighbour to the south, it at least now had some sort of green light.

Yet many at External Affairs remained hesitant to go forward with the project. Robertson captured the mood of this group when he wrote that "some of us are still old fashioned enough to have reservations about the whole trend, and cannot work up very much enthusiasm for organized Canadian participation in it." One contentious issue was that of "lingering suspicion of state-aided support for 'culture.'"[32] At the time, Canadians had not yet embraced the idea of state support for the arts, despite the persistent efforts of many composers and painters, writers and actors, who laboured to enrich their country's cultural life. Except for the support it gave to some key institutions (for example, the CBC, the NFB, and the NGC) and one-off initiatives (among others, the fourth centenary of Jacques Cartier's first voyage to Canada and the royal visit of 1939), governments saw few reasons to aid individual artists and private-sector institutions who could turn to philanthropists in time of need.[33] Although the war eventually gave cultural producers an added sense of purpose, "not simply as nation-builders or educators but as the custodians of the values their civilization was struggling to preserve," local arts communities across Canada were in the early 1940s still in the early stages of organizing to lobby governments to do more.[34]

Complicating matters was the sense that only a fine line separated information from propaganda, the latter evoking images of Nazi films and radio broadcasts or fabricated news stories. That Brazil was governed by a president with fascist sympathies did not help defuse these concerns, and may even have made External Affairs more reluctant to wholeheartedly support T. da G. Aranha and Désy's project. Canada had already taken the path of propaganda, notably with its Wartime Information Board, but strategists liked to think that they were neither deceitful nor treacherous with their messaging. The euphemistic use of the term "information" held much appeal to them since it better aligned with the approach that the United States and Great Britain publicly appeared to be taking. The distinction they made between white propaganda (ostensibly fair and objective information originating from a verifiable source), grey propaganda (unattributed information that conveys a particular viewpoint to advance the interests of the sponsoring party), and black propaganda (falsely attributed information meant to embarrass or stir up dissent) revealed a broad spectrum of practices.[35] Canada may have championed the first of the three, but it was nonetheless engaged in disseminating propaganda, or rather influencing "attitudes of large numbers of people on controversial issues of relevance to a group."[36] External Affairs' lack of enthusiasm evidently had more to do with the perception that the Vargas regime's illiberal politics and intentions were opaque, if not dubious.

The biggest obstacle to moving forward was arguably Ottawa's lack of jurisdiction over educational matters. Section 93 of the Constitution Act, 1867, stipulated that provincial legislatures held the exclusive right to make laws in relation to education. Quebec fiercely guarded its jurisdiction in this area. By the 1940s, the predominantly French-speaking province had developed a vast network of student exchange relationships and teaching partnerships with France. Having travelled across the Atlantic on many occasions as a student and later as a professor, Désy was a product of this privileged connection. Having taught constitutional law, he was also certainly aware of the challenges that the Canada-Brazil cultural agreement would pose to External Affairs. That is presumably why he reworked the five-point agreement, substituting a harmless clause indicating that the two governments would "consider favourably the exchange of students, technicians, professors and lecturers" for three separate clauses that detailed potential scholarship allocations.[37] Yet Robertson still feared "the political objections to what might be regarded as a Federal initiative in the educational field," and he also doubted that a state-supported agency was the right vehicle "for fostering intellectual contacts and activities in the general field of international cultural cooperation."[38] He needed more convincing.

Désy finally had a chance to discuss the topic face to face with his colleagues during a short stint back in Ottawa in November of 1943. Robertson, Escott Reid, Kenneth Rae, and Frederick H. Soward represented External Affairs while Grierson, Geoffrey C. Andrew, and Allan Anderson spoke for the Wartime Information Board. The group raised a number of points in opposition to the project: (1) the fear of setting a precedent in the Americas where none existed within the Commonwealth; (2) discomfort with the notion of exporting culture in a manner reminiscent of fascist propaganda; (3) concerns with the "danger of admitting undesirable propaganda into Canada virtually under government sponsorship"; (4) ambivalence vis-à-vis the "value of 'exporting culture'"; and (5) apprehension at the thought of encroaching upon areas of provincial competence. The last point might have sealed the fate of the agreement had the attendees not realized that the question of competence was the one area where a precedent might be necessary since "culture" had been left unassigned in the Constitution. They remarked that "here there was the risk that if the federal government took no action the provinces might come to make cultural working arrangements abroad on the basis of their educational powers."[39] The need to protect Canada's prerogatives in the area of international cultural relations sufficed to rally everyone behind the agreement.

Things moved swiftly after that meeting. The legal division of External Affairs reworked Désy's draft from a year earlier and submitted it to the Itamaraty for approval. It now read as follows:

> It is considered that, in the relations between the two countries, there should be a recognition of the desirability of promoting a greater mutual knowledge and wider comprehension of the respective peoples, their cultures, traditions, and institutions.
>
> In particular the Government welcomes efforts made: to encourage and facilitate the exchange of official, scientific and technical publications, reviews, newspaper articles, books, et cetera; and to encourage and facilitate the organization and presentation of artistic exhibitions, concerts, lectures, radio programs, films, and other activities and contacts.

> To this end the Government of Canada is resolved, within its constitutional powers, and by such means as are at its disposal, to encourage intellectual and cultural activities of reciprocal value in furthering the understanding of one country by the other.[40]

The Exchange of Notes between Canada and Brazil Constituting an Agreement for the Promotion of Cultural Relations between the Two Countries was signed on 24 May 1944 at a ceremony held in Rio de Janeiro.

The news was well-received in Brazil, with various newspapers reporting on the event, which featured speeches by Désy and Minister of Foreign Affairs Oswaldo Aranha.[41] There were no such celebrations in Canada, and the few reporters in that country who mentioned the agreement simply reprinted Prime Minister William Lyon Mackenzie King's announcement to Parliament, on 5 June, that he would soon table the exchange of notes.[42] No efforts were made to disseminate the document or publicize it. Copies were not sent to Ottawa's reference and legislative libraries, presumably because of "wartime shortages of materials."[43] None of this was surprising considering External Affairs' lack of enthusiasm.

The Ottawa-based newspaper *Le Droit* nonetheless took an interest in the matter. On 26 May, a week before King made his official announcement, one of its reporters shared the news on the front page that a pioneering cultural agreement had been signed between Canada and Brazil.[44] Its source was the Brazilian ambassador to Canada, Cyro de Freitas Vale, Vargas's third representative in the country since 1941. His predecessors, João Alberto Lins de Barros and Caio de Mello Franco, had each served roughly a year as ministers plenipotentiary so they were limited in what they could accomplish to further cultural relations. Vale, who held the post of ambassador to Germany until Brazil's entry into the war in 1942, had arrived in Ottawa just in time for the legation's elevation to embassy status, and he was eager to hype this latest initiative by Désy and his colleagues in the Itamaraty. *Le Droit* then published a subsequent piece summarizing the terms of the agreement, as explained by King, adding that Canada had much to offer the world despite its youthfulness: "In this moment when all are preaching for international collaboration, we could not hope for a better way to promote common understanding between peoples than through cultural relations."[45] It was a sound argument, and one that External Affairs had overlooked.

Slowly but surely, then, the word got out. The Canadian Arts Council's Elizabeth Wood was but one of many who reached out to External Affairs for more details. Why were copies of the exchange of notes not readily available? Were the terms of the agreement confidential? M.J. Patry, of the political and literary magazine *L'Oeil*, J. Robert Kaine, president of the Hispanic studies group Cercle Cervantes de Québec, and Walter Herbert, director of Canada Foundation, also requested copies and asked if other similar agreements had been signed with other countries. Even the CBC-IS thought that this was newsworthy material, but External Affairs continued to politely insist that it did not wish to bring too much attention to the exchange of notes due to a combination of constitutional difficulties and fears that other South American countries would press Canada for similar deals. Having told Wood not to distribute the document too widely, MacDermot made a similar request to the representative from CBC-IS: "I should appreciate it, therefore, if you would give publicity to the enclosed Agreement only in your broadcast to Brazil."[46]

External Affairs' insistence that circulation of the agreement be limited was counterintuitive if one of the motivating factors for signing it was to send a message to provinces that the managing of international cultural relations was a federal responsibility. It is revealing that Désy's immediate successors – James Scott MacDonald, Herbert Coleman, Sydney Pierce, and Arthur Irwin – never managed to replicate the close bonds established in the 1940s in the absence of support from Ottawa. It is true that most were unenthusiastic about their being posted in Brazil.[47] They were also less equipped than their French-speaking Catholic predecessor to exploit the idea of cultural affinities so as to nurture close relationships with Brazilians throughout the 1950s. In any case, they would not have been in a position to take advantage of the cultural agreement since most people at External Affairs forgot its existence within a decade.

The decision to burry the exchange of notes would haunt Ottawa in the early 1960s. The failure to publicize the document, as well as the neglect of the precedent it set, would result in Quebec doing exactly what External Affairs had sought to prevent in 1944: the province would establish cultural working arrangements abroad on the basis of its educational powers. The 1961 opening of the Maison du Québec in Paris would be one of many symbolic actions taken to challenge Ottawa's effort to reserve for itself the right to speak for all Canadians on the world stage. The Canadian government, instead of holding the initiative, would find itself reacting to Quebec's foray into the realm of international cultural relations.

## INSTITUTO BRASIL-CANADÁ

In the short term, External Affairs' neglect of cultural diplomacy allowed individuals on the ground to continue operating under the radar. The whirlwind of activities did, however, capture the attention of the British diplomatic corps in Rio de Janeiro. Philip M. Broadmead, counsellor at the embassy, followed closely the work of the Canadians, informing his superiors in London that Désy's "expression of satisfaction at the conclusion of the agreement was more than formal" since he had "shown himself to be very keen on all forms of cultural activities … which has undoubtedly pleased Brazilians." Pursuing the Vargas regime's strategy of trying to accumulate goodwill through bilateral cultural agreements, T. da G. Aranha apparently reached out to Broadmead with the "hope that the United Kingdom would follow the example of the Canadian Government."[48] This was wishful thinking; the British were preoccupied with more urgent wartime matters. They were also unlikely to lay claim to a portion of the cultural terrain in Brazil since they knew that it would raise eyebrows in the United States. The British Council took a genuine interest in Canada's cultural rapprochement with the South American giant, because a strong performance by a leading Dominion there was likely to benefit the entire Commonwealth family.

Not everyone was confident, though, that Canadians were mature enough to deliver on that front. Malcolm MacDonald, high commissioner to Canada, shared with others in the British Foreign Office the patronizing opinion that Canadians had much work to do before they could speak with a unified voice on the international stage.[49] Charles E. Shuckburgh, in a memorandum prepared for London, further explained that Canada's inability to articulate and perform its self-designated status as a "catalyst-nation" revealed "the characteristic uncertainty of the country's position" as both an American nation and a member of the Commonwealth. According to him, it also revealed deep schisms among continentalists, imperialists, and autonomists. As for French Canadians, he refused to believe that they had the vision and the means to act upon their so-called racial affinity with South Americans. "They have failed, partly through their own narrowness of outlook and partly by deliberate localism, to create in Quebec or Montreal centres of attraction for modern French thought and culture on this continent," Shuckburgh wrote disparagingly. He did, however, note that Désy might eventually succeed in projecting an engaging image of Canada in Brazil, and that he "may well play a part in making … 'Latin affinity' … something more of a reality than it has hitherto been."[50]

In his assessment of French Canadians, Shuckburgh merely echoed some of Désy's Anglophile colleagues in Ottawa, not all of whom were sympathetic to French-speaking Catholics. "Cultural paradigms," no less than institutional and policy imperatives, were important factors in identifying who was deemed most capable to stand for Canada and determining how to engage with the world.[51] Those who worked at External Affairs, MacDermot included, often reverted to racial and religious stereotypes when articulating their perception of – and expectations toward – the Global South.[52] Colleagues who spoke a different language (French) and held another set of beliefs (Catholicism) were viewed dismissively through a similar lens, as the subtext of Shuckburgh's correspondence suggests.

The Instituto Brasil-Canadá, inaugurated in Rio de Janeiro on 14 June 1944, was one of the venues Désy used to display the intellectual and cultural proficiency of Canadians, particularly those from Quebec and about whom Shuckburgh and others had doubts. It was meant to serve "as a clearing-house for all activities of a cultural nature which can be more easily directed by an organisation outside the Embassy." Mindful that he should not overstretch himself, Désy reassured his less adventurous colleagues in Ottawa that the intention was to make the initiative "a largely Brazilian affair."[53] Needless to say, they agreed on that point.[54] The notion that the institute could operate independently with little to no government involvement was, however, illusory. The Canadian ambassador held the title of honorary president, which was an acknowledgment of his role in founding the organization and providing it with momentum. Building from a narrow network of personal and professional contacts, including members of the Itamaraty, he solicited the support of an ever-growing range of prominent individuals and groups. Invariably, he handled some of the heavy lifting and fundraising himself, which brought in donations from affluent friends in Brazil as well as representatives at the Light and the Royal Bank of Canada. He himself added $15,000 to the organization's coffers – money he raised "from private firms and individuals" while he was undergoing medical treatment in Canada in the fall of 1943.[55]

The institute brought together a cohort of Francophile men from Rio de Janeiro's elite intellectual and economic circles, most of them with connections to the Vargas regime and, thereby, a vested interest in supporting cultural diplomacy initiatives that could enhance the image of the Estado Novo. Executive officers included the rector of the Universidade do Brasil (Raul Leitão da Cunha, who was elected president of the institute), a high-ranking federal judge (Edgard Costa, who served as vice-president), the head of the Federal Savings Bank and future president of Brazil (Carlos Luz, as secretary), an industrialist turned patron of the arts and literature (Raymundo Ottoni de Castro Maya, with the title of treasurer), and Vargas's attorney general (Gabriel de Resende Passos, who would serve as the Deliberative Committee's director).[56]

Cunha's speech on the day of the inauguration signalled that the Instituto Brasil-Canadá would serve as a conduit to amplify the tropes deployed to advance Canada-Brazil relations. Artfully and self-assuredly, the institute's president charmed the Canadians in attendance by revisiting Voltaire's oft-cited *Candide*, reminding them that their country had progressed from a "few acres of snow" to become "one of the great powers, materially and spiritually rich."[57] Overall, his speech expressed confidence in the institute's ability to help Brazilians and Canadians better understand their shared past and destiny as ethnically diverse, peace-driven peoples. The two nations had important roles to play in the postwar world, so they had much to gain by co-operating and acknowledging each other's potential, he implicitly argued. It was a prescriptive message informed by the individual and collective aspirations of those present.

Cunha was not the only person that day to speak about Canadian and Brazilian exceptionalism with an eye toward the future. Oswaldo Aranha, honorary president like Désy, was somewhat more direct in depicting Brazil as a sister nation and a wartime ally capable of leadership. His speech on 14 June echoed the one he gave on the day that the cultural agreement was signed. Both were framed in the context of the war with an emphasis on the two countries' ability to exert a positive influence in the world. Not only were Canadians and Brazilians making enormous sacrifices to "free Europe from tyranny ... [and] permit relations between peoples to be carried on as they are in America," they also stood as exemplars of tolerance. By highlighting the two nations' diverse populace, their "common formation of Latin origin," and their "faith in Christian ideals," he sought to arouse reciprocal feelings of trust and admiration, with the ultimate aim of nurturing further economic and political ties. His speech was about seeking recognition for the Estado Novo's wartime domestic and foreign efforts as much as it was about setting expectations for expanding the two countries' partnership. Much of it was rhetoric and hyperbole meant to cajole "a good and loyal neighbour" into siding with Brazil in preparing the terrain for the postwar world, within the framework of Pan-Americanism and internationalism.[58]

Cunha, Aranha, and their Rio de Janeiro colleagues were soon joined by a like-minded cohort who established, on 13 December 1944, a branch of the Instituto Brasil-Canadá in São Paulo. They came from similar backgrounds in industry, politics, and academia.[59] Berenguer Cesar, former counsellor of the Brazilian embassy in Ottawa, delivered the main address on inauguration day. He was no less explicit than Aranha had been in setting expectations for the future and highlighting that Brazil was demarcating itself as the sole South American country to send troops to Europe to fight alongside Canada "with the same arms, against the same enemies, for the same ideals." He continued: "It is good to study each other better ... and to esteem each other better. This is the principal objective of the Brazil-Canada Institute. Racial or economic rivalries do not exist between us. We are two free peoples, two nations which look confidently into the future. A wide road is opening before us."[60] Like his colleagues in Rio de Janeiro and São Paulo, Cesar saw the institute as a tool for consolidating the reputation of the Vargas regime and placing Brazil in a position of leadership in the hemisphere.

Désy, by contrast, appeared less concerned with getting Brazilians to endorse Canada's short- or long-term foreign policy goals than he was with occupying the spotlight and creating opportunities for his French-Canadian compatriots to share the stage with him. In other words, he prioritized projection over engagement in the ways that he approached the bilateral agreement, the "pride" of his career, and the Instituto Brasil-Canadá, an exceptional vehicle for "promoting a wider knowledge of Canada."[61] Unlike his counterparts, he did not dwell on the war during the speeches that he gave on 24 May 1944 and on the inauguration days of the Rio de Janeiro and São Paulo branches of the institute, possibly to avoid having to make false equivalences between the two countries' human and material contributions to the war in Europe and the Pacific.[62] His speeches were intentionally impressionistic, rather than prescriptively detailed.

In addition to mobilizing the usual tropes (*latinité*, family, Catholicism, and *métissage* as expressed through the idea of a compact between "two founding races"), Désy seized the moment to articulate a more explicitly nationalistic vision of Canadians' (and incidentally French Canadians') place in the world. Considering the extent of the United States' cultural penetration of South America, he knew that Brazilians would respond favourably to his call to frame the bilateral agreement as an instrument for "preserving" and "broadening" their "autochthonous cultures."[63] "We are equally sensitive with regard to questions of honour, autonomy, and independence," he told his interlocutors.[64] Dansereau and Tannehill's visit the previous year had laid the necessary groundwork for this particular reading of the cultural agreement by playing on the interplay between difference and sameness. The institute's first two scholarship recipients, the political scientist Marcel Roussin and the painter Jacques de Tonnancour, lent their voices to this effort.

## MARCEL ROUSSIN, PHD

As a guest of the Instituto Brasil-Canadá, Marcel Roussin travelled to Rio de Janeiro with the hope of making the experience a stepping stone for his career.[65] He belonged to a younger generation of French-Canadian, Catholic intellectuals that was walking in the footsteps of prominent elite figures – people like Désy, Édouard Montpetit, and Raoul Dandurand – who envisioned Quebec playing a crucial role in Canada's passage from colony to nation. Born in 1918, Roussin earned a bachelor of arts from the Séminaire de Joliette before relocating to Montreal, where he spent two years studying international law. He then undertook graduate studies in political science, completing his master's degree in 1941 and successfully defending his doctoral dissertation four years later.[66] A sessional lecturer at the Université d'Ottawa, he represented the institution at the National Federation of Catholic Universities, a position that entailed coordinating "Pax Romana propaganda" in the southern hemisphere.[67] Having learned Spanish and Portuguese in short order, he established his reputation as a South Americanist through a series of articles published in *L'Action catholique*, *Les Carnets victoriens*, *L'Étoile du Nord*, and *Le Jour*.

The young scholar had a wide-ranging grasp of political and economic topics pertaining to South America as a whole, but he focused his attention on Brazil, presumably because of the opportunities that

Désy was creating there for French Canadians. Starting in 1943, Roussin began advocating for the creation of a Comité Canada-Brésil to entice his compatriots into supporting closer relations with the South American giant. The commonality of feelings, identities, and desires that he claimed existed between the two nations rested on Brazilians' adherence to Western Christian values and their knowledge of the French language, which allowed them to go "anywhere in the world where one finds civilized peoples." His was a normative view that favoured certain elements of Brazilian society over others. At the same time, Roussin was intrigued by what he saw as the country's exoticism. He was, no doubt, referring to himself when he remarked that "among Canadians too, burns this flame of Brazil, producing a feverish desire to travel to Rio and Sao-Paulo, to stroll along Copacabana beach, and to admire the Christ of Corcovado standing out against the night sky."[68] He already had his eyes set on a research trip there, so his championing of Canada-Brazil relations was part of a broader strategy to call attention to his work and enthusiasm.

Roussin's self-promotion efforts were successful even if they did not always bring about the desired outcomes. A case in point was his attempt to script a series on South America for Radio-Canada. He had hoped that the project would bring his expertise to the attention of the broadcaster's listenership or, at the very least, its program directors. The project, however, did not take off. Roussin might nonetheless have been instrumental in getting some airtime for Freitas Vale. The Brazilian ambassador and his predecessor, Franco, took note of Roussin's "sympathetic disposition" toward their country and the ostensibly "disinterested nature" of his intentions.[69] Hence their support for the idea of sending him on a research trip to Rio de Janeiro.

Plans were in the works as early as the summer of 1942 and they involved Désy, the Itamaraty, Brazil's diplomatic corps in Canada, and Hector Perrier, Quebec's provincial secretary. The correspondence between and among the various parties reveals how proactive Roussin was in seeking endorsement and setting things in motion for his scholarship overseas. It also indicates that the project was initially framed in terms of a rapprochement between Brazil and Quebec, rather than Canada. This was certainly due to an awareness of the constitutional difficulties that accompanied questions of international student exchange programs. The fact that Désy, T. da G. Aranha, and Franco were debating this question in 1942 and 1943 suggests that this was perhaps also a strategy to force Ottawa's hand amid discussions about the two countries' bilateral cultural agreement. Or could it be that they were pursuing alternate avenues in the event that External Affairs refused to act on the cultural diplomacy file?

In any event, Quebec would have held the initiative had it not failed to act. On 4 June 1943, Franco wrote to Perrier with the news that his government was open to offering a scholarship to Roussin if such a gesture could pave the way to further reciprocal exchanges. Désy had endorsed the young scholar's candidature and signalled his willingness to work with his colleagues in Quebec to help move the dossier forward. Roussin, through his publication record, showed that he was "a real friend of Brazil," Franco told Perrier, adding that he could also play the role of "propagandist for his province."[70] The provincial secretary was slow to respond to the offer, in part, because he was distracted by a filibuster launched in opposition to a planned state-owned beet sugar plant south of Montreal.[71] Funds had been set aside for Roussin by the fall of 1943 and it was just a matter of deciding on the proper channels through which to funnel the money. The signing of the cultural agreement in 1944 provided the answer: the scholarship would be awarded via the Instituto Brasil-Canadá. Quebec had missed the boat.

Roussin was not alone in trying to take advantage of Canada's hemispheric moment to carve a greater place at home and abroad for French Canadians. The O'Leary brothers, Émile-Dostaler and Walter-Patrice, were exceptionally effective in rallying people around the idea that Quebec's *latinité* qualified it for leadership on continental matters.[72] They had honed their organizing skills during the Great Depression with Jeunesses patriotes du Canada français, a separatist organization with fascist leanings. In 1939, they orchestrated a rapprochement between French-Canadian nationalists and Catholic militants in Mexico with the creation of the Unión Cultural México-Canadá Francés. The organization's Montreal chapter subsequently adopted a new name – Union culturelle des Latins d'Amérique (UCLA) – to reflect its broader mandate to (a) establish direct and ongoing contact with the people of South America, and (b) develop cultural, educational, social, and commercial relations with them.

The O'Leary brothers may have appeared to embrace internationalism, but their goal was to further their nationalist agenda. By locating "French Canada at the crux of Canadian-Latin American diplomatic relations," they sought to ensure the survival of the *fait français*.[73] Their use of the trope of *latinité* was ineluctably tied to two other markers of identity: the French language and Catholicism. Like Désy, they were pursuing transnational collaborations to advance a politico-cultural project rooted in identity politics. That said, they were disinclined to imagine Quebec thriving as a sub-national actor on the international stage, determined as they were to see the province chart its own path out of the shadow of the Anglosphere. Their outreach efforts also masked an apparent, conservative *repli culturel* that was at odds with the cosmopolitan internationalism that Désy and his cultural ambassadors embraced.

The UCLA was not a fringe organization that one could easily dismiss. Ottawa took note of the zealousness with which the organization's members networked with representatives from the industrial, cultural, business, government, and university sectors to elevate French-speaking, Catholic Quebec as a key player in continental affairs.[74] For the O'Leary brothers, 1943 was an especially productive year. While External Affairs debated the pros and cons of signing a cultural agreement with Brazil, their organization screened films on South American topics, compiled books and records for a projected library, offered Portuguese and Spanish language classes, sponsored public talks, and convened its 250 or so members to themed evening dances. The O'Leary brothers also coordinated propaganda campaigns to publicize their work throughout the hemisphere. They used their contacts in municipal and provincial governments to be part of the welcoming committees assembled for official visits by foreign dignitaries. Their annual conference, Journées d'Amérique latine, served as a forum in which UCLA's members, government officials, and representatives from South American embassies, legations, and consuls in Canada could meet and converse. Their multi-pronged strategy positioned them as the prime movers for Quebec's rapprochement with its neighbours to the south at a time when External Affairs thought it could still hold the initiative.[75]

Roussin could not ignore the group since it was a legitimate vehicle for asserting his expert status. He was, however, ideologically closer to Désy than to the O'Leary brothers. If anyone in Ottawa doubted where his loyalties lay, he reassured them during his intervention at the 1943 Journées d'Amérique latine. Held at the Cercle universitaire de Montréal, in the city's downtown core, the two-day conference brought together more than thirty presenters around six panels dealing with three key themes: economics, cultural affairs, and political relations. Titled "L'Amérique du Sud et les relations diplomatiques,"

Roussin's paper placed French Canadians' search for an international identity squarely within the history of Canada's pursuit of autonomy while pleading with those in attendance not to implicate others in the country's internal squabbles. "We may be predisposed to act as bridge builders between Canada and South America, but we must exercise caution in this work, just like diplomats; we need to show composure," he remarked. "The Canada that is at war now, is neither French, nor English, it is Canada," Roussin added, before reminding the audience that "from an international standpoint, we are all Canadians."[76] Speaking on behalf of External Affairs on this occasion, Roussin was unlikely to be critical of the path chosen by the likes of Désy, especially since the ambassador was hard at work trying to secure his scholarship.

The young scholar thus positioned himself adroitly vis-à-vis the UCLA's vision of an imagined community exclusive to French-speaking, Catholic Quebec. What seemed like a benign alternate proposition in fact threatened the pan-Canadian, bicultural ideals that animated efforts in Brazil and of which Roussin was a direct beneficiary. As Maurice Demers explains in his study of Quebec-Mexico relations, French-Canadian nationalists sought to overcome their marginal status in North America by creating a "symbolic space" outside of that occupied by Canada in its relationship to the Anglosphere. Through the UCLA, they crafted "a meaningful and authoritative imagined community with an international reach to counter the geopolitics imposed by central governing authorities."[77] Although they failed to make a lasting impact on Canada's and Quebec's approaches to the making of international relations, they – like Désy and his impromptu ambassadors – understood the importance of culture in responding to asymmetrical power dynamics.

Once in Brazil, Roussin was surprisingly invisible. It was a striking contrast to the public persona he had developed prior to departing Canada on 23 May 1945. It also did not align with the idea of a Canadian-Brazilian imagined community, which he had championed alongside Désy. Newspapers in Rio de Janeiro did not seem to notice his presence. How could they if he was not engaging with his hosts? He unexpectedly had little to report to Canadian publications about Brazilian political and socio-economic developments. He had been a prolific contributor on these topics in the past, even advocating for the creation of a Comité Canada-Brésil, but he was largely silent during his short stay in the southern hemisphere.

Much was happening in Brazil at the time that should have been of interest to Roussin and worth writing about. The first squadrons of the Força Expedicionaria Brasileira (Brazilian Expeditionary Force) were beginning to return from Italy, where they had fought valiantly, most with the United States Army and some under the command of Harold Alexander, 1st Earl of Tunis and future governor general of Canada. The Partido Comunista do Brasil (Communist Party of Brazil) was also making its return. Founded in 1922, it had rallied people on the left under the guidance of the Communist International, gathering sufficient support to stage a coup against the government in 1935. It had failed, thus playing in the hands of Vargas, who then declared a state of emergency in order to begin consolidating his dictatorship. Communists returned to the national stage in 1945 with the president promising elections for October. Many doubted he would relinquish power, and so the military left him no choice but to resign. The war was bringing democracy back to Brazil.

Roussin was less interested in writing from the perspective of a true friend of Brazil, as Franco had hoped, than he was in substantiating, for his compatriots back home, the idea that French Canadians were especially qualified to enact leadership. He thus acted as a propagandist for his province by highlighting the important work that the group Quatuor alouette and Quebec-based Dominican fathers were doing in Brazil. The latter had just established themselves in São Paulo, and Roussin felt that it was crucial that "families and friends back home be kept informed of the work accomplished and the devotion shown by these spiritual ambassadors, so that they could support their mission and pray for them."[78] Likewise for Quatuor alouette, a folkloric vocal ensemble from Montreal, on tour in Brazil at the invitation of Désy. The concert reviews he submitted to *La Presse* applauded the singers as eminent dignitaries. Praising Désy, he clearly enjoyed the sense of family that he felt around his French-speaking, Catholic co-envoys.[79]

A certain *mal du pays* comes through the reports that Roussin sent back home. His experience of Rio de Janeiro was not what he expected. As a scholarship recipient, he intended to spend a full year overseas, but he shortened his stay to six months, apparently for health reasons.[80] Although it is unclear what he suffered from, his dislike of urban life in Brazil must have made matters worse. He weighed his words carefully in public forums, but his private notes reveal the extent to which his northern gaze informed his perception of Brazilians. The following excerpt is telling:

> *Human life*. Brazilians have no sense of values. They disregard life as much as the individual. At night, cars brush against you at 50 miles an hour with their lights off … On the street, people shoot at each other with revolvers about this and that. They let poor disabled peoples drag themselves on their knees on sidewalks, but they erect monuments, and make propaganda … Few Brazilians know how to read, but all those who can have written a book and compose verses.
>
> *At mass*, they sing just about anything. This morning, 29 July 1945, at the N.S. Church of Copacabana, a baritone sang an Ave Maria to the tune of Jocelyn's Lullaby, and a tenor sang the second part of the Sanctus … omitting the first, and it all ended in a waltz. Not to mention a young negro, who feels obliged to dance barefoot in the main aisle, going back and forth, among the faithful. The Creator must have regrets sometimes.[81]

In this entry and many others dealing with topics ranging from tramways to fashion and culture, Roussin describes urban life in Brazil as disorganized and rudimentary as well as deficient on questions of morality and religion. Privately, then, he articulated his contempt for Brazilians who, because of their place on the periphery of the industrialized North, were destined in his eyes to fail in their efforts at emulation.

Going from attraction to repulsion, Roussin's ambivalence toward his hosts reflected his perception of Brazil as a distant stage where – through an encounter with an Other – he could perform, and thus validate and propagate, a boastful self-image centred on white normativity.[82] His ethnocentric gaze reflected his belief that Canadians were politically, economically, and culturally more advanced than Brazilians. He obviously could not say so publicly for fear of creating a diplomatic incident. Roussin was careful not to undermine Désy's efforts or upset the Brazilian diplomats who had supported him in Canada and with whom he was likely to interact again in the future in his capacity as a political scientist. Accordingly, he avoided discussing Brazilian current affairs, focusing instead on the French-Canadian – official and impromptu – ambassadors with whom he associated. In discussing the work that they were doing, he could project authority and display expertise on the unfamiliar topic of cultural diplomacy. Implicitly, Roussin suggested, by association, that he was himself doing similarly important work.

The signing of the 1944 agreement marked a turning point. It provided a framework for expanding the tools and the range of activities with which to project Canada's image abroad. It had been a lengthy process due, in part, to External Affairs' lukewarm interest in culture and the fact that Brazil did not rank high on the department's list of international priorities. Official bilateral cultural relations between the two countries were off to a slow, uneventful start. Yet Désy managed to keep the momentum going on the ground in Rio de Janeiro and São Paulo. A promising recruit, Roussin did not quite deliver as a guest of the Instituto Brasil-Canadá. He did, however, help publicize among the readers of Quebec's French-language newspapers the work that his fellow French Canadians were doing in the South. His reporting was a sincere endorsement of their efforts even if it concealed deep prejudice toward Brazilians. Prioritizing performance and projection over engagement, the young scholar sought the familiar in Brazil while adopting an essentializing outlook to deal with difference. "Brazilians create for themselves an air of exoticism, and we can't blame them for trying to escape, even if only in their mind, this poor country," he penned in his travel book. In Roussin's telling, even Rio de Janeiro's world-famous "Copacabana beach … is no better than those of Pointe-Claire or Murray Bay."[83] Cracks were beginning to appear in Désy's carefully crafted cultural project.

# 4
# Familiar Folks

"When one arrives to Rio through the bay, what is most striking is the imposing statue of Christ the Redeemer, which can be seen from throughout the city, in the same way that Montrealers can see the cross on Mount Royal," explained Émile Lamarre to Oscar Richer, journalist at *La Presse*, in December of 1945.[1] The singer had just returned from a two-month tour of Brazil with his bandmates from Quatuor alouette: Jules Jacob, André Trottier, and Roger Filiatrault. They were not mere amateurs, as the renowned folklorist Marius Barbeau pointed out after their performance at the 1942 edition of the US-American National Folk Festival, which was held in Washington and New York that year.[2] The four men were folklorists themselves, and their project to give a "Fine Interpretation and Artistic Vulgarizing of French Canadian Folklore" intertwined with their desire to articulate an antimodernist vision of the world through music, much of it infused with Catholic faith and values.[3]

Filiatrault and Jean Désy were cousins, but that alone did not explain the group's presence in Brazil in October and November of 1945. A regular fixture on radio airwaves, Quatuor alouette was extremely popular in Quebec. Moreover, its members possessed experience as cultural ambassadors, having performed in France during the 1934 celebrations organized for the fourth centenary of Jacques Cartier's first voyage to Canada, as well as in the United States, where they twice acted as official Quebec delegates to the National Folk Festival (in 1942 and 1943). Désy invited Quatuor alouette to Brazil to inject life into the musically imagined community that Jean Danserau and Muriel Tannehill had inspired two years earlier. It was a departure from "serious music," but he was optimistic that the group's repertoire and stage presence would resonate with Brazilians.

Much happened between August 1943, when Dansereau and Tannehill left Rio de Janeiro, and October 1945, when Quatuor alouette disembarked there. In that time, Désy graduated from minister plenipotentiary to ambassador and the two countries cemented their friendship with a pioneering cultural agreement. Brazil also deployed soldiers to the Mediterranean theatre as a show of support for the United States, Canada, and their wartime allies. No other South American country committed troops to the conflict. President Getúlio Vargas's participation in the defeat of the Axis powers was much celebrated, but it also brought into focus the evident contradiction of a dictatorship fighting undemocratic fascist regimes overseas.[4] His ongoing reluctance to commit to a return to democracy fuelled a range of domestic discontents, from the spectre of a subversive fifth column to the threat of a military coup. Yet the Estado Novo held strong, in part due to the support it was receiving from the Catholic Church.[5]

It is revealing that the members of Quatuor alouette were more inclined to capitalize on the shared religion of Brazilians and French Canadians than adopt a critical posture vis-à-vis the dictatorship in this pivotal period. In Brazil, they performed folk songs that spoke of nostalgia for an idyllic time, the sanctity of *bonne entente* and community, the picturesque and majestic Canadian landscape, and the importance of traditional values in changing times. The tour also provided them with the opportunity to expand and attach new meanings to their repertoire: more so than usual, it revolved around their Catholic heritage. The fact that Quatuor alouette arrived in Rio de Janeiro at the same time as missionaries from the congregation Les Frères du Sacré Coeur was pure coincidence, but the serendipity of the encounter delighted both parties. It inspired the singers to lend their voices to the cause of their ordained brothers. In doing so, Quatuor alouette took cultural diplomacy in an unforeseen direction, causing some disharmony with the embassy's mandate by placing religion squarely at the heart of the two countries' cultural relations in the closing months of the Vargas era.[6]

## MISSIONS TO BRAZIL

In Rio de Janeiro as in Montreal, the Catholic Church exerted its influence from on high. The erection of a cross atop Mount Royal and the statue of Christ on Corcovado Mountain were reminders that religion had shaped the two cities' histories. The story of the former originates in 1643 when Paul de Chomedey, sieur de Maisonneuve and founder of Ville-Marie (now Montreal), asked his god to protect the settlement from the rising waters of the Saint Lawrence River, promising to plant a cross on the city's highest point as a sign of gratitude. The threat passed, and in 1924 the Société Saint-Jean-Baptiste revisited the sieur's pledge with a thirty-metre-high illuminated structure.[7] Brazilians had poured the concrete base of their statue of Christ two years earlier in a similar display of their Catholic faith. Despite getting an early start, they only completed the project in 1931. Work had begun on the centenary of their country's independence thanks to the persistent efforts of prominent Catholic figures. The timing was opportunistic, and it conveyed the church's desire to reassert itself as a unifying and stabilizing force three decades after the First Republic put forward the principle of separation between church and state.[8]

The Catholic Church in Brazil traces its origins to the sixteenth century, when religious orders – Franciscans, Dominicans, and Jesuits – established themselves throughout the land. The Franciscans were the first to lay roots in an official manner; their establishment of a bishopric in 1552 promptly set a pattern of co-operation between subsequent religious orders and the colonial regime. These groups were instrumental in helping impose the Portuguese language and system of governance across much of the territory, although there were occasional tensions with settlers, many of whom were disinclined to support efforts to proselytize Indigenous communities. Catholicism became Brazil's official religion when the country achieved its independence in 1822, but the alliance did not last long. The end of Dom Pedro II's reign in 1889 saw the dawn of an era of secular government. The setbacks that religious groups experienced in the early years of the First Republic did not, however, prevent them from establishing additional bishoprics. Catholic Action groups, among others, were especially zealous in assisting the political Right, promoting a discourse of order and discipline that fed into the nationalism and anti-communism upon which the Estado Novo would thrive in the 1930s.[9]

Vargas's ascent to power signalled the beginning of a new era for the Catholic Church, which endorsed his centralizing and corporatist approach to governance. The president, who many "believed to be an agnostic," understood that the church could be a valued ally in his national reconstruction efforts.[10] Not only could it help legitimize his regime among pious segments of the population, but it could also provide much-needed cost-saving assistance in educating Brazilians and instilling in them a sense of patriotism. During the Vargas era, church and state worked in tandem, becoming "mutually-legitimating allies in the face of perceived ideological threats such as 'anarchic liberalism' and 'atheistic communism.'" This "reciprocal legitimation" did not just manifest itself in sermons and political speeches, explains Marcelo Campos Hazan, but also "played out musically" through vast programs aimed at popularizing liturgy, which acted as a "musical simulacrum of the authoritarian order," and Orpheonic singing, which "aimed at suppressing dissent, infusing obedience, and subordinating the urban masses to their political and musical leaders."[11] Religion and music mixed synergistically during this period.

The Catholic Church's growing role and visibility were not without complications. The effort to augment its influence among Brazilians of German origins is a case in point. The persistence of ethnic enclaves in the southern states of Rio de Janeiro, Rio Grande do Sul, and Espírito Santo, sustained in part by religious leaders, was difficult to reconcile with the national vision that was at the core of the Estado Novo. As Brazil slid toward war against Germany, these populations became an obvious security concern. Accordingly, lawmakers moved to prohibit the clergy from preaching in the language of belligerent nations.[12] This was followed by education reforms aimed at nationalizing curricula and restricting the use of foreign languages in classrooms.[13] Careful not to antagonize clergy members, the Vargas regime sought to make them allies in the fight against Nazism. For instance, Dom Joan Becker, archbishop of Rio Grande do Sul, reportedly of German origin, showed his support in a circular in which he warned against the "doctrinary errors of neo-pagan Nazis" who were spreading "poisonous and corrosive" ideologies that seeped "into the spirit, intoxicating the brain and the more holier truths." Faith and patriotism, he reminded his flock, were one and the same.[14]

The Canadian diplomatic corps in Brazil was keeping a close watch on Nazi sympathizers among the clergy there. Désy was encouraged by Becker's circular, but he felt that the situation was bound to deteriorate without further reinforcement. He was therefore pleased to learn from Prime Minister William Lyon Mackenzie King that Father Marcel-Marie Desmarais, a member of the Dominican Order and a celebrity broadcaster in Quebec, was on his way to South America.[15] Desmarais travelled from country to country to distribute copies of a theological treatise, known as the *Piana*, that the war had made scarce. In Rio de Janeiro, he networked with other Dominicans and the broader Catholic leadership, lending his name to their fight against Nazism.[16] Désy and his staff offered their visitor a platform by way of their contacts in the press. On 22 April 1942, Brazilian newspapers reprinted segments of Desmarais's "Para lá do patriotismo." In it, he urged Brazilians to support the war against Germany if they wanted to hold on to their hard-won freedom and human dignity. Patriotism demanded it, he argued. Sensing perhaps that his argument would sound hollow in the context of Brazil's own dictatorial turn, he added that a more urgent reason for siding with the Allies was "to defend God himself."[17] Religion had previously factored into the making of diplomacy in Brazil, with Désy occasionally highlighting the shared Catholicism of Brazilians and French Canadians, but it had never moved centre stage in this way.

French-Canadian missionaries had been to South America before, but most had little to no contact with Ottawa's official envoys until the 1940s. The Soeurs de la Providence were pioneers in sending five of their members to Chile in 1853. The delegation, however, represented "but a few grains of sand in the Catholic desert of Latin America."[18] Pope Benedict XV's *Maximum illud*, a 1919 apostolic letter that outlined the work that needed to be done to propagate the faith in the aftermath of the devastating First World War, inspired groups in Quebec to train and organize their members to serve as ambassadors of Christ. Publications such as *Le Précurseur* and *Missions-étrangères du Québec* soon sprung up, providing congregations with a means to publicize their work, recruit new candidates, and amass donations for their planned missions abroad, from China to Japan and India, but also to South America, where there was at the time an insufficient number of Catholic leaders and missionaries to meet the spiritual needs of a growing pious population.[19]

French Canadians' experience with missionary work would be a factor in the transformation of Quebec society from the 1950s onward. It would open a window onto the world and bring increased awareness to human rights and social justice issues, first in the Global South and then at home. That said, the missionaries who travelled overseas during the first half of the twentieth century were from an older, more conservative generation. Their paternalistic and normative Eurocentric word view reflected their belief in the superiority of Roman Catholicism and Western culture.[20] The missionaries who travelled to South America in the 1940s were thus less likely to be transformed by their travels, and less likely – in the beginning, at least – to adopt an internationalist ethos and embrace new, progressive ideas to promote dialogue and action in support of local populations.[21]

An unexpected turn of events brought Desmarais back to Brazil as head of mission in the fall of 1944. He and his colleagues – Étienne-M. Laporte and Gustave-René Picher – were there to establish a new home for missionaries who had left or were expected to soon leave wartime Japan. The Dominicans had been present in the Pacific since 1928, but they were no longer welcome at the close of 1941. The rise of ultranationalism and concerns over security, which had only heightened after Pearl Harbor, resulted in the internment and expulsion of missionaries, many of them French Canadians. Laporte and Picher were among the fortunate few who managed to leave Japan in the early months of the war.[22]

In the spring of 1945, Desmarais, Laporte, and Picher moved into a villa located in Santo Amaro, in the south of São Paulo, where they prepared for the arrival of close to thirty of their colleagues still presumed to be interned in Japan. In charge of their own territory, they focused their energy on schools and universities as well as hospitals. Of primary interest were Brazilian intellectuals who could be counted upon to undertake proselytizing work themselves on the outskirts of the city and in its impoverished neighbourhoods. The group inaugurated its retreat centre that fall. It was a large, twenty-room building that included a vast garden and a chapel already popular among the local clergy. Marcel Roussin, who was still in Brazil at the time, wrote enthusiastically about the event for *La Presse*, praising Quebec's "spiritual ambassadors" and expressing his joy at being in their company.[23]

Like Roussin, Desmarais felt most at ease, even uplifted, among fellow French Canadians. He, too, was finding it difficult to adapt to the oppressive heat and what he saw as Brazilians' unreliability. "Tomorrow" is their favourite word, he complained.[24] His nerves raw and jumping at the sound of samba, the music of the *favelas*, he found commuting through the city to be both hazardous and disconcerting. Japan having formally surrendered on 2 September 1945, he was in all likelihood relieved to learn that the Dominican missionaries there had been released and given permission to stay. The news compelled Laporte and Picher to sail back to the Pacific, leaving Desmarais with the task of shutting down their short-lived operation before his return to Quebec.[25]

## THE SEARCH FOR THE FOLK

The decision to invite Quatuor alouette to Brazil in 1945 was a judicious one considering how religion was beginning to factor into Canada-Brazil relations. The four singers wore their Catholicism on their sleeves. As folklorists, they weaved it into origin stories of Quebec as a folk society. A composite term, "folklore" refers to a somewhat homogeneous social group (folk) and the totality of its cultural manifestations (lore). A product of the investigative gaze, folklore is a "constructed term," or an "essentialist abstraction," that first appeared during the Romantic period.[26] In the eighteenth century, the Prussian-born philosopher Johann Gottfried von Herder proposed to place the folk at the heart of a nascent Germanic nationalism that aimed to cope with the disruptive effects of industrialization and foreign influences on society. His championing of traditional local expressive cultures (from language to poetry and music) inspired others, such as German academics Jacob and Wilhelm Grimm, to pursue the search for a fixed – thus stable and enduring – national essence. In posing the question of selfhood and nationhood versus Otherness, folklorists such as Herder and the Grimm brothers searched for order and purpose in ways that betrayed their discomfort with the world as it changed around them.

A similar uneasiness inspired folklorists at the turn of the twentieth century. Responding to a multifarious combination of phenomena (from industrialization to urbanization, population migration, leftist agitation, changing socio-cultural mores, and shifting power centres), they searched for an idyllic corporeal entity that could serve as a model they could cling to, perhaps even emulate, in the face of disquieting change. Francis James Child and John Lomax were folklore studies pioneers whose work on music contributed to the invention of the folk, a repository and passive transmitter of expressive cultures whom experts could mine, document, display, and comment on by drawing from anthropological and literary approaches. Folklorists could be one or all of the following: academics, cultural producers, or educators. In those capacities, they harnessed the potential of information technologies to record, preserve, frame, and disseminate their findings. Their projects were as much about constructing a past that could offset the more disruptive aspects of modernization, economic hardship, and war as it was about finding anchors for the nation and the social order within which they thrived as elite members of society.[27]

Folklore studies developed under a similar set of circumstances in Brazil, where *Brasilidade* demanded a re-engagement with both Indigenous folklore and Afro-Brazilian expressive cultures. The search for the folk there coincided with the search for a national essence that could foster national unity, guard against cultural imperialism, respond to the challenges posed by non-Portuguese immigration, and offset the destabilizing effects of industrialization on the social order. The country's North and Northeast became coveted sites for fieldwork, because they were wellsprings of pre-Columbian and diasporic heritage. They were also the sites of the first Portuguese settlements, those that followed Pedro Álvares Cabral's landing in what is now Bahia. Hence the feeling of "*saudade*, or longing," that accompanied evocations of the Northeast, a region that many considered "the cradle of Brazilian civilization."[28]

Mario de Andrade was at the centre of folklore studies in Brazil, even if he initially refused to consider himself a folklorist.[29] The São Paulo artist and intellectual played a pivotal role in documenting – and theorizing about – expressive cultures from throughout the country. As the founding director of São Paulo's Departamento de Cultura (Department of Culture), he organized and sent a folklore research mission to the North and the Northeast in 1938. It returned with recordings of 1,000 melodies, loads of musical instruments, close to 18,000 textual documents (from notebooks to notations and lyrics), cult objects, over 1,000 photographs, and 19 films.[30] Andrade also founded a music library, the Discoteca Pública, which handled the cataloguing, preservation, display, and dissemination of the documents and items his mission had collected. As such, he actively sought out and mobilized source materials that he and others would exploit – through poems, novels, and music – to reimagine Brazil as an exceptional nation capable of "creating a cultural (if not a biologically) *mestiço* people."[31]

As for folklorists in Canada, they operated within the framework of the Anglo-American folklore matrix that developed around Child's and Lomax's research.[32] Systematic fieldwork began in 1910 when the anthropologist and linguist Edward Sapir became involved in the Geological Survey of Canada, which then included the Victoria Memorial Museum (later renamed National Museum of Canada). As the founding director of the Anthropological Division, he initiated a vast study of Indigenous languages and expressive cultures, including music. Returning from Great Britain, where he had studied on a Rhodes Scholarship, Marius Barbeau joined Sapir in 1911 to conduct research. A chance encounter with Franz Uri Boas, the renowned German-American anthropologist and one of Sapir's former mentors, inspired Barbeau to set his gaze beyond the "native races" and to study the distinctive history and contours of French-Canadian folklore.[33] If French Canadians were legitimate research objects, so were the Scots of Nova Scotia, as folklorist William Roy MacKenzie might have argued. His work on British Isles ballads preserved in the province was in the Child tradition, although he came on the scene a little too early to ride the anti-modernist wave of the 1920s and '30s. His successor, Helen Creighton, had better luck and timing in constructing and popularizing an essentialist past for Nova Scotia.[34]

Barbeau set himself apart from his professional and semi-professional colleagues with his ability to combine research and public scholarship in both French and English Canada. Born in 1883 in Sainte-Marie, Quebec, he first studied law at the Université Laval before transitioning to anthropology while in Great Britain. Following his meeting with Boas in 1913, he began fieldwork in Quebec with the intent of better understanding how French-Canadian folk tales intersected with the expressive culture of the Wyandot people. Music, especially, captured his interest. His mother, an organist with the local parish, had taught him the rudiments on the piano, which proved handy in preparing transcriptions, harmonizations, and arrangements for the folk songs that he was recording. Johann-Baptist Beck, a philologist with an interest in troubadours, the English composer Arthur Somervell, and the Canadian-born composer Ernest MacMillan, among others, provided assistance with some of that work.[35] Barbeau's *Folk Songs of French Canada* (co-authored with Sapir in 1925) was a product of these efforts.[36]

Barbeau reinvented himself as a cultural producer to convey the significance of his research in the aftermath of the First World War and amid fast-paced industrialization. He started organizing and staging lecture-recitals at which he sought to popularize French-Canadian folklore and to educate audiences about the merits of a music that spoke of *terroir* and an idyllic past. The rural landscapes of yesteryear that his work evoked were in stark contrast with the dense and often disorienting modern cities of the present. The folk songs that he discussed and presented on stage were meant to serve as reassuring connections to ostensibly purer, more authentic times.[37] Whether it was the Veillées du bon vieux temps, held at Montreal's Bibliothèque Saint-Sulpice in 1919 and 1920, or the concerts presented under the auspices of the Canadian Pacific Railway (CPR) Festival, organized by publicity agent John Murray Gibbon between 1927 and 1931, Barbeau tirelessly conveyed his anti-modernist vision to elite audiences throughout Canada.[38]

Désy found inspiration in this work. In 1945, he published an article on Canadian folklore in *Brasil Musical*, a prestigious publication read by members of the country's cultural elites. In it, he outlined the history of French-Canadian folk songs, those imported from France in the seventeenth century and others invented in the New World by explorers, missionaries, and settlers. Borrowing from Barbeau, he proposed a taxonomy that accounted for variations in melody, wording, and pronunciation: lullabies, love songs, dialogues and vaudevilles, humorous songs, dance and work tunes, and religious hymns. Désy explained to the readers of *Brasil Musical* that generations of French Canadians had nurtured the collective memory of this material. He stressed the nomadic character of the songs as if they had a life of their own – a life from which one could draw lessons about survival and endurance as well as the need for anchors in order to adapt and thrive.[39] Turning to Irish, Scottish, and English folk songs, he argued that the heterogeneity of Canada's repertoire spoke of diversity and *bonne entente*, even *métissage*. It was an apt vehicle for telling stories to others about the Canadian experience.

Désy's focus on settler colonists informed his deliberately reductive understanding of Brazil's musical past. In his *Brasil Musical* article, he wrote about popular Brazilian songs such as "A canoa virou" and "Entrei na roda," emphasizing their Spanish, Italian, and French origins. As for works originating from Africa, he briefly noted that their presence in Brazil could be explained by "the size of the black race established in this country."[40] It is revealing that Désy made references neither to Black Canadians nor to the two countries' role in the transatlantic slave trade. By avoiding both topics, Désy could present Canada as having been forever white and free of racism. Accordingly, he also made no mention of Indigenous expressive cultures. He made a similar point in a separate article, published in *Correio da Manhã*, in which he highlighted similarities between the French-Canadian lullaby "Courte paille" and the Luso-Brazilian folk song "Caterineta."[41] The narrative that Désy deployed in both publications foregrounded a musically imagined community with clear zones of exclusions. It served as an instructive prelude to Quatuor alouette's tour of Brazil.

## IN UNISON WITH QUATUOR ALOUETTE

Founded in 1930 by Roger Filiatrault and André Trottier, Quatuor alouette was a product of the flurry of activity that followed Barbeau everywhere he went. The group entered the limelight after a chance encounter with Oscar O'Brien, who had just stepped in as artistic director for the Veillées du bon vieux temps. He was replacing Charles Marchand, folklorist and baritone with the Troubadours de Bytown, whose death had left a sudden void in the organization. Quatuor alouette impressed O'Brien with their professionalism and their mastery of the repertoire that Barbeau had assembled over the years. Desirous to pursue Marchand's work, the group and O'Brien joined forces. They gave their first concert at Montreal's Salle des artisans canadiens-français on 29 May 1932. Their success was not long coming. The four singers, coached by their artistic director, became a regular fixture on radio airwaves, performing throughout Canada as well as in Europe and the United States.[42]

Born in 1892, Oscar O'Brien was an educator and a musician whose chosen instruments were the piano and the organ. He began collaborating with Marchand in 1915, accompanying him in his efforts to elevate folk singing to the status of a legitimate art form. He harmonized and prepared arrangements for hundreds of songs in accordance with the vision that Barbeau put forward in his publications and during events such as the Veillées du bon vieux temps. On 4 December 1933, Quatuor alouette and O'Brien organized a lecture-recital at the École technique de Montréal. He asked the audience: Is folk music worthy of attention? Is it genuinely beautiful? Can it be the basis of our national music? These were rhetorical questions since O'Brien was already convinced that folk music would not be studied, discussed, and performed so assiduously if it did not have intrinsic value. Its poetic and musical qualities lay in understated yet evocative images that only true art conveyed, he argued. Hence its popularity. It travelled through space and across time, from one generation to another, anchored in the *terroir* so that artists could harvest its fruits. According to O'Brien, folk singers and composers made audible the nation's essence.[43] His line of argument was evidently self-serving. Still, there is little doubt that he believed in the potency of music as a means of coping with the frenzied pace of change that characterized the interwar years.

The singers' overseas experience played an important part in their reception at home, and it made them exceptional candidates for Désy's cultural diplomacy. In 1934, they accompanied the official Canadian delegation to Paris for the fourth centenary of Jacques Cartier's first voyage to Canada.[44] They performed as a quartet most of the time, although other singers joined in on a few occasions.[45] The highlight of that first trip to Europe was their performance of "Panis angelicus" at Notre-Dame de Paris and at Saint-Malo Cathedral, where Cartier had received his blessings before sailing across the Atlantic.[46] Filiatrault and his associates returned to Europe in 1937 equipped with a better understanding of their status as cultural ambassadors. With the support of provincial secretary Joseph-Henri-Albiny Paquette and Quebec's Office du tourisme, the group travelled to France and Belgium under the patronage of Philippe Roy, Canada's minister plenipotentiary in France, who helped promote a picturesque and inviting image of both the province and the country to French-speaking elites and prospective migrants.[47]

It is at this point that Désy enters the Quatuor alouette story. At the time, he was counsellor at the Paris legation and could then provide some assistance to Filiatrault, his cousin, by reaching out to influential people he knew in the press and in broadcasting.[48] The tour, which lasted from 25 September to 20 November, included thirteen concerts, not counting those that the group gave at sea in the stunning Mayfair Lounge of the *Empress of Britain*. "These young men did excellent propaganda for French Canada in France," Désy reported back to Paquette.[49] By writing to the provincial secretary, he was hoping to help facilitate other such opportunities for his cousin's increasingly popular and experienced vocal ensemble. It is possible that 1937 was also the year when he discovered what he could accomplish in diplomacy through culture.

The four singers and their artistic director were skillful self-promoters themselves, and they understood early on the career-building advantages of aligning their artistic vision with the political and cultural future of their fellow French Canadians. In a letter to the renowned composer Wilfrid Pelletier, O'Brien explained that Quatuor alouette was pursuing "a national *oeuvre*" and that their battle had two fronts: the first concerned the need to prevent amateurs from tarnishing the art of folk music, while the second consisted of confronting the snobbery of those who failed to understand its importance as a form of national expression.[50] They were in a sense making the argument that their approach was founded on erudition and good taste, and that it was therefore compatible with the cultural preferences of the elites – which is something Désy evidently believed.

The group also lobbied Quebec's Office du tourisme to secure support for concerts in the United States. Hector Perrier, the newly elected provincial secretary, responded favourably to their request by allocating them funding for the 1942 and 1943 editions of the US-American National Folk Festival ($600 and $500, respectively).[51] As had been the case in Europe, the Canadian legation provided assistance on the ground. First Lady Eleanor Roosevelt reportedly described the folk singers as "marvellous" after hearing them perform.[52] Enthused, O'Brien hoped to see Canada, and thus Quatuor alouette, participate in more of these events. "The fact of seeing all the people of the North hemisphere, from Alaska to Panama," he wrote, "united in a spirit of good will, expressing themselves through the medium of their songs and dances, each in their own traditional way, this, I think, would be the greatest lesson of tolerance and understanding ever given to the whole world."[53]

The singers and O'Brien were convinced that their work was of great importance in the context of the Second World War. They performed often to boost morale and to denounce fascism, notably as part of a concert organized in 1942 at the Montreal Forum by the Quebec Committee for Allied Victory. They also appeared on wartime broadcasts, including on the US-American Columbia Broadcasting System's *Millions for Defence*.[54] In New York, the group recorded material destined for the French Resistance.[55]

Being a cultural ambassador in these turbulent times had its advantages, as Filiatrault was to find out. In the summer of 1943, he received a request from the Canadian Army that he take a series of medical examinations to determine whether he was fit for battle. Prime Minister King had held a plebiscite a year earlier to ask Canadians if they would allow him to break his promise regarding conscription. The Yes side won, but it was an uncertain victory, with the majority of French Canadians voting No. "Not necessarily conscription, but conscription if necessary," King had told them.[56] Voluntary enlistment numbers were high enough at the time to delay the imposition of forced military service, but not for long. Much to his dismay, Filiatrault found himself face to face with the possibility of being conscripted overseas. Immediately, he reached out to people of influence who could attest to his important role as an artist: among others, Pelletier, Édouard Montpetit, Sister Marie-Stéphane, and Joseph Morin, the director of Quebec's Service de ciné-photographie.[57] "Without any pretension, I consider myself more useful to the nation in my role as a teacher … and by partaking in national propaganda at home and abroad, as a singer interpreting our folk songs in the ranks of Quatuor alouette," Filiatrault pleaded.[58] The arguments and letters must have been compelling, since he avoided enlistment, and was thereafter free to pursue his role as a national and war propagandist.[59]

Quatuor alouette went through a change of leadership on the eve of its trip to Brazil. In 1945, O'Brien embarked on a different journey by entering the Benedictine monastery of Saint-Benoît-du-Lac. Roger Filiatrault thus found himself stepping into his departed colleague's shoes while continuing as the group's baritone. Born in Montreal in 1905, he first learned the piano and the violin before committing himself entirely to singing. In Brussels, he studied voice and choral conducting at the Royal Conservatory. One of his teachers, Désiré Defauw, would go on to direct the OCSM from 1941 to 1952. In Paris, Filiatrault studied the physiology of the voice. Back in Montreal, he founded Quatuor alouette and subsequently started teaching at the ESMO, the Université de Montréal, and the Université d'Ottawa. Like his three other colleagues in the group, he found his calling in the study, performance, and teaching of folk music. Their first decade and a half together reached its apex with a highly acclaimed recital at Montreal's Plateau Hall, which was filled to capacity. Thinking back on the work accomplished since 1930, Filiatrault noted proudly a few months before leaving for Brazil that the experience disproved the proverb claiming that "no one is a prophet in his own country."[60]

The four singers were ideal candidates for the kind of musical diplomacy that Désy was now deploying. The initiative was entirely his, in that External Affairs and the Itamaraty appeared to have played only a minimal role in the tour's organization. The same was true for the provincial secretary, despite the fact that Ottawa enclosed the following note in Filiatrault's passport: "The bearer … is proceeding to Brazil on an official cultural mission on behalf of the Government of the Province of Quebec, Canada."[61] Was this a gesture meant to acknowledge Perrier's earlier efforts on behalf of Quatuor alouette, or did someone, within the group or its entourage, request that there be some official recognition that the impromptu ambassadors would represent, first and foremost, French Canada? There is no evidence to support either hypothesis, except for an intriguing letter that Désy sent to Premier Maurice Duplessis at the end of the tour. In it, he provided a list of Quatuor alouette's multiple engagements while praising the singers for their professionalism. It is revealing that he made no mention of their ambassadorial role, on behalf of either Quebec or Canada, when highlighting the warm reception that the group received throughout Brazil.[62] He was walking a fine line between promoting French-Canadian culture and projecting Canada.

That said, the contract stipulated clearly that the agreement was between Désy and Quatuor alouette, the latter agreeing to travel – all expenses paid – to Brazil to give an unspecified number of performances for a minimum of two months. The weekly fee was fixed at $600, with all living expenses covered by the ambassador. The contract also included a note to the effect that Désy would essentially act as an impresario, collecting payments and remitting to the group any amount collected in excess of the costs incurred by the embassy.[63] In the end, Filiatrault and his colleagues received $970 in travel expenses and $6,000 for ten weeks of work, which suggests that no other party contributed financially to the tour and that Désy either broke even or lost some money with this experiment.[64]

The terms of the contract were such that the embassy had plenty of reasons to keep Quatuor alouette busy in Brazil. The four singers had their work cut out for them. On 4 September, they boarded a train from Montreal to New York, where the steamship *Jose Menendez* awaited them. They arrived in Rio de Janeiro a month later, on 5 October, to the great pleasure of Désy, who organized a reception for them. The group had its premiere at the Teatro Municipal the following Monday. It then travelled to Petrópolis, which was then a summer retreat for the who's who of Brazilian "high" society. It gave two concerts at the prestigious resort hotel Palácio Quitandinha before returning to Rio de Janeiro for a two-week residence at the Cassino da Urca (Urca Casino). The tour also included a short stint in São Paulo for a recital at the city's own Teatro Municipal (Municipal Theatre). Désy squeezed in additional performances here and there, including at the Conservatório Brasileiro de Música (Brazilian Conservatory of Music) and at the MES, and finally a concert at the

Igreja da Glória (Church of Glória). If that was not enough, Quatuor alouette appeared more than a dozen times on radio, thanks to the enthusiastic support of Rádio Tupi, Rádio Gazetta, and the hosts of *Ondas Musicais*, the musical program of Canada's own the Light.[65]

The group's busy itinerary was not just about balancing the budget. It was also about giving shape and substance to the musically imagined Canadian-Brazilian community that Désy was envisioning. Since arriving in Rio de Janeiro in 1941, he had been stressing similarities between the two nations: focusing on their so-called exceptionalism as former white settler colonies; their resource-rich and picturesque landscapes; their shared spirit of community and family; their Latin and Catholic heritage; and – taking cues from Brazilian discourses on *métissage* – their exemplary commitment to *bonne entente*. Désy instrumentalized Brazil's and Canada's differences to stress, paradoxically, their shared uniqueness vis-à-vis the rest of the hemisphere. Yet he did so by underscoring whiteness as the normative link between the two countries.

Désy reverted to writing, as he had done with Jean Dansereau and Muriel Tannehill, to make sure that people understood how to engage with Quatuor alouette's stage and radio performances: his article in *Brasil Musical* served that purpose, as did the program notes that he prepared for the group's Rio de Janeiro debut. The ambassador turned cultural promoter explained that the folk singers' repertoire reflected Canada's French heritage, but also the "precious contribution of Celtic lyricism and Anglo-Saxon joviality." Their songs were "from a good race and a respectable genealogy."[66] In other words, Quatuor alouette's repertoire was respectable because it was rooted in white European culture. The story it told was one that started with white settlers. The history it celebrated was that of discovery, colonization, and proselytization.

Quatuor alouette had a vast repertoire to work with. It was a collection of material that conveyed an anti-modernist image of Quebec with discernable pan-Canadianist and religious undertones, but also an implicit celebration of settler colonialism. Most of the titles fell under the following categories: (1) old French songs; (2) French folk songs preserved in Canada; (3) folk songs originating from Canada; and (4) Irish, Scottish, and English folk songs preserved in Canada. The group complemented this material with a selection of religious works, including "Panis angelicus," "Ave Maria," and "Tantum ergo." It had performed "Panis angelicus" on numerous occasions, most notably on its 1934 trip to France and during its fifteenth-anniversary concert at Plateau Hall, but otherwise it reserved its religious works for special occasions such as Christmas or Easter.[67] Also included in the repertoire was "Tenaouiche tenaga, ouichka," a derogatory song that mocked Indigenous languages. As for English-language songs, Filiatrault and his bandmates performed them infrequently. "Annie Laurie," "Believe Me, if All Those Endearing Young Charms," and "Drink to Me Only with Thine Eyes" were favourites of the group, who normally featured them in its "Empire" potpourri or in a program segment titled "Old Irish, Scots, and English Songs."[68]

For its debut concert in Rio de Janeiro, Quatuor alouette put together a program that reflected the breadth and scope of its repertoire, as described by Désy. The group performed its "Empire" collection and even sang "Vive la Brésilienne," likely a playful rendition of the widely popular hymn "Vive la Canadienne."[69] Efforts to promote the singers using the trope of *métissage* resulted in some unusual visual contrasts, such as ads that featured them wearing traditional French-Canadian attire, including the colourful *ceinture fléchée*, with illustrations of the Brazilian landscape juxtaposed against a drawing of the Canadian Rockies, pine trees, or even a mounted police officer.[70]

The singers, however, promptly gave precedence to their French-Canadian identity on stage and on the airwaves. The journalist Mary Newton remembered fondly one of their performances at the Cassino da Urca: "Dressed in the heavy, colorful garb of the northwoodsman, they stood in front of a big mural of the Canadian countryside in this gay night club setting, and sang the beautiful, old songs of 'New France.'" "Night after night," she added, "the gay crowds applauded melodies of the Quebec lumber camps, of the country parishes, of family groups around their kitchen fireside and of school children playing in the convent yard."[71] The host of *Ondas Musicais* intended to introduce them as French Canadians rather than Canadians, because of such performances, but someone inside the organization edited the script to stress the fact that Filiatrault and his colleagues were, above all, cultural ambassadors for Canada. "~~French~~ Canadians are natural born singers," the host explained before noting that their music "conveyed the essence of their race." The group did perform its "Empire" potpourri on the show, but it noted that those works were not "technically speaking folklore."[72] Subsequent broadcasts on the airwaves of Rádio Gazetta and Rádio Tupi featured no English-language material.[73] French became the language of choice to "intensify the shared understanding and to further strengthen the relations that unite the peoples of Brazil and Canada."[74] The singers were manifestly on an official cultural mission for Quebec even if the tour was taking place under the auspices of the Canadian embassy.

If Désy's *Dîner canadien* was an attempt to rectify the situation, it failed. On 12 November, the ambassador and his wife, Corinne de Boucherville, hosted an elaborate dinner in the main hall of the Associação Brasileira de Imprensa; this was the same room where Danscreau and Tannchill had performed on Dominion Day in 1943. More than two hundred guests attended the event. They came from either the diplomatic corps or belonged to Brazil's highest political, economic, and cultural circles. Those present included the British ambassador, the US-American ambassador, France's cultural attaché, Brazil's minister of foreign affairs, and Rio de Janeiro's mayor. The invitation card that the Désys sent to them featured a variety of illustrations that doubled as national symbols: a Canadian moose, a beaver, maple groves, snowshoes, and snowflakes, as well as men and women seen fishing, farming, and baking.[75] It provided hints about the extensive menu that awaited the guests. The *Dîner canadien* offered a taste of Quebec with its apple juice, Gaspé salmon, pork stew and pie, leg of lamb, potatoes, brown beans with bacon, cheese, and maple ice cream. Seagram's whisky was possibly the most Canadian of all the items, and it, too, originated from Quebec.[76]

Culture was front and centre throughout the evening. Quatuor alouette served as the artistic aperitif with its "songs about drinking" and "songs about eating."[77] Rather than interrupting the dinner with a formal speech, Désy opted to print and distribute a text titled "Discours qui ne sera pas prononcé par l'Ambassadeur du Canada." In it, he explained that gastronomy is a "civilized act," an "art that has its traditions and its disciplines," all of which represent "the faculty of adaptation to the geographical environment." Désy added: "Good dishes and good wines are made for smart and educated stomachs." With this *Dîner canadien*, he ventured into the unknown territory of culinary diplomacy, subsumed here within the broader framework of cultural diplomacy. Not forgetting that this initiative was meant to complement his musical nation-branding efforts (in addition to complimenting Brazilians in attendance), he concluded by noting that his "ancestors – who knew how to live, eat, and drink – would digest while singing."[78] Quatuor alouette took care of that part of the program with its "songs about digesting."

This fanciful affair spoke more about the persistence of the *fait français* in North America than it did of Canada's so-called culture of *métissage*. French expatriate Jean-Gérard Fleury certainly thought so, as he explained to the middlebrow readers of the Montreal-based *La Revue populaire*. He was essentially corroborating *La Presse*, which described the event as a great success.[79] Conflating Quebec with Canada, Fleury explained that the Désys had shown their guests "how much this British dominion had remained French in tastes and thoughts." He noted that Brazilians welcomed this cultural rapprochement, because the war had cut them off from France: Quebec culture – and Quebec cheese – were valid substitutes, according to him. Fleury also reserved praises for Quatuor alouette's performance. "It does not matter that France is not rich in nickel or uranium, in Rocky Mountains; it has something much better: the loyalty of an entire people, whose life, art, and cuisine bear witness to the vitality and eternal greatness of the motherland," he wrote.[80] Canada, or perhaps more so Quebec, no longer seemed to be a mere surrogate of the old imperial motherland: it now appeared as its extension, if not its new, sub-imperial incarnation. Perhaps inadvertently, Désy had emphasized Quebec's distinctiveness at the expense of the country of which he was the official representative in Brazil. It is revealing of External Affairs' laissez-faire approach and lack of interest in cultural matters that no one in Ottawa noticed that the tour had taken a somewhat unexpected turn.

Even more so than food, Catholicism set French Canadians apart – a cultural trait that the singers were more than willing to emphasize while in Brazil. Désy must have been struck by the frequency with which Filiatrault and his colleagues turned to religious material during the tour. "Le curé de notre village" continued to be a favourite, but other, less popular works, which the group had neglected in the past, now found themselves on set lists destined for Brazilian audiences. Quatuor alouette's radio performances are a case in point. On 9 October, it sang "Grâces soient rendues" followed by a series of works that told stories from the lives of Jesus Christ and the Virgin Mary.[81] Two weeks later, it opened with a triptych: "Notre Père," "Panis angelicus," and "Sanctus et benedictus."[82] As for the group's concert at Rio de Janeiro's Igreja da Glória, it received extra attention in the form of a broadcast. Inaugurated in 1739, the church was a Brazilian landmark visited assiduously in the past by the imperial family, including Dom Pedro II, who was baptized there. The program included the above triptych augmented with "Hymne des Frères Moraves" and "D'où viens-tu bergère."[83] On 30 October, the singers celebrated Christmas on the airwaves, two months early, with a selection that included "Le fils du roi de gloire" and "Allons bergers, partons tous."[84]

The new friends that Quatuor alouette made en route to Brazil likely influenced its musical choices. The four singers were not the only French Canadians aboard the *Jose Menendez*. Missionaries from the congregation Les Frères du Sacré Coeur were also headed to Brazil to begin work in the small interior city of Campanha. The two parties bonded, with the missionaries teaching Portuguese to the singers in exchange for informal classes on the physiology of the voice. Quatuor alouette also gave impromptu performances on the deck on Sundays, to the great pleasure of its fellow travellers. Filiatrault was pleased with the opportunity to sing "Panis angelicus" in such a setting. "When it comes to good deeds, the group does the right thing without the need for prayers," he noted humorously in his diary.[85] On 1 October, he and his colleagues offered a free recital, which featured three Brazilian songs that they had learned while at sea: "Nesta rua," "As bonecas," and "O café."[86] They must have lacked confidence in Portuguese, because they only performed them infrequently in Brazil and with mixed results.[87]

The encounter left a deep impression on Quatuor alouette, even if the two parties went their separate ways upon arriving in Rio de Janeiro. The missionaries made sure to remind the singers that they formed part of the group's audience in Brazil and Canada. They attended its debut concert at the Teatro Municipal and listened with great interest to its radio performances. They sent letters of congratulations, and even invited Filiatrault, Lamarre, Trottier, and Jacob to their Sacré Coeur mission in the state of Minas Gerais.[88] The four men could not make it to the interior, but they did visit the Pères de Sainte-Croix, who had set up operations in the suburbs of São Paulo at the beginning of the year. They also visited the Dominican mission before Laporte, Picher, and Desmarais abandoned it. Filiatrault maintained some correspondence with them and carried with him photos he took at their retreat centre, one of which showed the group posing cheerfully in front of a lush palm tree.[89] Impromptu ambassadors themselves, these missionaries from Quebec conflated their religious and national identities while encouraging the four singers to do the same.

Filiatrault and his colleagues had heard that message before. On the eve of their departure for Brazil, Dom Raoul Hamel from the Benedictine monastery of Saint-Benoît-du-Lac, the same community that O'Brien had joined, sent an article to *Le Devoir* in which he addressed the group and congratulated them for their "national *oeuvre*." He commended the singers for promoting "a living, rhythmic unity, founded on a spiritual, objective outlook" – a form of communion that differed from lower forms of togetherness rooted in material concerns, he insisted.[90] It is this difference and this spiritual calling that animated the four artists in Brazil.

Quatuor alouette thus felt compelled to augment its set lists with songs that spoke of the civilizing mission of settler colonialism – namely, "Danse indienne no. 1," "Danse indienne no. 2," and "Noël Huron." The first two originated from northern Ontario and reportedly featured the primitive sound of Indigenous folklore. The third revealed the "melodic evolution" of that music "under the influence of Canada's missionaries."[91] The group sang them in that order – in other words, chronologically – to make the case that Indigenous expressive cultures survive only through sublimation. The selection echoed Désy's assertion that Quatuor alouette's repertoire was a rare opportunity to hear Canada's "first civilizing and civilized songs."[92] As for "Tenaouiche tenaga, ouichka," the group chose not to perform it in Brazil despite the fact that it had sung it on numerous occasions prior to the tour: on stage in the United States during the National Folk Festival, at Montreal's Plateau Hall, and on Canadian airwaves.[93] Filiatrault and his colleagues perhaps felt that the song's blatant racism would be difficult to reconcile with the trope of *métissage* at the heart of Désy's musically imagined Canadian-Brazilian community.

Quatuor alouette's final recital on Sunday, 18 November, best exemplified the tone and scope of the tour. Held in São Paulo's Teatro Municipal, the concert featured only French-language material and it began with *La légende dorée*, a succession of short works evoking the life of Jesus Christ.[94] A reporter from *A Gazeta* remarked that the singers succeeded, through their heartfelt rendition of French-Canadian folklore, in engaging the captivated audience. His review of the concert praised Filiatrault and his colleagues for bringing to life a unique, musically imagined Canadian-Brazilian community: "In the room, the spectators and the artists banded together, like friends trying wholeheartedly to please each other." He continued: "Such togetherness is rare, even in the most homogeneous circles, as in families: but most striking in this spontaneous pact of friendship was the enthusiasm with which all sang the song of the Alouette – the imperishable and symbolic bird, image of conviviality and bravery, of everlasting confidence in life and in God."[95] The sonorous community thus imagined was one that was united in faith. If it differed from that initially imagined by Désy, it is because of the agency he afforded to his cultural ambassadors.

The above report from *A Gazeta* shows the local press responding favourably to this latest round of musical diplomacy. Reporters once again used the tropes of family and friendship, but also Catholicism.[96] The spontaneity and raw authenticity of Quatuor alouette's music sparked their interest, because it was soulful and conveyed the "pulse of the collectivity."[97] If art was "the revelation of the moral and material greatness of peoples," they argued, then there is no "other manifestation more expressive than the human voice to evoke and exalt the riches of the earth and the virtues of the peoples themselves."[98] French-language newspapers in Quebec were equally thrilled, showing even greater interest in the tour once self-congratulatory reports from Brazil started trickling in. *La Presse* praised the four singers for having so brilliantly fulfilled their mandate as "ambassadors of Canadian folklore," while *Le Devoir* noted approvingly that Quatuor alouette had brought "honour to our race."[99] As for Canada's English-language newspapers, they took little to no interest in the tour.[100] In hindsight, one could argue that the *Montreal Star* demonstrated clairvoyance when it referred – inadvertently, perhaps – to the four singers as "missionaries" instead of ambassadors on the eve of their voyage to Brazil.[101]

As an exercise in musical diplomacy, Quatuor alouette's tour was undoubtedly one-sided in terms of how it centred on French-speaking, Catholic Quebec rather than fostering any genuine dialogue with Brazilians. As an exercise in musical nation branding, it showed how vulnerable Canada's image was in the hands of non-state actors with a mission of their own. The four singers proved surprisingly adept at promoting their own agenda without inexorably undermining Désy's own efforts to advance the embassy's objectives. They excelled at disseminating their anti-modernist vision of the world while supporting their ordained compatriots. More striking is the ease with which they navigated cultural life in Brazil, and how uncritical they were of the Vargas regime's fascist leanings, possibly because of how familiar the country seemed to them when looked at through the trope of Catholicism. Examining the group's extensive records of its two-month tour, you would not know that Brazilians were going through dramatic changes in the fall of 1945. On 29 October, the military responded to the growing anti-dictatorship sentiment by forcing Vargas, who appeared to stall on his promise of restoring democracy, to resign. It placed José Linhares, president of the Supremo Tribunal Federal (Supreme Federal Court), at the helm of the country and tasked him with organizing proper elections before the end of the year. None of the events preceding or following the coup d'état that ended the Estado Novo interfered with Quatuor alouette's national performance. The music carried on as the Vargas era ended and the Fourth Brazilian Republic rose on the horizon.

# 5
# Vista Points

It was with a profound sense of accomplishment that Jean Désy wrote to President Getúlio Vargas, on 4 December 1944, to thank him for attending *Pintura Canadense Contemporânea*, the first ever pan-Canadian visual arts exhibition in South America.[1] Held in both Rio de Janeiro and São Paulo at the turn of 1945, the event featured a compelling showcase of handicrafts and folk art in addition to 190 paintings by 75 artists. Approximately 50,000 people thus learned about Canada, "this great, friendly, and allied country from the north."[2] Désy scored a major coup with this initiative, thanks to his many partners: External Affairs, the NGC, the Department of Trade and Commerce, galleries in Montreal and Toronto, the Quebec government, the Instituto Brasil-Canadá, the Itamaraty, and the MES. "It was the common work of us all," Désy told Minister of Trade and Commerce James MacKinnon, that allowed the embassy to further "the propaganda of Canada at a time when it is extremely important, commercially, as well as politically, to keep Canada on the map in this country."[3]

The visual arts were a means to illustrate the stories about Canada that Désy and his impromptu cultural ambassadors had been telling Brazilians since the establishment of diplomatic relations between the two countries. The success of *Pintura Canadense Contemporânea* was such that the embassy organized a follow-up exhibition in 1946: *Arte Gráfica do Canadá*, which further revealed "the potentialities of Canada."[4] The two exhibitions underlined the so-called exceptionalism of white settlers who had grown as a distinct nation and were now building centres of culture that might one day rival those of the former imperial metropoles, Paris and London. The events spoke of Canadians' ability to negotiate the interplay between tradition and modernity as well as between authenticity and cosmopolitanism. They conveyed a commitment to democracy, liberalism, and *bonne entente*. They did so eloquently in ways that called attention to the country's vast resources, its youthful promise, know-how, and friendliness at a time of great expectation and renewal when the world was transitioning from war to peace – or dictatorship to democracy, as was the case in Brazil.

The use of the visual arts as an instrument of diplomacy did not signal a departure from earlier efforts. Paintings, engravings, and sculptures had already found their way to Rio de Janeiro for display at the embassy or at the ambassador's official residence. The scope of these exhibitions, however, was unprecedented. The same was true of the range of partners and contributing artists, all with a stake in Canada's projection abroad. *Pintura Canadense Contemporânea* and *Arte Gráfica do Canadá* revealed what could be accomplished when, in the absence of initiative from Ottawa, one resorted to directed improvisation. The two events proved to be effective venues for disseminating a coherent and sophisticated image that matched Canada's leadership aspirations, even if it was at times difficult for stakeholders, including audiences, to assimilate the full breadth of the ideologies and meanings conveyed through the works assembled under the embassy's patronage.[5] This was no small feat, considering that the potential for dissonance – such as that caused by Marcel Roussin and Quatuor alouette – tended to be proportional to the number of protagonists involved.

A successful cultural diplomacy is not so much one that leads to immediate, actionable outcomes as one that mobilizes civil society and accommodates different, even competing, agendas to advance a long-term vision. This latest experiment energized cultural elites and institutions in Canada, alerting them to the realm of possibilities opened up by state-funded international cultural relations. Harry Orr McCurry, director of the NGC, was among those who responded to Désy's invitation to lead the way in the face of External Affairs' perfunctory interest in cultural matters. Called to lend a helping hand on more than one occasion, he wasted no opportunity to assert the gallery's prerogatives when it came to overseas exhibitions, underscoring the need for appropriate protocols and adequate resources to communicate Canada's achievements more effectively to foreign publics.

*Pintura Canadense Contemporânea* and *Arte Gráfica do Canadá* also appealed to artists in Toronto and Montreal. The war had limited their ability to show their work – if not domestically, at least internationally – in addition to making it impossible for them to perfect their art in Europe's cultural centres. Montreal's Jacques de Tonnancour, a young painter whose dream of making it in Paris was shattered by the war, was a direct beneficiary of Canada's cultural rapprochement with Brazil. Compared to the "City of Light," Rio de Janeiro was an unlikely site for consecration, but the artist still hoped that the experience would help him find and consolidate his place among Quebec's most accomplished painters. Like Roussin, he travelled south as a guest of the Instituto Brasil-Canadá to define himself in relation to and against a Brazilian Other. One of *Pintura Canadense Contemporânea*'s stars, he inherited the role of concertmaster in the follow-up exhibition, which he helped plan with high hopes for his future. De Tonnancour and McCurry were in effect doing diplomacy from below amid a surprisingly harmonious alignment of interests and priorities in the space opened by the 1944 cultural agreement.

## OUTLINES OF CANADA

No institution was better positioned than the NGC to disseminate stories about Canadians in cultural capitals around the world prior to the 1940s. Established in 1880, it was the product of a period of rapid socio-economic transformation and growing national consciousness, which saw the country's elites mobilize culture to consolidate their influence and edify the nation. The gallery was first attached to the Royal Canadian Academy of Arts, an organization with a somewhat exclusive membership. This arrangement was both a source of prestige and an impediment in that it was incongruent with the NGC's mission to bring a broad array of artists together and to inculcate Canadians with a taste for the arts. After a plodding start, the gallery's prospects improved dramatically in the early 1910s, thanks to gradual budget increases (from $10,000 to $30,000) and the appointment of Nottingham-born Eric Brown as full-time curator and director. The institution's move from the second floor of the Government Fisheries Building to the newly built Victoria Memorial Museum also did much to improve the spirits of its personnel. In 1913, an act of Parliament incorporated the gallery, giving it the necessary autonomy and resources (its budget would soon rise to $100,000) to build its collections and establish its reputation at home and abroad.[6]

The NGC's ascendency resulted from Brown's untiring efforts to acquire, write about, and display works by domestic artists, not just international ones. It was also intimately tied to the rise of the Toronto-based landscape painters who came to prominence in the second half of the 1910s, just before they became known as the Group of Seven: Franklin Carmichael, Lawren Harris, A.Y. Jackson, Frank Johnston, Arthur Lismer, J.E.H. MacDonald, and Frederick Varley. Early on, Brown perceptively focused his attention on their work, because of how it captured the Canadian wilderness in mesmerizing, familiar tones informed by an attachment to tradition as much as a passion for modernism. That the prices for these paintings were within the range of the gallery's budget served as a further incentive for closer relations between the artists and Brown. The Group of Seven officially came together in May of 1920 at an exhibition held at the Art Gallery of Toronto. The catalogue that they prepared for the occasion opened with a manifesto-like foreword that highlighted the group's commitment to interpreting the "spirit" of the "nation's growth." "Art must grow and flower in the land before the country will be a real home for its people," the document read.[7] Presented in such terms, it was hardly surprising that the group found a home at the NGC.

Brown's early inclination to harness the symbolic value of the Group of Seven was arguably nowhere more apparent than at the 1924 British Empire Exhibition held in London. By then, he was actively involved in promoting them according to his strongly held belief that their collective work revealed how superbly Canada could measure "her art against the other British Dominions."[8] The gallery did not focus exclusively on the Group of Seven; it showed a total of 270 works by 108 artists. But it certainly called attention to the group and Tom Thomson (who was associated with them until his untimely death in 1917) by featuring their contributions in a separate salon. Ross King, the group's biographer, remarks that Canadians sought approval in Great Britain to refute accusations of parochialism and to overcome their "national inferiority complex."[9] As an exercise in nation building and nation branding, it doubtlessly bolstered their confidence in Canada's ability to play a leadership role, even if only culturally, within the imperial family.

The gallery was not alone in speaking for Canada at the colonial exhibition. In fact, Brown's display of the country's art was part of a larger effort spearheaded by the Canadian Government Exhibition Commission (CGEC). Established in 1901, the agency operated as a branch of the Department of Fisheries until the Department of Trade and

Commerce took it under its wing in 1928. The commission's presence in London was consistent with its mandate to advertise Canada abroad. The Canadian Pavilion (a 300-by-400-foot structure filled with elaborate displays of mineral and industrial goods, murals depicting vast landscapes, a model railway, and working dioramas) conveyed Canadians' growing confidence in the aftermath of the First World War and, incidentally, their pursuit of a national identity that could resonate internationally. Rather than foregrounding regional or provincial displays of natural resources and industries, the CGEC promoted a unified vision of Canada. In other words, the exhibition went beyond the usual promotion of tourism, investments, and immigration to articulate a "national narrative of material and cultural progress within a land of peace and plenty."[10] The intent was to make an impression not only on the foreign publics who visited the pavilion, but also on those Canadians who visited or read about the British Empire Exhibition.

The CGEC was among the first agencies to participate in the projection of Canada abroad, but that did not make it a trendsetter. An instrument of the state, it operated as part of a bureaucracy that insulated its staff from the cultural elites who were pushing the country in new directions as it entered the twentieth century. The commission's efforts to advance a post-Victorian image of Canada were timid at first, despite its reliance on modern marketing strategies. Up until the late 1920s, it disseminated a "staples vision of Canada" that "conveyed the message that the new nation was one of fertility, abundance, and opportunity." It did so by using samples of staple goods that signified the "bounty of Canadian agriculture, forest, fisheries, and mines." The CGEC eventually embraced modernism in its architecture and display designs, as well as in its use of films, photographs, and elaborate maps, but it did so without ever breaking new ground or pushing Ottawa to do more to support the arts at home and abroad. In the end, bureaucratic imperatives, budgetary considerations, and looming deadlines dictated the aesthetic and politico-cultural choices it made.[11]

The responsibility for renewing the aesthetic language with which to talk about the country thus fell on the NGC. Compared with music, for instance, the visual arts may have been privileged in terms of their ability to attract government patronage, but that support should not be overstated.[12] Whatever the gallery managed to accomplish in the years leading up to the Second World War was thanks to the patience, intuition, and resourcefulness of Brown, who could count on like-minded artists and a supportive board of trustees. His death on 6 April 1939, on the eve of the war, would have crippled the institution had it not been for Harry Orr McCurry, the director's right-hand man for two decades. An Ottawa-born career civil servant, McCurry arrived at the NGC from the Department of Public Works to "oversee accounts" in 1919. He was a strong advocate of outreach programs in addition to sharing with Brown a commitment to making the visual arts central to how Canadians understood themselves and their place in the world. He was the obvious choice to take the helm of the gallery in 1939. McCurry was neither creative nor inclined to take bold initiatives, but he did excel as an "organizer and consolidator" when "fortuitous circumstances" or the "leadership of others" presented him with opportunities to carry on his predecessor's vision.[13]

McCurry was therefore equipped to advance – or at the very least prevent others from encroaching upon – the NGC's mission when he took over. The early 1940s were challenging years for the institution. Its acquisition budget was slashed, and its operating funds were reduced to a minimum in the wake of Brown's passing. Moreover, McCurry and his associates had to adopt a conservative style in managing the gallery since its board of trustees never reached quorum during the meetings that it held throughout the war.[14] Yet they did continue to fulfill requests for lithographs and various reproductions, in addition to acquiring works dealing with Canada's war experience (among others, Hubert Rogers's depiction of the Quebec Conference and a selection of Jack Nichols's drawings). They also did their best to arrange modest in-house and travelling exhibitions, which helped bring visibility to the NGC (notably the *Canadian Society of Painters in Water Colour* and the *Royal Canadian Academy* exhibitions). In this context, Désy's leadership in Brazil was welcomed, but with some reservations. McCurry was not particularly eager to let a diplomat take the lead on cultural matters. The South American giant was also not on his radar. But here, perhaps, was an opportunity to capture the attention of External Affairs and educate its staff about the important role that the gallery could play in the making of international relations.

## MODERNIST MONTREAL

While the NGC sought to maintain momentum amid war, Montreal's artistic life was bursting with activities. Canada's largest city was thriving despite the threat of conscription looming on the horizon. For the most part, French Canadians were disposed to believe Prime

Minister William Lyon Mackenzie King's promise not to impose overseas military service. All hoped to avoid a repeat of 1917, when the government of Robert Borden pushed ahead with its Military Service Act, effectively prompting thousands to take part in riots that left dozens wounded and five dead. Provincial Liberal leader Adélard Godbout was a direct beneficiary of King's popularity. His electoral victory in 1939 substituted progressive politics for the arch-conservative Union nationale regime of Maurice Duplessis. Optimism pervaded large segments of Quebec society, particularly in Montreal, where abundant resources were pumped into war industries and transportation infrastructure. Debates about democracy, human rights, and internationalism flourished with the return of expats and the arrival of European artists and intellectuals fleeing advancing Nazi troops. To be sure, there were voices of disruption and division, notably among right-leaning nationalists who, fearing another conscription crisis, looked upon Liberals with distrust.[15] But overall, the air was filled with promises of a new era that would see the city develop into a formidable metropolis.

The Contemporary Arts Society was the driving force behind Montreal's visual arts scene during the war. Established in the winter of 1939 as an artist collective, it saw itself more as a vehicle to educate publics and lobby governments than an exhibition society. It championed modernism in the arts (from fauvism to expressionism and cubism) as an antidote to academicism, which it argued stifled the creativity of young painters who were trying to comprehend the world through their own subjective depictions of urban life. The organization's founding father, the painter and critic John Lyman, believed in the need to mount an opposition to the conservative art establishment in Quebec, because of its paralyzing influence on both artists and publics. He also "disliked the exalted claims made for the Group of Seven, which he felt was having a repressive effect on the development of art" in Canada. The Contemporary Arts Society was a means of tackling these two issues. Before long, it expanded its activities with a first exhibition in accordance with its mandate "to give support to contemporary trends in art and to further the artistic interests of its members by any means at its disposal."[16] Paul-Émile Borduas, the future *enfant terrible* of the Quebec art world, was among the participating artists.

The recruitment of French-speaking painters was integral to the Contemporary Arts Society's establishment of a common front. It energized the organization and helped transform the local scene. In the early 1940s, modern art proved a potent catalyst for bridging linguistic and aesthetic divides. As an expression of humanism, it fostered a universalist outlook that many deemed necessary if Quebec were to undergo a program of cultural *rattrapage*. The idea that the province was abnormal in its development, lacking as it was in the realm of culture, at least when compared to its neighbours to the west and to the south, or across the Atlantic, had many adherents at the time, including French Canadians, who were but a handful among the organization's twenty-six members in 1939.[17] Yet that did not prevent Borduas from joining the executive committee as vice-president. In fact, the support he received from Lyman was a testament to his rising authority and the power of his artistic vision.

Born in 1905 just south of Montreal, in Saint-Hilaire, Paul-Émile Borduas developed an interest in art as an apprentice with the painter Ozias Leduc, who specialized in church decorations. The aspiring artist subsequently attended Montreal's École des beaux-arts before sojourning in France. There, he became fascinated with the surrealists despite having no contact with the group; his time overseas was divided between studying at the Parisian Ateliers d'art sacré and decorating churches in the northeast department of Meuse. By 1937, he was back in Montreal and teaching at the École du meuble, an applied art school where he started to experiment with modern techniques. Within a few years, he built a strong following of students who were equally committed to deploying new aesthetic languages.[18] Several of them eventually joined the Contemporary Arts Society as non-voting "junior artists," a new membership category that allowed the organization "to continue a natural course of evolution, in which new artistic practices and the rapidly growing strength of the French painting community received its due."[19]

French Canadians were well represented in another category created for non-artists: that of "associate membership."[20] The most prominent member of that group was the educator and critic Maurice Gagnon, a colleague of Borduas at the École du meuble, who perfected his education in Paris under the supervision of art historian Henri Focillon. In his capacity as secretary of the Contemporary Arts Society, he was actively involved in promoting modernism in the arts through lectures and exhibitions. Gagnon was a progressive Catholic who saw no contradiction between the search for self-expression and the moral demands that social life placed on individuals. On the contrary, such a pursuit could reveal one's soul and spirituality in ways that he believed were consistent with the principles of personalism, an intellectual movement that originated in France and emphasized the inherent worth of the individual as foundational to the vitality of communities.[21] Gagnon demystified what became known as *art vivant*, by opposition to the stagnant art of academicism, through an interpretative framework that he deployed in a series of articles published in *La Revue moderne*. He also wrote books on the topic, including his 1940 *Peinture moderne*, in addition to editing a series for Montreal's Édition de l'arbre.[22] In these works, Gagnon championed the stance taken by his Contemporary Arts Society colleagues, in the process giving them and himself further authority, while filling the important discursive void that emerged when art books and magazines stopped flowing from Paris to Montreal after the fall of France in May of 1940.[23]

The early years of the war marked the apex of a transitional period that had begun a decade earlier under the impulse of a new partnership between adventurous artists and far-sighted critics. Prior to the 1930s, the visual arts in Quebec centred mostly on landscapes and depictions of rural life, some of it seen timidly through the modern lens of Impressionism. These works continued for the most part to crystallize "the agriculturalist Catholic ideal associated with the French Canadian mission in North America."[24] Increasingly, however, painters like Borduas and Adrien Hébert, among others, turned to universalist and cosmopolitan themes about the human experience with the support of "left-leaning Christians," such as Gagnon, who "rejected the authoritarianism of Québec's Catholic establishment."[25] Their promotion of an *art vivant*, an idea that originated at the turn of the 1930s and gained momentum during the war, expressed their desire to occupy a place of importance as mediators between the past and the present, or as liaisons between the Old and New Worlds.

The return from France of Alfred Pellan, in the early months of 1940, further galvanized the city's cultural milieu, including the Contemporary Arts Society, which the painter promptly joined. In November and December of that year, he showed his work as a member of the organization in the *Art of Our Day in Canada* exhibition. His presence felt "like a blood transfusion," said one of his colleagues. "It had an explosive effect," confided another.[26] Born in Quebec City on 16 May 1906, Pellan developed an interest in painting at an early age. In 1926, after distinguishing himself at the École des beaux-arts de Québec, he received a scholarship to continue his studies in France. In the space of a decade, he managed to exhibit his work in prominent Parisian galleries, hold his first solo show, and earn first prize at the 1935 exposition of mural art. Pellan considered coming back home in 1936 to teach at his alma mater, but he was considered too modern for the institution. In any case, he preferred the company of Pablo Picasso, Henri Matisse, and other prominent figures of the European avant-garde. But the outbreak of the Second World War thwarted his plan to stay overseas. Back in Montreal, he accepted a teaching position at the École des beaux-arts, then under the directorship of the conservative Charles Maillard, who hoped to contain Pellan's influence while capitalizing on his popularity. A head-to-head clash ensued, which led to Maillard resigning from his job in 1945. Gagnon, in his 1943 book on Pellan, had warned that the painter could not be co-opted and that his attitude as a modernist was pure, particularly in the ways with which he creatively harnessed the past in the present with an eye on the future.[27] Pellan, he argued, embodied the spirit and potentialities of Montreal in the early 1940s.

The French-Canadian contingent of the Contemporary Arts Society felt especially emboldened in 1940s Catholic Quebec, because it could also claim the support of the French intellectual Marie-Alain Couturier, a Dominican friar turned respected stained-glass artist. The Catholic priest was on an assignment in New York when the Second World War broke out. Rather than sailing back across the ocean, Couturier travelled north to Montreal, where he discovered a booming visual arts scene partly inspired by Catholic personalism and fervently opposed to academicism, like he was. To him, "academic formulas" were consonant with the notion of "official" art, which he associated with fascism and cancerous forms of nationalism.[28] Couturier's views were well-received among those who both shared his dislike of the collaborationist Vichy regime and were becoming increasingly impatient with the clerico-nationalist establishment in Quebec. Couturier soon found himself teaching alongside Borduas and Gagnon at the École du meuble, lecturing at events sponsored by the Contemporary Arts Society, and helping organize *art vivant* exhibitions. Whereas Pellan gave the city's French-Canadian painters confidence and inspiration, Couturier joined Gagnon in providing them with ideological legitimacy and a sense of purpose amid trying times.

CANADIAN ART IN BRAZIL

Désy, to his credit, could feel the pulse of the city and grasp the sense of purpose that animated its artistic community at a time when the NGC, faced with the impossibility of launching bold new projects, was disposed to consider outside proposals. Brazil offered a distant stage where energies could be channelled, even if only temporarily and without great expectations regarding mid- or long-term prospects there. The stage, however, had to be set. Displaying Pellan's *Canada East* and *Canada West* on the walls of the legation's waiting room conveyed a clear message about the country's *fait français* and its vivacious maturity. Upon learning of the initiative, McCurry commended Désy for "setting a very important precedent," which he hoped would be "widely followed."[29] At the diplomat's request, he prepared and sent a bundle of paintings, etchings, and wood engravings to decorate the official residence and other rooms of the legation in Rio de Janeiro. Surrounded by Pellan's murals and the works of Clarence A. Gagnon, Walter J. Phillips, and David B. Milne, Désy was confident that he could convince his "Brazilians friends" that Canada could "produce something more than wheat, salmon, and apples."[30]

*Pintura Canadense Contemporânea* saw Désy turn to directed improvisation to amplify that message and to mobilize potential allies in government and various art institutions. The exhibition travelled to two cities over a period of two months: it began at Rio de Janeiro's Museu Nacional de Belas Artes (National Museum of Fine Arts), from 25 November to 15 December 1944, and ended at São Paulo's Galeria Prestes Maia (Prestes Maia Gallery), from 9 January to 25 January 1945. The inclusion of a section on folk art might have struck some as odd, considering the emphasis on the contemporary in the event's name, but it served to contextualize and illustrate the idea that Canadians possessed a rapidly evolving, authentic, and vigorous national art. Close to fifty thousand people looked at colonial and late nineteenth-century handicrafts (from fabrics to embroidery, ceramics, and wooden sculptures) before making their way through various other rooms to contemplate 190 paintings by the likes of Borduas, Gagnon, Jackson, Leduc, Lyman, Milne, Pellan, Thomson, and the promising young painter Jacques de Tonnancour.[31]

Although it was conceived as a pan-Canadian exhibition, *Pintura Canadense Contemporânea* leaned heavily on artists from Toronto and Montreal. The latter city captured the bulk of the attention. The emphasis placed on Quebec in the folk art section ensured that visitors gravitated primarily toward French-Canadian painters. Those with money to spend did the same. Twenty-one of the thirty works sold were by Quebec-based French-speaking artists: de Tonnancour, Fleurimond Constantineau, Jacques Blouin, Marc-Aurèle Fortin, Denise Gadbois, and Marius Plamondon, among others.[32] Overall, Désy deemed the exhibition a popular and critical success, a vindication of his unorthodox approach to diplomacy.

It was difficult to imagine the success of the enterprise as not lying squarely on the ambassador's shoulders, irrespective of the elaborate nature of the exhibition or the number of contributors and sponsors it called upon. Désy made sure that Brazilian and Canadian observers saw *Pintura Canadense Contemporânea* as a reflection of his leadership, stature, and erudition, all of which he hoped would reflect positively on Canada. This was a function of his persistent efforts to conflate his personal and national identities as if he were the embodiment of Canada's image in South America. In many ways, he very much embodied that image, but only because he had free rein to shape it and exert influence on its reception.

This level of personal involvement was consistent with the emphasis he had placed on the tropes of family and friendship in the making of Canada-Brazil relations. It was also a reflection of Désy's sense of self-importance as both a cultural mediator and a patron of the arts in the context of Montreal's growing openness to the world. The journalists who ventured through the rooms of the Museu Nacional de Belas Artes and the Galeria Prestes Maia praised Désy as a "magician" and a "charming guide" who "irradiates intelligence and sympathy." "Mr Désy," wrote *Illustração Brasileira*'s Michel B. Kamenka, "is the spiritual father and the indefatigable and persevering animator of fine undertakings."[33] Hyperbole or not, such flattering comments made for great publicity, both in Brazil and at home.

Not only did Désy orchestrate the whole affair, acting as liaison between the various parties involved and playing tour guide when on site, he also helped curate the folk art section so that visitors experienced it as a didactic journey through Canadian history. He employed the same strategy that he used when preparing the stage for Jean Dansereau and Muriel Tannehill as well as Quatuor alouette, communicating with the gallery-going public through articles that served as the basis for program notes that he himself put together. In "A pequena indústria de arte no Canadá," published in the magazine *A Vida*, he described a resilient, pious, and industrious French-Canadian nation engaged in the celebration of its past through the preservation of handicrafts – in other words, a people attached to its traditions and able to look confidently toward the future with "fervour, sincerity, and faith."[34] Désy included a lightly edited version of the article in the exhibition catalogue for *Pintura Canadense Contemporânea*. It articulated a narrative of spiritual growth and progress centred around the arts. "Thus speaks this New France that one cannot visit … without loving her," wrote a reporter who responded heartily to the first part of her journey through the exhibition.[35]

The reference to New France was not merely anecdotal since most of the handicrafts spoke of the experience of French-speaking white settlers. The program notes and displays were explicit on that point, highlighting the work accomplished by farmers, artisans, and religious congregations to cultivate the land and establish communities on it. The story told by *Pintura Canadense Contemporânea* began with the foundation of permanent settlements in the seventeenth century. The discourse of disappearance was prevalent throughout the entire exhibition, with Indigenous cultural practices and symbols relegated to the distant past in the form of "Indian reminiscences." Visitors thus marvelled at the intricate finger-weaving patterns of the *ceinture fléchée*, or Pellan's and Edwin Holgate's respective depictions of totem poles. According to the reviews, most people came out thinking that the exhibition revealed but "memories of the contact with the Iroquois and the Hurons through the products of their indigenous popular art."[36]

Underlying this narrative, albeit subtly, was the assumption that Indigenous peoples were not deserving of the same rights as the settlers who moved across unceded territories, complicit in what the Canadian Historical Association recognizes today as a cultural genocide.[37] An exercise in self-representation, the exhibition acted in part as an appendage to the colonial project that was forcing thousands of First Nations, Métis, and Inuit children into residential schools. Sustaining the dispossession and eradication of these communities was a discursive and symbolic regime that depicted them either as existing outside the nation or as a disappearing presence in the cultural terrain.

*Pintura Canadense Contemporânea* foregrounded white settlers and their descendants as formidable history makers and thus the only protagonists of consequence in the constant evolution of Canada.

The qualities attributed to the paintings on display were presumably also those of the country where they originated: authenticity, sharpness of focus, innovation, and youthful impetus – qualities that presumably qualified Canada for leadership. The diplomatic corps in Brazil hoped that the energies and resources invested in this elaborate cultural diplomacy initiative would be construed as further evidence of the country's capabilities and noble intentions. They were therefore pleased to read that journalists valued the exhibition as a cultural gift and a cordial sign of goodwill. Valerie Vally, in a piece published in *Correio da Manhã*, best synthesized what was accomplished in nation-branding terms: "From this collection of works, gradually and so happily set out, arises, as a gust of fresh air, the figure of a nation strong, industrious, of a sound cheerfulness." Her colleague Amora Maciel, from *Correio da Noite*, concurred when he wrote that Canada's "artistic productions" revealed a "hospitable land, which possesses many credentials to assert itself in the new world … that the Atlantic Charter will bring us."[38] Not only did the exhibition put the spotlight on the country's *fait français*, it also lent credence to the idea that Canadians had what it took to lead by example after the war.

The local press in Rio de Janeiro and São Paulo were full of praise for Canadians. Notwithstanding the momentous efforts that went into making the exhibition a success, the opposite would have been surprising considering that the entire project was organized under the official seal of the Vargas regime, with logistical support coming from the Itamaraty and the MES. Still, journalists recognized *Pintura Canadense Contemporânea* for what it was: a brilliant exercise in cultural diplomacy. "What lasts, what unites, what produces fraternal spirit is, undoubtedly, cultural and artistic understanding in which the elite is more interested; and it is through the action of this elite that great influence is exercised upon nations," wrote *O Estado de São Paulo*'s Mario Guastini in his glowing review of the exhibition. Brazilians were well versed in the art of diplomacy. They knew how to decipher initiatives such as this and how to respond to them. "Really Canadian art is the best ambassador this … country has sent us until today," noted Kamenka, who was prompt to add: "After Mr. Désy – naturally."[39] In compiling these positive reviews in a neatly bound bilingual volume destined for distribution back home, the Canadian ambassador hoped that they would encourage the Canadian and Quebec governments to do more for the arts.

McCurry, too, saw an opportunity here to convince External Affairs that art exhibitions abroad were "an exceedingly effective means of promoting interest in Canada and Canadian affairs."[40] He was determined to use the occasion to assert the NGC's prerogatives in that area. *Pintura Canadense Contemporânea* owed a lot of its success to McCurry, who, despite not being in charge of operations, understood that it was in everyone's best interest to spare no effort.[41] Not only did he assist Désy in putting together a representative selection of works from coast to coast, but he also helped coordinate shipping logistics, in addition to pushing for more realistic deadlines in response to initial plans to stage the exhibition in July. Moreover, he wrote the preface to the program, in which he gracefully applauded Désy "for his energy and enterprise." Knowing that copies of the text would circulate in Ottawa, he emphasized his and Désy's point that works of art are "among the most effective impersonal envoys to a country."[42] In case the message did not get through, McCurry restated his point in a separate letter to External Affairs. In it, he laid out his expectations that proper consultation and "orderly planning" would be the *sine qua non* of future events.[43] This was his way of making it clear that the NGC was best equipped to handle cultural diplomacy initiatives of that nature.

In the short term, Quebec artists were the ones who reaped most of the benefits from the exhibition.[44] Of all the Contemporary Arts Society members, Pellan was singled out for accolades, thanks in part to his *Canada East* and *Canada West*. No surprise there. Brazilians had either seen the two works in the embassy, or they had read about them in magazines such as *Sombra* and *A Vida*, which meant that they had some prior knowledge on which they could rely to confidently approach these works. Placed side by side – first on the walls of the Rio de Janeiro museum and then at the São Paulo gallery – the paintings caught everyone's attention. As for de Tonnancour, he distinguished himself as a promising young artist who, although "still groping for a purely personal style," was destined to be "recognized as one of the best modern Canadian painters."[45] Faith in his potential was such that he sold three of his six paintings on display in Brazil.[46] In the end, the Montrealers stole the show despite the attempt to feature artists from all provinces.[47] McCurry might have encouraged such an outcome by highlighting in the catalogue the fact that the meeting of Anglo-Saxon and Latin cultural sensibilities in Montreal "will undoubtedly produce a Canadian school of painters of unusual power and interest."[48] Brazilian critics echoed his comments when they wrote of "the deep coldness of British interpretation and the intense brilliancy of French painting," a contrast that the "genius of a young nation" had "synthetized admirably in rich and expressive forms."[49]

## MONTREAL'S JACQUES DE TONNANCOUR

*Pintura Canadense Contemporânea* brought visibility to de Tonnancour, but the exhibition was not the sole reason why he secured one of the scholarships offered by the Instituto Brasil-Canadá in 1945. His persistent lobbying and mastery of the art of self-promotion was the other. The young painter had tried unsuccessfully in the past to obtain government funding to pursue his studies overseas, preferably in France. The war, however, shattered his hope of crossing the Atlantic to walk in the footsteps of Borduas and Pellan. He was therefore intrigued when he learned that the Brazilian government was setting funds aside for early-career artists and scholars who wished to travel to Rio de Janeiro to acquire new experience. In April of 1945, he received news that Désy had secured for him a one-year scholarship.[50] Montreal journalists were thrilled to report that a representative from the city's visual arts milieu would be travelling south. They were also quick to criticize the governments of Canada and Quebec for failing to support domestic talent.[51]

Montrealers discovered de Tonnancour, the painter, through his association with the Contemporary Arts Society. Before that, they knew him primarily for his art write-ups in publications such as *La Nouvelle relève*, *Relations*, and *Amérique française*. Joining the organization allowed him to measure his work as an artist and a critic against those of Borduas and Gagnon, whom he looked up to. Born in Montreal in 1917, he spent his early twenties at the École des beaux-arts de Montréal. Disillusioned by the conservative and regionalist mindset of his teachers, he eventually dropped out of school. He admired Picasso and the Group of Seven, but he felt a special affinity with Goodridge Roberts, a close associate of Lyman, and Pellan, with whom he associated from 1941 onward. In November of 1942, he showed his work as a new member of the Contemporary Arts Society during an exhibition held at the Art Association of Montreal. His *Femme assise* caught the eye of the NGC, who promptly purchased it for its collection. De Tonnancour held his first solo show shortly after, in April of 1943, at Montreal's Dominion Gallery.[52] He had arrived on the scene.

De Tonnancour would soon join Roussin in Rio de Janeiro, also a guest of the Instituto Brasil-Canadá, with the similar goal of elevating his status by taking on the role of impromptu ambassador.[53] "No one is a prophet in one's own country," he thought after witnessing the warm reception accorded to Pellan upon his return from Paris.[54] In his eyes, Brazil was an unlikely site for consecration, but it would have to do since a trip to wartime France was out of the question. "I am really itching to get out of the country," he confided to *Le Canada*'s Eloi de Grandmont.[55] McCurry and he had been in touch to settle payment for the paintings sold during *Pintura Canadense Contemporânea*. He was evidently encouraged by reports that Brazilians saw him as a potential "Matisse of tomorrow."[56] Details of his upcoming trip, including what would be expected of him, were still fuzzy. Yet the "adventure" was "worthwhile," he told McCurry on the eve of his departure.[57]

The Instituto Brasil-Canadá's new guest arrived in August of 1945, barely four months after learning that he was the recipient of a scholarship. The Brazilian art correspondent Michel B. Kamenka took the initiative, possibly with a nudge from Désy or the Itamaraty, to prepare a feature on the young painter in case the country's cultural elites did not remember him from the exhibition that had closed in São Paulo in January. Here was an artist deserving of attention, he wrote, encouraging *Planalto*'s readership to follow the Canadian envoy on his journey.[58]

De Tonnancour was easy to find. He spent most of his time atop Santa Teresa hill, in Désy's garage, where he set up his studio for a better view of Botafogo Bay and its beachfront neighbourhood. He was also present at most of the social functions and cultural events organized by the embassy. His talent was put to good use on more than one occasion. He designed, for instance, stunning programs for Quatuor alouette's debut concert and the Désys's *Dîner canadien*.[59] He also lectured on cultural life in Canada at the invitation of the MES, which arranged for a copy of his speech to appear in the "Pensamento da América" supplement of the Rio de Janeiro daily *A Manhã*.[60] Whereas Roussin was mostly absent in Brazil, de Tonnancour kept a public profile to bring attention to his work.

By taking such an active part in the projection of Canada abroad, de Tonnancour was effectively writing himself into the story of his country's hemispheric moment. This trip was an opportunity for him to take his place in the world as a French-Canadian artist. In an interview conducted on the eve of his departure from Montreal, he explained that he intended to "better situate the Canadian people toward others ... to better situate himself on his own plane." He added: "You can guess what I am getting at: those qualities that are authentically mine (and thus Canadian), which must be conveyed in the most universal form that I can imagine."[61] Ultimately, he hoped that the intensity of urban life in Brazil, once tamed and juxtaposed against its surrounding landscape, would help him cast a different gaze on the world, including his own. From his vantage point atop Santa Teresa hill, he could dominate Rio de Janeiro with his commanding and essentializing tourist gaze. He had, by his own admission, to adopt that posture if he wanted to shut out the buzzing city life and take in the immensity of the hills, bays, and ocean that surrounded him: "There as a painter, I had no choice but to assume the perspective of a tourist."[62] By venturing into this foreign tropical environment, he sought to define himself both in relation to and against a Brazilian Other with the hope of consolidating his place within Montreal's cultural milieu. Denied the possibly of consecration in Paris, he travelled south to capture Rio de Janeiro on canvas as one conquers a city.

De Tonnancour's drawings and paintings in Brazil fell in two categories: landscapes and female figures. He approached both with apprehension. "The light, the mountains, the vegetation, the sea, the women," he noted, "so far surpassed what one accepts as normal or even as exceptional in the current run of our life that the painter finds himself cast into the midst of an agonizing problem: how to create beauty in a world which, as far as visual order goes, is already overflowing with beauty." His response to this dilemma was to "take nature and twist its neck," because true works of art can only occur following the "death of the natural elements and their resurrection transfigured in the painting."[63] Botafogo Bay and the Pão de Açúcar, the iconic peak found at the mouth of Guanabara Bay, were focal points of his work, although he also occasionally travelled to other elevated parts of the city to capture a broader sweep of the landscape. He was likely pleased to read that Marc Berkowitz, cultural correspondent for *Brazil Herald*, enjoyed his work and saw in it something of the "great Matisse's *joie de vivre*." The piece, however, was not all praise. Indeed, the author added that de Tonnancour's panoramas, with their "strong, almost primitive colours," formed in his opinion "the only right approach from a foreign artist to the Brazilian landscape if he has lived in Brazil for a relatively very short time."[64] This was a backhanded compliment if ever there was one.

Those Brazilians who were following the Canadian envoy's journey were finally able to see what he had been working on in the late spring and summer of 1946. The *Arte Gráfica do Canadá* exhibition was held first in São Paulo, at the Biblioteca Pública (Public Library), between 26 May and 8 June. The event was a teaser of sorts for a more substantial event scheduled to take place in Rio de Janeiro, between 7 and 19 August, at the gallery of the MES. The São Paulo exhibition featured but four items by de Tonnancour. The real show was in the capital, and it included an entire section dedicated to his corpus of Rio de Janeiro works, forty-one in total.[65]

*Arte Gráfica do Canadá* was initially supposed to take place in May of 1945 at the inauguration of the exhibition room of the Museu Nacional de Belas Artes, but there was insufficient time. Once again, McCurry saved the show. He managed to push deadlines and provided crucial assistance in selecting the works and soliciting the assistance of galleries and associations throughout Canada.[66] Not everyone was enthusiastic about the project. For example, Douglas Duncan, co-founder of Toronto's Picture Loan Society, suggested that this "sub rosa business" be abandoned as it was likely to "cause a lot of ill will" among those not consulted and not considered for inclusion. In his mind, it was not worth the trouble.[67] Lyman and Pellan, on the other hand, were amenable to help due to Désy's earlier efforts to spotlight the Contemporary Arts Society. Likewise for de Tonnancour, who had the fortune of being on the ground in Brazil when it all came together in the early months of 1946.

One prominent Brazilian was notably absent: Vargas. Forced to resign in the closing months of 1945, the former president had returned to his native Rio Grande do Sul. His successor, Eurico Gaspar Dutra, had won the popular vote in the December general election. The former minister and close associate of Vargas would lead the country in its passage from dictatorship to democracy, and he would continue to nurture those relationships established during the Estado Novo. Canada would remain a friend deserving of support and an audience.

Occurring so soon after *Pintura Canadense Contemporânea*, the new exhibition could do little more than add colour and depth to the stories Canadians were telling through the visual arts. At best, it was an opportunity to emphasize key elements of the narrative put forth by Désy and his staff since 1941. Once again, journalists generously showered Canada with praise, noting that its "embassy of art and culture" was unique in Rio de Janeiro. Hyperbole abounded, as when Kamenka referred to the art on display as the product of a "heroic tradition." "An important contribution towards the progress of civilization," added *Vamos Ler*'s Oswaldo Teixeira, who saw in the exhibition a reflection of Canadians' "civilizing attitude" and true patriotism. Such reviews amplified the normative undertone that ran through the embassy's cultural initiatives. Brazilian arts correspondents may have been sincere in their enthusiasm, but they also understood that polite niceties were necessary to spur generative cultural conversations. They were very much literate in matters of cultural diplomacy and knew that such an exhibition functioned as an "energetic, expressive and cordial hand-shake."[68]

Significantly, a portion of the spotlight was on female artists whose works spoke of both tradition and modernity. *Pintura Canadense Contemporânea* had introduced the sisters of the Order of Saint Ursula as key actors in the national narrative, in part because of their almost maternal role in documenting and preserving Indigenous crafts. Simone Hudon's contributions to *Arte Gráfica do Canadá* – among others, *St Francis of Assisi* and *Cheminées à Québec* – helped create a narrative bridge between the two exhibitions. Echoing fellow reporters who wrote about Canadians' civilizing mission, Olga Obry noted: "Feminine art in Canada has a long tradition, for were not the Ursulines … the first ones to carry the French knowledge of arts and crafts to the New World – teaching the little Indian girls of the most northerly of all American countries the beauties of perfect embroidery and weaving, and raising the simple manual skill to the level of pure art?" *A Gazeta*'s correspondent was either consciously repeating the official narrative about Canada's past or had absorbed it uncritically. One thing is certain, she knew that women were generally assigned but secondary roles in that story, hence her effort to draw a line from the Ursulines to Hudon while magnifying the latter's robust technique, which in her eyes justified the artist's inclusion alongside her male peers. Hudon's woodcuts and etchings, Obry wrote, "might be thought masculine were it not for the tenderness and feminine emotionalism which can be read 'between the lines.'"[69]

Reporters' interest in Canadian female artists was not confined to folk art and handicrafts. The presence of Denyse Gadbois, a young painter who was married to embassy secretary Roger Chaput, brought attention to the modernist inclinations of her generation. Not only did her participation reveal "a fine artistic feeling" and "uncommon vigour," it also underscored women's unacknowledged role in the making of international relations since she was part of the team that organized the exhibition. In other words, it offered a rebuttal to the patronizing language used to depict women as passive actors who played merely symbolic roles. A case in point was Corinne de Boucherville, who, despite wearing many important hats as a diplomatic wife, was generally cast as a lady engaging in delicate work on behalf of Désy. Even worse, she was often objectified in ways that denied her any agency. Reflecting on his meeting with the ambassadress in the gallery of the MES, Teixeira, although well-intentioned, reduced her to another object among the decor, noting that she "added beauty and charm to the exhibition," like some stunning eighteenth-century portrait. The positive language used to describe Gadbois's contributions, both as an artist and as a member of the organizing committee, was a refreshing exception to such belittling comments.[70]

Most of the attention, however, was directed toward de Tonnancour, the unequivocal star of the show. Virtually unknown in Brazil two years earlier, he was now one of the central figures in the two countries' rapprochement. A guest of the Instituto Brasil-Canadá, he was featured prominently in *Arte Gráfica do Canadá* as it travelled from São Paulo to Rio de Janeiro. In both places, he was offered a stage from which to lecture on his country's cultural life. In the capital city, he presided over what amounted to a solo show of his work held within the larger pan-Canadian exhibition. De Tonnancour's voice took up much space in the catalogue. His "Notes on the Graphic Arts" informed visitors that the works on display demonstrated that Canadians were "worthy of contributing to the artistic production of the world." The painter stayed on message when he drew parallels between Canada's achievements in the arts and its cultural leadership credentials. The same was true regarding his reference to the healthy and productive fusion of "the French and English Canadian temperaments," an image that by 1946 was verging on cliché. In celebrating his country's cultural maturity, de Tonnancour was essentially highlighting the individual contributions of artists like himself who were pushing the nation forward after it had "lagged" far too long "behind the march of progress."[71] A year in Brazil had taught him how to tell a compelling story about Canada, and how to situate himself squarely in the middle of it as both narrator and protagonist.

By assuming such a position, de Tonnancour claimed the exhibition's triumph as his own – a necessary prerequisite of his successful return home. It was all the better if praise for *Arte Gráfica do Canadá* came from a French expat with some degree of authority. Born in Algiers and educated in Paris, Émile Gaudissard obtained success as a painter and a sculptor before trying his hand at architecture. In Brazil during the war, he earnestly followed the Canadian embassy's cultural undertakings. In his view, Désy and his impromptu ambassadors were doing the essential work of maintaining the prestige of French culture at a time when Paris was besieged by fascists. Canada is helping France in "her time of trouble," he wrote in *Brasil Portugal*. Referring to the exhibition, Gaudissard added: "In making Canada known in Brazil, Jean Désy has imported a little of the fragrance of my France, an ancient perfume of days gone by, the perfume of old France so perfectly preserved in Canada."[72] In the same way that the *Dîner canadien* foregrounded the persistence of the *fait français* in North America, validating Canada's image as a nation still intimately attached to France, the graphic arts exhibition presented Montreal as slowly transcending its status as a surrogate of Paris to assume the position of a leading metropolis of the French-speaking world.

With the war over, de Tonnancour was so eager to return home that he apparently refused an offer to stay in Rio de Janeiro for another year. He was, moreover, sure that he had accomplished what he set out to do. "We have sought and we have found ourselves," he wrote in the exhibition catalogue.[73] What he also meant was that he had accumulated whatever credentials he felt was needed to occupy a place of some prominence among Montreal's cultural elites. De Tonnancour did not leave much behind regarding his impressions of Brazil. It is therefore impossible to know how he experienced the country's transition to democracy and peacetime. There is no evidence to suggest that it impacted his work there. De Tonnancour did, however, later complain to a friend that the trip likely cost him opportunities in France, although he did not specify how. The country also provided little in terms of creative enrichment: "It is about the present, and therefore too circumscribed."[74] Notwithstanding this feeling of regret, Brazil did confer visibility upon his work, which helped him gain recognition from critics and his peers back home. McCurry arguably approached Brazil from a similar perspective in an effort to advance the NGC's mission and nudge External Affairs into doing more for the arts. In the absence of decisive action from Ottawa, de Tonnancour, McCurry, and others enacted agency by joining Désy and turning the various opportunities presented in Brazil to their advantage, improvising their way through their country's nascent cultural diplomacy, learning in the process how to harmonize and tread the fine line between politics and aesthetics as they pursued their multi-faceted agendas.

# 6

# The Art of Counterpoint

Ernest MacMillan was a towering figure of Canada's musical life when he departed for Brazil in the summer of 1946. At the helm of the Toronto Symphony Orchestra (TSO) since 1931, he was knighted by King George V for his service to music, some of which involved transcribing material for Marius Barbeau and preparing arrangements for John Murray Gibbon's CPR Festival. He was undoubtedly flattered when Jean Désy invited him to Rio de Janeiro for a series of concerts with the OSB. He embraced the status of cultural ambassador offered to him with the hope that the dissemination of Canadian music overseas would create additional work and funding opportunities for artists at home. But whatever high hopes he had for his time in Brazil, the reality on the ground kept them in check. "Rio is the most beautiful city I have ever seen," he wrote in his diary. It is also "the most exasperating," he added more tellingly.[1] Repetitive administrative, scheduling, and rehearsal problems with the orchestra were at the root of some of his frustrations, although city life in the tropics also brought its share of discomfort and unpredictability.

This latest attempt at cultural diplomacy took place in the early months of the Fourth Brazilian Republic. The Estado Novo had just ended with a fragile, some would say timid, return to democracy under the presidency of former minister of war Eurico Gaspar Dutra. Concerns over leftist agitation may have been growing, but there were few signs of the emerging Cold War in Rio de Janeiro at the time.[2] Things certainly looked quiet compared to 1944 and 1945, at least from the embassy's perspective. The closing years of the dictatorship had seen occasional civil unrest, continuous political intrigue, heightened fears of a coup, and desperate political manoeuvring by

Getúlio Vargas's regime. "The situation is very speculative and I do not believe the atmosphere has been more tense since I came to Brazil," Désy had reported to Ottawa in the summer of 1944.[3] However alarming the situation, it had not been dire enough to warrant halting the embassy's experiments with music and the visual arts. External Affairs had neither interfered nor requested that Désy explain his cultural campaigns, which indicated that there was little appetite in Ottawa for his intelligence gathering and his unorthodox approach to diplomacy. The situation had not changed by 1946. Canadian-Brazilian cultural relations continued on their established course as if detached from the larger geopolitical context of the immediate postwar years.

MacMillan did not travel alone to Brazil. Claude Champagne joined him at the request of Désy, who planned to present a sophisticated image of a bicultural Canada by getting the two composers to perform each other's works. Having them take turns conducting the OSB would be a means of adding resonance to past cultural encounters: specifically, Champagne and Francisco Mignone's exchange of musical gifts, as well as Jean Dansereau and Arnaldo Estrella's joint radio performance on Dominion Day 1943. The tour was an attempt to revisit the musically imagined Canadian-Brazilian community that was in the making before Quatuor alouette's trip to Brazil. It chimed well with the Itamaraty's own take on musical diplomacy, which revolved around works by the likes of Heitor Villa-Lobos and sought to convey the message that Brazil was sufficiently mature to participate in the concert of nations, or rather that it was – like its world-renowned maestro – a worthy interlocutor on the international stage. Brazil's musical life was evidently much more diverse and complex than it appeared to those listening in from outside. The same was true for Canada. In both cases, the decision to amplify "serious music" to drown out vernacular sounds was a conscious one, and it made audible the structuring power of race and class in the two countries' rapprochement.

A thorough examination of MacMillan and Champagne's national performance in Brazil reveals just how tenuous were the metaphors deployed to further Canada-Brazil relations. In Rio de Janeiro, the two impromptu ambassadors sought to cement their status as cosmopolitan artists while bringing prestige to Canada. They accomplished this, in part, by mingling with the city's male-dominated "high" art milieu. As representatives of their country's so-called two founding races, they embodied Britishness and *latinité* through the ostensibly apolitical language of folk-infused "serious music." Their parallel efforts aligned with the trope of *métissage*, but did so, once again, through the prism of whiteness. Oscillating between nationalism and universalism, between difference and sameness, they approached Brazil by way of a northern gaze, which led them to feel ambivalence toward their hosts – MacMillan, more so than Champagne. Further undermining the project of a musically imagined Canadian-Brazilian community was the fact that they followed separate paths in Brazil rather than collaborating on a multi-day program, as originally planned. Instead of *bonne entente*, the tour displayed, with a resounding irony, Canada's "two solitudes."

## THE SOUND OF BRAZIL

The crucial role that composers and musicians played in the two countries' cultural rapprochement was a reflection of how important music was to Brazilians. Through the Vargas era and beyond, it was a potent instrument for rallying peoples around a shared sense of identity and a commitment to patriotic values. It was also a core component of the strategies deployed to remedy Brazil's image problem. Domestically, vernacular genres such as samba shared the spotlight with Antônio Carlos Gomes's Luso-Brazilian operatic storytelling and Villa-Lobos's odes to *Brasilidade*. On international stages, however, there was sufficient bandwidth to accommodate only "serious music." The sound of Brazil intended for the world differed from that which Brazilians enjoyed at home. This "dissociation" was a striking one, but it served its purposes.[4]

The Vargas regime was adept at picking up on musical trends to disseminate its ideologies and create national symbols. By the time Canada opened its legation in 1941, samba had become the national sound of Brazil. Although it traced its origins to the early colonial period, the music emerged in the middle of the nineteenth century among African slaves, notably in the northern region of Bahia. Developing from and morphing with *candombe*, *lundú*, and *maxíxe*, among others, it acquired its own distinctive character once it arrived in Rio de Janeiro, absorbed elements of other vernacular styles, and became an integral component of the city's pre-Lenten Carnival. Samba owed its rise to pre-eminence in part to an Afro-Brazilian musician named Ernesto dos Santos (alias Donga) and whose "Pelo telefone" is regarded as the genre's first recording. The 1916 work was met with controversy from the start, with critics and musicians questioning Dongas's claim of authorship and what they saw as his fame-seeking intentions. This brought into focus the racial and class politics surrounding samba.[5] Bryan McCann, in his chronicle of the flourishing of Brazilian popular music, explains:

> Much of the debate in the samba world concerned questions of the origins and nurturing grounds of the genre, with some sambistas claiming that samba was music of the *cidade*, or city, and others contending that it was originally and primarily music of the *morro*, or hill. Both were collective terms, with *cidade* standing for the various working and middle-class, white and mixed-race neighbourhoods of downtown Rio as well as for the city's radio stations and recording studios, and *morro* for the predominantly black favelas. The polemic regarding these two vaguely defined locations explicitly treated questions of style, and implicitly involved more sensitive questions of class and race.[6]

A hybrid and malleable genre, samba was ripe for appropriation by the time Vargas rose to power.

Its symbolic significance and popularity were such that it quickly became one of the preferred soundtracks of the Estado Novo. Supported initially by municipal governments, samba schools and Carnival received federal sponsorship under Vargas. The regime's Rádio Nacional, in conjunction with the DIP, prioritized *morro*-esque samba, because it spoke more directly to the idea of *Brasilidade* and could thus foster social cohesion and national unity.[7] Rádio Nacional carefully curated its programming to inculcate civic values among its listenership. For instance, songs with lyrics that romanticized images of *malandros* (nonconformist, law-defying troublemakers) received little to no airplay. The broadcaster and the DIP did not stop at censoring works; they also commissioned songs that "helped popularize and commercialize hyperpatriotic lyrics that complemented the Vargas regime's goals of civic renewals and social uplift."[8] Sambistas, of course, could not be completely silenced or co-opted. Their music continued to be regarded as a means of collective self-affirmation and resistance in various public arenas that lay beyond the gaze of the state apparatus.[9] It could accommodate competing interpretations and agendas while effectively linking the past to the present in the national imaginary.

One of samba's most notorious ambassadors in North America was Carmen Miranda. Born into a white family in northern Portugal but raised in Rio de Janeiro, she was barely twenty when she recorded "Prá você gostar de mim," her second single and the one that catapulted her to fame in 1930. Her popularity grew as her appearances on radio and in movies multiplied. By the end of the decade, she had performed in four domestic films and earned an invitation to perform on Broadway in *The Streets of Paris*, taking her musicians along for the trip and getting the Brazilian government to cover their fare from Rio de Janeiro to New York.[10] A goodwill ambassador in her own right, she was a guest of George Orson Welles on his *Hello Americans*, a Good Neighbor radio series on Latin America. She also starred in a series of lucrative films for Hollywood's Twentieth Century Fox. These productions capitalized on her exotic image, which centred on her expressive features, foreign accent, and colourful clothing, including her signature fruit hat and beaded jewelry. Although she continued to record singles, cinema became the medium through which she promoted her samba-inspired tunes. By the end of 1945, she had acted in nine feature films, one of which, *Springtime in the Rockies* (Irving Cummings, 1942), was set in Canada.

Miranda's informal ambassadorial work left some of her compatriots perplexed. Many felt that she was complicit in propagating damaging stereotypes that were at odds with the sophisticated image of themselves that the Brazilian elites wished to foreground. More problematically, they saw her as an embodied image of a colonized Brazil.[11] Yet there was more to her performances than met the eye. In the United States, Miranda was "systematically Brazilianizing her material" through (often improvised) coded messages meant to assert her independence and communicate her attachment to Brazil.[12] These acts of resistance, however, could only accomplish so much. As a white performer, she continued, ipso facto, to symbolically embody "the image of a *mestiço* Brazil" in ways that were non-threatening to North American audiences.[13] The spectacle sold movie tickets and singles; it also brought samba to North America. And yet, not all Brazilians were at ease with the path taken and the images conveyed.

The Itamaraty was reactive more than proactive during most of this period. Its reluctance to use samba and other vernacular sounds for diplomatic and nation-branding purposes resulted from the need to find a balance between projecting an image of Brazil as a modern racial democracy and avoiding bringing attention to domestic tensions that could reveal how fragile the construct of *Brasilidade* was. As Daryle Williams explains in his study of the Vargas era, the regime "tried to seduce and discipline the foreign imagination of Brazilian culture against significant internal debate over the look and meaning of Brazilianness."[14] This did not preclude supporting Miranda and her musicians, although government support for their New York debut was the exception rather than the rule. That Vargas purportedly told them to "display musical honesty" was an indication that samba had the potential to disrupt Brazil's image overseas.[15] The connection between the Itamaraty's musical diplomacy and the "Golden Age of Samba" was a loose one that probably rested more on Vargas's personal relationship to Miranda than it did on the government's efforts to boost coffee exports using music.[16]

If the Itamaraty was not keen to promote samba, it was at least curious about the potential of "serious music." It learned much from the DIP, the MES, and the DIC, all of whom shared – however imperfectly – responsibility for "cultural relations with other countries, the diffusion of Brazilian culture, and the publicizing of useful knowledge ... in the principal foreign centers." Inadequate budgets and a lack of coordination often impeded their efforts, which ranged from supporting touring musicians, inviting foreign artists, financing cultural events, sponsoring private organizations, and sending both records and musical scores to embassies and consular offices overseas. Brazil's return to democracy and the subsequent dismantling of the DIP brought about significant changes on the cultural diplomacy front. In 1946, the Dutra government centralized and further institutionalized operations through the newly established Divisão Cultural do Itamaraty (Cultural Division of the Itamaraty), an agency that actively recruited composers and cultural producers in the pursuit of Brazil's national interest.[17] Notwithstanding their shortcomings, Vargas's and Dutra's respective cultural apparatuses looked impressive when compared to that of Canada.

The Itamaraty could count on practitioners who understood how the projection of a more engaging image of Brazil could benefit their careers. Founded in 1940 by a "group of Brazilian idealists," the OSB saw itself as the vehicle through which Brazilians could demonstrate their cultural sophistication and *savoir faire*.[18] Conceived as a great patriotic endeavour, it sought to educate the masses and promote national pride and unity through its performance of works by Brazilian composers and its mastery of the canon of Western music. Supported by Vargas, the orchestra championed musical nationalism through a program of religious and youth concerts, radio broadcasts, and cross-country tours. It also aimed to energize musical life in Brazil by providing a forum for interaction with visiting composers, which also helped to advance the country's cultural diplomacy agenda.[19]

Launched in 1944, the magazine *Brasil Musical* served similar purposes by featuring Brazilian artists and opening its pages to foreign composers and writers. Published exclusively in Portuguese, the overseas reach of this high-budget magazine was somewhat limited, although it did manage to favourably position Brazil's national musical culture by placing Brazilian artists alongside some of the great names in the world of "serious music." *Brasil Musical*, like the OSB, was conceived partly as a vehicle for promoting a positive image of Brazil – an image intended for cosmopolitan artists and intellectuals deemed most likely to influence perceptions of the South American giant in their own country.[20]

It is revealing of the defective state of the Estado Novo's cultural diplomacy that its first musical ambassador to Canada travelled with the support of a US-American organization: Columbia Concerts.[21] Or was this sheer opportunism? Born in Rio de Janeiro in 1908, Arnaldo Estrella mastered the art of the piano at the Escola Nacional de Música (National School of Music), where he familiarized himself with the works of Villa-Lobos. A connoisseur when it came to Frédéric Chopin and Johannes Brahms, Estrella was first and foremost a champion of Brazilian music. He found himself travelling north in the winter of 1943 after winning a Columbia Concerts competition held to promote better cultural relations between the United States and Brazil. It is not clear who proposed to bring Estrella to Canada, but plans were in place a full month prior to the pianist's New York debut on 7 February.[22] Burdened with a busy schedule, Estrella managed to cross into Canada on 30 March for a one-off performance of Brazilian works on the airwaves of Radio-Canada.[23] Brazilian diplomats in Montreal reported enthusiastically about their compatriot's "superior technique and Brazilian sensibility" at the piano.[24] The press, however, failed to take note of the event since it was poorly promoted. Estrella nonetheless managed to meet with Champagne, who had just finished his "Quadrilha brasileira." On vacation in Montreal at the time, Désy organized a reception for the Brazilian pianist. The idea of having him premiere Champagne's composition in Brazil was likely born that day.

José Siqueira followed a similar route to Canada with no more luck than Estrella. Born in 1907 in the small town of Conceição, in the northern part of the country, he acquired his musical education in the army and then at Rio de Janeiro's Instituto Nacional de Música. He started making a name for himself as a composer and conductor in the 1930s, but his career really took off with the OSB, of which he was the director and a founding member. In 1943, he travelled to the United States at the invitation of Nelson Rockefeller. He was due to travel north again, to meet with composers Leopold Stokowsky and Karl Krueger, when he reached out to the DCI for assistance in October of 1945. At the time, no one gave any serious thought to the idea of having him perform in Canada, at least not until Désy got involved.[25]

A performance by Siqueira in Toronto or Montreal would make a splendid prelude to Champagne and MacMillan's trip to Brazil, Désy thought. On 6 December, he contacted MacMillan to see if he could arrange for the Brazilian composer to direct the TSO in January of 1946.[26] He also wrote to Champagne to inquire about the possibility of organizing something in Montreal. Whereas Champagne managed to secure a Radio-Canada performance for Siqueira, MacMillan failed to generate opportunities for his Brazilian counterpart on such short notice. The situation caused him much anxiety since Désy had just shared the news that plans were being made to bring him and Champagne to Brazil. Siqueira appeared somewhat annoyed in his correspondence; that was at least how it was read by MacMillan, who felt that his reputation and that of the TSO were being damaged unnecessarily. Seemingly indulging in self-importance, MacMillan voiced his frustration to External Affairs in a letter that evoked the likelihood of a diplomatic incident. He may have been exaggerating, but he was trying to make the point that more could be done to facilitate cultural exchanges and that better planning would be consistent with Canada's efforts to project a positive image overseas. There were also domestic power dynamics at work in this episode: "Montreal will get the credit and Toronto the blame," MacMillan complained.[27] In the end, Siqueira's radio performance, on 30 January, went largely unnoticed, although it probably earned Champagne additional goodwill in Brazil.[28]

## A CANADIAN MUSICAL MOSAIC

In 1946, Canada's musical life still bore the indelible mark of its colonial origins. As Paul Helmer explains in his study of the country's musical development, it "was bifurcated in a manner that reflected its history: there was an anglophone community oriented towards London and Edinburgh, and a francophone community oriented towards Paris, with Montreal serving as the geographical synapse of the two."[29] Toronto and Montreal had their own music schools, music faculties, and orchestras with which to assert their identities, if not dominance, on the national stage. The CBC often served as a conduit for these efforts although it was itself a potential competitor since it also employed artists and had its own orchestra. In this contest, each city could count on the patronage of a wealthy family eager to help Canadian talent graduate from musical salons to concert stages: the Massey family, who established Toronto's Massey Hall in 1894, and the Athanase family, who helped found the OCSM in 1934. The composers and musicians who travelled to Great Britain and France to perfect their training, and those who crossed into the United States to pursue lucrative opportunities, helped energize local music scenes. This was true for both Toronto and Montreal, but also for other emerging cultural hubs: among others, Quebec City, Halifax, and Vancouver.

The permeability of the border between Canada and the United States was of significance in the development of an elitist, cosmopolitan culture in Canada during the interwar years. It permitted the circulation of people (touring orchestras), sounds (radio broadcasts), and funds (philanthropic endeavours) – all of which encouraged the professionalization, institutionalization, and modernization of musical life in urban cultural centres. Philanthropic organizations such as the Carnegie Corporation and the Rockefeller Foundation played an especially important role by providing Canadians with the means and the skills necessary to advance from a private approach to cultural patronage to one increasingly dependent on corporate and state structures. These transnational exchanges brought into focus a commonality of values among those who defined themselves as members of a cosmopolitan elite – most of them "white, financially comfortable, middle-aged males."[30]

The music pouring over the border was not always to the taste of this elite. This was particularly true of samba, which had travelled all the way from Brazil. Canadians could not have missed the phenomenon if they tuned in to the stations broadcasting from the United States or if they lived near or in a city that had a dance hall, a concert venue, or a movie theatre in the 1940s. In Canada, the age of modernity, with its radio airwaves and silver screens, combined with the ease of cross-border movement and the shared language reality for much of the population, had accelerated a massive degree of cultural penetration that had begun shortly after the First World War.[31] Because of the ready access that Canadians had to cultural products coming in from the United States, the State Department did not expend any energy or resources northward during the Good Neighbor era.[32] This state of affairs did not shelter Canadians from exposure to the sounds that circulated throughout the hemisphere as a result of their neighbours' cultural offensive in Brazil.

The singer Alys Robi was among those who fell under the spell of samba. Born Alice Robitaille in a working-class family, she was seven years old when she performed in *Ten Nights in a Bar Room*, a professional stage adaptation of a US-American novel from the mid-nineteenth century. She soon began winning contests, which led to a growing number of appearances on radio. In 1935, Robi relocated to Montreal, where she performed alongside Rose Ouellette (alias La Poune) at Théâtre national, later moving on to bigger and better opportunities, notably on the road with promoter Jean Grimaldi. Significantly, she rose to fame in the rest of Canada in 1944 with her performances on *Latin American Serenade*, a CBC show of which she was the star. French Canadians had long been interested in the music of South America, which they discovered through sheet music, dance manuals, and early recordings.[33] The UCLA did its part with its program of cultural events.[34] A member of the organization, Robi brought Quebec's Latinophilia to the national stage through the medium of radio.[35]

However, arguably the most decisive factor that brought South American music to the limelight in Canada was the popularity of Miranda's Hollywood film performances. It was these productions that inspired Robi to incorporate Brazilian songs into her repertoire.[36] In December of 1944, she travelled to New York for her first studio session with RCA Victor. She intended to record English-language versions of some of the works that she was using to conquer new publics, including the Brazilian song "Tico-tico no fubá," but the label thought it preferable to prioritize French-language versions. The market for such material had quickly become saturated, so RCA Victor was most likely trying to capitalize on Robi's difference as a French Canadian.

"Tico-tico no fubá" had first been popularized through the Walt Disney animation film *Saludos Amigos* (Wilfred Jackson et al., 1942). In 1944, Ethel Smith's rendition, which was featured in *Bathing Beauty* (George Sidney, 1944), climbed through US-American pop charts. It was followed shortly after by the Andrews Sisters' jazzed-up version. Because Miranda had yet to record her own single of the song, Robi's French-language version fulfilled listeners' desire for the exotic.[37]

In the mid- to late 1940s, Robi found herself in the ambiguous position of performing two roles simultaneously: transcultural mediator and exotic Other. Regarding the first, she introduced North American audiences to South American works. Many of these either originated from Brazil or were inspired by samba: among others, "Tico-tico no fubá," "Aquarela do Brasil," "Samba," and "Chica chica boom chic." Robi's genuine interest in the music was evidenced by her trips to Mexico and her correspondence with the Brazilian composer Ary Barroso, whose permission she sought before translating some of his songs into French.[38] According to her biographer, she intended to bring Canada's "two solitudes around a Brazilian samba."[39] Robi's difference marked her as an exotic Other in ways that ostensibly legitimized – and rendered authentic – her performance of this material. The American entertainer Jack Benny, with whom she shared the stage in 1943, referred to her as the Canadian – or Quebec's own – "Carmen Miranda." The moniker was misleading since Robi never wore extravagant attire, yet it proved an effective shorthand for introducing her to audiences in the early 1940s.[40] It may have even contributed to her being invited to Hollywood to discuss potential projects with film executives. There, Robi met Miranda, who was both friendly and, it turned out, a Francophile.[41]

Robi incidentally disrupted the musically imagined Canadian-Brazilian community that Désy championed through his cultural diplomacy. However problematic were parts of the singer's Brazil-inflected repertoire, her success revealed that popular music was a legitimate vehicle with which to mediate new connections to the nation and to the world, even if the sounds that inspired her came filtered – and thus somewhat distorted and essentialized – through US-American media. Désy apparently did not take note of Robi's formidable career. If he had, he would have disapproved of her appropriation of a vernacular genre rooted in Afro-Brazilian culture. The French-Canadian singer did not end up taking the place of Miranda on the big screen, nor did she ever tour Brazil.[42] Although her music did chart briefly there, Brazilians seemed unaware of Robi's reputation as "Canada's Carmen Miranda," with one critic for *Diario da Noite* comparing her instead to a lesser version of the famous Wisconsin-born cabaret singer Hildegarde.[43]

What caught the Canadian elites' attention in the early 1940s was their country's growing proficiency in the realm of "serious music." This development was due in part to the arrival of European artists fleeing both war and persecution by totalitarian regimes. Their presence in cities like Toronto and Montreal provided impetus to local efforts to establish a modern cosmopolitan culture. Between 1933 and 1942, thirty-eight musicians arrived in Canada – a small number that does not quite capture the breadth of the contributions they made to the country's musical life.[44] Born in Vienna, the pianist and harpsichordist Greta Kraus fled the Nazis in 1938. She relocated to Toronto, where she established her reputation as a stellar performer and a dedicated educator. The Mannheim-born cellist Lotte Brott also arrived in Canada in 1938, performing with the McGill String Quartet and the OCSM throughout the 1940s. Born in Berlin, the pianist Helmut Blume escaped to England in 1939 and was interned and then transferred to Canada. Released in 1942, he participated in wartime propaganda broadcasts and made his mark as an instructor and administrator in the Faculty of Music at McGill University.

These individuals, and many others like them, injected new life into Canada's thriving culture of classical music. Their experience, Helmer argues, is "essentially a story of liberation." According to him, it is also a story of decolonization in that they encouraged Canadians to think beyond French-English binaries: "Émigré musicians helped us to move beyond a colonial mentality by opening our musical consciousness and giving us a new appreciation of the rich tapestry that constitutes the Canadian mosaic." "Their efforts," he adds, "brought about a Canadianization of our musical life."[45] Yet to describe Canada's wartime and postwar musical life as a mosaic would be to look at the past through the prism of the ideology of multiculturalism, which was still foreign to people like Désy, MacMillan, and Champagne in 1946.

Between the wars and through to the mid-1940s, Canada's cultural elites continued to seek inspiration in the works of folklorists who prioritized source material that spoke of the country's white settler origins. During this period, composers turned to melodic or thematic elements that they could quote or incorporate into their works to evoke Canadian life and spaces. Theirs was not a systematic or concerted effort. No one composer was positioned to take centre stage and move the country's musical development beyond its "early nationalism" phase.[46] No government body was volunteering to support them in the spirit of musical nationalism. In this context, Barbeau's contribution to the development of folk-infused art music was crucial. His efforts, like Gibbon's, provided incentives for composers to begin transcribing folk songs to create vocal and instrumental arrangements. Their 1927 and 1928 editions of the Quebec City CPR Festival saw MacMillan and Champagne contributing "Two Sketches for String Quartet" and "Suite canadienne," respectively. MacMillan went on to focus intently on English-Canadian and Irish folk songs with the encouragement of Barbeau while Champagne continued exploring French-Canadian folklore.[47] The international connections and émigré contributions discussed above energized the two composers, but they did not make them any less interested in folk material, especially Champagne, who was from Quebec, where the search for origin stories remained strong.[48]

## MUSICAL ENVOYS FROM CANADA'S TWO SOLITUDES

Sir Ernest MacMillan, as many people called him, was a central figure in the emergence of a distinctive "serious music" culture in Canada. Born in 1893 in Mimico, Ontario, he grew up in a Presbyterian family. A minister and hymnist, his father encouraged him to play the organ at church. In 1905, MacMillan accompanied his family to Scotland, where he perfected his musical education. Back in Canada in 1908, he was once again eastbound, although this time he was headed to Paris to study the piano. He was in Germany for a music festival when the First World War broke out. Interned at Ruhleben as an enemy alien for the duration of the conflict, he used that time to refine and develop his organizational, compositional, and conducting skills with musicians whom he assembled into impromptu orchestras. After the armistice, he was released from the detention camp and sent back to Canada, where he began a prolific teaching and administrative career in addition to taking up the position of conductor at the TSO.

Upon his return, MacMillan devoted himself to improving his country's cultural life. He collaborated with Barbeau and Gibbon in their efforts to find a place for folk materials within the nation's emerging repertoire of classical music. He accepted the knighthood awarded to him in 1935 not because he was an imperialist, but because the title was an "acknowledgment of the growing importance of music in public life."[49] Throughout the 1930s, MacMillan tirelessly called attention to the need for more funding, better coordination, and greater promotion of the strategies deployed to train musicians, disseminate their works, and educate the public about the value of "serious music."[50] He subsequently helped establish the Canadian Music Council, whose mandate was to place the sonic arts squarely at the heart of the nation's future.[51] The Canada that he embraced was one that was characterized, above all, by its Britishness.[52] As Helmer explains: "A super musician and a consummate gentleman, MacMillan was a prime example of the British domination of the musical scene in Toronto and to some extent across Canada."[53]

Wilfrid Pelletier was "MacMillan's francophone counterpart," according to Helmer.[54] Born in Montreal in 1896, he played percussion with local bands in his youth before learning rudiments on the piano. With the help of a private instructor, he rose through the ranks of the city's small music community to secure a position with the National Theatre's orchestra. He won the Prix d'Europe in 1915, but he had to wait until the following autumn to cross the Atlantic due to the war raging overseas. In 1917, he made his way to New York, where he found work as a *répétiteur* at the Metropolitan Opera. Within just a few years, he was conducting orchestras himself and giving performances throughout the United States. He was one of the Metropolitan Opera's regular conductors when news reached him that he was needed back in Canada. Montreal philanthropists wanted him to serve as artistic director for a new orchestra whose mandate would in part be to feature Quebec-born and Quebec-trained soloists and composers, particularly Prix d'Europe recipients. Pelletier participated in the creation of the OCSM out of a sense of national pride and to repay his debt to the burgeoning cultural elite that had made it possible for him to travel overseas almost two decades earlier. Like MacMillan, he believed that more could be done to train aspiring musicians and to initiate the broader public to "serious music." The opening of the CMQM in 1943 was an important step in trying to address both objectives.[55]

That said, MacMillan's true counterpart in 1940s Quebec was arguably Claude Champagne.[56] Born in 1891, the Montreal-born composer-educator adopted the violin as his primary instrument. Educated at the Dominion College of Music and the Conservatoire national de musique, he first made a name for himself as a teacher and performer. Champagne completed his first composition in 1914, but it is his "Hercule et Omphale," a 1918 symphonic poem, that caught the attention of Montreal's cultural elites. Between 1921 and 1928, he studied in Europe – first in Belgium and then in Paris – where he premiered the work to great acclaim. From there, he composed "Suite canadienne," which won one of the prizes awarded during the May 1928 edition of the Quebec City CPR Festival for works inspired by French-Canadian folk melodies.[57] Back home in 1929, Champagne focused his energies on teaching and helping to reform music education. He was instrumental in preparing the terrain for the provincial law to which the CMQM owed its existence. In his capacity as assistant director of the new institution, he strove to elevate the city's musical life and to prepare future generations for successful careers within the province and beyond.[58] Champagne moved in the same social and cultural circles as Désy, which is how he found himself tasked with writing "Quadrilha brasileira" and helping arrange opportunities for Siqueira. He was therefore better positioned than Pelletier to accompany MacMillan to Brazil in 1946.[59]

The initial plan for the joint MacMillan-Champagne tour was a clear indication that Désy's latest musical nation-branding effort was designed with both domestic and foreign audiences in mind. The ambassador invited the composers to Brazil for two concerts that would launch the OSB's 1946 musical season in Rio de Janeiro. They were expected to share a two-part program according to which MacMillan would direct works by French-Canadian composers while Champagne would handle the English-Canadian repertoire. The former would begin the first concert and end the program on the second night. Désy insisted that this scheme would provide a great example of *bonne entente* and intercultural exchange "for both compatriots and foreigners."[60] On the one hand, the initiative was meant to further substantiate the trope of *métissage*. On the other, it was meant as a rebuttal of the two solitude thesis, which caught national attention following the 1945 publication of Hugh MacLennan's *Two Solitudes*, a novel about the impossibility of communication between French- and English-speaking Canadians.[61] Hence the suggestion that the concerts be broadcast on Brazilian airwaves and then relayed to the CBC.

Désy was inviting Champagne and MacMillan as his official guests "with the assistance of his friends in Brazil." External Affairs was not too keen to contribute to the project, despite agreeing to provide some logistical support. Quebec, on the other hand, offered $4,000 to help cover costs for one of the concerts. As for Ontario, it declined to help, possibly because the predominantly English-speaking province could not see how a tour framed as a "Cultural Propaganda Movement" with "no commercial character whatsoever" could benefit Ontarians with marginal ties to South America and whose cultural standing in Canada seemed secure.[62] The discrepancy between each province's response to the project was another indication that the idea of a Canada-Brazil cultural rapprochement resonated more with French Canadians.

The difficulties encountered by MacMillan and Champagne in planning for the tour revealed the extent to which Désy's musical diplomacy was improvised. The two composers first heard about the project in the summer of 1945. Details were sketchy; there were talks of a shared program to be performed with the OSB on two consecutive nights, but also mentions of potential concerts in various venues throughout Rio de Janeiro, performances on the airwaves, and lectures at the Escola Nacional de Música. The concerts were to take place in May, although they were later postponed to June, then July, and finally August. There was no guarantee that the calendar would not change again.

Whereas Champagne was happy to keep his schedule open until full details were available, MacMillan was becoming increasingly impatient with the fact that Désy could confirm neither the dates nor the financial terms. He had also asked about conducting more concerts since he thought that it was "absurd" to travel all the way to Brazil only to perform a shared program twice. It did not help that External Affairs was no more informed than him. MacMillan had "*not yet given up hope*" although he was clearly exasperated by the slow pace at which things were moving.[63] As for Champagne, he was "rather surprised, and worried," by the fact that his Toronto counterpart seemed to have second thoughts regarding the tour.[64] His personal relationship with Désy gave him confidence that everything would work out in the end. On 10 April 1946, he wrote to MacMillan to remind him that "boosting Canadian music abroad" was important. He added: "Of course, with you, being a professional conductor, the case may be a little different, but I feel sure if you will visualize the 'overall' good it will do Canada, you will think it a very worthy gesture."[65] Champagne appeared to doubt MacMillan's willingness to put his career at the full service of the nation. In the end, Canada seemed barely more capable than Brazil of organizing such a tour on its own since MacMillan only agreed to go after Columbia Concerts got involved and negotiated terms for him.

External Affairs, more so than Désy, was to blame for the haphazard way in which the tour was organized – at least that is what MacMillan believed. He did not need Champagne to lecture him on cultural diplomacy. "He is preaching to the converted," he told one correspondent during this period.[66] MacMillan had resisted the temptation to walk away from the project to avoid embarrassing "our Ambassador in his genuine efforts to promote international good will."[67] External Affairs had told Désy and MacMillan that Ottawa did not have the resources to support such a tour in the immediate aftermath of the war. The department's resources were stretched so thin that it could only make partial photostats of the scores needed in Brazil.[68] MacMillan, who had been actively campaigning for public support for the arts, was disappointed that it could not do more to support Canadian artists by ensuring the best of conditions when performing abroad. More importantly, he felt that Ottawa was failing them by not keeping up with less developed nations that had already equipped themselves with a sophisticated cultural diplomacy apparatus. "I am not wishing to plague you personally but I do think your Department ought to be kept reminded of the absolute necessity for doing something reasonably adequate to promote better international relations through music," he told Terence W.L. MacDermot.[69]

Although MacMillan made frequent references to music's ability to foster international co-operation, his lobbying efforts were aimed primarily at creating opportunities for artists like himself and those he was working with as a conductor and educator. The insistence with which he brought these matters to External Affairs was less about creating a musically imagined Canadian-Brazilian community than about creating the conditions for the projection of an appealing image of Canada that corresponded to the high rank he thought the country maintained in the concert of nations. In that sense, he was not much different than Siqueira, who also championed musical nation branding to consolidate his career and elevate his country's status on the international stage.

Amid these developments, MacMillan and Champagne came to embody the power dynamics that existed between Montreal and Toronto. The two composers collaborated somewhat reluctantly throughout the year that it took to conclude the details of the tour. MacMillan politely expressed his reservations regarding the original two-part program by indicating that having conductors share a stage was destabilizing for both the orchestra and the audience.[70] He also mentioned that it would be more appropriate for him to headline the first concert, which suggests that his indisposition had to do with practicality as much as status.[71] He shared some of his concerns in private correspondence with Désy, who indiscreetly kept Champagne in the loop. The ambassador and the French-Canadian composer were on a first-name basis and spent time together in Montreal during the summer of 1945. Proximity and familiarity informed Champagne's response to Désy's proposal. The opposite was true for MacMillan.

Latent tensions between the two composers, especially in light of MacMillan's reluctance to commit to the project until April of 1946, resulted in the initial plan being scrapped. Citing health reasons, Champagne told his diplomat friend that he preferred to focus on teaching while in Brazil and that it would be best to let MacMillan handle the concerts with the OSB.[72] Final details for the tour were agreed on just weeks prior to departure: MacMillan would conduct eight concerts while Champagne would give eight lectures at the Escola Nacional de Música. The latter would also conduct two concerts: one in the auditorium of the MES and the other at Cine-Rex, a movie theatre that also hosted music events. The tour would be about the two solitudes after all.

The trope of *métissage* was a doubtful metaphor as evidenced by the works performed by the two composers in Brazil. Siqueira confused Champagne and MacMillan by telling them that he was looking forward to their shared program of "Canadian and British music."[73] More than a semantic mistake, the use of these adjectives suggested that he associated Canadian culture primarily with French Canada. Correspondingly, he assumed that the culture of English-speaking Canadians was still very much colonial in its adherence to Britishness. Thinking that Siqueira actually meant works by British composers, Champagne told MacMillan that works by French composers would then have to be incorporated into the program to ensure equal representation.[74] That was before the initial musical scheme fell apart. Désy ultimately agreed to let the two composers conduct their own affairs, although he encouraged them to include Canadian works in their respective selections.

For his Rio de Janeiro debut, Champagne performed his "Berceuse" alongside Czech (Bedřich Smetana), Russian (Nikolai Rimsky-Korsakov), and French (Arthur Honegger and Henri Rabaud) works. He dedicated his second concert entirely to Canadian composers, all of them from Quebec. Aside from his own "Two Sketches for String Quartet" and a one-off performance of Champagne's "Danse canadienne," MacMillan performed mostly compositions associated with the core canon of "serious music" (from Ludwig van Beethoven to Franz Schubert and Gustav Theodore Holst, among others). Whereas Champagne focused on Quebec's cultural output and its connections to both France and the musical nationalisms of Smetana and Rimsky-Korsakov, MacMillan made his case for the cosmopolitan universalism of Western "high" culture. Two solitudes indeed.[75]

Coverage of the tour inevitably reflected this polarization. The Brazilian press welcomed MacMillan and Champagne as "guests of maestro Siqueira" and "messengers from Canada," but it also emphasized their difference from each other by noting that they embodied distinct musical manifestations of – rather than mere variations on – Canada's musical culture.[76] Reporters often found themselves discussing the two composers simultaneously since they were in Brazil at the same time.[77] Yet this made it easier to consistently juxtapose MacMillan's connections to the English-speaking world against Champagne's connections to the French-speaking world. Viewed through the prism of the Brazilian press, then, Toronto and Montreal appeared to be worlds apart, especially with MacMillan and Champagne following their own itineraries in Rio de Janeiro.

The fact that Ontario newspapers took an interest in the tour did not mean that Désy was more successful in his efforts to have an image of national unity reflected back toward Canada. English-language newspapers had for the most part shown no interest in Désy's earlier cultural diplomacy initiatives, but MacMillan's successes with the OSB were cause for celebration. Most reporters, however, failed to take note of Champagne's presence in Brazil.[78] French-language newspapers did no better in that they focused on Montreal's envoy and his ambassador friend rather than engaging with the image of *bonne entente* and the trope of *métissage* that initially informed the project.

Did this jeopardize the musically imagined Canadian-Brazilian community then in the making? As was the case with other aspects of the tour, the way in which the two composers engaged with their hosts' culture differed. MacMillan thought it appropriate to ask Désy and Siqueira, shortly before the trip, whether he should include a Brazilian composition in one of his concerts. He was therefore shocked to learn that Brazil's government had passed a law requiring all conductors to feature at least one Brazilian work in their programs.[79] Coming as it did at the last minute, this new restriction became an additional source of annoyance.

Not everyone in Brazil thought that the law was a good idea since it generally meant that visiting conductors usually picked compositions that were easy to play and could be learned quickly. The result was that audiences were often confronted with lesser-quality works that did not quite reflect the richness of their country's musical culture.[80] Still, the law forced foreign artists to familiarize themselves with the Brazilian repertoire, which meant that some of them became informal ambassadors for Brazil when they returned home. In Rio de Janeiro, MacMillan performed Siqueira's "Crepúsculo" and "Dança brasileira" as well as Villa-Lobos's "Caixinha de boas."[81] Champagne, on the other hand, was above the law. Neither of his two concerts included Brazilian works, although he did share the stage with Siqueira, who opened the Cine-Rex program with works by Carl Maria von Weber and Wolfgang Amadeus Mozart. It is possible that Champagne was exempted because he performed in non-conventional concert venues and was friendly with Siqueira. His reputation was also in good standing thanks to his "Quadrilha brasileira."

The two impromptu ambassadors gravitated in and around predominantly male political and cultural circles in Rio de Janeiro. They befriended and developed collegial relationships with the likes of Villa-Lobos, Francisco Mignone, and Oscar Lorenzo Fernández – towering figures to whom the two composers needed to measure up. MacMillan's onstage performances provided evidence that he was up to the task, according to Brazilian music critics.[82] Not only had he grown into an accomplished and widely respected composer-educator, he had also survived a German internment camp during the First World War and had been awarded a knighthood.[83] His "vigorous artistic attitude," objective outlook, and even temperament allowed him to wrest control and guide the OSB to "one of the biggest musical triumphs" ever experienced in Rio de Janeiro.[84] This journalistic hyperbole was thought to capture the full measure of the man. In a parallel way, he and Champagne were pictured in the Canadian press smoking with radiant, victorious smiles.[85] A similar photo of Champagne with Villa-Lobos further highlighted the androcentric nature of this cultural encounter.[86] Pipe and cigar smoking were practices that reinforced one's sense of masculine and bourgeois identity. It was also a marker of sociability as the Champagne and Villa-Lobos picture seemed to suggest.[87] This representation helped depict the French-Canadian composer as being on par with his Brazilian counterpart, whom the press described as the "arbiter" and "absolute ruler of things musical in his country."[88]

Triumphant or not, the tour saw the OSB put MacMillan's manful authority to the test. Although he successfully surmounted obstacles with vigour and valour during live concerts (from inexperienced musicians struggling through hard passages to horns playing out of tune), he found himself discouraged and enervated, even powerless, during rehearsals.[89] The problems he faced ranged from the missing key needed to open the piano to the double booking of rehearsal halls, delayed payments of conductor fees, missing and incomplete scores, as well as rehearsal and concert calendars that kept changing. Most tiring were the musicians themselves. MacMillan sympathized with them in that he recognized that they were underpaid and overworked, but he still reprimanded them for their indiscipline, lack of focus, and frequent absences. "Musicians are a bit like children anywhere, but here perhaps more than elsewhere," he wrote in his diary.[90] Being old did not shield them from criticism: "The oldest player must have been 75 and seemed very short-sighted; he was certainly abysmally stupid."[91] Echoing Marcel Roussin's disparaging remarks, he described the OSB as a sub-par orchestra from a city whose musical standards were below those of a true metropolis.[92]

MacMillan's ambivalence vis-à-vis Brazilians concerned not just their heedlessness and their unresponsiveness to his authority; they were a disconcerting Other in a disorienting city. Rio de Janeiro had, at first, seemed familiar, with its layout, cafés, and buildings reminding MacMillan of Paris: in his eyes, the Avenida Presidente Vargas was a little bit like the Avenue des Champs-Élysées and the Teatro Municipal was a "miniature of the Paris Opera."[93] He was also surprised that the city was not as ethnically diverse as he had imagined it, but that was due to the fact that he spent most of his time in elite white circles.[94] Rio de Janeiro's problem, according to MacMillan, was that it had none of the comforts that Toronto offered. His first room did not have a bath. The room he subsequently moved into had plumbing issues, which forced him on one occasion – and to his great chagrin – to conduct a concert un-bathed. "Even toilets call for patience," he wrote in his diary.[95] Brazilians mishandled his laundry and his mail when they did not overcharge for cabs and stamps. He complained of their attitude, their unreliability, and their inability to hold promises.[96] "How so apparently lacka daisical a race managed to build Rio I don't know," he noted in his diary with exasperation.[97]

Growing increasingly disenchanted with his hosts, MacMillan feared being contaminated by what he considered to be their flawed character.

He conceded that this "sweeping generalization" applied primarily to Brazilians, although "visitors and foreigners of brief residence" were susceptible "to be infected by the Brazilian attitude." His compatriots were also at risk since improvidence "was beginning even to creep into the Canadian embassy." Fortunately for him, he could turn to Désy and his chargé d'affaires, Benjamin Rogers, who provided unceasing support as "the only solid ground in a country of quicksands." Like Roussin, MacMillan sought comfort in the familiar and criticized Brazilians for not living up to the standards that he set for them through his northern gaze. Reflecting on his experience in Brazil, he penned the following words in his diary: "Never in my life have I wished more ardently to get away from a place, unless perhaps Ruhleben."[98] Apparently, Rio de Janeiro was hardly more bearable than a detention camp in wartime Germany.

Champagne did not leave behind a tour diary detailing his impressions of Brazil, but it is reasonable to assume that his experience of Rio de Janeiro was more enjoyable than that of MacMillan's since he concentrated his activities on lecturing, which put him into contact with fellow composers and educators, many of whom were Francophiles. Unlike MacMillan, he felt "very much at home" in the city because of its "European atmosphere," its "cosmopolitan spirit," and the supposed absence of "race discrimination."[99] Champagne's positive depiction of the city reflected, of course, the fact that he spent most of his time among the elites and had few contacts with musicians who often came from less privileged background. Besides, he was not going to undermine Désy's work by disparaging a people with whom Canadians were expected to engage. Such behaviour would also have been ungrateful, considering the high esteem in which Brazilians held him because of his closeness to the ambassador and the assistance he provided to Siqueira during his trip to Canada earlier that year. In attendance during one of MacMillan's concerts, Champagne was honoured with a long ovation by the "*habitués*" of the Teatro Municipal.[100] By using a French term to describe the concert hall's loyal audience, *Jornal do Brasil*'s Francisco Cavalcanti underlined the continued importance of *latinité* and Paris-derived "high" culture in Canadian-Brazilian relations. In fact, Désy and his many impromptu ambassadors had been so successful at dislocating Britishness from the centre of Canada's international image that many Brazilians now assumed that all Canadians spoke French as their first or second language.[101]

If there is one thing that MacMillan and Champagne agreed on, it was that Brazilians were exemplary in terms of their engagement with culture and their support for the arts. The two composers returned inspired – but also somewhat embarrassed, even angered – that Brazil, a country on the periphery of the world as they knew it, had progressed more than Canada on the question of state-funded aid to artists.[102] This realization certainly destabilized their sense of themselves as dignified cultural representatives of a great modern North Atlantic nation. The interviews that they gave to the press upon returning home revealed the urgency with which they sought to tackle that issue. Champagne was surely romanticizing what he had witnessed in Brazil when he stated that "music predominates above all else," but the point that he was trying to make was that governments had a responsibility to subsidize artists if they wished to see Canadians take their rightful place in the concert of nations.[103] "Brazil is far ahead of Canada so far as creative musical activity is concerned," he told Thomas Archer, as if trying to engender shock among the *Montreal Gazette*'s readership.[104] Given his seeming animosity, MacMillan should not have been forthcoming in talking about Brazil, but he felt the need to qualify his compatriot's statement in an interview with the *Globe and Mail*: "They are far ahead of us as far as opera and the ballet are concerned, but I think their symphonic tradition has perhaps lagged behind ours."[105] Overall, though, he concurred with Champagne. The "unimaginative people" at External Affairs, he thought, carried part of the blame for failing to understand "the place that cultural propaganda can and should take in foreign (or for that matter, any) relations."[106]

Concerned as they were with seeking validation in their search for an international identity, Canadians were quick to shift the discussion to other matters. The *Globe and Mail*, in the aftermath of the tour, wrote jubilantly that Brazilians were now more "inclined to think of Canada as a nation of artists, poets and musicians, rather than to harbour the more frequent foreign notion that Canada is a glacial land inhabited by trappers, Eskimos and the Royal Canadian Mounted Police."[107] Désy deserved much credit for this, argued *Mayfair*'s George Austen, who attributed the diplomat's success to two things: "A real interest in Canadian painters and musicians, and a combination of showmanship and hard work that would get him a hearing as a press agent, let alone as the ambassador of a friendly power."[108] Désy, however, was not alone in making an impression in Brazil. The many cultural ambassadors that he mobilized had plenty of opportunities to enact agency too. The projection of Canada abroad was, as a result, a largely contested affair. Between *bonne entente* and two solitudes, the latter predominated in 1946. And while Champagne and MacMillan took part in the acts of national projection and national self-representation, Othering Brazilians in the process, they also served as a conduit through which Brazil's own impromptu ambassadors propagated their ideas and works. Having failed to help Siqueira in the winter of 1946, MacMillan indicated that he would do his best to reciprocate upon returning home. In March of 1947, he wrote to his counterpart to let him know that he had just introduced his "Danças brasileiras [1 and 5]" to an appreciative Toronto audience.[109] Candidly and with the satisfaction of having accomplished one of his goals, Siqueira replied: "I hope you will go on playing Brazilian composers since the public seemed to like it."[110] Brazilians were evidently not passive actors in this story, as the next (and final) chapter demonstrates.

# 7
# Circular (Re)Transmissions

On 12 March 1953, Jean Désy found himself in the unenviable position of having to testify in front of the House of Commons Standing Committee on External Affairs to discuss the recent activities of the CBC-IS. He was there in his capacity as director general of the organization, a title he held since January of the previous year. He had left Brazil in 1947 to continue his diplomatic career in Italy. Désy was weighing his options for the future when External Affairs recalled him to help reorganize the CBC-IS so that its programming better aligned with the department's foreign policy orientation. He might as well have kept his ambassador and impresario titles since the standing committee had convened him to explain why he had spent close to $25,000 on the production of a concert and a recording by Heitor Villa-Lobos at Montreal's Plateau Hall.[1] Held on 17 December 1952, the event in question, which was broadcast live to South America, had marked the culmination of a decade-long history of cultural relations between Canada and Brazil, but not everyone agreed that this had been a sound investment of taxpayers' money.

The Royal Commission on National Development in the Arts, Letters, and Sciences had published its report less than two years earlier, and Désy had found in it plenty of arguments to support his most recent initiative. Launched on 8 April 1949, the commission had as its mandate to report on the significance and state of culture from coast to coast while making recommendations on how best to promote and support those "institutions which express national feeling, promote common understanding, and add to the variety and richness of Canadian life."[2] Through its proceedings, it gave voice to artists, administrators, producers, and patrons of the arts who put forward the argument that "high culture" was fundamental to the pursuit of nationhood and that it was therefore the best safeguard against both the tyranny of totalitarian ideologies and the "illiberal menace of mass culture."[3] This was for them a "moment of cultural consolidation," and so they seized the occasion by laying out "measures to further imprint a cultured national design" in accordance with their sense of place in the world.[4]

Désy saw in the Massey Commission a vindication of his earlier experiments in cultural diplomacy, as well as an opportunity to energize Canadian participation in the cultural Cold War, particularly since the report characterized the CBC-IS as the "most important agency" engaged in the projection of Canada abroad. Hence its recommendation that (a) "the International Service ... be continued and expanded with a view to increasing the knowledge and understanding of Canada abroad," and (b) that "every effort be made to use for this purpose as often as possible the service of Canadians eminent in various fields."[5] Quoting from the report, the ambassador turned administrator evoked the urgent need to enrich the country's cultural life and make it better known throughout the world. To do so, it was incumbent on Canada to listen and reciprocate in its relationships with other nations. As far as Désy was concerned, there was no better way to accumulate international goodwill.[6] As he was quick to point out, the commissioners did emphasize that the "promotion of a knowledge of Canada abroad is not a luxury but an obligation," and that Canadians had neglected their "distant neighbours, taking little and giving less." Not only that, they argued that the use of culture in international relations was an effective means of countering "false propaganda" by hostile regimes.[7]

The Villa-Lobos concert, coming as it did during the Cold War and amid a period of heightened cultural nationalism, exposed the limits of the metaphors and technologies deployed to project Canada abroad. While commentators distinguished between psychological warfare (the dissemination of information for propaganda purposes) and broadcasting (the dissemination of ostensibly apolitical, objective information), the international service performed a less apparent, but equally crucial, third role – namely, that of an instrument for nation branding.[8] From the mid-1940s onward, the CBC-IS used shortwave transmissions to tell stories about Canadians and the place they occupied, or thought they ought to occupy, in the world. Its mastery of radio technology and enterprising use of transcription records, combined with the staging of sophisticated mediated events, also put Canadian *savoir faire* and economic power on display while facilitating the transnational circulation of sounds and musicians, all of which were meant to shape perceptions of the country. In this context, the elaborate 1952 broadcast concert was about the projection of Canadian identity more than Brazilian music. But the negative reviews it received and the controversy over costs that surrounded it revealed that Canadians had yet to reach a consensus on what to project (and how) after a decade of performances on Brazilian stages.[9]

## RADIO DIPLOMACY

Canada entered the international broadcasting arena as a novice player in 1945.[10] The first breakthroughs in shortwave transmissions occurred decades earlier when radio amateurs in the United States and Great Britain established transatlantic communication with one another. From the First World War onward, radio technology developed at a rapid pace with commercial broadcasters competing for limited space on the airwaves, which they also shared with military organizations. Believing that high-powered, low-frequency long-wave transmissions held greater potential, regulators forced amateurs into the upper portion of the radio spectrum to prevent them from creating interference in military and commercial communication. Radio amateurs were not discouraged by this. They subsequently experimented successfully across long distances, using high frequencies that bounced off the ionosphere over thousands of kilometres, to the great surprise of observers who had yet to fully understand the physics of radio communication in the early 1920s.[11]

The commercial potential of shortwave radio may not have been apparent at the time, but imperial governments were quick to realize that long-distance communication could serve to link together their colonial holdings. At the turn of the 1930s, the British, the French, the Belgians, and the Dutch began experimenting with shortwave broadcasts aimed at their colonies.[12] As for the Soviet Union, it turned to broadcasting to convey the meaning and promises of the communist revolution to the world. Established in 1929, its Radio Moscow pioneered the use of airwaves for propaganda purposes. Other nations, most notably Germany and Italy, followed suit with greater vigour and belligerence as the clouds of war rolled over Europe in the late 1930s.[13] Canadians had much catching up to do, and time was short.[14]

Although Great Britain was ahead of the curve, it was still a reluctant participant in the propaganda contest that was unfolding on the airwaves. Its first official foray into the world of shortwave communication occurred in 1926 when the Marconi Company, in conjunction with the British Post Office, established an imperial radio network that reached across the ocean to Canada. The following year, the network expanded to include Australia, South Africa, and India. In the 1930s, the British extended their reach beyond the Commonwealth in an effort to maintain their influence throughout the world. The competition was fierce, with Germany and Italy using the airwaves to disseminate anti-British propaganda in multiple languages. The British Broadcasting Corporation Overseas Service (BBC-OS) rose to the challenge. By the 1940s, it was transmitting content in forty-five languages to counter disinformation, maintain alliance relationships, discredit Axis propaganda, and shape public opinion in other countries through ostensibly impartial news.[15]

In the United States, radio amateurs, commercial broadcasters, and the State Department found ways to coexist, even co-operate, in the upper portion of the radio spectrum. Joint private-public approaches to economic and cultural expansion in South America helped consolidate US-American "hegemony in hemispheric communications" during the Good Neighbor era.[16] In the 1940s, Nelson Rockefeller's OCIAA joined the fold with its radio division, whose task it was to amplify transmissions throughout the region, analyze Axis propaganda, and create engaging content for audiences south of the Rio Grande.[17] The State Department pursued its incursion into the realm of international broadcasting with the launch, in February of 1942, of a station that would soon become known as the Voice of America.[18] Brazil was one of the main targets of these efforts, because of its economic and strategic importance for hemispheric stability and defence. US-American priorities and concerns were communicated in large part through the medium of radio, a process facilitated by the fact that Getúlio Vargas welcomed co-operation in the field of communications as part of his bargaining strategies with major Western powers.

When it came to radio, Brazilians were engaged, practical, and purposeful. In 1922, they celebrated a century of independence with a world expo that attracted participants from fourteen countries, including Belgium, France, England, Portugal, and the United States. The festivities began with a special broadcast, a national first, from atop Corcovado Mountain. The event was a perfect display of Brazilian prowess, one that reinforced the image of economic, political, and cultural progress that the Brazilian government wished to foreground during its Exposição Internacional do Centenário da Independência (Independence Centenary International Exposition). The Westinghouse Electric and Manufacturing Company – with some assistance from Canada's the Light – helped the country enter the age of radio in a spectacular way on that occasion.[19]

Following Vargas's rise to power in 1930, broadcasting in Brazil went through a rapid phase of expansion that was carefully scripted through regulatory mechanisms, state censorship, and adroit negotiations with various North American organizations. For example, the DIP demonstrated pragmatism when it opted to discuss broadcasting opportunities with Columbia Broadcasting System executives.[20] By allowing US-American commercial broadcasters to develop and maintain relations with affiliate stations in Brazil, Vargas permitted an influx of expertise and equipment that would greatly enhance the Estado Novo's own broadcasting capabilities.[21] Radio helped unite a dispersed population, a large portion of which was illiterate, around the regime's nation-building project. The MES participated actively in these efforts using its own station, Rádio MES, to deploy a range of education programming and to disseminate musical works that conveyed the spirit of ***Brasilidade***.[22]

The Vargas regime then turned its attention to international broadcasting. Having acquired the popular Rádio Nacional, it wished to direct some of its programming outward in hopes of seducing foreign audiences with a positive image of Brazil.[23] On 31 December 1942, Rádio Nacional beamed its content out into the world for the first time, a feat celebrated as a "victorious initiative."[24] Its inaugural broadcast revealed Brazilians' confidence and pride in their national musical culture. It also provided an indication of the countries and regions that Vargas and the Itamaraty considered priorities: the trilingual, four-part program was aimed at Latin America, Portugal, England, and the United States. Scheduled from 11:00 p.m. to midnight, the North American transmission focused exclusively on music except for a brief introduction by US-American ambassador Jefferson Caffery.[25] It is likely that the signal travelled north of the forty-ninth parallel, although few people would have been listening at that time of day in this early phase of Canada's rapprochement with Brazil.

## THE CBC-IS

It took another two years for the CBC-IS to launch its own Voice of Canada and join the international broadcasters club. Established in 1936 through an act of Parliament, the CBC concerned itself exclusively with the domestic stage in the years leading up to the Second World War. The projection of Canada abroad was not in the plans of the Crown corporation, even though Canadians had been allocated shortwave frequencies at the 1932 International Telecommunications Conference. Yet voices within both the CBC and External Affairs soon rose to advocate for a broader mandate for the institution.[26] First, it was imperative that Canada "occupy" the frequencies assigned to it by the international community to prevent other countries from taking them over. Failure to do so would result in Canadians being "shut out of the field."[27] Second, national prestige was at stake since the country was lagging behind others in the competition taking place on radio airwaves.[28] Canada needed to "take her rightful place among the nations of the world" to ensure continuous economic growth.[29] Canadians needed to be heard and noticed if they wanted to enhance and develop trade relations. Projecting an appealing and esteemed image would help them accumulate goodwill and occupy a position of pre-eminence as the world prepared for life after war. There were internal benefits as well, and they ranged from partaking in program exchanges to extending the reach of French-language broadcasts to "contribute to a better understanding between the two mother races in Canada."[30]

Wartime exigencies evidently factored into these debates. Some commentators argued that international broadcasting could help Canada keep its soldiers and allies informed about its national war efforts. It could also complement the broadcasts deployed by the United States and Great Britain to discredit Axis propaganda. Canada's presence on the airwaves was needed to ensure uninterrupted transmissions in the event that BBC-OS stations were damaged. This would permit the relaying of critical information to combatants at the front and the resistance in occupied territories.[31] Canadians of European origins would have a role to play in inviting their former compatriots to embrace "peace and understanding" over war.[32] Canadians were well equipped to disseminate such a message argued CBC assistant manager Augustin Frigon: "The experience of our country in reconciling differences of race and religion and our unique background of a joint cultural heritage constitute a message which can unobtrusively and profitably be made available in the world's present troubled state and in the period of reconstruction, when peace has been restored."[33] These arguments suggest that psychological warfare on the airwaves was about defeating belligerent foes and defending liberal democracy as much as it was about branding Canada and accumulating goodwill to help the country get noticed as a key player in the North Atlantic triangle.

Ottawa finally decided to move ahead with the project after carefully considering the briefs presented to the House of Commons Standing Committee on Radio Broadcasting in 1938, 1939, and 1942. On 18 September 1942, the Privy Council recommended that immediate actions be taken to establish "two 50 kW short wave transmitters, three directional antennas and associated apparatus" in Sackville, New Brunswick.[34] Already occupied by a CBC-owned radio station, the site was ideal because it was at a safe distance from the disruptive electromagnetic field generated by the magnetic pole and it offered "high ground conductivity for the antenna arrays," which needed to reach Europe, Africa, and South America.[35] As per the directives outlined in Order-in-Council 8168, the CBC was put in charge of the international service, with operational funds coming from direct parliamentary grants and External Affairs acting as a consultant on programming content.

One of the first questions that needed answering was one of emphasis: Which regions should Canada prioritize? Unable to predict how much longer the conflict would last, External Affairs and CBC-IS representatives decided to plan for both wartime and postwar needs, prioritizing first the United Kingdom and Commonwealth, followed (in order of importance) by South America, France, China and the Far East, and Russia and Central Europe.[36] Delays in network construction, and the growing realization that peace was still a distant prospect, resulted in wartime imperatives being placed squarely ahead of postwar considerations. On 8 March 1944, Undersecretary of State for External Affairs Norman A. Robertson sent Frigon a revised priority list with the United Kingdom at the top followed by the whole of Europe. In this new hierarchy, South America slipped to sixth place.[37] Finally, on 25 February 1945, Prime Minister William Lyon Mackenzie King officially inaugurated the CBC-IS when he announced on air that "Tonight ... Canada enters the world radio arena."[38]

The advent of the Cold War brought about another shuffling of priorities. The CBC-IS initially beamed its broadcasts in French, English, and German. It soon added programming in Dutch, Slovak,

Swedish, Norwegian, Danish, Spanish, Portuguese, and Italian. By 1952, tensions between the Eastern and the Western Blocs had reached such proportions that the CBC-IS launched Russian and Ukrainian programs.[39] In this context, the term "psychological warfare" was often used synonymously with "political warfare," and it referred to the dissemination of content to shape – to one's advantage – public opinions and attitudes in other countries.[40] The CBC-IS was entering its third phase after just ten years of existence: it initially sent messages of support to Canadian forces in war-torn Europe, and then concentrated resources on promoting postwar "peaceful international collaboration," but recent developments now required that it take part in the "war of ideas" against communism.[41]

Canada's entry into the world radio arena came with its share of complications, which the Cold War exacerbated. First, the expansion of services – from the lengthening of the broadcast schedule to the creation of programs in an increasing number of languages – created budget headaches in the immediate postwar years since the funds set aside for peacetime transmissions were insufficient. This led CBC-IS representatives to seek additional grants by highlighting the "comparative cheapness and effectiveness of radio as a potent weapon in the arsenal of defence."[42] They were, in other words, making the argument that shortwave radio was an economical way to fight the Cold War against the Eastern Bloc. Another source of concern was the need for more effective coordination. Which of the two, External Affairs or the CBC-IS, had the authority to determine who the primary targeted audiences were and what was appropriate content for a specific situation?[43] Questions regarding the policy aspects of international broadcasting and the effectiveness of the service in accomplishing its stated goals urgently needed to be answered. Between 1942 and 1951, liaison between the CBC-IS and External Affairs was imperfect, with the two experimenting with different approaches, all of which "met with varying degrees of success."[44]

This situation exposed the broadcaster to various attacks, the most serious being that it had been infiltrated by communists whose "pinkish influence" was damaging Canada's image overseas.[45] In January and October of 1951, Robert Keyserlingk of the Catholic daily *The Ensign* attacked the CBC-IS in print and on the air, claiming that the organization's neutral tone could mislead countries behind the Iron Curtain into thinking that Canada was sympathetic to their cause. The broadcaster, he claimed, was guilty of adopting an "anti-anti-communist slant."[46] However unfounded or sordid the accusation, it caused considerable anxiety within the institution in the aftermath of the red scare that had plagued the NFB just a few years earlier.[47]

In 1945, Igor Gouzenko, a cipher clerk at the Soviet Union's embassy in Ottawa, defected with documents that revealed the existence of Soviet spy rings at the heart of the Canadian state, plunging Canada into the escalating Cold War confrontation between the communist Soviet Union and the US-led Western democracies. As a climate of national insecurity gripped the country, the NFB and its progressive workforce became a target of the Royal Canadian Mounted Police. Caught in the bullseye of a royal commission investigating leaks of confidential information, the institution fell prey to an anti-communist witch hunt that resulted in substantial purges despite little to no evidence of subversive activities taking place within its walls.[48] In this context, External Affairs could not afford to dismiss *The Ensign*'s accusations without first doing some housecleaning at the CBC-IS.

Désy's appointment to the newly created position of director general constituted an effort on the part of External Affairs to deal with this crisis in direction, authority, and trust among the international service.[49] The former ambassador had some relevant experience in the broadcasting policy field. In 1927, he had joined colleagues from Ottawa at a meeting held in the United States to discuss the allocation of wavelengths in North America.[50] He had also helped extend the reach of the CBC-IS's southbound transmissions in Brazil when they began in 1945. Told that he would maintain his rank and status at External Affairs while "on loan" to the broadcaster, Désy served for eighteen months (from 1 January 1952 to 15 July of the following year).[51] During this period, he undertook a major overhaul of the organization by bringing what previously were relatively autonomous language sections under the control of an expansive administrative structure. He then recruited Yvon Beaulne, a foreign service officer who had worked with him in Italy, to handle the circulation of classified materials back and forth between Ottawa and the CBC-IS's offices in Montreal. He also helped improve communication with External Affairs through the creation of a Political Coordination Unit that had "as its primary responsibility the provision of policy guidance."[52] These changes allowed him to fix the CBC-IS's image problem without having to fire or demote anyone.[53]

But while bringing administrative order to the international service, Désy was also emboldened by the Massey Commission's report and seized the opportunity to advance his own dearest passions by ensuring that more attention was lavished on music and the coverage of South America. However, the heavy hand with which he approached his job, combined with External Affairs' intrusiveness into the everyday operations of the broadcaster, alienated many people within the organization. According to the institutional biographers of the CBC-IS, Désy's ostentatious, tactless, and condescending managerial style as director general demoralized his employees.[54] Similarly, they claimed that his elitist posture translated into grandiloquent, self-serving undertakings that were difficult to reconcile with Ottawa's foreign policy goals. Accused of being a "big spender" who "never lost sight of his own personal interests," Désy was especially tarnished by the 1952 Villa-Lobos concert, which his critics dismissed as a "pet project" emblematic of his wasteful "flair for the extravagant."[55] Yet, while an easy target, this focus on Désy's personality does not explain fully the ambitious nature of Canada's postwar radio diplomacy and Brazil's place in it.

## SOUTHBOUND TRANSMISSIONS

The cultural Cold War unfolding on the airwaves in Europe, and the need to defend the CBC-IS against accusations that it was soft on communism, mobilized much of the organization's resources at the turn of the 1950s. South America nonetheless remained on everyone's radar, in accordance with the broadcaster's mandate. The order-in-council to which the CBC-IS owed its existence had outlined that southbound transmissions would help promote internationalism while projecting an engaging image of Canada to complement diplomatic relations in countries such as Brazil, Chile, and Argentina.[56] Parliamentary debates echoed those views since Axis propaganda threatened to undermine Canadians' emerging economic ties in the region.[57] On 26 April 1944, Assistant Undersecretary of State Hugh L. Keenleyside sought to reassure Canada's ambassadors in Rio de Janeiro, Santiago, and Buenos Aires that services would be in operation by January of the next year despite the fact that the continent was slipping down the list of priorities.[58] The aggressive timeline turned out to be the result of wishful thinking. Experimental broadcasts did, however, begin on 12 August 1945.[59]

In Brazil at the time, Désy immediately understood that shortwave transmissions would make a wonderful addition to his cultural diplomacy arsenal.[60] "Word has been received that the new short-wave programs beamed to Latin America ... come in loud and clear," announced the CBC-IS one week after the launch of the experimental broadcast.[61] Benjamin Rogers, chargé d'affaires at the Rio de Janeiro embassy, was among those who volunteered constructive criticism. "I think particular attention should be paid to the musical tastes of Brazilians and Latin Americans in general," he wrote. "The competition with American, British, French, Spanish, Argentine, and other short wave broadcasts is going to be intense and unless the C.B.C. programmes are as good or better," Rogers continued, "the great expense in building this station will be lost. People are only going to listen to the best."[62] An ally of Désy since the opening of the legation in 1941, he was rarely in the limelight. But his part in the making of Canada's cultural diplomacy was no less consequential because of that. Having taken advantage of Brazil's radio infrastructure in the past, he and Désy arranged for domestic broadcasters to record and replay CBC-IS programs to reach larger sections of the population. They were thus able to further disseminate the Voice of Canada, which aired for thirty minutes every Sunday evening at 9:00 p.m.[63]

The CBC-IS arrived in Brazil at a pivotal moment in the country's history. It was a period characterized by growing instability, factionalism, and economic hardship. The Fourth Brazilian Republic saw a return of the Partido Comunista do Brasil, which collected 10 per cent of the popular vote in the 1945 general election that saw Eurico Gaspar Dutra come ahead of other candidates, thanks in part to the endorsement he received from Vargas. Brazil had enriched itself somewhat during the Second World War, but its fortunes decreased significantly in the immediate postwar years. Its foreign reserves depleted, the government resorted to promoting staple exports rather than continuing the push to industrialize and modernize the economy. Faced with stagnating, even decreasing, standards of living, workers turned an increasingly sympathetic ear to left-leaning organizations until President Dutra, with the encouragement of the United States, moved to crack down on the Communists and terminate diplomatic relations with the Soviet Union. As Robert M. Levine explains in his history of Brazil, the former general's "somber presidential style subdued the heated political atmosphere that had been generated at the end of Vargas's tenure."[64] Yet it also extended "the shadow of the Estado Nôvo ... over a newly democratic Brazil."[65]

When he arrived at the CBC-IS in 1952, then, Désy found himself looking at a Brazil that was both strangely familiar and confoundingly different from the one he had previously known, especially since Vargas had returned to power, succeeding Dutra as a duly elected leader. The former dictator had defeated a divided opposition during the general election of 1950 through his forceful use of populist rhetoric and his skillful manipulation of the recently founded Partido Trabalhista Brasileiro (Brazilian Labour Party). His nationalist and interventionist platform worried both champions of liberal internationalism and hardened anti-communist nationalists in Brazil. Unable to revert to presidential decrees, as he had done in the past, Vargas was finding it difficult to overcome congressional opposition to unite the country and reverse its economic decline in the early 1950s.[66]

The man who replaced Désy in Brazil, James Scott MacDonald, was not one to pursue bold initiatives. External Affairs initially struggled "to find a suitably qualified person ... who would be willing or able to accept the appointment at short notice."[67] The post had been vacant for several months and time was of the essence since the governor general of Canada, Harold Alexander, 1st Earl Alexander of Tunis, was due to visit Brazil in June of 1948. Rogers, who had remained in Rio de Janeiro, was becoming impatient, and he felt that the Itamaraty was bound to take offence at the delay. With External Affairs since 1927, MacDonald held the title of high commissioner in Newfoundland when he was approached for the post. He had no particular interest in going to Brazil, but he accepted the assignment, in part, because Newfoundlanders were about to vote on whether or not to join Confederation. All involved believed that it was better for Canada's representative to leave the island while the whole process played itself out. By sending him to Brazil, Ottawa could make two friends with one gift.[68]

Possibly taking cues from his chargé d'affaires, the new ambassador seemed disposed to learn from Brazilians on matters of cultural diplomacy. He was particularly interested in the DCI, because the problems that it tackled were similar to those faced by Canadians: "Both of us fall in the group of countries which have neither a colourful, ancient civilization ... nor yet a modern culture like that of the United Kingdom, the United States or France whose literature, press, radio, films, etc., are distributed on such an extensive scale by ordinary commercial agencies that they practically monopolize interest and rule out effective competition from official cultural agencies operating with meagre funds."[69] In Brazil for only two years, however, MacDonald did not have the will to turn curiosity into action. External Affairs did not mind, and they made that clear by telling him that he did not need to follow his predecessor's methods.[70]

It took Francisco Matarazzo Sobrinho to jolt MacDonald into action. In the summer of 1950, the president of São Paulo's Museu de Arte Moderna (Museum of Modern Art) contacted the embassy to secure Canadian participation in the first edition of the Bienal Internacional de Arte (International Art Biennial), which was scheduled to take place in March of the following year. Bringing the world to his city by hosting an international event was an expedient and cost-effective way for Sobrinho to project a positive and engaging image of Brazil. Harry Orr McCurry, director of the NGC, was uninterested: the institution had other commitments and there was too little time to prepare an adequate selection of works. News that the event had been postponed, coupled with continued lobbying by the biennial's organizers, compelled MacDonald and C.J. Van Tighem, Canadian consul in São Paulo, to nudge McCurry into finding a solution. In the end, he agreed to send a "small token exhibition" comprised of works from twenty-one painters: from Lionel LeMoine Fitzerald to Marian Dale Scott and Jacques de Tonnancour, to name but a few.[71]

Canadians' half-hearted contribution to the biennial was a repeat of an earlier scenario. In the winter of 1950, the embassy received an invitation to submit a selection of works for inclusion in an exhibition sponsored by the Conselho Nacional de Proteção aos Índios (National Council for the Protection of Indians). The initiative caught MacDonald's attention, and he convinced Ottawa's National Museum to send artifacts to the first and the second editions of the council's exhibition (19–26 April 1950 and 19–26 April 1951). The items – a pair of moccasins, a beaded bag, a tobacco pouch, and a soapstone cooking pot, among others – were "attractively displayed" both years, but they were lacking in contextual information. To make matters worse, the speech that Ottawa prepared for the 1951 exhibition was but an excerpt from a 1930 edition of *The Cambridge History of the British Empire*, which offered "an unwholesome picture of how Canadian Indians lived 20 or better still 50 years ago."[72] Such negligence was in keeping with the practice of relegating Indigenous peoples to the past to better erase their presence in the present. MacDonald was nonetheless dismayed by the incompetence, and it discouraged him from doing more on the cultural diplomacy front.[73]

Aside from these tepid efforts, the embassy's priority was to emphasize Canadian autonomy in international affairs, something that the visit of the 1st Earl Alexander of Tunis threatened to undermine. Brazilian authorities had invited him in part because the Força Expedicionária Brasileira had fought under his command during the Second World War. MacDonald had been in the country for only twelve days when his distinguished guest arrived on 11 June. The governor general's week-long stay included the usual social functions and ceremonies attended by members of the Canadian and British communities. Of significance was a special event during which he presented British war decorations to the soldiers who had served in the Mediterranean theatre. Since the British embassy in Rio de Janeiro was keen to capitalize on the visit, Rogers and MacDonald had to carefully script the entire trip so that it was branded primarily as a Canadian-Brazilian affair.[74]

MacDonald hosted another important visitor during his short tenure in the country: Hugh W. Morrison, supervisor of the CBC-IS's Latin American Section. In his post since 1 April 1948, he hoped to expand services to the region.[75] Seeking to understand the radio landscape there, he visited nine countries and thirteen cities in November and December of 1950. His itinerary included a short stop in São Paulo (5–10 December) and a one-week stay in Rio de Janeiro (10–17 December). The CBC-IS's daily programming schedule for Brazil included a range of content (general continuity, news bulletin, commentaries and news talks, expository talks, music, the answering of audience mail, and feature programs) that elicited enthusiastic responses.[76] Audience mail received from South America tripled between 1948 and 1950: from 1,842 to 5,472 letters, with 40 per cent of them coming from Brazil.[77] Most of these were favourable, and they highlighted the clarity of the transmissions, the quality of the content, and the positive image of Canada that the CBC-IS was helping disseminate. One fervent listener confided, "Two languages, but one heart – that is the Canadian people! The way you attract your listeners with your programs is winning more and more new friends and admirers for Canada."[78]

The broadcaster badly needed positive feedback like this to deal with the crisis in which it was embroiled at the turn of the 1950s.[79] Couching his discussion of broadcasting in the language of the Cold War, Morrison argued in his post-trip report that Canada had a role to play on the airwaves, even if only as a junior partner to the United

States and Great Britain in the war of ideas. Keeping in mind the need for ammunition to deal with accusations that the CBC-IS was soft on communism, Morrison emphasized that trade and "considerations of human brotherhood" are but two reasons why broadcasts should be maintained at their current level, if not increased. A more important incentive, he explained at a luncheon of the Canadian Inter-American Association, was "to preserve our inherited system of government by consent of the governed, by showing our friendly neighbors that we are reasonably happy and healthy under such a system and that we have no aggressive designs upon their territory or fanatical plan to convert them to our individual national way, willy-nilly."[80] According to him, South America was a "politically combustible area" that could very well "become another Far East" since "communism and its agents" were everywhere, "lying in wait."[81]

Morrison was overstating his case, at least with regard to Brazil, where anti-communism had become de facto state policy. As a matter of fact, reports coming out of the embassy in Rio de Janeiro suggest that ultranationalism and authoritarianism were a bigger threat to the country's democratic institutions than communism.[82] Morrison may have lacked a proper understanding of the politico-cultural landscape in Brazil, but he nonetheless collected ample evidence to demonstrate that the CBC-IS had a role to play on the airwaves. His discussion of the BBC-OS and Voice of America broadcasts reflected his faith in Canada's middle power capabilities, which he sought to validate through a comparative analysis of shortwave transmissions aimed at Brazil. Canadian broadcasts could be heard daily for thirty minutes on two frequencies, he explained. Voice of America transmissions followed a similar schedule using four frequencies. As for the BBC-OS, it disseminated its hours-long programs using three frequencies. Morrison remarked that the CBC-IS's counterparts thus had a greater presence on the airwaves, which explained why they were "easier" to find even though the discrepancy in programming times and frequencies did not mean that their transmissions were "better." Morrison proudly noted that Canada received more letters from Brazil than the United States did: "Remembering that we are heavily outnumbered in frequencies this is no small achievement."[83] That said, he nurtured no illusions that Canadians could compete with their southern neighbour. Yet, he insisted that the role of CBC-IS was likely to grow since the BBC-OS and the Voice of America were increasingly focusing their attention on Cold War Europe.[84]

Morrison was not alone in making these points. Internal correspondence from 1951 stressed that the maintenance of southbound shortwave transmissions was crucial: "While the Latin America area cannot be considered to have the same *primary* political importance as Europe, it has its own urgency which cannot be ignored without risk."[85] The overall broadcast schedule for 1952 suggests that such concerns were taken seriously. It is true that total weekly broadcast hours to Europe (fifty-nine hours and fifty minutes) were more than those allocated to South America (twenty-nine hours and ten minutes), but this was also the result of needing to reach a more diverse population using a greater number of languages – eleven for Europe and four for Central and South America. In fact, weekly Portuguese-language programming totalled eight hours and ten minutes, which surpassed any other language service aimed at Europe except for French (also eight hours and ten minutes), English (eight hours and forty-five minutes), and Czech (nine hours and forty-five minutes).[86]

Music was a key component of the CBC-IS's strategy in South America due to its ostensibly apolitical and inconspicuous nature. At the turn of the 1950s, it represented approximately 38 per cent of the content beamed toward Brazil compared to 31 per cent for the rest of South America. What most differentiated the broadcasts in Portuguese from those in Spanish was the exclusive focus on "serious music" and folk songs. Jazz and other popular genres were notably absent from the schedule prepared for Brazilian audiences.[87] Morrison's musical choices were consistent with those championed by Désy. Observing that there was "more than a surfeit of popular music on local Latin American stations," and that he could well "imagine that shortwave listeners would seek relief," he argued for "continuance of serious and folk music" on the airwaves and through the mailing of transcription records.[88] Sound discs prepared specifically for distribution to overseas broadcasters, these records made it possible to reach larger publics while providing an easy solution to the fidelity issues that arose when transmitting music programs over long distances using shortwave bands. They were also economical since they could be reproduced and used repeatedly, unlike a live performance.

The CBC-IS thus fulfilled an important need when it launched its first series of transcription records in 1949. By December 1952, the Transcription Service had produced more than eighty albums featuring works by a variety of Canadian artists: among others, composers Ernest MacMillan and Claude Champagne, folk singers Alan Mills and Quatuor alouette, jazz pianist Oscar Peterson, as well as pop singers Gisele and Alys Robi.[89] Désy, however, believed that more could be done to use music to better align the CBC-IS's programming with the policy priorities of External Affairs when he reinvented himself as an international broadcaster.

## NORTHBOUND BRAZILIANS

The CBC-IS approached Brazilians with the assumption that their musical tastes were as sophisticated and informed as those of Canadians, particularly when it came to popular sounds coming through the Voice of America; and if they were not, they could at least be shaped in this image. The broadcaster's musical choices reflected the Canadian cultural elites' expectation that their South American counterparts would share their liberal humanist and "highbrow" nationalist ideals. In the context of the Cold War and Brazil's faltering return to democracy, such programming concealed normative undertones. It also betrayed Canadians' desire to validate their self-image as model international citizens and stalwarts of democracy worthy of emulation. On the one hand, this approach required Othering Brazilians who were at the receiving end of southbound transmissions. On the other, it called for fruitful exchanges with prominent individuals with whom Canada's cultural elites could identify. Villa-Lobos was a first-rate interlocutor in this regard due to his extensive experience as a cultural ambassador as well as his fearsome reputation on the world stage, where he confidently proclaimed his difference.[90] Moreover, he had taken a keen interest in Désy's early cultural diplomacy initiatives, whether it was to provide a venue for Quatuor alouette at the MES or helping Champagne network with Brazilian colleagues. The ambassador had made sure to thank him personally before leaving his post for Italy.[91] He also intended to reciprocate at the first opportunity.

This was easier said than done. Part of the problem, some argued sardonically, was that Brazilians were lacking in effectiveness and efficiency. What was more difficult to recognize was that Canada was never a priority for Brazilian artists, who saw the United States as a more promising stage for career-building purposes. For many of them, travelling north of the forty-ninth parallel was either an afterthought or an opportunity to explore, but only once firmer plans had been established south of the border. This was the case with Arnaldo Estrella in 1943, and José Siqueira a few years later, both of whom travelled to Canada following invitations to perform in the United States.[92]

Villa-Lobos was an exception since he had taken great care to insert a few Canadian dates in his 1944–45 tour of the Americas, which the Itamaraty intended to support. He originally planned to spend two weeks in Canada performing four concerts. However, the tour did not include Canada in the end.[93] Exasperated by the missed opportunity, Désy later confided to MacMillan: "I do not understand why Brazilian artists go to Canada and the United States without making arrangements a long time in advance through the usual agencies."[94]

Notwithstanding these problems, Brazilian composers managed to have their works heard in Toronto and Montreal by exploiting the connections that they were making with Canadians. For instance, Villa-Lobos was encouraged to learn that Wilfrid Pelletier was disseminating his music after a short stint in Brazil in 1946. The two had met when the Metropolitan Opera visited Rio de Janeiro. There primarily to accompany his wife, singer Rose Bampton, Pelletier made the most of the trip by familiarizing himself with his hosts' national musical culture and music education system. Back in Quebec, he used Villa-Lobos's reputation as a patriotic "artist-worker" to nudge Premier Maurice Duplessis into paying attention to the important work that composers and educators were doing in the province. "I was pleased to learn that you really were a music lover," he wrote, before explaining that he had purchased for him a record by "a Brazilian composer who does extraordinary work for the advancement of music in his country."[95]

Pelletier returned with scores too, not just records. On 22 and 23 October 1946, he premiered Villa-Lobos's "Bachiana brasileira no. 1" to great acclaim at Montreal's Plateau Hall. The two-night concert was organized under the patronage of Désy and Omer Côté, Hector Perrier's successor as provincial secretary. The program that the OCSM put together appealed to the audience's taste for the exotic by describing the composer's music as displaying "a certain primitive quality in keeping with one who was in his youth near to the jungles of the Amazon." At the same time, it provided reassurance that the music adhered to Western European norms: "In spite of his most natural leaning towards his native folk music, Villa-Lobos regards J.S. Bach as the one foundation on which the entire structure of music should rest."[96] The concerts were a critical success. To reviewers, "Bachiana brasileira no. 1" was an enthrallingly original yet comprehensible work, particularly when tamed and performed under the baton of one of their own.[97]

Pelletier was not alone in promoting Villa-Lobos in Canada. One of the Brazilian composer's chief supporters was the Montreal-born pianist Ellen Ballon. She was the only woman to travel alone to Brazil as a Canadian impromptu ambassador, and she did so mostly on her own initiative. The embassy appears to have provided some logistical support, although the evidence – or lack thereof – suggests that she was relegated to the margins of Désy's androcentric musically imagined Canadian-Brazilian community.[98] Born in 1898 of Russian parents, Ballon was a child prodigy who studied at the McGill Conservatory before continuing her training in New York. From there, she travelled throughout North America and then Europe. She settled in London, where she remained until the outbreak of the Second World War. Ballon met Villa-Lobos in the United States in 1945. Fascinated by his growing aura in the context of musical Pan-Americanism, and taking advantage of Canada's cultural rapprochement with Brazil, she astutely commissioned the composer to write a piano concerto, which he promptly accepted out of recognition of her talent. After agreeing to the terms of the project, Villa-Lobos wrote his "Concerto de piano e orquestra no. 1" and dedicated it to Ballon. He then arranged for the Itamaraty to invite her to premiere the work in Rio de Janeiro on 11 October 1946.[99]

The Canadian press enthusiastically framed the event within the context of Canadian-Brazilian cultural relations, even though it had not been orchestrated by the embassy. The *Montreal Daily Star* boastfully noted that Ballon, a "cosmopolite" who worked mostly "outside the Dominion," always kept her "identity as a Canadian."[100] This collaboration demonstrated the ability of non-state actors to advance their own agendas by interjecting themselves within interstate cultural relations. Villa-Lobos, of course, understood this very well, and he counted on Ballon to help promote his name in North America by premiering "Concerto de piano e orquestra no. 1" there.

Villa-Lobos's name was becoming familiar to music connoisseurs as a result of Pelletier's and Ballon's efforts. The Canadian premiere of "Concerto de piano e orquestra no. 1," on 28 October 1947, served as an important precedent for Villa-Lobos's 1952 concert at Plateau Hall. It was the first instance during which the many components of Canada's musical diplomacy coalesced to render more tangible the project of a musically imagined Canadian-Brazilian community.[101] Désiré Defauw, artistic director of the OCSM, held the baton while Ballon sat at the piano. The CBC-IS beamed the concert to South

America with Désy's encouragement.[102] P.W. Cook, Morrison's predecessor at the Latin American Section, had written to External Affairs to see if Prime Minister King would consider either attending the performance or recording a short message for shortwave radio listeners in Brazil. King politely declined for fear of setting a precedent and because he thought it "better to stay out of such things altogether."[103] Villa-Lobos could not be there either, although he did send a message to be relayed on the airwaves. In it, he stated that music was "one of the principal elements towards the conclusion of an understanding of peace between men." Ever cordial, he saluted "Canada for the splendid initiative of using music as an excellent vehicle for an understanding between the nations of the world."[104]

The *Montreal Gazette*'s Thomas Archer was profoundly impressed by the scope and sophistication of the event, noting that it was "a hearing that had definite significance and meaning" in the ways it brought audiences together around the shared experience of music. He was especially invigorated by Defauw and Ballon's performance, which made accessible the "luxuriant, generous music," as well as "extravagant" and "lusty tunes" of Villa-Lobos.[105] The composer's exoticism, his Otherness, was intriguing and inspiring, rather than unsettling or threatening, when framed in such a way by the CBC-IS in collaboration with its state and non-state partners. Brazilian diplomats were evidently pleased, especially since Canadians, independent of state sponsorship, were doing propaganda work for them.[106]

Everyone expected the 1952 concert to be received just as enthusiastically considering that it was the continuation of these earlier initiatives, albeit augmented with the presence of the maestro himself. It was also to be the culmination of a decade-long cultural rapprochement. Although the CBC-IS was in the midst of a crisis in 1952, Désy and the diplomatic corps in Brazil continued to believe that the institution had an important role to play in creating a climate conducive to healthy diplomatic and economic relations in South America. They saw music as central to these efforts. "It offers analogies with what we call the great concert of nature, the harmony of spheres and of worlds," Désy told a group of music students on the eve of Villa-Lobos's visit.[107]

On 14 December, the Brazilian composer settled in Montreal and addressed representatives from the media. A believer in the mediating potential of music, Villa-Lobos lent credence to Désy's vision of a musically imagined Canadian-Brazilian community when he described the former ambassador as an "honorary Brazilian."[108] During the press conference, he emphasized how important it was to negotiate the tension between patriotism and universalism using the principles of humanism. His music, he explained, was rooted in the lived experiences of the peoples of Brazil. Through the "transfiguration" of folklore, he could transform the nation – perhaps even humanity.[109] "I am the maestro of the world," he had said prior to leaving for Canada.[110] There was some arrogance in his posturing, but it did not offend journalists, who either thought that it was part of his exotic persona or believed that Canadians had it in themselves to perform a somewhat similar role. Expectations were high with many hoping that the concert would energize the city's cultural life. Pelletier and Ballon having set the stage, audiences were expected to find themselves at home in Villa-Lobos's musical universe.

Villa-Lobos's Canadian debut took place at Plateau Hall on 17 December. Organized under the auspices of the CBC-IS, the concert fell outside the regular programming of the OCSM. The Brazilian composer led the orchestra through four compositions: his own "Bachianas brasileiras no. 7" and "Choros no. 6" followed by "La voz de la calles de padro," a Chilean symphonic poem by Humberto Allende, and "Obertura criolla," by the Argentinian composer Ernesto Drangosch. Although Désy framed the event as a gesture of reciprocity, Villa-Lobos declined to perform his concerto for piano with Ballon and he seemed to have given no thought to performing Canadian works.[111] The event thus took the form of a South American evening with Villa-Lobos asserting his predominance over his continental counterparts. His own compositions took up most of the program and overshadowed – in terms of both colour and sophistication – the other two works, which critics dismissed as being of little significance.

Written in 1926, "Choros no. 6" was a sort of *Brasilophonia* in that it proposed a musical synthesis of Brazil's social and cultural history, from the jungles of the Amazon to the coasts of Bahia and the streets of Rio de Janeiro. "Bachianas brasileiras no. 7" borrowed from the Baroque period, and most notably from Johann Sebastian Bach's approach to counterpoint, to revisit and transfigure an array of Brazilian vernacular sounds. It was part of a series composed to champion *Brasilidade* during the Vargas era. Bach's music, Villa-Lobos claimed, was a music of mediation that could help bring "all races" together.[112] It had universal appeal, but its inventive use of counterpoint – the interweaving of apparently distinct melodic lines – gave it added resonance in Brazil, where it could be redeployed to imagine a mosaic-like national musical culture. There was an obvious tension, if not a paradox, between Villa-Lobos's universalism and his musical nationalism, noted *Le Devoir* in its negative review of the concert.[113]

The Montreal daily was not alone in expressing skepticism and disappointment in the days following the event. Music critics agreed that this had been a sub-par performance, although they stressed that the orchestra was not at fault. It is true that the musicians were unfamiliar with the works and that they did not have enough time to rehearse. But the sound at Plateau Hall was deficient and the stage could barely hold the group, which had to accommodate additional instruments as required by the scores.[114] The problem was the music itself. It was colourful and intricate, but it also lacked direction, restraint, and finesse. Its points of references were foreign and difficult to assimilate if not completely disorienting and incomprehensible. It was tiresome and overwhelming to the senses. The great length of Villa-Lobos's compositions "struck me as a sort of musical knitting in which he forgot the normal length of sleeves," observed the *Montreal Star*'s Eric McLean.[115] As for *Le Canada*'s Paul Roussel, he complained of leaving the concert hall with the same feeling that one gets after eating too copious a meal.[116] The only favourable review appeared in *La Patrie*. Its music critic had nurtured no illusions of a musically imagined Canadian-Brazilian community; the composer was an exotic Other and his concert had been nothing more than a voyage to a distant land.[117] Performed under Villa-Lobos's baton, "Choros no. 6" and "Bachianas brasileiras no. 7" sounded worlds apart from the other works that Canadians had discovered through Pelletier, Ballon, and Defauw.

The consensus, then, was that Villa-Lobos's difference posed problems. In trying to situate the Brazilian composer vis-à-vis his Canadian counterparts, the local press constructed a masculine Other that was more likely to favour emotionality over rationality, primitive ardour over enlightened self-command, and flamboyance over humility. In discussing the performance, music critics choose to favour certain biographical elements over others, such as Villa-Lobos's primitivist inclinations and his proximity to the musicians who populated Rio de Janeiro's nightlife or Minas Gerais's interior. Seeking to further emphasize the distance between the composer's musical world and the musical life of their city, they challenged his masculine identity by deploying emasculating gendered metaphors. It is revealing, indeed, that the critics for *Le Canada* and the *Montreal Star* referred to knitting and cooking in their respective reviews of the concert. Roussel pressed on by describing Villa-Lobos as a chatterbox while McLean lamented that this was "not a concert to ask a man to."[118]

Music critics were not alone in expressing discontent and questioning Désy's motive for wasting taxpayer money in this way.[119] The CBC-IS had its own dissenters. Patricia FitzGerald, music producer at the Transcription Service, did not hesitate to share her thoughts. She had already given her letter of resignation, so this was a "heart-breaking final assignment" for her.[120] FitzGerald insisted that the event had cost too much, both financially and from a musical nation-branding perspective. She believed that the venue had been a poor choice, one that had made it impossible to properly capture the performance. This was problematic since the CBC-IS broadcast the concert to Brazil and planned to make a transcription record with it. According to her, the orchestra's less-than-satisfactory performance and the poor quality of the recording threatened to damage Canada's image. Also, the event monopolized scarce resources that could have been used to produce three transcription records by local artists. More importantly, FitzGerald firmly opposed the idea of adding a foreign composer to her carefully curated catalogue. Désy might have been an "honorary Brazilian," but this did not justify placing Villa-Lobos alongside the dozens of Canadian artists whose music she had engraved on vinyl records.[121] Ultimately, the event exposed the fact that Canadians – whether they worked at the CBC-IS or not – had yet to agree on how best to conduct cultural diplomacy on the airwaves. Clearly, better lines of communication were needed between the various parties concerned.

Désy had some explaining to do once it became known that the whole venture cost close to $25,000. The House of Commons Standing Committee on External Affairs questioned him on the matter. The discussion that ensued demonstrated the extent to which Canadian-Brazilian cultural relations had been – in Désy's mind, at least – a conduit for the performance of middle power aspirations. In his responses, he insisted that Canada needed to show that it had the means and *savoir faire* to reciprocate if it wished to continue accumulating goodwill and to speak with authority on the international stage. Canadians could not afford to fail their test with Brazil, the only country with which they had a cultural agreement at the time, since people were listening. The former ambassador brushed aside concerns regarding the budget by pointing out that there was nothing abnormal about it since it included a broadcast to South America and the production of a transcription record. Brazilians, he noted, had invested far more money than Canadians in the two countries' cultural rapprochement, providing tremendous support to touring artists such as Quatuor alouette and MacMillan in addition to hosting various art exhibitions.

Quoting from the report of the Massey Commission, Désy emphasized that Canada's projection abroad was "an obligation" that also entailed reciprocation. Canadians' poor performance on that front was "particularly illustrated by our relations with Brazil," he argued. Reading again from the document, he said that "exchanges with other nations in the fields of the arts and letters will help us make our reasonable contribution to civilized life and since these exchanges move in both directions, we ourselves will benefit by what we receive." Canada, Désy insisted, had much to offer the world, and it was through interactions and comparisons with others that Canadians could assess both their strengths and the true value of their contributions.[122] The data he provided indicated that business executives, professionals, and workers were listening in greater numbers each year in Brazil; 300,000 synchronized their shortwave receivers daily while three times that number did so for special CBC-IS broadcasts such as those prepared for Dominion Day, Brazil's Independence Day, or visits by eminent artists like Villa Lobos.[123] Canada's image was at stake, he concluded dramatically.

With the crisis plaguing the CBC-IS in the early 1950s, Désy and his colleagues in broadcasting and government thought it pertinent to revert to Cold War tropes while also highlighting the economic benefits of southbound transmissions, even if these were unquantifiable. In their presentation to the committee, they further emphasized the middle power argument by depicting the CBC-IS as a junior, but also critical, partner in international broadcasting. With the Voice of America and the BBC-OS focusing on the "war of ideas" in Europe and the Middle East, the CBC-IS could expect to become the voice of liberal democracy and the English-speaking world in South America. Secretary of State for External Affairs Lester B. Pearson stressed that ongoing efforts and coordination with these Cold War allies were key to making sure that "what we do in this field dovetails into a general scheme of propaganda."[124] Désy reassured the committee members that his team was equipped to deal with the "Niagara of teletypes" coming from the United States and Great Britain. Morrison and others at the CBC-IS had argued for the continuance of southbound transmissions to counteract potential threats to the political and economic stability of the region. Désy emphasized that point and added that service to "friendly countries" like Brazil was a cost-effective means of maintaining control of Canada's image and those of its allies. He brashly added: "Listeners will be inclined to attach more importance to the Voice of Canada, because our country, although a world power, has no extra-territorial ambition except international peace and co-operation."[125] His intervention left many unswayed, including Gordon Graydon, a Progressive Conservative member of Parliament, who stated that such a costly initiative should not be repeated "without thinking deeply about it."[126]

The lukewarm response was due to the fact that Brazil did not rank high on Canadians' list of international priorities. It was also because the relationship was not delivering on the economic front. The 1937 exchange of notes had helped spark the two countries' rapprochement, paving the way to reciprocal diplomatic exchanges and a formal trade agreement in 1941. The war years had been lucrative, but things then went south as the Brazilian government reverted to import restrictions to deal with its postwar currency and debt problems. Canadian exports to Brazil duly dropped by 50 per cent between 1947 and 1950. At the turn of 1952, experts in Ottawa worried that the South American giant, dragged down by substantial arrears, would default on its payment obligations to Canada.[127] In this context, politicians like Graydon could not help but see the concert's $25,000 bill as both untimely and wasteful.

Brazilian diplomats in Canada, perplexed as they were by the whole affair, did not seem concerned about the economic question. Notwithstanding their willingness to engage with the trope of *métissage* deployed through Désy's cultural diplomacy, the fact is that they had long been aware of the tensions between French-speaking Canadians and their English-speaking counterparts, which precluded the emergence of a genuine national culture and impeded efforts to project a coherent image of the country overseas. Caio de Mello Franco, Brazil's minister in Ottawa, characterized the Canadian political arena as opposing an "ardent English mistrust" to a "proud French inferiority complex."[128] His colleague F.C. de Bittencourt Berenguer thought it was an accurate description, noting that the "incomprehension among Canadians of these two races" was "total" and that neither party seemed willing to work toward a common understanding.[129] Further reports corroborated this unequivocally bleak picture of Canada.[130]

Brazilian state actors demonstrated acuity in their analysis of the Canadian cultural landscape. Far from being credulous spectators, they complemented their discussion of the "racial origins" of Canada's population with a series of post–Massey Commission reports about the country's "cultural deficiency."[131] They commended the CBC for trying to connect communities from coast to coast through its broadcasts, dissemination of records, and organization of music festivals.[132] They doubted, however, that government bodies could spur a sustained "cultural recovery" that would see French and English Canadians come together around a shared national culture. Raul de Sá Barbosa, third secretary at the embassy, recognized the validity of the points raised by the commissioners in their introductory chapter on the forces of geography, whether it concerned the need to resist US-American cultural hegemony or the challenge of uniting a sparse population dispersed over an immense territory. Yet, the bigger challenge, in his mind, was addressing the tension between the two groups separated by language and history.[133] Their concentration in Quebec and Ontario made a nationwide culture unviable, which in turn perpetuated a colonial mentality whereby each group was set in its ways with little chance of reconciliation, let alone engagement with the diasporas that populated the rest of the country. Brazil, such reports suggested, could teach Canada a thing or two about national unity, racial democracy, and cultural autonomy.[134]

The members of Brazil's diplomatic corps could hardly have been surprised at the response to the Villa-Lobos concert. In fact, it validated the observations that they had made over the years, and it provided added justification for Villa-Lobos's visit to Canada. They perceptively observed that the event had been about projecting Canadian identity more than anything else. They thus saw the controversy surrounding it as an opportunity for Canadians to learn something about themselves. In his report, Barbosa built on earlier observations regarding French-English tensions and the inchoate state of Canadian culture to explain why critics failed to grasp the social and symbolic significance of the maestro's music. He began with a dismally depressing portrait of the country's musical landscape: from conservative orchestras playing unimaginative repertoires to inadequate government support for the arts, which limited opportunities and fostered ignorance. Returning to the negative reviews of the concert, he asked: "How do we explain this? How do we explain the lack of interest, this neglect, this deficiency?" A colonial mindset and national immaturity, he answered.

Ironically, the conclusion that he and his colleagues reached was that the Villa-Lobos concert had been a necessary cultural shock, a potentially transformative experience that could accelerate Canadians' passage to modernity and true nationhood.[135]

No doubt, this was not what the Massey Commission had in mind when it claimed that Canadians would benefit from the bi-directional flow of culture that the projection of Canada abroad encouraged. This also was not the outcome that Désy envisioned for an event meant to be remembered as the crowning achievement of his decade-long cultural diplomacy with Brazil. Although he succeeded in placing French Canada front and centre in the country's international image, he failed to substantiate the trope of *métissage* on which he relied to convince Brazilians and his compatriots that they all shared the ideal of racial democracy and *bonne entente*. That *Brasilidade* was a construct did not seem apparent to Canadian observers, who underestimated Brazilians' ability to dissect the stories directed at them via music and shortwave transmissions. Part of the problem was a lack of reciprocity, but it was also an insufficient disposition to listening, both of which betrayed Canadians' assumption that their interlocutors would be an easy public. Misplaced confidence and a self-serving approach to cultural relations partly explained the inability of the two nations to properly synchronize their activities. The CBC-IS simply amplified these unaligned signals. If a truly successful cultural diplomacy is one that finds widespread public support at home, then this latest episode in Canadian-Brazilian cultural relations was evidence that the battle would be an uphill affair.[136]

# Conclusion

The Conservative Party of Canada had to make a hasty decision about a pair of paintings by Quebec's Alfred Pellan in the summer of 2011. Commissioned by Jean Désy seven decades earlier, *Canada East* and *Canada West* had found their way back north following a refurnishing of the Rio de Janeiro embassy in 1960. There was nothing controversial about the two works, which had greeted visitors to the Lester B. Pearson Building, home of Foreign Affairs and International Trade Canada (known today as Global Affairs Canada), since it opened in 1973. The problem was that they did not quite reflect the image that then prime minister Stephen Harper wished to put forward on the eve of a visit by Prince William and his wife, Kate Middleton, the Duchess of Cambridge. The order to remove the paintings came from Minister John Baird amid a formidable "royal scramble" that saw officials and staffers erecting portraits of Queen Elizabeth across federal offices at home and abroad. The Lester B. Pearson Building carried considerable symbolism as the site where Conservatives were deploying their imperialist brand of nationalism. Hence the decision to give a facelift to its lobby by substituting a mounted picture of the monarch for Pellan's paintings. As if to further drive home its point, the government re-designated the structure where the works stood as the "Sovereign's Wall."[1]

Observers in Quebec were quick to denounce what they considered to be a political blunder. Notwithstanding the fact that Parliament was in recess, the Bloc Québécois was in no position to mount a resistance since the party had been nearly wiped off the political landscape during the May 2011 federal election. The provincial Parti Québécois (PQ) thus took it upon itself to denounce the Conservatives for seemingly manifesting contempt for Quebecers' contributions to Canadian culture. Yves-François Blanchet, the PQ's cultural critic at the time, led the charge. He conceded that Baird probably did not intend to insult, but that the removal nonetheless conveyed the message that his party was profoundly ignorant about Quebec.[2] The poet and essayist Paul Chamberland, who co-founded the left-nationalist magazine *Parti pris* in the 1960s, took to *Le Devoir* to decry this "hostile act," which he saw as a subtle display of power intended to silence and subjugate a creative people.[3] In the midst of the scandal, the PQ called for the repatriation of the paintings; in this, it had the support of the Musée national des beaux-arts du Québec, which looked forward to augmenting its collection with two largely unknown works by one of the province's main champions of modernist art. The rushed and negligent promotion of Anglophilia in Ottawa had fired up the nationalist agenda in Quebec. Baird remained unmoved. He would not comment on the whereabouts of the works, reasserting instead his promise to find them a suitable home.

What is particularly striking about this episode is the incongruity between the various readings of *Canada East* and *Canada West*. On the one hand, the PQ looked at the two works through a nationalist lens, assigning them meaning as symbols of Quebecers' self-affirmation in their passage to modernity and, in due course, self-governing nationhood. On the other hand, Baird and his colleagues approached the paintings somewhat carelessly, because of what they saw as their apparent lack of meaning. Although they returned Pellan's art to the Lester B. Pearson Building after winning the 2015 federal election, Justin Trudeau and his Liberals were no more *au fait* with the history and significance of the works. John Babcock, spokesperson for Global Affairs Canada, remarked prosaically that the reinstallation showed "continued interest in representing the best of Canada at every opportunity."[4] His intervention may have been well-intentioned, but it confirmed how little everyone knew about the paintings. Indeed, no one seemed cognizant of the fact that they had been part of a broader campaign aimed at situating Quebec, with Montreal as a noteworthy cultural centre in its own right, at the heart of the country's emerging international identity in South America, and more specifically Brazil, where Pellan's art hung with symbolic importance for nearly two decades.[5]

An unexpected opportunity to learn something about Canada's feeble approach to cultural diplomacy followed these events when

Trudeau's Liberals manifested their intention to rebrand Canada and retune its soft power on the world stage.[6] In the fall of 2017, the Standing Senate Committee on Foreign Affairs and International Trade launched a study on the "impact and utilization of Canadian culture and arts in Canadian foreign policy and diplomacy."[7] One of the experts that it invited was the University of Southern California scholar Nicholas J. Cull. In his 30 May 2018 testimony, Cull outlined four core approaches to cultural diplomacy. The first, "cultural gift," consists of selecting a valued cultural element that is representative of Canada and offering it to foreign audiences to solicit their attention and earn their admiration. "Cultural information" is the dissemination of lesser-known works and practices to provide depth and nuance to Canada's image in countries where there is either a lack of information or an abundance of misinformation. Third, "cultural capacity building" is the allocation of resources to help foreign audiences fulfill needs that they may have in the realm of culture. Finally, "cultural dialogue" aims to promote person-to-person interactions through various fora. Cull told the Senate committee that a "well-planned piece of cultural diplomacy can actually hit all four of these marks." He added, however, that a truly effective practice is one that is attuned to the needs and realities of others: "It isn't enough to think who Canada would like to be in the world."[8] Listening, he suggested, is the *sine qua non* of successful international cultural relations.

What Cull no doubt understood implicitly, even if he omitted to mention it explicitly in his testimony, is that it is also important to listen to the past. In this regard, the silences in political and scholarly discourse surrounding the pioneering efforts undertaken in Brazil are striking. This state of affairs is partly a function of the sustained attention accorded to Quebec in the aftermath of the 1961 opening of the Maison du Québec in Paris, a move that signalled the province's determination to develop an international identity in defiance of Ottawa's jurisdictional authority on matters of international relations.[9] The neglect of the precedents set in Brazil, a blind spot on the periphery of the North Atlantic world, was a result of External Affairs' persistent efforts to downplay, if not to bury outright, the 1944 bilateral cultural agreement so as to stay clear of constitutional difficulties and to avoid having other countries seek similar agreements. It is true that the department was trying to make do with scarce resources. But its staff also lacked imagination, as evidenced by how quickly they lost sight of what could be accomplished, domestically and internationally, by using culture as an instrument of diplomacy. Their inability to examine and reflect on the southbound projection of a bicultural image of Canada may have inadvertently lent credence to claims that Ottawa lacked the means and vision to adequately represent French Canadians overseas.[10]

External Affairs' early track record in the realm of cultural diplomacy was marred by missed opportunities and missed connections. L.A.D. Stephens's 1967 report on Canadian information and press activities abroad, published in the wake of the establishment of the Cultural Affairs Division, is a good example. The history of the information programs does not amount to "a brilliant record but [it] is marked by a great deal of conscientious endeavour by employees ... who worked with a bare minimum of government policy to guide them, in the face of frequent indifference from their own departmental leadership and almost always with a level of resources which permitted only threshold operations," conceded Stephens.[11] Ironically, his chronicle failed to even mention, let alone consider in any depth, Désy and his pioneering experiments in Brazil.[12] The oversight is difficult to explain. If the 1944 bilateral cultural agreement and its supporting documentation had been set aside by the mid-1960s, they certainly had not been lost. A revealing note appeared at the time in the margins of the minutes for the 1943 meeting during which the decision was made to go ahead with the exchange of notes with Brazil for fear, in part, that inaction would open the door to provinces entering into cultural agreements of their own on the basis of their jurisdictional powers. "So true now in 1965," the note reads.[13] Not only were textual records handy, but Yvon Beaulne, Canadian ambassador to Brazil in 1967 (incidentally, also Désy's right-hand man in Italy and at the CBC-IS), repeatedly brought up the question of cultural relations with his colleagues in Ottawa, who eventually replied that there was "little immediate prospect of increased activity in this area."[14]

While some officials were no doubt demoralized or, at best, less than inspired by such indifference, others, such as Désy, saw it as an opportunity to experiment under the radar. As a diplomat and a bureaucrat working from both inside and outside the power apparatus, he was single-minded in his devotion to the idea of culture as a force for mutual understanding between peoples and as an expression of national authenticity. Diplomatic work is a form of apostolate, he reflected while on his last assignment in Paris in 1954.[15] An ambitious French-speaking Catholic with intimate ties to Montreal's elite, he held a liberal humanist vision of Canadian culture and championed the image of Canada as a bicultural and bilingual federal state rooted in the "exceptional" histories of two white settler societies. His personal and social identities were relational as well as malleable, particularly when juxtaposed against those of his counterparts in Brazil. Like the artists that he worked with, many of whom were friends or family, he pursued several agendas simultaneously, modulating his performance of nation to make it correspond with his evolving sense of self.[16]

From this perspective, Désy was no different than the impromptu ambassadors who took part in Canada's hemispheric moment to advance their careers while helping to enrich cultural life at home. These included Pellan and the artistic couple of Jean Dansereau and Muriel Tannehill, whom Désy promoted together with Quatuor alouette, Jacques de Tonnancour, Claude Champagne, and Ernest MacMillan, but also Ellen Ballon and Wilfrid Pelletier, even Alys Robi, who acted independently, in distinct domestic and international settings, to adopt a posture of being-in-the-world. Similar in some respects and different in many others, each and every one of these individuals represent a point of entry in the constellation of mediations that connected Brazil to Canada and Quebec, or Rio de Janeiro to Toronto and Montreal, among other locales.

Looked at through the prism of this constellation, the above cast of protagonists reveals the extent to which Brazil served as a distant stage on which to mediate old and new connections to the idea of nation. It draws attention to the competing sets of values, attitudes, and perceptions with which Canadians approached the cultural Other, musical or otherwise, at home and abroad. Their self-conscious efforts to activate music and the visual arts as instruments of diplomacy were largely improvised affairs that foregrounded whiteness and revolved around the tropes of *latinité*, family, *métissage*, and Catholicism. Canada's official and impromptu ambassadors negotiated the tension between difference and sameness, as well as between nationalism and universalism, in their concomitant search for a national and an international identity. Mediated events added resonance to these efforts. They also amplified the dissonance between the discursive and symbolic connections deployed in Brazil and their reception in Canada.

Going back to what Cull told the Senate committee, it is obvious that the efforts undertaken in Brazil were too focused on "who Canada would like to be" and not enough on "listening to the foreign public, finding out what the world needs, and then thinking how Canada's interests intersect with this need."[17] It is also evident that Brazilian interlocutors were not treated entirely as equals if we consider, for instance, the response to Heitor Villa-Lobos's 1952 performance in Montreal. That said, the protagonists of this story did demonstrate remarkable goodwill and readiness, particularly in cases where they were able to hit the four marks that Cull identified. By way of illustration, Champagne's "Quadrilha brasileira" was a splendid "cultural gift." His performance of folk-infused works in Brazil conveyed "cultural information" about Quebec and its relationship to the rest of Canada. The courses that he taught at the Escola Nacional de Música constituted a form of "cultural capacity building," which doubled as "cultural dialogue" if we consider his extracurricular activities, notably as a guest of Villa-Lobos and José Siqueira at various events. De Tonnancour was no less resourceful in fulfilling his mission, whether it was through his pictorial interpretation of the beachfront neighbourhood of Botafogo, the public talks that he gave parallel to the *Arte Gráfica do Canadá* exhibition, or his multi-faceted contributions to official embassy events, such as the *Dîner canadien*.

If these efforts did not achieve widespread popular support at home, let alone in the staid East Block headquarters of External Affairs, it was because too few people were genuinely listening and willing to consider the possibilities for growth that a more inclusive and interconnected world entailed. To the extent that all international relations are intercultural relations, the reluctance to build on – and to learn from – the experiments described in *Distant Stage* was to some extent both a failure of diplomacy and a missed opportunity to advance the domestic agenda using an international stage.[18] As for those who kept an eye and an ear on the world, leaving behind creative works for us to critically examine and enjoy, they did provide ample evidence of the mediating potential of music and the visual arts, both locally and globally. The decision to be imaginative and to tune in (or not) is now ours to make.

# Notes

## INTRODUCTION

1 Unless otherwise specified, all references to seasons are from the perspective of North America.
2 Jean Désy to N. Robertson, 2 October 1942, MG26-J1, vol. 323, no. 274402, LAC; Memorandum for the Prime Minister, 19 October 1942, MG26-J1, vol. 323, no. 274403, LAC.
3 Renditions of these two works can be heard on the following recordings: André-Sébastien Savoie, *Pianofiesta*, n.d., Radio Canada International RCI 418, 33⅓ rpm LP, and Claude Champagne, *Anthologie de la musique canadienne*, 1982, Radio-Canada International ACM-30, 4 x 33⅓ rpm LPs. See also "A Rádio Nacional homenageia o Canadá," *A Noite*, 1 July 1943, 2.
4 The use of the term "French Canadian" here reflects common usage at the time. It centres exclusively on Quebec and refers predominantly to Catholic, French-speaking descendants of white settlers.
5 Exchange of Notes between Canada and Brazil Constituting an Agreement for the Promotion of Cultural Relations between the Two Countries, 24 May 1944, Treaty Series 1944, no. 15, 3.
6 Proper nouns will appear here in their original Portuguese (or in French, for those Quebec-based organizations and agencies with no official English names).
7 The cultural initiatives listed in these paragraphs are discussed at length in subsequent chapters of the book.
8 Hall, *Radio Canada International*, 89–93, and Siegel, *Radio Canada International*, 118–19.

9 Ellen Ballon to Heitor Villa-Lobos, 3 March 1945, Correspondencia – Ellen Ballon, MVL; Ellen Ballon to Heitor Villa-Lobos, 5 June 1946, Correspondencia – Ellen Ballon, MVL.

10 Jessica C.E. Gienow-Hecht's multi-volume series *Explorations in Culture and International History* offers several case studies that illustrate this point. Notable collections of essays in the series include Gienow-Hecht and Donfried, *Searching for a Cultural Diplomacy*, Gienow-Hecht and Schumacher, *Culture and International History*, and Gienow-Hecht, *Decentering America*.

11 Nye, *Soft Power*, x. Brazilians often refer to the citizens of the United States as *norte-americanos*, a demonym that does not quite capture the diversity of North America, sidelining Canada in the same way that "American" obfuscates the other peoples of the hemisphere. For that reason, "US-American," "Canadian," and "Brazilian" will be used throughout the book.

12 Frank A. Ninkovich and Emily S. Rosenberg pioneered the study of cultural diplomacy in the early 1980s by shedding light on the strategies developed by philanthropists, private entrepreneurs, and state actors to export US-American culture in the defence of the national interest during the first half of the twentieth century. Writing in a post-détente context, the two scholars provided the backstory to the state-centric propaganda campaigns deployed by the United States government to stop communism in its tracks. From then on, the Cold War came to occupy a central place in the historiography, as demonstrated by the abundance of works dealing with the importance of cultural productions (from abstract art to ballet and jazz, among other forms) in the ideological rivalry that pitted the United States against the Soviet Union. See Ninkovich, *The Diplomacy of Ideas*, and Rosenberg, *Spreading the American Dream*. See also Hart, *Empire of Ideas*; Arndt, *The First Resort of Kings*; Cull, *The Cold War and the United States Information Agency*; Caute, *The Dancer Defects*; Saunders, *Who Paid the Piper?*; Nilsen, *Projecting America*; Hixson, *Parting the Curtain*; Wagnleitner, *Coca-Colonization and the Cold War*; Scott-Smith and Krabbendam, *The Cultural Cold War in Western Europe*; Krenn, *Fall-Out Shelters for the Human Spirit*; Falk, *Upstaging the Cold War*; Osgood, *Total Cold War*; Barnhisel, *Cold War Modernists*; Davenport, *Jazz Diplomacy*; Eschen, *Satchmo Blows Up the World*; Poiger, *Jazz, Rock, and Rebels*; and Carr, "Diplomatic Notes."

13 Villanueva Rivas, "Theorizing Cultural Diplomacy All the Way Down," 691. See also Iriye, "Culture and International History"; Sevin, Metzgar, and Hayden, "The Scholarship of Public Diplomacy"; Ayhan, "The

Boundaries of Public Diplomacy and Nonstate actors"; and Reus-Smit, *On Cultural Diversity*.

14 Nicholas J. Cull, cited in Standing Senate Committee on Foreign Affairs and International Trade, *Proceedings*.

15 Cull, "Public Diplomacy," 34.

16 Hall, "Cultural Studies," 527.

17 Cooper, "Canadian Cultural Diplomacy," 6.

18 The doctrine found its clearest expression in a 1965 speech given by Paul Gérin Lajoie, the nèo-nationalist deputy premier. For a detailed and nuanced analysis of the topic, see Meren, *With Friends Like These*, 207–37. Quebec's challenge to Ottawa's prerogatives in international affairs spurred a broad literature on diplomatic history that has focused nearly exclusively on either Quebec-France bilateral relations or Quebec-Canada-France triangular dynamics. See, among others, Harvey, "Les relations culturelles entre la France et le Canada (1760–1960)"; Paquin, *Histoire des relations internationales du Québec*; Mesli and Carel, *50 ans d'échanges culturels France-Québec*; and Gendron, *Towards a Francophone Community*.

19 Prior to 1966, External Affairs' Information Division handled press inquiries in addition to taking care of disseminating press releases and reference material to foreign outlets, but poor communication with the Department of Trade and Commerce and agencies such as the NFB and the CBC-IS, whose mandate also involved projecting Canada abroad, often impeded this work. The department's efforts were for the most part "less than inspired and less than effective" until the establishment of the Cultural Affairs Division. Stephens, *Study of Canadian Government Information Abroad*, chap. 9, p. 1.

20 Robert Bothwell's survey of Canadian international relations is indicative of the ease with which diplomatic historians promptly dismiss South American countries as being of no consequence to Canadians' relationship to the world. Regarding Brazil, he writes that the country was "on the fringes of the world, as most Canadians saw it, unfamiliar and exceedingly distant to all but a few Canadian investors. Latin America, Brazil included, was a caricature of democracy, governed more by dictators than by civilian politicians, its societies remote and incomprehensible." Bothwell, *Alliance and Illusion*, 20.

21 The field's preoccupation with North American and transatlantic questions has contributed to a neglect of hemispheric affairs until recently. Rosana Barbosa's contributions to the thin literature on Canada-Brazil relations are thus important ones. To a great degree, her synthesis of the

dynamic between the two countries reproduces the motifs that characterize dominant narratives in Canadian diplomatic history, although it also successfully brings to the fore a neglected history worth pursuing. See Barbosa, *Brazil and Canada*, and Barbosa, "Brazilian and Canadian Relations." The literature on Canadians' relationship to Brazil also includes Smith and Greer, "Monarchism, an Emerging Canadian Identity, and the 1866 British North American Trade Mission to the West Indies and Brazil"; Zucchi, *Mad Flight?*; and Glass, "Connections between Canada and Brazil Before World War One."

22 Key recent works include Carr, "No Political Significance of Any Kind"; Cavell, "Canadiana Abroad"; Smith, "Art and the Invention of North America, 1985–2012"; Miller, "An Ancillary Weapon"; Hansson, "Dancing Into Hearts and Minds"; Fernández Tabío, Wright, and Wylie, *Other Diplomacies, Other Ties*; McKercher and Van Huizen, *Undiplomatic History*; Cull and Hawes, *Canada's Public Diplomacy*; and Webb, "How to Raise a Curtain." See also the *Journal of Curatorial Studies*'s third issue from 2016, titled "Curating Cultural Diplomacy" and guest-edited by Lynda Jessup and Sarah E.K. Smith.

23 Incidentally, *Distant Stage* responds to Jessica C.E. Gienow-Hecht's call for the "internationalization" of cultural diplomacy studies, which requires "decentering" the United States, to deepen our understanding of how individuals and groups from – or sometimes representing – different nations engaged with one another using culture. Gienow-Hecht, "On the Diversity of Knowledge and the Community of Thought," 14, and Gienow-Hecht, "Introduction," 7.

24 For succinct histories of wartime Quebec, see Dickinson and Young, *A Short History of Quebec*, 271–304, as well as Gossage and Little, *An Illustrated History of Quebec*, 197–231.

25 Helmer, *Growing with Canada*; Keillor, *Music in Canada*. There were also significant developments taking place in the realm of jazz; see especially Mills, "Democracy in Music."

26 Carney, "Modern Art, the Local, and the Global"; Lamonde and Trépanier, *L'Avènement de la modernité culturelle au Québec*; Berg, *Literature and Painting in Quebec*.

27 Zimmermann, "Global Intellectual Elites," 550.

28 The discourse of *survivance* in Quebec was founded on a defensive form of nationalism, and it gained currency following both the failure of the rebellions of 1837–38 and the ascendency of ultramontanism.

29 "Tory to the core and convinced that Canada's national interests were best served within the comforting embrace of the British Empire, Sir

Joseph Pope ... had only modest ambitions for his new ministry," contend Greg Donaghy and Michael K. Carroll. Donaghy and Carroll, "Introduction," 2. See also Pope, *Public Servant.*

30 Two works shed considerable light on the experience and beliefs that informed O.D. Skelton's approach to foreign policy: Ferguson, *Remaking Liberalism*, and Hillmer, *O.D. Skelton.*

31 Hilliker, *Canada's Department of External Affairs*, 189–90.

32 Murray, "Canada's First Diplomatic Missions in Latin America," 162.

33 "Intercâmbio comercial do Brasil com o Canadá em 1941," 30 September 1941, 36/5/03, AHI.

34 Trade Agreement between Canada and Brazil, 17 October 1941, Treaty Series 1941, no. 18, 2.

35 McDowall, *The Light*, 4.

36 Ogelsby, *Gringos from the Far North*, 129.

37 Chapnick, "The Canadian Middle Power Myth," 188. See also Chapnick, "Middle Power No More?," and Chapnick, *The Middle Power Project.*

38 The following works interrogate Brazil's claims to "middlepowerhood": Burges, "Mistaking Brazil for a Middle Power," and Fox, *The Politics of Attraction.*

39 The concept of a North Atlantic triangle is used here to highlight the influence that the United States and Great Britain had on Canada's external relations (and thus on Canadians' views of the world). It is not meant to overstate Ottawa's importance in the triangular interplays first analyzed by John Bartlet Brebner in 1945. Tony McCulloch explains: "Before 1945 the triangle was essentially isosceles – with two equal powers (Britain and the US) and a much weaker third. But since 1945, the North Atlantic triangle has become increasingly obtuse, with three very unequal powers – the US as the world's only superpower; Britain, still a great power, even now; and Canada, a middling power in most respects." McCulloch, "The North Atlantic Triangle," 206. See also Brebner, *North Atlantic Triangle.*

40 Rempel, *Counterweights*, 3. For more on the concept of counterweight in the Canadian context, see also Holmes, *Canada*, 12.

41 See Smith, *Brazil and the United States*; and Moura, *Autonomia na dependência.*

42 Rochlin, *Discovering the Americas*, 16.

43 Gabinete do Ministro, "Decreto N. 5.077: Aprova o regimento do Departamento de Imprensa e Propaganda (DIP)," 29 December 1939, GCg 1934.09.22, FGV-CPDOC. Unless otherwise specified, all translations are my own.

44 These numbers refer to disembarkations. For more details on estimates, consult the digital memorial at www.slavevoyages.org. See also: Skidmore, *Black into White*; Marx, *Making Race and Nation*; and Degler, *Neither Black nor White*.

45 For concise discussions of the dictatorship's place in – and long shadow over – the history of Brazil, see Skidmore, *Brazil*; Smith, *A History of Brazil*; and Hentchke, *Vargas and Brazil*.

46 Levine, *Father of the Poor?*, 61.

47 As Peter Wade explains: "The idea of race is just that – an idea. The notion that races exist with definable physical characteristics and, even more so, that some races are superior to others is the result of particular historical processes which … have their roots in the colonisation by European peoples of other areas of the world." Wade, *Race and Ethnicity in Latin America*, 12. Underscoring the fact that race is a social construct does not mean that racial thinking is a benign form of violence. Nor does it suggest that whiteness is a moot corollary to race. See Baldwin, Cameron, and Kobayashi, *Rethinking the Great White North*, as well as Madokoro, McKenzie, and Meren, *Dominion of Race*. Note that I decided not to use quotation marks throughout the text for "race," "racial," "white," and related terms in an effort to facilitate reading.

48 See Davis, *Avoiding the Dark*, 87.

49 The image of Brazil as a racial democracy traces its origins to the writings of Gilberto Freyre, specifically his *Casa-grande & senzala*, published in English under the title *The Masters and the Slaves*. Although not explicitly articulated in this 1933 book, the image gained traction during the Vargas era. See Freyre, *Casa-grande & senzala*, and Skidmore, *Black into White*, 209–18. Barbara Weinstein argues that the book was "successful because it did not directly challenge existing assumptions about whiteness and progress." It foregrounded "features of Brazilian culture … whose implications were highly gratifying to all but the most stiff-necked racists within Brazil's lettered classes." Weinstein, *The Color of Modernity*, 12–13.

50 Rochlin, *Discovering the Americas*, 37.

51 Minutes of Meeting on Cultural Relations with Latin America, 8 November 1943, RG25, vol. 3243, LAC.

52 Edward Said's contrapuntal analysis of artistic works (both what they say and what they leave unsaid) reveals the ways in which the making of culture intersects with overlapping histories of power and resistance to it. Said, *Culture and Imperialism*, xxii. Mary A. Renda makes a similar argument when she writes that "cultures are continually constituted and

reconstituted through relations of power, that they are neither monolithic nor static." Renda, *Taking Haiti*, 25.

53 Waligorska, "Music and Imagined Communities."

54 Vucetic, *The Anglosphere*, 3. For studies dealing with Canadians' sense of place in the world and their relationship to empire, see Buckner, *Canada and the End of Empire*; Buckner and Francis, *Canada and the British World*; Buckner and Francis, *Rediscovering the British World*; Hopkins, "Rethinking Decolonization"; and Meren, "The Tragedies of Canadian International History."

55 On this topic, see Igartua, *The Other Quiet Revolution*, 22–3. On the idea of Canada as a country free of racism, read Backhouse, *Colour-Coded*, 5–14; and Walker, *The African Canadian Legal Odyssey*.

56 The idea of "two founding races" subsisted beyond the 1950s, and it continued to frame understandings of French-English tensions even as Ottawa turned to biculturalism to foster national unity. Royal Commission on Bilingualism and Biculturalism, *Report*, xxi.

57 The term *métissage* used here must be understood strictly in the historical context of Canada-Brazil relations. It is not connected to claims of Indigeneity among French Canadians in Canada. On this topic, see Leroux, *Distorted Descent*, as well as Gaudry and Leroux, "White Settler Revisionism and Making Métis Everywhere."

58 "Dois grandes povos, duas pátrias irmãs," *Jornal do Commercio*, 18 July 1943, 10.

59 Notable Canadian works that examine how identity categories informed attitudes and perceptions in both the foreign policy apparatus and civil society include Price, *Orienting Canada*; Touhey, *Conflicting Visions*; Dubinsky, Perry, and Yu, *Within and Without the Nation*; Madokoro, McKenzie, and Meren, *Dominion of Race*; and Razack, *Dark Threats & White Knights*. See also Haglund, "And the Beat Goes On," and Wylie, *Perception of Cuba*.

60 "If diplomacy is theatre," writes James Ball, "it is also performative." Both are "arts of enactment that stabilize shared narratives to serve particular ends," he adds. Ball, *Theatre of State*, 5.

61 As Sean Mills explains, putting Canada's "fractured historiographies into dialogue with each other" is key to understanding "the shared cultural and political space and asymmetrical relations between English and French Canada, as well as their entanglements with other societies around the world." *Distant Stage* accomplishes that by examining French Canadians' entangled history with the Global South, underscoring the ways in which they helped shaped – and were themselves transformed by – Canada's

relationship to empire. Mills, "The End of Empire?" 355. See also Meren, "The Tragedies of Canadian International History," and Fahrni, "Reflections on the Place of Quebec in Historical Writing on Canada."

62 Cited in Szczepanik, "On the Ethnography of Media Production," 101.

63 See Born, "After Relational Aesthetics"; Born, "The Social and the Aesthetic"; and Born, "Music and the Materialization of Identities."

64 Born and Hesmondhalgh, "Introduction," 6.

65 Ernest MacMillan, diary, 7 August 1946, MUS 7, vol. 31, D.48, LAC.

66 Désy, *Les sentiers de la culture*, 29.

## CHAPTER ONE

1 Cited in Jean Désy to Secretary of State for External Affairs, 1 October 1941, RG25, vol. 2640, LAC.

2 Ibid. Emphasis in original.

3 Jean Désy to Secretary of State for External Affairs, 2 October 1941, RG25, vol. 2640, LAC.

4 Moura, *Autonomia na dependência*, 189. See also Vizentini, *Relações internacionais do Brasil*; Vizentini, *Relações exteriores do Brasil*; as well as Cervo and Bueno, *História da política exterior do Brasil.*

5 For a chronicle of the events leading from the revolution of 1930 to the establishment of the Estado Novo, see Skidmore, *Brazil*, 107–13.

6 Moura, *Sucessos e ilusões*, 24; Bethell, "Brazil," 33; Lafer, "Brazilian International Identity and Foreign Policy," 223–4; and Corsi, *Estado Novo*.

7 Joseph Smith explains: "The arrangement appeared restrictive but was particularly attractive to Brazil ... not only because it offered a signal opportunity to increase exports at a time of world economic depression, but also because it obviated the need to allocate scarce foreign exchange and gold reserves to finance foreign trade." Smith, *Brazil and the United States*, 108.

8 Tota, *O imperialismo sedutor*, 22.

9 Cited in Lochery, *Brazil*, 6.

10 According to Emily S. Rosenberg, liberal developmentalism had five dimensions: "(1) belief that other nations could and should replicate America's own developmental experience; (2) faith in private free enterprise; (3) support for free or open access for trade and investment; (4) promotion of free flow of information and culture; and (5) growing acceptance of governmental activity to protect free enterprise and to stimulate and regulate American participation in international economic and cultural exchange." Rosenberg, *Spreading the American Dream*, 7.

11 Smith, *Brazil and the United States*, 104.

12 Ibid., 107. Brazil's war experience is discussed in Seitenfus, *A entrada do Brasil na Segunda Guerra Mundial*, and Lochery, *Brazil.*

13 Oswaldo Aranha to Getúlio Vargas, 15 October 1935, GVC 1935.10.15, FGV-CPDOC.

14 Cited in L.D. Wilgress to O.D. Skelton, 7 February 1938, RG25, vol. 2630, LAC. Skelton informed Prime Minister King of these developments, but no follow-up ensued. See O.D. Skelton to L.D. Wilgress, 11 February 1938, RG25, vol. 2630, LAC.

15 Memorandum for the Prime Minister, 6 August 1938, RG25, vol. 2630, LAC.

16 Massey to Secretary of State for External Affairs, 25 May 1939, RG25, vol. 2630, LAC.

17 K.H. McCrimmon to Dr Keenleyside, 19 June 1940, RG25, vol. 2630, LAC.

18 Rochlin, *Discovering the Americas*, 12–22.

19 Frank M. Garcia, "Brazil President Predicts New Era," *Montreal Gazette*, 12 June 1940, 17.

20 Aluisio Martins Torres to O.D. Skelton, 14 June 1940, RG25, vol. 2640, LAC.

21 Hillmer, *O.D. Skelton*, 85.

22 Ferguson, *Remaking Liberalism*, 89.

23 Although Canadians held competing and evolving views regarding what constituted the national interest from the 1940s onward, they tended to focus on issues of sovereignty, economic growth, hemispheric stability, national unity, and liberal democracy. For a detailed discussion of these views, see Donaghy and Carroll, *In the National Interest.*

24 This view was shared by officials at External Affairs and the Department of Trade and Commerce. Rochlin, *Discovering the Americas*, 16. See also N.A. Robertson to Jean Désy, 7 July 1942, MG26-J4, vol. 232, no. 156953, LAC; and Jean Désy to Secretary of State for External Affairs, 20 April 1943, MG26-J1, vol. 339, no. 291949, LAC.

25 Ogelsby, *Gringos from the Far North*, 133, 136–7.

26 Armstrong and Nelles, *Southern Exposure*, 277, 282. Emphasis in original.

27 The following works pertinently argue that the activities of cosmopolitan capitalists in South America were consequential to the continued influence of empire as a structuring agent in Canadian international history: Hudson, "Imperial Designs"; Hastings, "Rounding Off Confederation"; Hastings, "The Limits of 'Brotherly Love'"; Dubinsky and Epprecht, "Canadian Businesses and the Business of Development in the 'Third World'"; and Valiani, "The Articulation of an Independent Foreign Policy."

28 McDowall, *The Light*, 335.

29 Ogelsby, *Gringos from the Far North*, 135; Barbosa, *Brazil and Canada*, 34.

30 K.H. McCrimmon to Oswaldo Aranha, 13 June 1937, OAcp 1937.06.13.1, FGV-CPDOC.
31 C.A. Sylvester to Miller Lash, 13 May 1938, MG28-III112, vol. 76, 011.4 pt 17, LAC. For an overview of Oswaldo Aranha's tenure at the head of the Itamaraty, consult Castro, *1808–2008 – Itamaraty*, 365–97.
32 K.H. McCrimmon to Dr Keenleyside, 19 June 1940, RG25, vol. 2630, LAC.
33 Copy on 261–40, September 1940, RG25, vol. 2630, LAC.
34 Cited in H.V. Barter to Col Walter Gow, 27 November 1940, MG28-III112, vol. 76, 011.4 pt 20, LAC. For the original Brazilian publication, see "O estabelecimento de relações diplomáticas entre o Canadá e o Brasil," *O Jornal*, 17 November 1940, 4.
35 K.H. McCrimmon to Sir Herbert Couzens, 3 February 1942, MG28-III112, vol. 325, 21, LAC.
36 "Brasil-Canadá," *A Notícia*, 21 November 1940, in MG28-III112, vol. 76, 011.4 pt 20, LAC.
37 Euzebio de Queiroz Mattoso, "Os tentaculos amigos do polvo," *O Jornal*, 30 June 1940, 3.
38 Jean Désy's views on this topic would change somewhat in the late stages of his career, as discussed in the conclusion. On this topic, see Fournier, "Édouard Montpetit et l'université moderne, ou l'échec d'une génération"; Fournier, *L'entrée dans la modernité*; and Fabre, "Un arc transatlantique et sa tangente ou comment se dessine un réseau intellectuel franco-québécois?"
39 Rudin, *Making History in Twentieth-Century Quebec*, 47.
40 Sarrazin, "Portrait de son Excellence Jean Désy," 9 September 1949, MG32-E2, vol. 1, LAC.
41 Liste des membres – Comité France-Amérique Montréal, 1925, P76/E1, 4, DGDAUdM.
42 Lacroix, *L'invention du retour d'Europe*, 266.
43 Ibid., 254–5. See also Fabre, "Un arc transatlantique et sa tangente ou comment se dessine un réseau intellectuel franco-québécois."
44 Hillmer, "National Independence and the National Interest," 15.
45 Apparently, "only one qualified candidate presented himself" for the competition organized for the post. See Hilliker, *Canada's Department of External Affairs*, 104. The internal correspondence suggests, however, that there "were a number of very good men from Ontario, Quebec, and the West." O.D. Skelton to Léon M. Gouin, 13 July 1925, RG25, vol. 2960, LAC.
46 Memorandum for the Prime Minister, 19 June 1943, MG26-J4, vol. 241, no. 162687, LAC. See also Hillmer, *O.D. Skelton*, 164; and Kelly, *The Good Fight*, 27.
47 See Lalande, *The Department of External Affairs and Biculturalism*.

48 Hillmer, "O.D. Skelton," 65.
49 Jean Désy to Doctor [Skelton], 5 October 1928, RG25, vol. 2960, LAC.
50 R. Dandurand to W.L. Mackenzie King, 6 July 1928, MG26-J1, vol. 180, no. 128988, LAC.
51 Betcherman, *Ernest Lapointe*, 125. See also MacFarlane, *Ernest Lapointe and Quebec's Influence on Canadian Foreign Policy*.
52 For a detailed outline of the events following the outbreak of war, see "Despatches and Documents Relative to the Invasion of Belgium and the Activities of the Canadian Legation during the Period of 10th May–28th October, 1940," in MG32-E2, vol. 3, LAC.
53 Jean Désy to Secretary of State for External Affairs, 23 September 1940, RG25, vol. 2960, LAC.
54 Jean Désy to Dr Skelton, 9 October 1940, RG25, vol. 2960, LAC.
55 R. Dandurand [to Prime Minister King], 12 February 1941, MG26-J1, vol. 303, no. 256505, LAC.
56 Jeffrey D. Needell uses the term to describe the cultural life of Rio de Janeiro's elites between 1898 and 1914. Julio Lucchesi Moraes relies on a similar time frame to study São Paulo's own *belle époque*. See Needell, *A Tropical Belle Époque*, and Moraes, *São Paulo, capital artística*.
57 Needell, *A Tropical Belle Époque*, 44–5.
58 See Felix and Juall, *Cultural Exchanges between Brazil and France*; Lessa, "L'influence intellectuelle française au Brésil"; and Suppo, "La politique culturelle française au Brésil entre les années 1920–1950."
59 Stam and Shohat, *Race in Translation*, 32. For further discussions of transatlantic phantasmatic projections: Félix and Juall, *Cultural Exchanges between Brazil and France*.
60 See Denning, *Noise Uprising*; Shaw, *Tropical Travels*; and Sadlier, *Brazil Imagined*.
61 Moraes, *São Paulo, capital artística*, 83–5.
62 Needell, *A Tropical Belle Époque*, 129.
63 Williams, *Culture Wars in Brazil*, 40–1.
64 Stam and Shohat, *Race in Translation*, 192.
65 See Naves, "Os regentes do Brasil no período Vargas," 124, and Appleby, *Heitor Villa-Lobos*, 81.
66 Wright, *Villa-Lobos*, 61.
67 Béhague, *Heitor Villa-Lobos*, 155.
68 Skidmore, *Black into White*, 179. Emphasis in original.
69 Davis, *Avoiding the Dark*, 94. See also Velloso, *Os intelectuais e a política cultural do Estado Novo*, and Oliveira, "Vargas, os intelectuais e as raízes da ordem."

70 Garcia, "Music and the Brazilian Estado Novo," 613.
71 Davis, *Avoiding the Dark*, 87.
72 Hillmer, *O.D. Skelton*, 85.
73 Jean Désy to Secretary of State for External Affairs, 18 February 1942, MG26-J1, vol. 323, no. 274237, LAC.
74 Skidmore, *Brazil*, 118; Turino, "Nationalism and Latin American Music," 188–9.
75 Jean Désy to Secretary of State for External Affairs, 18 February 1942, MG26-J1, vol. 323, no. 274237, LAC.
76 Jean Désy to Secretary of State for External Affairs, 1 October 1941, RG25, vol. 2640, LAC.
77 "Brasil-Canadá," *A Notícia*, 21 November 1940, in MG28-III112, vol. 76, 011.4 pt 20, LAC.
78 "Chegou falando o nosso idioma," *A Noite*, 11 September 1941, 3.
79 "Os alemãos conhecerão em breve o segredo da Conferencia de Quebec," *O Radical*, 26 August 1943, 5. See also Luiz Guimarães Chaves, "Duelo das duas raças: Os Canadenses franceses e o elemento canadense inglês," *Correio da Manhã – 2 Seção*, 23 April 1944, 1.
80 Lourival Fontes to Getúlio Vargas, 19 July 1943, GVC 1943.07.18, FGV/CPDOC.
81 Raul Leitão da Cunha, "Speech of Professor Raul Leitão da Cunha," n.d., RG25, vol. 3278, LAC.
82 "Chegou falando o nosso idioma," *A Noite*, 11 September 1941, 3.
83 Jean Désy, "Fondation de l'Institut Brésil-Canada," 14 June 1944, MG32-E2, vol. 1, LAC.
84 Jean Désy, "Speech of the Canadian Ambassador," 1944, RG25, vol. 3243, LAC.
85 Ibid.
86 Lake and Reynolds, *Drawing the Global Colour Line*, 2.
87 Anderson, "Traveling White," 68.
88 Lake and Reynolds, *Drawing the Global Colour Line*, 3. The co-editors of *Rethinking the Great White North* concur, and add that "whiteness in all its historical-geographic variability is fundamentally concerned with spatializing racial difference in ways that allow for its spatial practices to pass unquestioned." Baldwin, Cameron, and Kobayashi, "Introduction," 6.
89 Patrick Wolfe explains that settler colonialism adhered to a "logic of elimination" whereby the Indigenous Other had to make way for the colonizers, who could still recuperate Indigeneity – either as a referent to the past or as a differentiator vis-à-vis the metropole – to establish control of both coveted territories and narratives of occupation. Wolfe,

"Settler Colonialism and the Elimination of the Native," 387. See also Wolfe, *Traces of History*, and King, "The Erasure of Indigenous Thought in Foreign Policy."

90 Jean Désy, "Speech of the Canadian Ambassador," 1944, RG25, vol. 3243, LAC.

91 Viau, *Modern Painting in French Canada*, 42.

92 Robert, *Pellan*, 37, 39.

93 Cited in Alfred Pellan to F.P. Cosgrove, 18 March 1943, RG20. vol. 1323, LAC.

94 Hawker, *Tales of Ghosts*, 47.

95 A.Y. Jackson, "Rescuing Our Tottering Totems," *Maclean's*, 15 December 1927, 23.

96 Dawn, *National Visions, National Blindness*, 105, 142.

97 Maurice Gagnon, "Pintura," *A Vida*, May 1943, in RG20, vol. 1323, LAC.

98 Robert Ford, "Um Canadense pinta para o Brasil," *Sombra*, May 1943, 38–9.

99 Keillor, *Music in Canada*, 181–2.

100 Taylor, *Beyond Exoticism*, 70–1. For a discussion of how this plays out in Canada, see Robinson, *Hungry Listening*.

101 Desautels, "Quadrilha brasileira," 11.

102 The event is discussed in the following chapter. For more on the composer, read Barros, "Francisco Mignone e sua obra orquestral nacionalista," and Martins, "A pianística multifacetada de Francisco Mignone."

## CHAPTER TWO

1 Eugène Lapierre, "Le 1er juillet au Brésil. Échange d'oeuvres dans l'air," *Radiomonde*, 10 July 1943, 6.

2 H. Coutinho, "Uma oferta de arte do Canadá ao Brasil," *Jornal do Brasil*, 18 July 1943, 2.

3 "Música – expressão de harmonia continental," *Correio da Manhã*, 10 July 1943, 7.

4 Anderson, *Imagined Communities*, 145.

5 Mahiet, Ferraguto, and Ahrendt, "Introduction," 10.

6 Jean Désy to N. Robertson, 2 October 1942, MG26-J1, vol. 323, no. 274402, LAC.

7 Account statement – Alfred Pellan, 11 September 1942, RG20, vol. 1323, LAC.

8 Jean Désy to Secretary of State for External Affairs, 26 November 1941, MG26-J1, vol. 303, nos 256745 and 256748, LAC.

9 Jean Désy to Secretary of State for External Affairs, 29 October 1941, MG26-J1, vol. 303, no. 256738, LAC.

10 These numbers reflect total trade (imports for consumption plus exports of Canadian and foreign produce, excluding gold). Dominion Bureau of Statistics, *Trade of Canada*, 50–1.

11 Rochlin, *Discovering the Americas*, 16.

12 Jean Désy to Secretary of State for External Affairs, 6 January 1942, MG26-J1, vol. 323, no. 274189, LAC. See also Jean Désy to Secretary of State for External Affairs, 17 March 1942, MG26-J1, vol. 323, no. 274257, LAC.

13 Rio de Janeiro newspapers, some of which acted as mouthpieces for the dictatorship, launched a "Carioca Press Campaign for the Inclusion of Canada in the Conference." They celebrated the country's valiant and selfless war effort, which they argued qualified it for participation in the event. Jean Désy to Secretary of State for External Affairs, 3 February 1942, MG26-J1, vol. 323, no. 274223, LAC. See also Jean Désy to Secretary of State for External Affairs, 24 January 1942, MG26-J1, vol. 323, no. 274202, LAC.

14 Valiani, "The Articulation of an Independent Foreign Policy."

15 Ibid., 176.

16 Rochlin, *Discovering the Americas*, 19. For a discussion of the domestic and international factors that informed Canadians' hesitancy vis-à-vis Pan-American multilateralism post-1940s, see McKercher, "Southern Exposure"; Zorbas, *Diefenbaker and Latin America*; McKenna, *Canada and the OAS*; and McKercher, "'Ultimate Destiny' Delayed."

17 Secretary of State for External Affairs to Jean Désy, 19 December 1941, MG26-J1, vol. 303, no. 256756, LAC.

18 Smith, *Brazil and the United States*, 107.

19 Dinah Silveira de Quiroz, "A América mestiça," *Correio da Manhã*, 21 June 1944, 4. See also Jean Désy to Secretary of State for External Affairs, 23 June 1944, RG25, vol. 3276, LAC.

20 Cited in Jean Désy to Secretary of State for External Affairs, 15 May 1944, RG25, vol. 3276, LAC. The original Portuguese is *cocacolização*: Mauricio de Medeiros, "Ghettos para negros," *Diario Carioca*, 9 May 1944, 4. Scholars tend to situate the appearance of the term "coca-colonization" to the Cold War in Europe, but it already circulated in Brazil in the early to mid-1940s. See Wagnleitner, *Coca-Colonization and the Cold War*, and Kuisel, "Coca-Cola and the Cold War."

21 Jean Désy to Secretary of State for External Affairs, 25 April 1944, RG25, vol. 3276, LAC.

22 Jean Désy to Secretary of State for External Affairs, 15 May 1944, RG25, vol. 3276, LAC.
23 Jean Désy to Secretary of State for External Affairs, 15 March 1943, MG26-J1, vol. 339, no. 291942, LAC.
24 Noel Charles to David Scott, 29 March 1943, MG26-J1, vol. 339, no. 291947, LAC.
25 Jean Désy to Secretary of State for External Affairs, 29 March 1943, MG26-J1, vol. 339, no. 291946, LAC.
26 Jean Désy to Secretary of State for External Affairs, 15 March 1943, MG26-J1, vol. 339, no. 291943, LAC.
27 The Good Neighbor era followed a tumultuous period during which the United States meddled in the Mexican Revolution and interfered in the internal affairs of countries in Central America and the Caribbean to advance its economic interests. For a survey of American intervention in the region, see Schoultz, *Beneath the United States*, and Smith, *The United States and Latin America*.
28 Sadlier, *Americans All*, 10.
29 Campbell, "Shaping Solidarity," 25.
30 Campbell, "Creating Something Out of Nothing."
31 Jennifer L. Campbell further explains that "for all the talk of service and the self-effacing altruism, there was an underlying motivation for getting experts in the field of music on board with the division's policy – using musicians and musical exchange as an excuse to have more contact and discussion with foreign governmental officials." Campbell, "Shaping Solidarity," 40, 65.
32 An umbrella term, "popular music" evades easy definition. Roy Shuker's synthesis of scholarly debates on the topic provides the following working definition: "Essentially, all popular music consists of a hybrid of musical traditions, styles, and influences, and is also an economic product which is invested with ideological significance by many of its consumers. At the heart of the majority of various forms of popular music is a fundamental tension between the essential creativity of the act of 'making music' and the commercial nature of the bulk of its production and dissemination." Shuker, *Popular Music*, 228.
33 Applegate, "How German Is It?," 287, 295. See also DeNora, "Musical Patronage and Social Change in Beethoven's Vienna."
34 Levine, *Highbrow/Lowbrow*.
35 Gienow-Hecht, *Sound Diplomacy*, 11.
36 As Danielle Fosler-Lussier points out, it "was difficult for the United States to offer art music without drawing accusations that the music

was not truly American." Fosler-Lussier, *Music in America's Cold War Diplomacy*, 24.

37 Gienow-Hecht, *Sound Diplomacy*, 214.

38 Gienow-Hecht, "The World Is Ready to Listen," 19–20. As a Western construction, the concert hall itself is also important in creating the context for disciplining bodies into listening and viewing performances in specific ways. Cressman, "The Concert Hall as a Medium of Musical Culture."

39 Caute, *The Dancer Defects*, 379.

40 Hess, *Representing the Good Neighbor*, 187. Incidentally, the State Department complemented this approach with smaller initiatives such as the Pan-American Union's Music Division, which – although subordinated to US-American interests – valorized aspects of the republics' national folklore within a regional framework: Palomino, "Nationalist, Hemispheric, and Global."

41 Gienow-Hecht, *Sound Diplomacy*, 214. Carol A. Hess concedes that point when she writes, "I am by no means suggesting that Pan Americanist sameness-embracing was uniformly benign." Hess, *Representing the Good Neighbor*, 7.

42 Magaldi, *Music in Imperial Rio de Janeiro*, x–xii.

43 Magaldi, "Two Musical Representations of Brazil," 205.

44 Ibid., 205, 221. Vargas would later rehabilitate *Il Guarany*, turning the piece into a de facto substitute to Brazil's national anthem by playing it daily on *A Hora do Brasil*, the regime's national broadcast. See also Béhague, *The Beginnings of Musical Nationalism in Brazil*.

45 Béhague, *Heitor Villa-Lobos*, 151.

46 Hess, *Representing the Good Neighbor*, 86–7.

47 Magaldi, "Two Musical Representations of Brazil," 217.

48 Naves, *O violão azul*, 39–42. See also Belchior Rodrigues, "O maestro do mundo," 107–14.

49 Fléchet, *Villa-Lobos à Paris,* 121–2.

50 Appleby, *Heitor Villa-Lobos*, 79.

51 Magaldi, "Two Musical Representations of Brazil," 219.

52 Hess, *Representing the Good Neighbor*, 83, 105, 109, 126–7.

53 Beezley, "The Rise of Cultural Nationalism and Its Musical Expressions," 19.

54 Turino, *Nationalists, Cosmopolitans, and Popular Music in Zimbabwe*, 190. A common approach at the time consisted of a "reformist fusion of local, non-cosmopolitan instruments, sounds, and genres within a largely

cosmopolitan aesthetic, stylistic, and contextual frame." Turino, "Nationalism and Latin American Music," 175.

55 Béhague, *Heitor Villa-Lobos*, 153.

56 Garcia, "Music and the Brazilian Estado Novo," 623–4.

57 Naves, "Os regentes do Brasil no período Vargas," 140; Alencastro, "Villa-Lobos et la première période Vargas," 16–22; and Belchior Rodrigues, "O maestro do mundo," 159–62.

58 Naves, *O violão azul*, 31.

59 Béhague, *Heitor Villa-Lobos*, 150.

60 Naves, "O Brasil em uníssono," 41.

61 Belchior Rodrigues, "O maestro do mundo," 308–10.

62 "Teatro Municipal. Temporada lírica oficial," *Diario de Noticias*, 18 August 1942, 9.

63 Jean Désy to N. Robertson, 4 September 1942, MG26-J1, vol. 323, nos 274391 and 274393, LAC.

64 Jean Désy to N. Robertson, 16 September 1942, MG26-J1, vol. 323, no. 274399, LAC.

65 Jean Désy to Secretary of State for External Affairs, 18 November 1942, RG25, vol. 3124, LAC.

66 Léon Mayrand to Secretary of State for External Affairs, 25 October 1943, RG25, vol. 3124, LAC.

67 Bethune, "A Gift Fit for the King," *Maclean's*, 18 July 2011, 48–9.

68 Gallo, "Dansereau, Jean," 259. For more details on the Prix d'Europe: Laurendeau, *Cent ans de Prix d'Europe*; Barrière, *Les 100 ans du Prix d'Europe*; and Lefebvre, "Le milieu musical québécois et ses réseaux."

69 Wilfrid Pelletier to Jean Dufresne, 25 October 1938, MSS20, 2006-10-001\358, BAnQ. See also Wilfrid Pelletier to E. Leteille, 25 October 1938, MSS20, 2006-10-001\358, BAnQ.

70 Jean Désy's cousin, Sister Marie-Stéphane, founded the ESMO in 1932. Pelletier was the CMQM's first director with Champagne serving as assistant director.

71 Keillor, *Music in Canada*, 301–3.

72 See Riley and Smith, *Nation and Classical Music*.

73 "Música – expressão de harmonia continental," *Correio da Manhã*, 10 July 1943, 7; "A arte a serviço dos ideais panamericanos," *Diário de Noticias*, 18 July 1943, 2.

74 "Recital do pianista Jean Dansereau," 14 June 1943, in MG32-E2, vol. 1, LAC.

75 For a discussion of the artistic couple and postwar modernity, see Gronberg, "Sonia Delaunay's Simultaneous Fashions and the Modern Woman," 113.

76 Levine, *Father of the Poor?*, 61.

77 For example, "Chegou o primeiro ministro canadense no Brasil," *A Noite*, 22 September 1941, 1, and "Uma entrevista com o ministro do Canadá no Brasil," *Correio da Manhã*, 1 July 1942, 1.

78 Jean Désy to Dr Skelton, 9 October 1940, RG25, vol. 2960, LAC.

79 See "Inaugurado mais um posto de trabalho da Organização das voluntárias," *Vida Doméstica* 26, no. 345 (December 1946): 3; "Pró aliados," *Careta*, 13 December 1941, 24; "Legião brasileira de assistência," *A Manhã*, 23 September 1942, 7; and "Cavaleiros paulistas e cariocas em novo cotejo," *Gazeta de Notícias*, 13 August 1944, 8. See also Memorandum for the Prime Minister, 22 December 1942, MG26-J4, vol. 241, no. 162579, LAC.

80 Hantel-Fraser, *No Fixed Address*, 189.

81 Enloe, *Bananas, Beaches, and Bases*, 96.

82 "Uma nota tocante da cordialidade canadense-brasileira," *A Manhã*, 11 September 1941, 1.

83 Cited in "Uma entrevista com o ministro do Canadá no Brasil," *Correio da Manhã*, 1 July 1942, 1.

84 Jean Désy, "Fondation de l'Institut Brésil-Canada," 14 June 1944, MG32-E2, vol. 1, LAC.

85 Jean Désy to T. da Graça Aranha, 8 January 1943, 82/3/5 AHI.

86 "Hoje, inauguração dos programas 'Ondas Musicais,'" *Correio da Manhã*, 2 April 1940, 8.

87 See Jean Désy, "Jean Dansereau," *A Manhã*, 15 June 1943, 4, and "Recital do pianista Jean Dansereau," 14 June 1943, in MG32-E2, vol. 1, LAC.

88 "Ondas Musicais," O *Radical*, 1 June 1943, 23, and Ariel, "Brasil-Canadá," *A Noite*, 7 July 1943, 4.

89 "Jean Dansereau na cultural artística," *Gazeta de Notícias*, 16 June 1943, 9.

90 "Notas de arte," *Fon Fon*, 3 July 1943, 11.

91 Alda Caminha, "Jean Dansereau, um artista diferente," *Diario Carioca*, 27 June 1943, 2.

92 "Música – expressão de harmonia continental," *Correio da Manhã*, 10 July 1943, 7.

93 "Correio musical: O pianista Jean Dansereau na cultural artistica," *Correio da Manhã*, 16 June 1943, 11.

94 Ayres de Andrade, "Música: Recital de Jean Dansereau," O *Jornal*, 16 June 1943, 2.

95 "A arte a serviço dos ideais panamericanos," *Diário de Noticias*, 18 July 1943, 2.
96 "Dois grandes povos, duas pátrias irmãs," *Jornal do Commercio*, 18 July 1943, 10; Ariel, "Canadá," *A Noite*, 29 August 1943, 4; "Música – expressão de harmonia continental," *Correio da Manhã*, 10 July 1943, 7.
97 The piano was considered predominantly a female instrument, particularly within middle-class circles, where it was associated with housebound femininity. See Steblin, "The Gender Stereotyping of Musical Instruments in the Western Tradition."
98 "Correio musical: O pianista Jean Dansereau na cultural artistica," *Correio da Manhã*, 16 June 1943, 11. Dansereau was injecting virility in what could be constructed as a "feminine" genre, to use Jeffrey Kallberg's taxonomy. See Kallberg, *Chopin at the Boundaries*, ix.
99 As Graham Carr points out, pianists could rely on a repertoire of canonic works by male composers to enhance their "masculine authority" on stage. Carr, "Visualizing 'The Sound of Genius,'" 28. See also Boise, *Men, Masculinity, Music and Emotions*.
100 "A Rádio Nacional homenageia o Canadá," *A Noite*, 1 July 1943, 2.
101 Ariel, "Brasil-Canadá," *A Noite*, 7 July 1943, 4.
102 Cited in Sheila Ivert, "Jean Dansereau," *Carioca*, 26 June 1943, 62.
103 Jean Vallerand, "Jean Dansereau ou le nouveau Brésilien," *Le Canada*, 20 October 1943, 5. See also "Notre Canada connu au Brésil, rapporte M. Jean Dansereau," *La Presse*, 28 October 1943, 12, and Eugène Lapierre, "Le 1er juillet au Brésil. Échange d'oeuvres dans l'air," *Radiomonde*, 10 July 1943, 6.
104 Ariel, "Brasil-Canadá," *A Noite*, 7 July 1943, 4. See also H. Coutinho, "Uma oferta de arte do Canadá ao Brasil," *Jornal do Brasil*, 18 July 1943, 2.

## CHAPTER THREE

1 Elizabeth Wood to T.W.L. MacDermot, 12 February 1946, RG25, vol. 8502, LAC.
2 T.W.L. MacDermot to Elizabeth Wood, 4 March 1946, RG25, vol. 8502, LAC.
3 Suppo, "La politique culturelle française au Brésil entre les années 1920–1950," 23; Lessa, "L'influence intellectuelle française au Brésil," 17.
4 Lessa, "L'influence intellectuelle française au Brésil," 13, 237.
5 Vidal and de Luca, "Les Français au Brésil," 12; Vilela, "Les relations culturelles entre la France et le Brésil," 101.

6 Suppo, "La politique culturelle française au Brésil entre les années 1920–1950"; Lessa, "L'influence intellectuelle française au Brésil"; and Santomauro, "De Brésil to Brazil."
7 Ninkovich, *The Diplomacy of Ideas*, 29.
8 See Lessa, "A política cultural brasileira e a Sociedade das Nações"; Dumont, *L'Institut international de coopération intellectuelle et le Brésil*; Dumont, "De la coopération intellectuelle à la diplomatie culturelle"; and Rolland, "A instrumentalização das culturas estrangeiras no Estado Novo."
9 Ministério das Relações Exteriores, *Relatório: Ano de 1943*, 84–5. See also Santos, *Um novo olhar sobre o país vizinho*.
10 Dumont and Fléchet, "Brazilian Cultural Diplomacy in the Twentieth Century," 5, 7.
11 Ferreira, "Difusão cultural e projeção internacional," 87.
12 Roosevelt, "Address at Chautauqua, N.Y."
13 Rushton, "The Origins and Development of Canada's Public Diplomacy," 80.
14 Evans, *In the National Interest*, 6, 17.
15 Druick, *Projecting Canada*, 90.
16 Royal Commission on National Development in the Arts, Letters, and Sciences, *Report*, 256–8.
17 The CBC-IS is discussed at length in chapter 7.
18 Mosquin, "Advertising Canada Abroad."
19 Melnyk, *One Hundred Years of Canadian Cinema*, 41.
20 Jean Désy to Secretary of State for External Affairs, 1 October 1941, RG25, vol. 2640, LAC. Emphasis in original.
21 Ministério das Relações Exteriores, *Relatório: Ano de 1944*, 77.
22 Jean Désy to Secretary of State for External Affairs, 28 April 1944, RG25, vol. 2640, LAC.
23 T. Graça Aranha to Jean Désy, 9 December 1942, 82/3/11, AHI. See also T. Graça Aranha to Jean Désy, 9 June 1942, 82/3/11, AHI, and T. Graça Aranha to Jean Désy, 8 July 1942, 82/3/11, AHI.
24 Jean Désy to Secretary of State for External Affairs, 17 December 1942, RG25, vol. 3243, LAC.
25 Ogelsby, *Gringos from the Far North*, 52, and Rochlin, *Discovering the Americas*, 31.
26 Escott Reid to Canadian Minister in Washington, 8 January 1943, RG25, vol. 3243, LAC.
27 Canadian Minister in the United States to Secretary of State for External Affairs, 11 January 1943, RG25, vol. 3243, LAC.

28 N.A. Robertson to Jean Désy, 26 January 1943, RG25, vol. 3243, LAC.
29 Jean Désy to Secretary of State for External Affairs, 5 March 1943, RG25, vol. 3243, LAC.
30 H.F. Feaver to Canadian Minister in Washington, 6 April 1943, RG25, vol. 3243, LAC.
31 L.B. Pearson to Secretary of State for External Affairs, 14 May 1943, RG25, vol. 3243, LAC.
32 N.A. Robertson to Jean Désy, 18 August 1943, RG25, vol. 3243, LAC.
33 Ironically, philanthropic help often came from the United States: Brison, *Rockefeller, Carnegie & Canada*.
34 Tippett, *Making Culture*, 168.
35 Burtch, "The Sword and the Mind."
36 James L. Hall borrows this definition of propaganda from Ernst Kris and Nathan Leites. Cited in Hall, *Radio Canada International*, 34.
37 Jean Désy to Secretary of State for External Affairs, 17 December 1942, RG25, vol. 3243, LAC.
38 N.A. Robertson to Jean Désy, 18 August 1943, RG25, vol. 3243, LAC.
39 Minutes of Meeting on Cultural Relations with Latin America, 8 November 1943, RG25, vol. 3243, LAC. A young recruit at the time, Montreal-born Marcel Cadieux had recently alerted his colleagues at External Affairs that should they "ignore Quebec's special interest in France and Latin America, the province might be emboldened to pursue its own cultural diplomacy." Kelly, *The Good Fight*, 32.
40 Exchange of Notes between Canada and Brazil Constituting an Agreement for the Promotion of Cultural Relations between the Two Countries, Canada-Brazil, 24 May 1944, Treaty Series 1944, no. 15, 3.
41 See "Acordo cultural entre o Brasil e o Canadá," *O Jornal*, 25 May 1944, 3; "Fortalecendo os laços que unem as Américas," *Jornal do Brasil*, 25 May 1944, 8; and "As solenidades de ontem no Itamaratí," *Correio da Manhã*, 25 May 1944, 2.
42 For example, "Ottawa veut augmenter la pension et, de plus, réduire la limite d'âge," *Le Soleil*, 6 June 1944, 3, and "Ottawa Briefs," *Globe and Mail*, 6 June 1944, 7
43 See handwritten note dated 15 February 1946 at the bottom of the following letter: Elizabeth Wood to T.W.L. MacDermot, 12 February 1946, RG25, vol. 8502, LAC.
44 "Un traité culturel est signé entre le Canada et le Brésil," *Le Droit*, 26 May 1944, 1.
45 C. L'H, "Canada-Brésil," *Le Droit*, 6 June 1944, 3.

46 T.W.L. MacDermot to R.H. Meek, 7 May 1946, RG25, vol. 8502, LAC. See also M.J. Patry to Secretary of State for External Affairs, 21 June 1945, RG25, vol. 8502, LAC; G.W. Hilborn to J. Robert Kaine, 13 March 1945, RG25, vol. 8502, LAC; W.B. Herbert to T.W.L. Macdermot, 22 January 1946, RG25, vol. 8502, LAC; and R.H. Meek to T.W.L. MacDermot, 2 May 1946, RG25, vol. 8502, LAC.

47 Arthur Irwin did not seem to think much of Brazil's geopolitical importance when he indicated, upon learning of his posting there, that he "might be most useful" in another country where there is "substantive political work" to be done. Arthur Irwin to Secretary of State for External Affairs, 30 July 1956, MG31-E97, vol. 26, LAC. See also Fillion, "P.K. Page and the Art of Diplomacy."

48 Philip M. Broadmead to Anthony Eden, 29 May 1944, FO370, vol. 891, NA.

49 Malcolm MacDonald to Mr Attlee, 15 August 1942, FO370, vol. 764, NA.

50 C.E. Shuckburgh, "The Attitude of Canada Towards Pan-America in General and Latin America in Particular," memorandum attached to Malcolm MacDonald to Mr Attlee, 15 August 1942, FO370, vol. 764, NA.

51 Madokoro and McKenzie, "Writing Race into Canada's International History," 14.

52 See Touhey, *Conflicting Visions*; Lackenbauer, "Race, Gender, and International 'Relations'"; and Spooner, "Awakening Africa."

53 Jean Désy to Secretary of State for External Affairs, 23 June 1944, RG25, vol. 3278, LAC.

54 R.M.M. to Jean Désy, 11 July 1944, RG25, vol. 3278, LAC.

55 "Memorandum for the Prime Minister," 22 November 1943, RG25, vol. 3243, LAC.

56 Jean Désy to Secretary of State for External Affairs, 23 June 1944, RG25, vol. 3278, LAC.

57 Raul Leitão da Cunha, "Speech of Professor Raul Leitão da Cunha," n.d., RG25, vol. 3278, LAC.

58 Oswaldo Aranha, "Speech of Foreign Minister Oswaldo Aranha at the Inauguration of the Brazil-Canada Institute," n.d., RG25, vol. 3278, LAC; Oswaldo Aranha, "Speech of the Brazilian Foreign Minister," 1944, RG25, vol. 3243, LAC.

59 Jean Désy to Secretary of State for External Affairs, 20 December 1944, RG25, vol. 3278, LAC.

60 Berenguer Cesar, "Address by Minister Berenguer Cesar, Former Counsellor at the Brazilian Embassy, Ottawa, at the Inauguration of the Brazil-Canada Institute, São Paulo," 13 December 1944, RG25, vol. 3278, LAC.

61 Jean Désy, "Speech of the Canadian Ambassador," 1944, RG25, vol. 3243, LAC.
62 More than one million Canadians served in the war, compared to a little over twenty-five thousand for Brazil. Lochery, *Brazil*, 257; Stacey, *Canada and the Age of Conflict*, 370.
63 Jean Désy, "Speech of the Canadian Ambassador," 1944, RG25, vol. 3243, LAC.
64 Jean Désy, "Fondation de l'Institut Brésil-Canada," 14 June 1944, MG32 E2, vol. 1, LAC.
65 Exteriores to Embaixada em Ottawa, 5 April 1945, 37/03/08, AHI.
66 Roussin, "Nos voisins latins: Des raisons historiques et géographiques qui associent nos économies respectives"; Roussin, "Le Canada, fils et héritier de la coutume."
67 Marcel Rousin to Jean Désy, 11 November 1943, P232/1/5, CRCCFUO. On this topic, see Savard, "Pax Romana."
68 Marcel Roussin, "Pour un comité Canada-Brésil," *Le Droit*, 30 September 1943, in 36/05/04, AHI.
69 Caio de Mello Franco to Oswaldo Aranha, 14 October 1943, 36/05/04, AHI.
70 Caio de Mello Franco to Hector Perrier, 4 June 1943, 36/05/04, AHI.
71 Hector Perrier to Alphonse Fournier, 21 June 1943, P232/6/7, CRCCFUO.
72 As Maurice Demers explains, the O'Leary brothers' understanding of *latinité* sprung from *L'Action française*, a clerico-nationalist publication whose editor was the priest-historian Lionel Groulx. Demers, *Connected Struggles*, 76–81.
73 Ibid., 16. See also Lacroix, "Lien social, idéologie et cercles d'appartenance."
74 Maurice Demers notes that the Royal Canadian Mounted Police followed closely the activities of the O'Leary brothers and those of the UCLA: Demers, *Connected Struggles*, 94–100. See also "Memorandum for the Prime Minister," 17 July 1943, MG26-J4, vol. 275, no. 189389, LAC; and "Memorandum for the Prime Minister," 5 December 1943, MG26-J4, vol. 275, no. 189393, LAC.
75 For instance, consult the organization's annual report for 1942–43. Union des Latins d'Amérique, "Rapport général du secrétariat pour l'année se terminant le 1er oct. 1943," n.d., CLG40 P40/C4-4, BAnQ.
76 Cited in Union culturelle des Latins d'Amérique, *Rapport complet. Journées d'Amérique latine*, 1943, CLG40 P40/C4-5, BAnQ.
77 Demers, *Connected Struggles*, 86–7.
78 "Les Dominicains du Canada ouvrent une maison à São Paulo," *La Presse*, 5 December 1945, 16.

79 "La tournée triomphale du Quatuor alouette," *Le Devoir*, 3 November 1945, 7.

80 Osório Dutra to Secretário Geral, 25 October 1945, 135/05/07, AHI.

81 "Impressions et dépression … Rio de Janeiro," 1945, P232/10/03, CRCCFUO.

82 "Ambivalence" is the simultaneous desire for one thing and its opposite (in other words, it consists of the interplay between attraction and repulsion). The concept is closely related to "mimicry," which is when subalterns adopt the modes of being (the language, values, and appearance) of colonialist/imperialist agents to fulfill either a desire for assimilation or a need to resist. That process is often fraught with tension, and it tends to disrupt the racist gaze of those who seek to exert hegemonic power. Homi K. Bhabha further explains: "Colonial mimicry is the desire for a reformed, recognizable Other, *as a subject of difference that is almost the same, but not quite*. Which is to say that the discourse of mimicry is constructed around an *ambivalence*; in order to be effective, mimicry must continually produce its slippage, its excess, its difference." Bhabha, *The Location of Culture*, 86. Emphasis in original. See also Young, *Colonial Desire*, 133.

83 "Impressions et dépression … Rio de Janeiro," 1945, P232/10/03, CRCCFUO.

## CHAPTER FOUR

1 Cited in Oscar Richer, "Rio de Janeiro vu par le Quatuor," n.d., F454/6/6, AFEUL.

2 Marius Barbeau, "Folk-Songs from French Canada," 1942, F454/5/1, AFEUL.

3 Quatuor alouette, "Biography," n.d., F454/3/2.1, AFEUL.

4 Smith, *A History of Brazil*, 149.

5 Williams, "Church and State in Vargas's Brazil," 457.

6 In focusing partly on religion, this chapter echoes the arguments made by David Webster in his contribution to *Undiplomatic History*: "In short, religion needs to be read back into the study of Canada and the World." Webster, "Rethinking Religion's Role in Canadian Transnational Relations," 97.

7 Rumilly, *Histoire de la Société Saint-Jean-Baptiste de Montréal*.

8 Giumbelli, *Símbolos religiosos em controvérsia*; Giumbelli and Bosisio, "A política de um monumento."

9 Williams, "Church and State in Vargas's Brazil," 66, and Skidmore, *Brazil*, 111.

10 Levine, *Father of the Poor*, 36–7.

11 Hazan, "Religious Music and Church-State Relations in Brazil during the Vargas Era," 303, 305.

12 Jean Désy to Secretary of State for External Affairs, 4 February 1942, MG26-J1, vol. 323, no. 274231, LAC.

13 Bomeny, "Três decretos e um ministério," 152.

14 Cited in Jean Désy to Secretary of State for External Affairs, 4 February 1942, MG26-J1, vol. 323, no. 274231, LAC.

15 Letter to Jean Désy, 12 March 1942, MG26-J1, vol. 323, no. 274248, LAC. The decision to relocate had not been Desmarais's to make.

16 Desmarais, *La magie du passé*, 123–8, 162. The assignment had come from his superior, who felt perhaps that the priest was spending too much time under the spotlight and on the airwaves, where he saw himself as the "haut-parleur de Jésus."

17 "Para lá do patriotismo," *Diario de Noticias*, 22 April 1942, 3. Jean Désy to Secretary of State for External Affairs, 26 May 1942, RG25, vol. 2640, LAC.

18 Ogelsby, *Gringos from the Far North*, 201.

19 Goudreault, "Les missionnaires canadiens à l'étranger au XXe siècle"; LeGrand, "L'axe missionnaire catholique entre le Québec et l'Amérique latine"; Foisy, "Relire le catholicisme québécois au XXe siècle à partir des 'remarquables oubliés' que sont devenus les missionnaires."

20 Foisy, *Au risque de la conversion*, 215–16.

21 On the question of transnational solidarities and the transformative experience of missionary work, see also Burril and LeGrand, "Progressive Catholicism at Home and Abroad"; Demers, "Réimaginer les rapports nord-sud"; Desautels, "La représentation de l'Afrique dans le discours missionnaire canadien-français"; and Mills, *A Place in the Sun*.

22 On Canadian missionaries in Japan, see Ion, "Soul Searchers and Soft Power"; and Leclerc, "God's Envoys." Lionel Groulx dedicated a chapter on Brazil in his study of French-Canadian missionaries. Groulx, *Le Canada français missionnaire*, 347–57.

23 "Les Dominicains du Canada ouvrent une maison à São Paulo," *La Presse*, 5 December 1945, 16.

24 Desmarais, *La magie du passé*, 176.

25 Ibid., 234. See also Desmarais, *Mon voyage au Japon*.

26 Mitchell, *The North American Folk Music Revival*, 8. Ian McKay further explains: "As one of the great abstractions of Romanticism, 'the Folk' came to be regarded as the epitome of simple truth, work, and virtue, the antithesis of all that was overcivilized, tired, conventional, and insincere. The Folk were closer to nature … and could respond more spontaneously to 'natural music.' For romantic nationalists, the 'Folk' were those whose

very existence and culture testified to the possibility and necessity of the nation." McKay, *The Quest of the Folk*, 12, 14.

27 Cohen, *Rainbow Quest*, 8–38.

28 Davis, *Avoiding the Dark*, 62.

29 Andrade, *Música doce música*, 77.

30 Brumana, "Mario de Andrade y la Missão de pesquisas folclóricas."

31 Davis, *Avoiding the Dark*, 61.

32 "There was ... a complex and powerful Anglo-American folklore matrix, a common trans-Atlantic entropic sensibility that structured assumptions and methods in the study of the Folk and their supposed lore," argues McKay. McKay, *The Quest of the Folk*, 80.

33 "In the course of the late-nineteenth and early-twentieth centuries, Boas pioneered what he believed to be a science-based approach to anthropology ... This involved studying a unique culture in all its aspects, including art, languages, history, and religion. From his perspective, the French Canadians qualified as a culture and a history as a result of distinctive historical, social, and geographic conditions." Lerner, "Marius Barbeau and Sam Borenstein," 121.

34 McKay, *The Quest of the Folk*, 31–2, 50.

35 Keillor, "Marius Barbeau as a Promoter of Folk Music Performance and Composition."

36 Ernest Gagnon was a precursor whose work also inspired Marius Barbeau: Gagnon, *Chansons populaires du Canada*.

37 Haines, "Marius Barbeau et le Moyen-Âge," 187–8.

38 De Surmont, "Genèse de l'enquête ethnomusicologique collective au Canada français," 205.

39 Jean Désy, "O embaixador Jean Desy escreve para 'Brasil Musical' sôbre a música folclórica no Canadá," *Brasil Musical* 1, no. 8 (1945): 3.

40 Ibid.

41 Jean Désy, "As duas primas: 'Courte paille' e 'Caterineta,'" 9 August 1942, *Correio da Manhã*, 1.

42 Quatuor alouette, "The Alouette Vocal Quartette," n.d., F454/3/2.1, AFEUL.

43 Oscar O'Brien, "Causerie au sujet du folklore du Canada," 4 December 1933, F454/6/2, AFEUL.

44 The tour was most likely an initiative of the Paris-based Comité France-Amérique, which had created the Mission Jacques-Cartier early in 1934. Harvey, "Les relations culturelles entre la France et le Canada," 120; Lacroix, "Il faudrait que nous sachions être aussi cela," 116–17.

45 Gérard Gauthier, Paul Leduc, Antonio Dupras, Alexis Pepin, and Émile Boucher, who had been involved with the Troubadours de Bytown.

46 "Fête du quatrième centenaire de la découverte du Canada par Jacques Cartier," 10 July 1934, F454/6/4, AFEUL.
47 "Vers la terre canadienne: Drame et chants du terroir par le Quatuor alouette," 1937, F454/6/2, AFEUL.
48 Roger Filiatrault to Jean Désy, 10 October 1937, F454/6/1, AFEUL.
49 Jean Désy to J.H.A. Paquette, 24 November 1937, F454/6/1, AFEUL.
50 Oscar O'Brien to Wilfrid Pelletier, 7 December 1940, F454/5/1, AFEUL.
51 Jean Bruchési to Oscar O'Brien, 5 March 1942, F454/6/1, AFEUL; Chambre du conseil exécutif, "Arrêté en conseil no. 3411," 12 November 1943, F454/6/1, AFEUL.
52 Oscar O'Brien, "Rapport du voyage du Quatuor alouette," 1942, F454/6/1, AFEUL.
53 Oscar O'Brien to M.J. Pickering, 8 June 1942, F454/6/1, AFEUL.
54 Henry Letondal to Oscar O'Brien, 8 September 1941, F454/1/7.32, AFEUL.
55 Oscar O'Brien, "Rapport du voyage du Quatuor alouette," 1942, F454/6/1, AFEUL.
56 Cited in Henderson, "Angus L. Macdonald and the Conscription Crisis of 1944," 87. For more on the conscription crisis of 1944 and war on the home front in Montreal, see Durflinger, *Fighting from Home*; Burns, *Life on the Home Front*; and Fahrni, "The Second World War."
57 Roger Filiatrault, "E. 233438," 10 August 1943, F454/1/7, AFEUL.
58 Roger Filiatrault to Wilfrid Pelletier, 5 August 1943, F454/1/7, AFEUL.
59 A. de Gaspé Taché to Roger Filiatrault, 19 August 1944, F454/1/7, AFEUL.
60 Quatuor alouette, "The Alouette Vocal Quartette," n.d., F454/3/2.1, AFEUL.
61 "Passport," 1945–47, F454/1/1, AFEUL.
62 Jean Désy to Maurice Duplessis, 26 November 1945, F454/6/3, AFEUL.
63 "Contrat," 28 August 1945, F454/6/6, AFEUL.
64 "Rapport financier sur la tournée au Brésil," n.d., F454/6/6, AFEUL.
65 "Agenda," 1945, F454/1/2, AFEUL.
66 "Cultura artistica do Rio de Janeiro apresenta Le Quatuor alouette," 8 October 1945, 170P-600/5, SAGDUQÀM.
67 See set lists for broadcasts between 1 June 1944 and 4 October 1945, in F454/7/1.3, AFEUL.
68 "Catalogue complet du répertoire du Quatuor alouette," 1 July 1940, F454/8/1, AFEUL.
69 "Cultura artistica do Rio de Janeiro apresenta Le Quatuor alouette," 8 October 1945, 170P-600/5, SAGDUQÀM.
70 "Cotovias do Canadá," *Gazeta de Notícias*, 9 October 1945, 5; "Ménestrels do Canadá," *Diario de Noticias*, 16 October 1945, 3. For example, see "Canções do Canadá," *7 Dias*, 18 October 1945,

in F454/6/6, AFEUL, and "Hoje despedida ... do Quarteto alouette," *Correio da Manhã*, 24 October 1945, 13.

71 Newton, "Portrait of a Man," *Brazilian American*, 22 December 1945, 19, in MG32-E2, vol. 1, LAC.

72 "Le patrimoine musical du Canada français," 16 October 1945, F454/6/2, AFEUL. Strikethrough in original.

73 "Radio Gazeta: Quarteto Alouette," 16 November 1945, F454/6/6, AFEUL.

74 "Quarteto alouette: Audição do dia 18/10/945," 18 October 1945, F454/6/6, AFEUL.

75 *Dîner canadien*, n.d., P232/4/10, CRCCFUO. These were but a sample of the symbols that the Désys had at their disposal: Dawson, Gidney, and Wright, *Symbols of Canada*.

76 "Menu," 1945, P232/4/10, CRCCFUO.

77 "Le Quatuor alouette chante," 12 November 1945, P232/4/10, CRCCFUO.

78 "Discours qui ne sera pas prononcé par l'Ambassadeur du Canada," 12 November 1945, P232/4/10, CRCCFUO.

79 "Brillant succès du dîner canadien à Rio-de-Janeiro," *La Presse*, 14 November 1945, 3.

80 Jean-Gérard Fleury, "Le Canada reçoit le Brésil," *La Revue populaire*, December 1945, in F454/6/3, AFEUL.

81 "Programa no. 357," 9 October 1945, F454/6/6, AFEUL.

82 "Programa no. 359," 23 October 1945, F454/6/6, AFEUL.

83 "Le Quatuor alouette à l'Église Gloria," 14 October 1945, F454/6/2, AFEUL.

84 "Programa no. 360," 30 October 1945, F454/6/6, AFEUL.

85 Roger Filiatrault, diary, 9 September 1945, F454/6/6, AFEUL.

86 "Concert du Quatuor alouette," 1 October 1945, F454/6/2, AFEUL.

87 Marcel Roussin reported to the Quebec press that Brazilians responded with enthusiasm to Quatuor alouette's rendition of these songs, but Andrade Muncy, writing for *Jornal do Commercio*, thought otherwise. See "La tournée triomphale du Quatuor alouette," *Le Devoir*, 3 November 1945, 7, and Andrade Muncy, "Quatuor alouette," *Jornal do Commercio*, 10 October 1945, 2.

88 Frère Alfred to Quatuor alouette, 10 October 1945, F454/5/1, AFEUL; Frère Gérald to Quatuor alouette, 16 October 1945, F454/5/1, AFEUL.

89 Étienne-M. Laporte to Quatuor alouette, n.d., F454/5/1, AFEUL; "Album do Rio de Janeiro," n.d., F454/6/6, AFEUL.

90 Dom Raoul Hamel, "Pour la chanson populaire," *Le Devoir*, 1 September 1945, 8.

91 "Programa no. 358," 16 October 1945, F454/6/6, AFEUL.
92 "Cultura artistica do Rio de Janeiro apresenta Le Quatuor alouette," 8 October 1945, 170P-600/5, SAGDUQÀM.
93 See set lists available here: F454/6/1, AFEUL; F454/6/2, AFEUL; and F454/7/1.3, AFEUL.
94 "Teatro Municipal: Programa oficial," 18 November 1945, F454/6/2, AFEUL.
95 Jean Désy translated and sent this newspaper clipping to Quebec: "Quatuor alouette à Sao-Paulo," *L'Action catholique*, 15 December 1945, 4.
96 See "Vozes de um país amigo trazem ao Brasil mensagens de harmonia," *O Cruzeiro*, 29 October 1945, 62; "Vozes cheias de encanto interpretando lindas canções," *Vanguarda*, 15 October 1945, in F454/6/6, AFEUL; "Chega ao Rio o Quarteto alouette," *A Noticia*, 6 October 1945, in F454/6/6, AFEUL; and "Arte – cartão de visita dos povos," *Correio da Noite*, 29 October 1945, in F454/6/6, AFEUL.
97 "Músicas de ontem, melodias de sempre," *Brasil Portugal*, 23 October 1945, in F454/6/6, AFEUL.
98 "O folclore canadense através de doces canções entrelaçado os sentimentos de dois povos amigos," *A Noticia*, 16 October 1945, in F454/6/6, AFEUL. See also "O Quarteto alouette," *Correio da Manhã*, 24 October 1945, 11.
99 Roger Champoux, "Le Brésil est la terre de l'avenir," *La Presse*, 5 December 1945, 3; "La tournée triomphale du Quatuor alouette," *Le Devoir*, November 3, 1945, 7. *Passe-temps* was also full of praise: "La tournée triomphale du Quatuor alouette au pays du café," *Passe-temps*, February 1946, 5.
100 Most English-language papers contented themselves with printing the same press release prior to Quatuor alouette leaving for Brazil. See "Alouette Quartet Leaves for Brazil," *Sherbrooke Telegram*, 7 September 1945, in F454/6/3, AFEUL; "Alouette Quartet Heads for Brazil," *Leaside Tribune*, 13 September 1945, in F454/6/3, AFEUL; and "Alouette Quartet," *Toronto Saturday Night*, 15 September 1945, in F454/6/3, AFEUL.
101 "Peace Brings Changes for Many Musicians," *Montreal Star*, 1 September 1945, in F454/6/3, AFEUL.

## CHAPTER FIVE

1 Jean Désy to Getúlio Vargas, 4 December 1944, EH, vol. 190, PAC-4, AN.
2 Cited in *Canadian Art in Brazil*, 76.
3 Jean Désy to J.A. MacKinnon, 9 February 1945, RG20-3, vol. 1323, LAC.

4 Cited in *Canadian Graphic Arts in Brazil*, 96.
5 For more on the challenges of curating exhibits overseas, see Jessup and Smith, "Introduction," 283–4.
6 For a detailed history, see Ord, *The National Gallery of Canada*.
7 King, *Defiant Spirits*, 336, 341–2.
8 Ord, *The National Gallery of Canada*, 85.
9 King, *Defiant Spirits*, 407.
10 Clendinning, "Exhibiting a Nation," 104.
11 Mosquin, "Advertising Canada Abroad," 23–4, 282.
12 Tippett, *Making Culture*, 91.
13 Ord, *The National Gallery of Canada*, 98.
14 See the board of trustees minutes for 1942–46, available in vol. 343, file 8, NGCLA.
15 For example, Montreal's mayor, Camillien Houde, was arrested and put in a federal internment camp after inciting citizens to ignore the Canadian Registration Act and resist conscription. See Amyot, *Le Québec entre Pétain et de Gaulle*; Bergère, *Vichy au Canada*; and Comeau, *Le Bloc populaire*.
16 Edmonton Art Gallery, *The Contemporary Arts Society*, 6, 38.
17 Trépanier, *Peinture et modernité au Québec*, 16.
18 For a discussion of Paul-Émile Borduas from the perspective of the sociology of art, see Warren, *L'art vivant*.
19 Edmonton Art Gallery, *The Contemporary Arts Society*, 28.
20 Ibid., 12.
21 Gauvreau, *The Catholic Origins of Quebec's Quiet Revolution*, 23–4. See also Trépanier, "Les paramètres épistémologiques et idéologiques d'un premier discours sur la modernité," 36, and Cellard, "Avant *Refus global*," 85.
22 Trépanier, *Peinture et modernité au Québec*, 99–106.
23 The impact of the war on the book publishing industry is discussed at length in Michon, *Les éditeurs québécois et l'effort de guerre*, and Michon, *Histoire de l'édition littéraire au Québec*.
24 Trépanier, "La modernité artistique au Québec avant les ruptures 'avant-gardistes,'" 11.
25 Carney, "Modern Art, the Local, and the Global," 112.
26 Edmonton Art Gallery, *The Contemporary Arts Society*, 20.
27 Gagnon, *Pellan*, 42.
28 Carney, "Modern Art, the Local, and the Global," 112.
29 Director to Jean Désy, 3 February 1943, vol. 130, file 13, NGCLA.
30 Jean Désy to McCurry, 14 November 1941, vol. 130, file 13, NGCLA.
31 *Pintura Canadense Contemporânea*, 1944, RG20-3, vol. 1323, LAC. See also the embassy's reports: Jean Désy to J.A. MacKinnon, 9 February

1945, RG20-3, vol. 1323, LAC; Jean Désy to H.O. McCurry, 3 January 1945, vol. 304, file 4, NGCLA; and Jean Désy to H.O. McCurry, 30 January 1945, vol. 304, file 4, NGCLA.

32 Jean Désy to H.O. McCurry, 15 March 1945, vol. 304, file 4, NGCLA.

33 Cited in *Canadian Art in Brazil*, 66, 169, 183, 271.

34 Jean Désy, "A pequena indústria de arte no Canadá," December 1942, in MG32-E2, vol. 2, LAC.

35 Cited in *Canadian Art in Brazil*, 36.

36 Ibid., 7, 211.

37 See High, "Recognizing Genocide in Canada," and Carleton and Woolford, "Ignore Debaters and Denialists, Canada's Treatment of Indigenous Peoples Fits the Definition of Genocide."

38 Cited in *Canadian Art in Brazil*, 32, 62.

39 Ibid., 183, 225.

40 H.O. McCurry to T.W.L. MacDermot, 9 March 1945, vol. 304, file 4, NGCLA.

41 Letter from H.O. McCurry to various artists, 1 June 1944, vol. 304, file 4, NGCLA.

42 H.O. McCurry, "Duas palavras," in *Pintura Canadense Contemporânea*, 1944, RG20-3, vol. 1323, LAC. An English-language version of the text, dated 2 October 1944, is available in vol. 304, file 4, NGCLA.

43 H.O. McCurry to T.W.L. MacDermot, 9 March 1945, vol. 304, file 4, NGCLA. A more pointed criticism and a list of pre-emptive directives for future endeavours appear in the annual report for 1945–46: "Exhibitions of Canadian art in foreign countries have always played an important part in the National Gallery's activities in the past and are now considered by the Trustees as a vital part of their duties to the Canadian people arising out of the National Gallery Act. The proper arrangement of these exhibitions requires both selection by competent and impartial juries and the professional advice of a trained staff, in order that the highest standard may be maintained in the Canadian work sent abroad ... It is hardly necessary to mention here the curtailment of this activity during periods of war and of depression when the Gallery's appropriation was reduced, but conditions such as these ought not to hamper the arrangement of foreign exhibitions at a time when world relations are of such vital importance." "Annual Report of the Board of Trustees for the Fiscal Year 1945–46," n.d., vol. 98, file 2, NGCLA.

44 D.W.B, "Brazil Sees Canadian Art," *Canadian Art* 2, no. 3 (March 1945): 105.

45 Cited in *Canadian Art in Brazil*, 109.

46 Jean Désy to H.O. McCurry, 15 March 1945, vol. 304, file 4, NGCLA; H.O. McCurry to Jacques de Tonnancour, 17 May 1945, 170P-030/1, SAGDUQÀM. The three works sold were *Paysage laurentien*, *Nu couché*, and *Jeune fille assise*. A portion of the proceeds went to the Brazilian Red Cross.
47 D.W.B, "Brazil Sees Canadian Art," *Canadian Art* 2, no. 3 (March 1945): 105.
48 H.O. McCurry, "Duas palavras," in *Pintura Canadense Contemporânea*, 1944, RG20-3, vol. 1323, LAC.
49 Cited in *Canadian Art in Brazil*, 26.
50 J.E. Ribeiro to Jacques de Tonnancour, 16 April 1945, 170P-030/1, SAGDUQÀM.
51 "Canada-Brésil," *Bloc populaire*, 11 May 1945, in 170P-030/1, SAGDUQÀM.
52 For a brief outline of the gallery's history and its connection to the Contemporary Arts Society, see Houle, "La galerie Dominion." For a lengthier profile of the artist, Folch-Ribas, *Jacques de Tonnancour*.
53 The ecologist Pierre Dansereau, a close friend of Jean Désy, also visited Brazil as a guest of the Brazilian government in 1945–46: Palmer, de Sá, and Sá, "Ecology, International Cooperation, and the Biogeographic Configuration of Brazil."
54 Cited in Marc Berkowitz, "Cultural Activities: The Canadian Painter Jacques de Tonnancour," *Brazil Herald*, 22 May 1946, in 170P-600/6, SAGDUQÀM.
55 Cited in Eloi de Grandmont, "Jacques de Tonnancour est-il le fruit mûr de nos Beaux-Arts," *Le Canada*, 12 June 1945, 7.
56 Cited in *Canadian Art in Brazil*, 183.
57 Jacques de Tonnancour to H.O. McCurry, 22 May 1945, vol. 304, file 4, NGCLA.
58 Michel B. Kamenka, "De Tonnancour: Artista canadense-francês," *Planalto* 10 (August 1945): 27–33.
59 See "Le Quatuor alouette," 8 October 1945, in 170P-600/5, SAGDUQÀM, and "Discours qui ne sera pas prononcé par l'Ambassadeur du Canada," in 170P-600/5, SAGDUQÀM.
60 See "Conferencias sobre o Canadá," n.d., in 170P-600/6, SAGDUQÀM, and "O desenvolvimento da vida artística do Canadá," 7 July 1946, in 170P-600/6, SAGDUQÀM.
61 Cited in Eloi de Grandmont, "Jacques de Tonnancour est-il le fruit mûr de nos Beaux-Arts," *Le Canada*, 12 June 1945, 7.
62 Jacques de Tonnancour, "Rio de Janeiro – A Challenge," *Canadian Art* 4, no. 2 (March 1947): 57.

63 Ibid., 56. The piece appeared subsequently in *Diário de Noticias*: Jacques de Tonnancour, "Rio de Janeiro, um desafio," *Diario de Notícias – Letras, Artes, Idéias Gerais*, 24 August 1947, 1.
64 Marc Berkowitz, "Cultural Activities," *Brazil Herald*, 22 May 1946, in 170P-600/6, SAGDUQÀM.
65 For a copy of the catalogue, see *Artes Gráficas do Canadá*, 1946, in 170P-600/6, SAGDUQÀM. See also *Exposição de Jacques de Tonnancour*, 1946, in 170P-600/6, SAGDUQÀM.
66 H.O. McCurry to T.W.L. MacDermot, 15 March 1945, vol. 136, file 6, NGCLA.
67 Douglas Duncan to H.O. McCurry, 15 April 1945, vol. 136, file 6, NGCLA.
68 Cited *Canadian Graphic Arts in Brazil*, 25, 109, 124, 131.
69 Ibid., 146.
70 Ibid., 35, 41.
71 Ibid., 16.
72 Ibid., 137–8.
73 Ibid., 16.
74 Jacques de Tonnancour to Julien [Hébert], 1946, in 170P-030/18, SAGDUQÀM.

## CHAPTER SIX

1 Ernest MacMillan, diary, 16 September 1946, MUS 7, vol. 31, D.48, LAC.
2 Hilton, *Brazil and the Soviet Challenge*, 220–2.
3 Jean Désy to Secretary of State for External Affairs, 4 July 1944, RG25, vol. 2640, LAC.
4 Dumont and Fléchet, "Brazilian Cultural Diplomacy in the Twentieth Century," 7.
5 Hertzman, *Making Samba*, 3. See also Vianna, *The Mystery of Samba*.
6 McCann, *Hello, Hello Brazil*, 42.
7 Ibid.
8 Williams, *Culture Wars in Brazil*, 86.
9 McCann, *Hello, Hello Brazil*, 90. For more on the transnational circulation of vernacular music and the performative agency of the non-elites, see Denning, *Noise Uprising*; Shaw, *Tropical Travels*; and Seigel, *Uneven Encounters*.
10 Gil-Montero, *Brazilian Bombshell*, 70–2.
11 Darlene J. Sadlier explains that "Carmen Miranda overturned earlier Hollywood stereotypes of Latin Americans by playing a charismatic,

talented, and 'good-willed' Latin who enchants everyone around her." Sadlier adds that "by repeatedly playing that role, she became another kind of stereotype – a hybrid created by Hollywood of its image of Latin America on the order of the indigenous, exotic Other depicted in colonial texts." Sadlier, *Brazil Imagined*, 229.

12 McCann, *Hello, Hello Brazil*, 147.

13 Dunn, *Brutality Garden*, 28. See also Davis, *White Face, Black Mask*, 162.

14 Williams, *Culture Wars in Brazil*, 201.

15 Peronne and Dunn, "Chiclete com banana," 13.

16 Martha Gil-Montero advances some of these hypotheses in her biography of Carmen Miranda. See Gil-Montero, *Brazilian Bombshell*, 70–1, and Tinhorão, *História social da música popular brasileira*, 300–1. Charles A. Peronne and Christopher Dunn also write about the link between the "Golden Age of Samba" and musical diplomacy, which Anaïs Fléchet argues must not be overstated. See Peronne and Dunn, "Chiclete com banana," 10; and Fléchet, "As partituras da identidade," 237.

17 Dumont and Fléchet, "Brazilian Cultural Diplomacy in the Twentieth Century," 4, 5, 10. See also Crespo, "O Itamaraty e a cultura brasileira."

18 "Orquestra Sinfônica Brasileira – 1940–1943," n.d., GC 1355F, FGV-CPDOC.

19 "Orquestra Sinfônica Brasileira," n.d., Pasta 30/4, BANUFRJ.

20 João Batista, "Nossa plataforma," *Brasil Musical* 1, no. 1 (November 1944): 1–2.

21 "Le pianiste Estrella à Radio-Canada, le 30," *L'Avenir du Nord*, 26 March 1943, 4.

22 T. Graça Aranha to Caio de Mello Franco, 7 January 1943, 37/02/13, AHI.

23 "Le pianiste Estrella à Radio-Canada, le 30," *L'Avenir du Nord*, 26 March 1943, 4.

24 Letter to Oswaldo Aranha, 3 April 1943, 48-931, ACI.

25 José de Lima Siqueira to Diretor da Divisão de Cooperação Intelectual, 9 October 1945, 112/01/14, AHI.

26 Jean Désy to Ernest MacMillan, 6 December 1945, MUS 7, vol. 2, A.51, LAC.

27 Ernest MacMillan to T.W.L. MacDermot, 26 January 1946, MUS 7, vol. 2, A.51, LAC.

28 "Jose Siqueira," *Radiomonde*, 9 February 1946, 6.

29 Helmer, *Growing with Canada*, 83.

30 Brison, *Rockefeller, Carnegie & Canada*, 10, 12. See also Litt, *The Muses, the Masses, and the Massey Commission*, 21.

31 On this topic, see Edwardson, *Canadian Content*, 27–50.
32 Teigrob, *Warming Up to the Cold War*, 227.
33 Sévigny, "The Influence of Latin Music on the French-Canadian Popular Song and Dance Scene," 5.
34 See the following newsletter for the UCLA's member list and for examples of the organization's cultural activities: UCLA, *Union des Latins d'Amérique* 6, no. 17, 31 December 1947, CLG40 P40/C4-11, BAnQ.
35 John Patrick Leary traces Latinophilia to the cultural "rediscovery" of Latin America during the Good Neighbor era. He characterizes it as "exoticist in its fetishization of racial, national, and ethnic difference, anecdotal and observational in its use of evidence, and generally popular rather than scholarly in tone." Leary, *A Cultural History of Underdevelopment*, 112. In Quebec, Latinophilia also fed into nationalist sentiments with some French-Canadian intellectuals finding inspiration in the anti-imperialist struggles of the South American republics. Demers, "De l'exotisme à l'effet miroir."
36 Beaunoyer, *Fleur d'Alys*, 64.
37 A.H. Joseph to Alys Robi, 28 November 1944, MCQP1 S2-SS1-D28, MC.
38 Sévigny, "The Influence of Latin Music on the French-Canadian Popular Song and Dance Scene," 12. Many of these songs are featured on Alys Robi, *L'Anthologie*, 2004, Disques XXI-21 XXI-CD-2-1502, 3 x compact discs.
39 Beaunoyer, *Fleur d'Alys*, 75.
40 Ibid., 72. See also "Latin American Frolics," March 1943, MCQP1 S2-SS1-D11, MC.
41 Beaunoyer, *Fleur d'Alys*, 89–91. See also Marie-Jeanne Patry, "Alys Robi, reine de la chanson légère de chez nous," *L'Oeil*, 15 December 1945, 24.
42 A car accident derailed Alys Robi's career and prevented her from pursuing opportunities in the United States.
43 "Discos mais vendidos," *A Scena Muda*, 7 September 1948, 28, and Sylvio Tulio Cardoso, "Discos populares," *Diario da Noite*, 19 August 1948, 8.
44 Helmer, *Growing with Canada*, 9.
45 Ibid., 238, 241.
46 Proctor, *Canadian Music of the Twentieth Century*, 18. Keillor, *Music in Canada*, 302.
47 Keillor, "Marius Barbeau as a Promoter of Folk Music Performance and Composition," 147. Ethnographers and composers also collaborated in the effort to establish a sound library of Indigenous materials. Such work was often complicit with the state's efforts to advance the colonial project. Dylan Robinson explains that "ethnographers, folklorists, and

anthropologists undertook such collection under the auspices of feeling responsibility to document and preserve songs for fear that they would vanish in the onslaught of modernity." He adds: "What is today understood as the 'salvage paradigm' – a false ascription of the inevitable extinction of Indigenous cultural practices and the resultant desire to save them – was at the time motivated by a sense of ethnographic responsibility, a similar practice of best-intentionality that led to the establishment of the residential schools and the sixties scoop." Robinson, *Hungry Listening*, 153.

48 Keillor, *Music in Canada*, 302.

49 Morey, "Introduction," 11.

50 MacMillan, "Problems of Music in Canada," 92.

51 Although it was created at the end of the war, the Canadian Music Council only acquired its federal charter in 1949. See Schabas, *Sir Ernest MacMillan*, 202–5.

52 Morey, "Introduction," 9. See also Schabas, *Sir Ernest MacMillan*, 310.

53 Helmer, *Growing with Canada*, 84.

54 Ibid.

55 See Pelletier, *Une symphonie inachevée*.

56 See Keillor, *Music in Canada*, 181, and Schabas, *Sir Ernest MacMillan*, 94.

57 Incidentally, MacMillan also secured a prize with his "Six bergerettes du Bas Canada" that year.

58 For a discussion of Claude Champagne's importance, see Laurendeau, *Cent ans de Prix d'Europe*.

59 Incidentally, Wilfrid Pelletier was in Rio de Janeiro at the same time as Ernest MacMillan and Claude Champagne. He was accompanying his wife, opera singer Rose Bampton, who was performing with the Metropolitan Opera in Brazil. Jean Désy organized a recital at his house, with Pelletier and Champagne accompanying Bampton on the piano and organ, respectively. "Trois musiciens sont applaudis à Rio," *La Presse*, 7 September 1946, 55.

60 Claude Champagne to Ernest MacMillan, 5 September 1945, MUS 7, vol. 2, A.51, LAC.

61 MacLennan, *Two Solitudes*.

62 Claude Champagne to Ernest MacMillan, 5 September 1945, MUS 7, vol. 2, A.51, LAC. See also T.W.L. MacDermot to Dana Porter, 16 August 1945, RG25, vol. 3799, LAC; T.W.L. MacDermot to Jean Désy, 24 September 1945, RG25, vol. 3799, LAC.

63 Ernest MacMillan to T.W.L. MacDermot, 26 January 1946, MUS 7, vol. 2, A.51, LAC. Emphasis in original.

64 Claude Champagne to Ernest MacMillan, 7 November 1945, MUS 7, vol. 2, A.51, LAC.
65 Claude Champagne to Ernest MacMillan, 10 April 1946, MUS 7, vol. 2, A.51, LAC.
66 Ernest MacMillan to Bruno Zirato, 13 April 1946, MUS 7, vol. 2, A.51, LAC.
67 Ernest MacMillan to Bruno Zirato, 8 April 1946, MUS 7, vol. 2, A.51, LAC.
68 T.W.L. MacDermot to Ernest MacMillan, 23 January 1946, RG25, vol. 3799, LAC.
69 Ernest MacMillan to T.W.L. MacDermot, 26 January 1946, MUS 7, vol. 2, A.51, LAC.
70 Ernest MacMillan to Jean Désy, 30 August 1945, MUS 7, vol. 2, A.51, LAC.
71 Ernest MacMillan to Claude Champagne, 4 November 1945, MUS 7, vol. 2, A.51, LAC.
72 Letter to Jean Désy, 3 June 1946, MUS 29, vol. I3, LAC.
73 José Siqueira to Claude Champagne, 21 March 1946, MUS 29, vol. I3, LAC.
74 Claude Champagne to Ernest MacMillan, 17 April 1946, MUS 29, vol. I3, LAC.
75 Jean Désy submitted separate reports to the Department of External Affairs. See Jean Désy to Secretary of State for External Affairs, 24 September 1946, RG25, vol. 3799, LAC; and Jean Désy to Secretary of State for External Affairs, 3 September 1946, RG25, vol. 3799, LAC.
76 See "Mensageiros do Canadá," *Brasil Musical* 17 (1946): 19; Roberto Lyrafilho, "Os convidados do maestro Siqueira," *Revista da Semana*, 7 December 1946, 19; and "Sir Ernest MacMillan e Claude Champagne: Duas grandes expressões musicais do Canadá," *Diario Carioca*, 28 July 1946, 9.
77 See "Ondas Musicais dedicam a dois notáveis regentes canadenses," *O Jornal*, 30 July 1946, 6; and "A caminho do Rio dois notáveis musicistas canadenses," *A Notícia*, 26 July 1946, in MUS 7, vol. 108, LAC.
78 For example, see Charles Lynch, "Desy, MacMillan Give Brazilians Respect for Canada," *The Times*, 10 September 1946, in MUS 7, vol. 108, LAC; "Canadian Culture," *The News*, 26 September 1946, in MUS 7, vol. 108, LAC; and "Jean Desy Puts Canada on Map in Brazil," *Montreal Star*, 12 September 1946, in MUS 7, vol. 108, LAC.
79 Jose Siqueira to Ernest MacMillan, 16 May 1946, MUS 7, vol. 2, A.52, LAC; Secretary of Ernest MacMillan to Walter P. Brown, 12 June 1946, MUS 7, vol. 2, A.52, LAC.
80 Mariz, *Vida musical*, 171. Eugene Ormandy, William Steinberg, and Charles Munch were among the OSB's other guests in 1946.

81 Ernest MacMillan was also supposed to perform Francisco Mignone's "Congada," but the score never arrived from São Paulo: Marc Berkowitz, "Cultural Activities," *Brazil Herald*, 27 August 1946, in MUS 7, vol. 108, LAC.
82 For example, "A caminho do Rio dois notáveis musicistas canadenses," *A Notícia*, 26 July 1946, in MUS 7, vol. 108, LAC.
83 One journalist got the world wars mixed up and thought that Ernest MacMillan had survived a Nazi internment camp: "Maestro Sir Ernest MacMillan," *Jornal do Commercio*, 4 August 1946, in MUS 7, vol. 41, LAC.
84 Ayres de Andrade, "MacMillan e a Sinfônica Brasileira," *O Jornal*, 16 August 1946, in MUS 7, vol. 108, LAC. See also "Canadian Music for Brazilians," *The Examiner*, 12 September 1946, in MUS 7, vol. 108, LAC; D'or, "Música. Orquestra Sinfônica Brasileira," *Diàrio de Noticias*, 15 August 1946, 2.
85 "Canadiens à Rio-de-Janeiro," *La Patrie*, 8 October 1946, 10.
86 Thomas Archer, "Report from Brazil," *Montreal Gazette*, 28 September 1946, 10.
87 Claude Champagne is often pictured smoking in the press. See, for example, "Mensageiros do Canadá," *Brasil Musical* 17 (1946): 19, and Roberto Lyrafilho, "Os convidados do maestro Siqueira," *Revista da Semana*, 7 December 1946, 19. On the topic of smoking and masculine sociability, see Rudy, *The Freedom to Smoke*.
88 Thomas Archer, "Report from Brazil," *Montreal Gazette*, 28 September 1946, 10.
89 Ernest MacMillan, diary, 16 September 1946, MUS 7, vol. 31, D.48, LAC. See also Marc Berkowitz, "Cultural Activities," *Brazil Herald*, 15 August 1946, in MUS 7, vol. 108, LAC.
90 Ernest MacMillan, diary, 8 August 1946, MUS 7, vol. 31, D.48, LAC.
91 Ernest MacMillan, diary, 16 September 1946, MUS 7, vol. 31, D.48, LAC.
92 Ernest MacMillan, diary, 7 August 1946, MUS 7, vol. 31, D.48, LAC.
93 Ernest MacMillan, diary, 2 August 1946, MUS 7, vol. 31, D.48, LAC.
94 Ernest MacMillan, diary, 4–5 August 1946, MUS 7, vol. 31, D.48, LAC.
95 Ernest MacMillan, diary, 2 August 1946, MUS 7, vol. 31, D.48, LAC.
96 Ernest MacMillan, diary, 16 September 1946, MUS 7, vol. 31, D.48, LAC.
97 Ernest MacMillan, diary, 4–5 August 1946, MUS 7, vol. 31, D.48, LAC.
98 Ernest MacMillan, diary, 16 September 1946, MUS 7, vol. 31, D.48, LAC.
99 "Interview with Claude Champagne," n.d., MUS 29, vol. I3, LAC; Pierre de Grandpré, "Les Brésiliens vus par M. Claude Champagne," *Le Devoir*, 30 September 1946, 5.

100 Francisco Cavalcanti, "Ernest MacMillan, Claude Champagne e Gyorgy Sandor no Municipal," *Jornal do Brasil*, 15 August 1946, 8.

101 Charles Lynch, "Desy, MacMillan Give Brazilians Respect for Canada," *The Times*, 10 September 1946, in MUS 7, vol. 108, LAC. Emphasis in original.

102 Ernest MacMillan, diary, 4–5 August 1946, MUS 7, vol. 31, D.48, LAC.

103 Cited in Pierre de Grandpré, "Les Brésiliens vus par M. Claude Champagne," *Le Devoir*, 30 September 1946, 5.

104 Thomas Archer, "Report from Brazil," *Montreal Gazette*, 28 September 1946, 10.

105 "Jean Desy Puts Canada on Map in Brazil," *Montreal Star*, 12 September 1946, in MUS 7, vol. 108, LAC. See also Colin Sabiston, "Music Subsidy Solution Seen in Happy Medium," *Globe and Mail*, 2 October 1946, 21.

106 Ernest MacMillan, diary, 3 August 1946, MUS 7, vol. 31, D.48, LAC.

107 Charles Lynch, "Rio Welcomes Canadian Culture," *Globe and Mail*, 10 September 1946, 7.

108 George Austen, "Exterminating the Domesticated Bison," *Mayfair* 21, no. 1 (January 1947): 46.

109 Ernest MacMillan to José Siqueira, 19 October 1946, MUS 7, vol. 2, A.53, LAC.

110 José Siqueira to Ernest MacMillan, 17 March 1947, MUS 7, vol. 2, A.53, LAC.

## CHAPTER SEVEN

1 Inaugurated in 1931 in the heart of the city's Lafontaine Park, Plateau Hall was home to the OCSM in addition to hosting numerous other concerts, including those of Quatuor alouette and the Montreal Youth Symphony Orchestra. The venue's main floor and balcony had a combined capacity of more than fifteen hundred seats.

2 Royal Commission on National Development in the Arts, Letters, and Sciences, *Report*, xi.

3 Litt, *The Muses, the Masses, and the Massey Commission*, 250.

4 Edwardson, *Canadian Content*, 57. On this topic, see Tippett, *Making Culture*; Brison, *Rockefeller, Carnegie & Canada*; and Smith, "From Guthrie to Greenberg."

5 Royal Commission on National Development in the Arts, Letters, and Sciences, *Report*, 256, 366.

6 Standing Committee on External Affairs, *Minutes of Proceedings and Evidence No. 6*, 155.

7 Royal Commission on National Development in the Arts, Letters, and Sciences, *Report*, 254, 263.

8 For example, Bernard J. Hibbitts differentiates between the CBC-IS as "a broadcasting organization *per se*" and the CBC-IS as "a psychological instrument" when he writes that "the broadcast historian is equally interested in shortwave transmissions and transcriptions; he is as much concerned with broadcasts to Latin America as with broadcasts to the USSR. The student of foreign policy … must be far more sensitive to the explicitly political aspects of his subject – thus the concentration … on shortwave transmissions to European, and especially East European, targets." Hibbitts, "The CBC International Service as a Psychological Instrument of Canadian Foreign Policy in the Cold War," ix.

9 As Mary Vipond argues, media events of this type double as "inclusive and consensual ceremonies that bind together modern societies at special moments, transforming audiences into publics." The CBC's experience on that front, she adds, reveals that it also often served to "subtly (and sometimes not-so-subtly)" reinforce social hierarchies in addition to underscoring the broadcaster's "own role in the construction of Canadian identity." Vipond, "The Royal Tour of 1939 as a Media Event," 150.

10 For a discussion of the early history of domestic broadcasting, see Vipond, *Listening In*.

11 Fejes, *Imperialism, Media, and the Good Neighbor*, 44.

12 Seul and Ribeiro, "Revisiting Transnational Broadcasting," 367.

13 Rawnsley, *Radio Diplomacy and Propaganda*, 7.

14 The Canadian-born Reginald Fessenden reportedly was the first to broadcast a "voice message" in 1900. As Michael Nelson notes, the landmark event did not result in Canada becoming a pioneer in international radio. The country was slow to take advantage of the medium's potential, resulting in others taking the lead instead. Nelson, *War of the Black Heavens*, 111.

15 Seul and Ribeiro, "Revisiting Transnational Broadcasting," 368. See also Fejes, *Imperialism, Media, and the Good Neighbor*, 44–6, and Rawnsley, "Introduction to International Broadcasting and Public Diplomacy in the 21st Century," 43.

16 Fejes, *Imperialism, Media, and the Good Neighbor*, 4, 46–60. See also Rosenberg, *Spreading the American Dream*, 92–7.

17 Sadlier, *Americans All*, 27.

18 Cull, *The Cold War and the United States Information Agency*, 14. For a broader discussion of shortwave broadcasting, see Fox, *Latin American*

*Broadcasting*; Berg, *On the Short Waves*; and Berg, *Broadcasting for the Short Waves.*

19 Sousa, *Rádio e propaganda política*, 110. See also Coelho, *Educadores no rádio*, 33.

20 Tota, *O imperialismo sedutor*, 144–5.

21 These developments and collaboration with the United States contributed to the modernization, consolidation, and expansion of Brazil's broadcasting infrastructure. Sousa, *Rádio e propaganda política*, 131. See also Jambeiro, *Tempos de Vargas*.

22 As Thomas Turino explains, radio in Brazil performed the role that Benedict Anderson assigned to print capitalism in his study of the origins of nationalisms: Anderson, *Imagined Communities*, 44–6; and Turino, "Nationalism and Latin American Music," 187.

23 See Calabre, "Políticas públicas culturais de 1924 a 1945," 168, and Calabre, *Políticas culturais no Brasil*, 37–9.

24 R. Magalhães Junior, "A onda curta da Rádio Nacional representa uma grande vitoria do Brasil," *A Noite*, 2 February 1943, 1.

25 "Onça hoje e sempre," *A Noite*, 31 December 1942, 7.

26 Hall, *Radio Canada International*, 12, 15.

27 "Establishment of a Short Wave Station," 3 September 1941, in *International Broadcasting Service: Information Prepared on the Desirability of its Establishment, 1937–1942*, RG41, vol. 125, LAC.

28 L.W. Brockington to Prime Minister, 26 October 1937, in *International Broadcasting Service*, RG41, vol. 125, LAC. See also "Establishment of a Short Wave Station: Digest of Editorial Opinions," n.d., in *International Broadcasting Service*, RG41, vol. 125, LAC.

29 Augustin Frigon, "Report on the Desirability of Establishing a Short Wave Station in Canada," n.d., in *International Broadcasting Service*, RG41, vol. 125, LAC.

30 L.W. Brockington to Prime Minister, 26 October 1937, in *International Broadcasting Service*, RG41, vol. 125, LAC.

31 "Order-in-Council 8168," 18 September 1942, RG25, vol. 2203, LAC.

32 L.W. Brockington to Prime Minister, 26 October 1937, in *International Broadcasting Service*, RG41, vol. 125, LAC.

33 Augustin Frigon, "Report on the Desirability of Establishing a Short Wave Station in Canada," n.d., in *International Broadcasting Service*, RG41, vol. 125, LAC.

34 "Order-in-Council 8168," 18 September 1942, RG25, vol. 2203, LAC.

35 Hall, *Radio Canada International*, 17.

36 "Note for Mr. Robertson," 2 December 1942, RG25, vol. 2203, LAC.

37 N.A. Robertson to A. Frigon, 8 March 1944, RG25, vol. 2203, LAC.
38 Cited in Hall, *Radio Canada International*, 27.
39 For an overview of the early years of the CBC-IS and its shortwave broadcasts to Europe, see also Siegel, *Radio Canada International*; Olechowska, *The Age of International Radio*; and Hibbitts, "The CBC International Service as a Psychological Instrument of Canadian Foreign Policy in the Cold War."
40 Burtch, "The Sword and the Mind."
41 Standing Committee on External Affairs, *Minutes of Proceedings and Evidence No.* 2, 43.
42 "International Service of the CBC," 9 February 1951, RG41, vol. 125, LAC.
43 Hall, *Radio Canada International*, 56.
44 "Memorandum for the Establishment Board: Political Coordination Section – Proposed Establishment," 29 January 1953, RG25, vol. 4338, LAC.
45 A. Anderson to John E. Thompson, 19 May 1950, RG25, vol. 2203, LAC.
46 Cited in Hall, *Radio Canada International*, 56. See also I. Dilworth to A.D. Dunton, 18 October 1951, RG25, vol. 2203, LAC.
47 On this topic, see Whitaker and Marcuse, *Cold War Canada*.
48 For a detailed account of the purges at the NFB, see Whitaker, Kealey, and Parnaby, *Secret Service*, 192–5.
49 Hall, *Radio Canada International*, 60.
50 Vipond, *Listening In*, 159.
51 J.W. Pickersgill to Jean Désy, 5 October 1951, RG41, vol. 492, LAC; N.A. Robertson, "Minute of a Meeting of the Treasury Board – 31/1722," 26 March 1952, RG41, vol. 125, LAC. Jean Désy was most likely pleased to settle back in Montreal with his family. Not long before, he had declined a promotion to the post of undersecretary of state for external affairs, because he preferred moving to a predominantly French-speaking city (one with adequate and affordable schools for his children) after leaving Italy. The likelihood of the ambassadorial seat soon becoming vacant in Paris was probably also in the back of his mind. Désy did end up relocating to France to replace George Vanier in 1953. Jean Désy to Louis Saint-Laurent, 1 October 1948, MG26-L, vol. 89, LAC.
52 The idea of a "political intelligence unit" was already circulating within External Affairs in the summer of 1951. See J.K. Starnes to Mr. Ritchie, 24 July 1951, RG25, vol. 4338, LAC; and "Memorandum for the Establishment Board: Political Coordination Section – Proposed Establishment," 29 January 1953, RG25, vol. 4338, LAC.

53 Standing Committee on External Affairs, *Minutes of Proceedings and Evidence No. 6*, 150. For dismissals prior to Désy's appointment, see Hibbitts, "The CBC International Service as a Psychological Instrument of Canadian Foreign Policy in the Cold War," 47–8.
54 See Peers, *The Politics of Canadian Broadcasting*, 422.
55 Siegel, *Radio Canada International*, 116–18, and Hall, *Radio Canada International*, 64, 89.
56 "Order-in-Council 8168," 18 September 1942, RG25, vol. 2203, LAC.
57 "Establishment of a Short Wave Station: Extracts from Hansard," n.d., in *International Broadcasting Service*, RG41, vol. 125, LAC.
58 Hugh L. Keenleyside to Canadian Ambassador to Mexico, 26 April 1944, RG25, vol. 2203, LAC.
59 Peter Aylen to T.W.L. MacDermot, 11 July 1945, RG25, vol. 2215, LAC.
60 Jean Désy to Secretary of State for External Affairs, 5 July 1945, RG25, vol. 2215, LAC.
61 "International Service News: Canadian Broadcasts to South America Reported Strong and Well Received," 21 August 1945, RG25, vol. 2215, LAC.
62 Benjamin Rogers to Secretary of State for External Affairs, 22 August 1945, RG25, vol. 2215, LAC. Unfortunately, the documents concerning these test broadcasts do not provide information about the music that was played.
63 See Canadian Ambassador to Secretary of State for External Affairs, 27 November 1945, RG25, vol. 2215, LAC; and Canadian Broadcasting Corporation to Under-secretary of State for External Affairs, 24 December 1945, RG25, vol. 2215, LAC.
64 Levine, *Father of the Poor*, 78.
65 Skidmore, *Brazil*, 130.
66 For a discussion of Vargas's return to power, see Dalio, *O segundo governo Vargas*.
67 Department of Foreign Affairs and International Trade, *Documents*, 1871.
68 L.B. Pearson, Memorandum for the Prime Minister, 22 April 1948, RG25, vol. 6187, LAC.
69 J.S. MacDonald to Secretary of State for External Affairs, 22 August 1949, RG25, vol. 3749, LAC.
70 Secretary of State for External Affairs to High Commissioner for Canada in Newfoundland, 26 April 1948, RG25, vol. 6187, LAC.
71 H.C McCurry to Acyr Paes, 18 July 1951, vol. 150, file 10, NGCLA. A portion of the correspondence with Francisco Matarazzo Sobrinho is found in 014-2, 016-5, 016-7, 018-4, 018-8, 019-3, 019-5, 023-7, 023-8,

and 037-2, Museu de Arte Moderna de São Paulo Collection, FB. Kirsty Robertson and her colleagues are correct in noting that Canada's participation had more to do with diplomacy than aesthetics, but they overstate their point when they argue that the success of External Affairs in convincing the NGC to send works is evidence that the department saw Brazil "as a site of great appeal." Robertson et al., "More a Diplomatic than an Esthetic Event," 65.

72 J.S. MacDonald to Secretary of State for External Affairs, 28 April 1951, RG25, vol. 8270, LAC. External Affairs would do a better job at deploying Indigenous art as an instrument of diplomacy as part of the cultural Cold War in Europe. See Vorano, "Inuit Art."

73 The absence of Indigenous peoples in the making of Canadian-Brazilian relations at the time does not mean that they did not enact agency elsewhere. The following works shed an important light on the range of actions that they were taking on the diplomatic and cultural fronts: Raibmon, "Theatres of Contact"; Miller, "Petitioning the Great White Mother"; Rutherdale and Miller, "It's Our Country"; and Webster, "'Red Indians' in Geneva, 'Papuan Headhunters' in New York."

74 For example, see Benjamin Rogers to Secretary of State for External Affairs, 5 March 1948, MG27-IIIA1, vols 1–8, LAC; Benjamin Rogers to Secretary of State for External Affairs, 1 March 1948, MG27-IIIA1, vols 1–8, LAC; and James Scott MacDonald to Secretary of State for External Affairs, 18 June 1948, MG27-IIIA1, vols 1–8, LAC.

75 Secretary of State for External Affairs to Canadian Ambassador, 26 December 1945, RG25, vol. 2215, LAC. Regarding Brazil, the CBC-IS had begun beaming weekly thirty-minute experimental broadcasts using two frequencies in August of 1945. Shortly after taking office, Hugh W. Morrison authorized daily transmissions to better account for the country's importance in terms of both geography and population.

76 For example, see "Radialista canadense em visita a São Paulo," 7 December 1950, MG30-E408, vol. 3, LAC; and "Programas de músicas brasileiras no Canadá," 7 December 1950, MG30-E408, vol. 3, LAC.

77 "General Notes re. CBC International Service," n.d., RG41, vol. 127, LAC.

78 "Latin American Listeners to CBC: What They Say about Radio Programs from Canada (excerpts from 5,472 letters received from all 19 Republics during 1950)," n.d., RG25, vol. 2215, LAC.

79 I. Dilworth to A.D. Dunton, 18 October 1951, RG25, vol. 2203, LAC.

80 H.W. Morrison, "Address Given to the Canadian Inter-American Association," 22 January 1951, MG30-E408, vol. 6, LAC.

81 H.W. Morrison, "Report and Analysis of the Latin American Service, 1948–1950," 12 January 1951, MG30-E408, vol. 6, LAC.
82 McDonald and his successor, Ephraim Herbert Coleman (he arrived in Brazil in the closing months of 1951), shared that view. See Benjamin Rogers to Secretary of State for External Affairs, 14 May 1948, RG25, vol. 3246, LAC, and E.H. Coleman to Secretary of State for External Affairs, 9 September 1952, RG25, vol. 8054, LAC.
83 H.W. Morrison, "Report and Analysis of the Latin American Service, 1948–1950," 12 January 1951, MG30-E408, vol. 6, LAC.
84 Désy validated this observation in 1952: Jean Désy, "Report on My Work as Director-General of the International Service of the Canadian Broadcasting Corporation from January 1952 to July 1953," n.d., MG32-E2, vol. 3, LAC.
85 I. Dilworth, "International Service of the CBC," 9 February 1951, RG41, vol. 125, LAC. Emphasis in original.
86 Hall, *Radio Canada International*, 80–5.
87 "Latin American Transmission (Spanish & Portuguese): Time Breakdown for Different Types of Program at March 3, 1950," n.d., RG25, vol. 2203, LAC.
88 H.W. Morrison, "Report and Analysis of the Latin American Service, 1948–1950," 12 January 1951, MG30-E408, vol. 6, LAC.
89 See "Transcription Service Catalogue," n.d., MG30-E408, vol. 6, LAC.
90 Cited in "Minha personalidade é diferente," *Folha de Minas*, 12 December 1953, in Livro 31, MVL.
91 Jean Désy to Heitor Villa-Lobos, 8 September 1947, Correspondência – Embaixada do Canadá, MVL.
92 See Donald Manson to F.H. Soward, 4 January 1946, RG25, vol. 2215, LAC; Jean Désy to Secretary of State for External Affairs, 5 January 1946, RG25, vol. 2215, LAC; and Canadian Broadcasting Corporation to Under-secretary of State for External Affairs, 9 January 1946, RG25, vol. 2215, LAC. Désy initially tried to get the CBC-IS to invite Siqueira for a concert that could be broadcast to South America. He even arranged for Rádio MES to relay the performance, but the Canadian broadcaster could not locate the composer, who eventually contacted Champagne and MacMillan.
93 Heitor Villa-Lobos, "Exposição do plano de excursão artístico-educacional do maestro H. Villa-Lobos pelo continente americano," 10 August 1944, 49-512, ACI.
94 Jean Désy to Ernest MacMillan, 6 March 1947, MUS 7, vol. 2, A.51, LAC.

95 Wilfrid Pelletier to Maurice Duplessis, 5 November 1946, MSS20, 2006-10-001\358, BAnQ. At the time, the composer was concerned that Duplessis's return to power might jeopardize the work accomplished to modernize music education in Quebec. See Wilfrid Pelletier to Hector Perrier, 11 August 1944, P142, 2002-07-002\1-21, BAnQ; Hector Perrier to Wilfrid Pelletier, 17 August 17, 1944, P142, 2002-07-002\1-21, BAnQ.
96 "Concerts symphoniques de Montréal, 22-23 octobre 1946," n.d., OSM.
97 See Frank Coleman, "Pelletier Directs Unusual Program," *Montreal Gazette*, 23 October 1946, 3, and Marcel Valois, "Villa-Lobos révélé avec autorité par Wilfrid Pelletier," *La Presse*, 23 October 1946, 11.
98 P.W. Cook to Saul Rae, 15 September 1947, RG25, vol. 2215, LAC.
99 Ellen Ballon to Heitor Villa-Lobos, 3 March 1945, Correspondencia – Ellen Ballon, MVL. A later recording of the work can be heard on the following album: L'Orchestre de la Suisse romande with Ellen Ballon, *Villa-Lobos: Piano Concerto*, 1949, London Records LLP.7535, 33⅓ rpm LP.
100 "City Pianist Wins Success in Rio Concert," *Montreal Daily Star*, 26 October 1946, in MS-5-2/3.27, KLSCDU.
101 Heitor Villa-Lobos also performed "Descobrimento do Brasil" that night.
102 P.W. Cook to Saul Rae, 15 September 1947, RG25, vol. 2215, LAC.
103 A. Anderson to P.W. Cook, 22 September 1947, RG25, vol. 2215, LAC.
104 Thomas Archer, "Continuity for Villa-Lobos Concert," n.d., Pasta 33 – Programas, MVL.
105 Thomas Archer, "CBC Introduces Villa-Lobos Here," *Montreal Gazette*, 29 October 1947, 10.
106 Acyr Paes to Secretaria de Estado das Relações Exteriores, "Concerto de música de Villa-Lobos," 29 October 1947, 37/02/14, AHI.
107 Jean Désy, "Propos sur la musique," *Notre temps*, 25 October 1952, in MG32-E2, vol. 3, LAC. Prior to 1951, the school was known as the ESMO.
108 Cited in "Stravinsky Finest Says Villa-Lobos," *Montreal Gazette*, 15 December 1952, 15.
109 "Heitor Villa-Lobos entend servir l'humanité par la beauté de l'art musical," *La Patrie*, 15 December 1952, 15.
110 Cited in "Sou o maestro do mundo," *Diário da Bahia*, 16 December 1952, in Livro 31, MVL.
111 C.R. Delafield to Heitor Villa-Lobos, 9 October 1952, Correspondencia – Société Radio-Canada, MVL.
112 "Bach, mediador entre todas as raças," *O Globo*, 6 February 1945, in Livro 49, MVL. See also "Stravinsky Finest Says Villa-Lobos," *Montreal Gazette*, 15 December 1952, 15.

113 Jean Vallerand, "Heitor Villa-Lobos dirige au Plateau," *Le Devoir*, 19 December 1952, 6.

114 For example, Jean Hamelin, "Villa-Lobos dans quelques-unes de ses compositions," *La Presse*, 18 December 1952, 41.

115 Eric McLean, "Villa-Lobos Conducts Here," *Montreal Star*, 18 December 1952, OSM.

116 Paul Roussel, "Concert de musique sud-américaine dirigé par Villa-Lobos au Plateau," *Le Canada*, 19 December 1952, 15.

117 Maurice Huot, "Villa-Lobos déploie toutes les couleurs de sa palette orchestrale," *La Patrie*, 18 December 1952, 14.

118 Paul Roussel, "Concert de musique sud-américaine dirigé par Villa-Lobos au Plateau," *Le Canada*, 19 December 1952, 15; Eric McLean, "Villa-Lobos Conducts Here," *Montreal Star*, 18 December 1952, OSM.

119 Both the *Montreal Star* and *Le Devoir* wondered how much the event had cost and whether the funds could not have been better used elsewhere. See Eric McLean, "Villa-Lobos Conducts Here," *Montreal Star*, 18 December 1952, OSM, and Jean Vallerand, "Heitor Villa-Lobos dirige au Plateau," *Le Devoir*, December 19, 1952, 6.

120 Patricia FitzGerald to C.R. Delafield, 31 December 1952, MG30-E408, vol. 6, LAC.

121 A copy of the transcription record is available at LAC. L'Orchestre des concerts symphoniques de Montréal, with Heitor Villa-Lobos, *Program no. 87*, n.d., International Service of the Canadian Broadcasting Corporation S-7021-7022-7023, 33⅓ rpm 16-inch LP.

122 Cited in Standing Committee on External Affairs, *Minutes of Proceedings and Evidence No. 6*, 153–5.

123 Ibid., 140, 145.

124 Cited in Standing Committee on External Affairs, *Minutes of Proceedings and Evidence No. 1*, 12.

125 Cited in Standing Committee on External Affairs, *Minutes of Proceedings and Evidence No. 6*, 141, 151, 170.

126 Cited in Canada, *Débats de la Chambre des communes*, 5102.

127 International Trade Relations Division, "Summary of Information on Canadian-Brazilian Trade Relations," July 1951, RG25, vol. 6368, LAC; Wm. Frederick Bull to A.E. Ritchie, 10 August 1953, RG25, vol. 6368, LAC.

128 Caio de Mello Franco to Oswaldo Aranha, 21 February 1944, OAcp 1943.01.06.02, FGV/CPDOC.

129 F.C. de Bittencourt Berenguer to Oswaldo Aranha, "Origem racial da população do Canadá," 21 June 1944, 36/05/05, AHI.

130 Raul de Sá Barbosa to Oswaldo Aranha, "O mês cultural: Outubro de 1952," 13 November 1952, 37/01/11, AHI.
131 Raul de Sá Barbosa, "O mês cultural: Agôsto de 1952," 17 September 1952, 37/01/10, AHI.
132 Raul de Sá Barbosa, "O mês cultural: Dezembro de 1952," 13 January 1952, 37/01/12, AHI. See also Raul de Sá Barbosa, "O mês cultural: Novembro de 1952," 1 December 1952, 37/01/11, AHI.
133 Raul de Sá Barbosa, "O mês político: Abril-maio de 1952," 1 June 1952, 37/01/09, AHI.
134 Heitor Lyra to João Neves da Fontoura, "Discriminação racial no Canadá," 26 September 1952, 37/01/10, AHI.
135 Raul de Sá Barbosa, "O mês cultural: Dezembro de 1952," 13 January 1952, 37/01/12, AHI.
136 Potter, *Branding Canada*, 55.

## CONCLUSION

1 Jennifer Ditchburn, "The Royal Scramble for the Queen's Photo," *The Star*, 27 November 2011. For a discussion of the context behind the Conservatives' rebranding of Canada, see McKay and Swift, *Warrior Nation*, and Jeffrey, *Dismantling Canada*.
2 Jocelyne Richer, "Le Québec devrait rapatrier les toiles, dit le PQ," *Le Devoir*, 28 July 2011, A3.
3 Paul Chamberland, "La mise au rancart des Pellan, un acte manqué," *Le Devoir*, 29 July 2011, A8.
4 Cited in "Quebec Artist Returns to Government Lobby, Replacing Queen's Portrait," *Maclean's*, 9 November 2015.
5 To follow the story of *Canada East* and *Canada West* after 1947, see RG25, vol. 2885, LAC.
6 Evan Solomon, "The Soft Power of Justin Trudeau, Canada's Viral PM," *Maclean's*, 9 March 2016. See also Hawes, "We're Back," and Copeland, "Is Canada 'Back?'"
7 Standing Senate Committee on Foreign Affairs and International Trade, *Cultural Diplomacy at the Front Stage of Canada's Foreign Policy*, 9.
8 Nicholas J. Cull, cited in Standing Senate Committee on Foreign Affairs and International Trade, *Proceedings*.
9 Rushton, "The Origins and Development of Canada's Public Diplomacy," 86.
10 Jean Chapdelaine, Canada's ambassador to Brazil at the turn of the 1960s, was among those who were dissatisfied with External Affairs' approach

to both Quebec and cultural diplomacy. Inspired by Désy's pioneering efforts and frustrated by his colleagues' lack of vision, he defected, or rather jumped ship, in 1965 to assume the recently established position of délégué général du Québec in Paris. André Patry, one of the architects of Quebec's challenge to Ottawa in international affairs in the 1960s, also deepened his knowledge of diplomacy and intercultural relations in Brazil, first as a correspondent for Rio de Janeiro's *A Noite* and later as a visiting speaker. Aird, *André Patry et la présence du Québec dans le monde*, 25.

11 Stephens, *Study of Canadian Government Information Abroad*, chap. 1, p. 1. See also Stephens, *Information and Press Activities of the Department of External Affairs at Home and Abroad.*

12 Stephens's omission is surprising, since he himself reported on Désy's work in 1946, noting that the embassy's lecture series, organized jointly with the Instituto Brasil-Canadá, "constituted an ideal medium of propaganda." L.A.D. Stephens to Director of Canada Foundation, 11 June 1946, MG28-I, vol. 179, LAC.

13 Minutes of Meeting on Cultural Relations with Latin America, 8 November 1943, RG25, vol. 3243, LAC.

14 C.S. Gadd to Yvon Beaulne, 4 July 1968, RG25, vol. 8622, LAC. See also Yvon Beaulne to Under-secretary of State for External Affairs, 31 May 1968, RG25, vol. 8622, LAC.

15 Désy, *Les sentiers de la culture*, 115.

16 According to David Meren, "nationalist resentment" motivated Désy to lobby Premier Maurice Duplessis "to be appointed, even unofficially, Quebec's representative in Paris" in 1957. Meren, *With Friends Like These*, 149. Désy had gone through a controversy of sorts earlier in 1953 when the Progressive Conservative George Hees accused him of wanting to deny rights to new immigrants. The then director general of the CBC-IS had just given a speech in which he promoted the idea of pan-Canadian bilingualism by evoking the idea of French Canadians' inalienable rights as first settlers. However unpleasant the episode, Désy continued to believe in the project of a bicultural federalism, remaining at the service of Canada until the end of his diplomatic career. His lobbying of Duplessis might have been an effort to stay in Paris, since his posting there was coming to an end. After all, he had begun his academic and diplomatic careers there. He had also declined the offer to be the first French Canadian to occupy the post of undersecretary of state for external affairs, because he preferred raising his children in a city that had good and affordable French-language schools. He had also indicated that he wished

to stop moving to provide a more stable environment for his family. Personal and professional imperatives defined his trajectory as a diplomat. Jean Désy to Louis Saint-Laurent, 1 October 1948, MG26-L, vol. 89, LAC; "Le bilinguisme, facteur d'unité et de culture," *La Presse*, 7 April 1953, 17; "Chose que M. Désy n'a pas dite attaquée par un tory à Ottawa," *Le Canada*, 25 April 1953, 7.

17 Nicholas J. Cull, cited in Standing Senate Committee on Foreign Affairs and International Trade, *Proceedings*.

18 Akira Iriye writes, "A nation is a culture in that its inhabitants share certain consciousness – of their land, of their history, and of who they are. Since all nations are in this sense cultures, international relations become inter-cultural relations." Iriye, "Culture and International History," 242.

# Bibliography

## ARCHIVAL SOURCES AND SPECIAL COLLECTIONS

*Archives de folklore et d'ethnologie, Université Laval (AFEUL), Quebec City*

F454 Roger Filiatrault Fonds

*Arquivo Central do Itamaraty (ACI), Brasília*

Ministério das Relações Exteriores Fonds

*Arquivo Histórico do Itamaraty (AHI), Rio de Janeiro*

Ministério das Relações Exteriores Fonds

*Arquivo Nacional (AN), Rio de Janeiro*

EH Agência Nacional Fonds

*Biblioteca Alberto Nepomuceno, Universidade Federal do Rio de Janeiro (BANUFRJ), Rio de Janeiro*

30 José Siqueira Fonds

*Bibliothèque et Archives nationales du Québec (BAnQ), Montreal*

CLG40 Dostaler et Walter-Patrice O'Leary Fonds
MSS20 Wilfrid Pelletier Fonds

P48 Conrad Poirier Fonds
P142 Hector Perrier Fonds

*Centre de recherche en civilisation canadienne-française, Université d'Ottawa (CRCCFUO), Ottawa*

P232 Marcel Roussin Fonds

*Division de la gestion de documents et des archives, Université de Montréal (DGDAUDM), Montreal*

P76 Comité France-Amérique de Montréal Fonds

*Fundação Bienal (FB), São Paulo*

Museu de Arte Moderna de São Paulo Collection

*Fundação Getúlio Vargas, Centro de Pesquisa e Documentação de História Contemporânea do Brasil (FGV-CPDOC), Rio de Janeiro*

GC Gustavo Capanema Collection
GV Getúlio Vargas Collection
OA Oswaldo Aranha Collection

*Killam Library Special Collections, Dalhousie University (KLSCDU), Halifax*

MS-5-2 Ellen Ballon Music Collection

*Library and Archives Canada (LAC), Ottawa*

MG26-J1 and MG26-J4 William Lyon Mackenzie King Fonds
MG26-L Louis St. Laurent Fonds
MG27-IIIA1 Harold Rupert Leofric George Alexander, 1st Earl Alexander of Tunis Fonds
MG28-I Canada Foundation Fonds
MG28-III112 Brascan Limited Fonds
MG30-E408 Hugh Whitney Morrison Fonds
MG31-E97 W. Arthur Irwin Fonds
MG32-E2 Jean Désy Fonds
MUS 7 Sir Ernest MacMillan Fonds
MUS 29 Claude Champagne Fonds

RG20-3 Department of Industry, Trade, and Commerce Fonds
RG25 Department of External Affairs Fonds
RG41 Canadian Broadcasting Corporation Fonds

*Musée de la civilisation (MC), Quebec City*

MCQP1 Lady Alys Robi Fonds

*Museu Villa-Lobos (MVL), Rio de Janeiro*

Heitor Villa-Lobos Collection

*National Archives (NA), London*

FO370 Foreign Office Fonds

*National Gallery of Canada Library and Archives (NGCLA), Ottawa*

National Gallery of Canada Fonds

*Orchestre symphonique de Montréal (OSM), Montreal*

Orchestre symphonique de Montréal Records

*Service des archives et de gestion des documents, Université du Québec à Montréal (SAGDUQÀM), Montreal*

170P Jacques de Tonnancour Fonds

## NEWSPAPERS AND MAGAZINES

*7 Dias* (n.p.)
*A Manhã* (Rio de Janeiro)
*A Noite* (Rio de Janeiro)
*L'Action catholique* (Quebec City)
*L'Avenir du Nord* (Saint-Jérôme, QC)
*Bloc Populaire* (Montreal)
*Brasil Musical* (Rio de Janeiro)
*Brasil Portugal* (n.p.)
*Brazil Herald* (Rio de Janeiro)
*Brazilian American* (n.p.)
*Le Canada* (Montreal)
*Canadian Art* (Ottawa)
*Careta* (Rio de Janeiro)
*Carioca* (Rio de Janeiro)
*Correio da Manhã* (Rio de Janeiro)
*Correio da Noite* (Rio de Janeio)
*O Cruzeiro* (Rio de Janeiro)
*Le Devoir* (Montreal)
*Diário Carioca* (Rio de Janeiro)
*Diário da Bahia* (Salvador)
*Diário da Noite* (Rio de Janeiro)

*Diário de Notícias* (Rio de Janeiro)
*Le Droit* (Ottawa)
*The Ensign* (Montreal)
*O Estado de São Paulo*
*The Examiner* (Peterborough, ON)
*Folha de Minas* (Belo Horizonte)
*Fon Fon* (Rio de Janeiro)
*Gazeta de Notícias* (Rio de Janeiro)
*Globe and Mail* (Toronto)
*O Globo* (Rio de Janeiro)
*Illustração Brasileira* (Rio de Janeiro)
*O Jornal* (Rio de Janeiro)
*Jornal do Brasil* (Rio de Janeiro)
*Jornal do Commercio* (Rio de Janeiro)
*Leaside Tribune* (Toronto)
*Maclean's* (Toronto)
*Mayfair* (Toronto and Montreal)
*Montreal Daily Star*
*Montreal Gazette*
*Montreal Star*
*The News* (Indian Head, SK)
*A Notícia* (Joinville, BR)
*Notre temps* (Montreal)
*L'Oeil* (Montreal)
*Passe-temps* (Montreal)
*La Patrie* (Montreal)
*Planalto* (São Paulo)
*La Presse* (Montreal)
*O Radical* (Rio de Janeiro)
*Radiomonde* (Montreal)
*Revista da Semana* (Rio de Janeiro)
*La Revue moderne* (Montreal)
*La Revue populaire* (Montreal)
*A Scena Muda* (Rio de Janeiro)
*Sherbrooke Telegram* (Sherbrooke, QC)
*Le Soleil* (Quebec City)
*Sombra* (Rio de Janeiro)
*The Star* (Toronto)
*The Times* (Trail, BC)
*Toronto Saturday Night*
*Vamos Ler* (Rio de Janeiro)
*Vanguarda* (Cássia, BR)
*A Vida* (Rio de Janeiro)
*Vida Doméstica* (Rio de Janeiro)

## SOUND RECORDINGS

Champagne, Claude. *Anthologie de la musique canadienne*. Radio-Canada International, ACM-30, 1982, 4 x 33⅓ rpm LPs.

L'Orchestre de la Suisse romande with Ellen Ballon. *Villa-Lobos: Piano Concerto*. London Records, LLP.7535, 1949, 33⅓ rpm LP.

L'Orchestre des concerts symphoniques de Montréal with Heitor Villa-Lobos. *Program no. 87*. International Service of the Canadian Broadcasting Corporation, S-7021-7022-7023, n.d., 33⅓ rpm 16-inch LP.

Robi, Alys. *L'Anthologie*. Disques XXI-21, XXI-CD-2-1502, 2004, 3 x compact discs.

Savoie, André-Sébastien. *PianoFiesta*. Radio-Canada International, RCI 418, n.d., 33⅓ rpm LP.

## GOVERNMENT DOCUMENTS

Canada. *Débats de la Chambre des communes*. 7th Session, 21st Parliament, vol. 5 (1952–53). Ottawa: Edmond Cloutier, Queen's Printer, 1953.

*Canadian Art in Brazil*. Rio de Janeiro: s.n., 1945.

*Canadian Graphic Arts in Brazil*. Rio de Janeiro: s.n., 1946.

Department of Foreign Affairs and International Trade. *Documents: External Relations*. Vol. 14, *1948*. Ottawa: Roger Duhamel, Queen's Printer, 1967.

Dominion Bureau of Statistics. *Trade of Canada: Year Ended December 31, 1942*. Vol. 1, *Summary and Analytical Tables*. Ottawa: Edmond Cloutier, Printer to the King, 1943.

Exchange of Notes between Canada and Brazil Constituting an Agreement for the Promotion of Cultural Relations between the Two Countries. Treaty Series 1944, no. 15. 24 May 1944.

Ministério das Relações Exteriores. *Relatório: Ano de 1943*. Rio de Janeiro: Imprensa Nacional, 1944.

– *Relatório: Ano de 1944*. Rio de Janeiro: Imprensa Nacional, 1949.

Roosevelt, Franklin Delano. "Address at Chautauqua, N.Y." *American Presidency Project*. https://www.presidency.ucsb.edu/documents/address-chautauqua-ny.

Royal Commission on Bilingualism and Biculturalism. *Report of the Royal Commission on Bilingualism and Biculturalism. General Introduction: Book 1*. Ottawa: Roger Duhamel, Queen's Printer, 1967.

Royal Commission on National Development in the Arts, Letters, and Sciences. *Report of the Royal Commission on National Development in the Arts, Letters, and Sciences, 1949–1951*. Ottawa: Edmond Cloutier, Printer to the King, 1951.

Standing Committee on External Affairs. *Minutes of Proceedings and Evidence No. 1: Main Estimates of the Department of External Affairs – Departmental Administration*. 7th Session, 21st Parliament, 19 and 23 February 1953. Ottawa: Edmond Cloutier, Queen's Printer, 1953.

– *Minutes of Proceedings and Evidence No. 2: Main Estimates of the Department of External Affairs – Departmental Administration*. 7th Session, 21st Parliament, 26 February 1953. Ottawa: Edmond Cloutier, Queen's Printer, 1953.

– *Minutes of Proceedings and Evidence No. 6: International Service of the Canadian Broadcasting Corporation*. 7th Session, 21st Parliament, 12 March 1953. Ottawa: Edmond Cloutier, Queen's Printer, 1953.

Standing Senate Committee on Foreign Affairs and International Trade. *Cultural Diplomacy at the Front Stage of Canada's Foreign Policy*. Ottawa: Standing Senate Committee on Foreign Affairs and International Trade, 2019. https://sencanada.ca/content/sen/committee/421/AEFA/Reports/Report_CulturalDiplomacy_e.pdf.

– *Proceedings: Issue No. 47 – Evidence – Meeting of May 30, 2018*. 1st Session, 42nd Parliament, 30 May 2018. https://sencanada.ca/en/Content/Sen/Committee/421/AEFA/47ev-54119-e.

Trade Agreement between Canada and Brazil. Treaty Series 1941, no. 18. 17 October 1941.

## PRINTED AND ONLINE SOURCES

Aird, Robert. *André Patry et la présence du Québec dans le monde*. Montreal: VLB éditeur, 2005.

Alencastro, Luiz Felipe de. "Villa-Lobos et la première période Vargas (1930–1945)." In *Villa-Lobos: Des sources de l'oeuvre aux échos contemporains*, edited by Luiz Felipe de Alencastro, Anaïs Fléchet, Juliana Pimentel, and Danièle Pistone, 11–24. Paris: Honoré Champion éditeur, 2012.

Amyot, Éric. *Le Québec entre Pétain et de Gaulle: Vichy, la France libre et les Canadiens français, 1940–1945*. Montreal: Fides, 1999.

Anderson, Benedict. *Imagined Communities*. Rev. ed. London: Verso, 2006.

Anderson, Warwick. "Traveling White." In *Re-Orienting Whiteness*, edited by Leigh Boucher, Jane Carey, and Katherine Ellinghaus, 65–72. New York: Palgrave Macmillan, 2009.

Andrade, Mario de. *Música doce música*. São Paulo: L.G. Miranda, 1934.

Appleby, David P. *Heitor Villa-Lobos: A Life (1887–1959)*. Lanham, MD: Scarecrow Press, 2002.

Applegate, Celia. "How German Is It? Nationalism and the Idea of Serious Music in the Early Nineteenth Century." *19th-Century Music* 21, no. 3 (1998): 274–96.

Armstrong, Christopher, and H.V. Nelles. *Southern Exposure: Canadian Promoters in Latin America and the Caribbean, 1896–1930*. Toronto: University of Toronto Press, 1988.

Arndt, Richard T. *The First Resort of Kings: American Cultural Diplomacy in the Twentieth Century*. Dulles, VA: Potomac Books, 2005.

Ayhan, Kadir Jun. "The Boundaries of Public Diplomacy and Nonstate Actors: A Taxonomy of Perspectives." *International Studies Perspectives* 20, no. 1 (2019): 63–83.

Backhouse, Constance. *Colour-Coded: A Legal History of Racism in Canada, 1900–1950*. Toronto: University of Toronto Press, 1999.

Baldwin, Andrew, Laura Cameron, and Audrey Kobayashi. "Introduction: Spatializing History, Historicizing Whiteness." In *Rethinking the Great White North: Race, Nature, and the Historical Geographies of Whiteness in Canada*, edited by Andrew Baldwin, Laura Cameron, and Audrey Kobayashi, 1–15. Vancouver: UBC Press, 2011.

– eds. *Rethinking the Great White North: Race, Nature, and the Historical Geographies of Whiteness in Canada*. Vancouver: UBC Press, 2011.

Ball, James. *Theatre of State: A Dramaturgy of the United Nations*. Chicago: Northwestern University Press, 2019.

Barbosa, Rosana. *Brazil and Canada: Economic, Political, and Migratory Ties, 1820s to 1970s*. London: Lexington Books, 2017.

– "Brazilian and Canadian Relations: A Historical Survey." In *Brazil and Canada in the Americas*, edited by Rosana Barbosa, 31–54. Halifax: Gorsebrook Research Institute, 2007.

Barnhisel, Greg. *Cold War Modernists: Art, Literature, and American Cultural Diplomacy*. New York: Columbia University Press, 2015.

Barrière, Mireille, ed. *Les 100 ans du Prix d'Europe: Le soutien de l'État à la musique de Lomer Gouin à la Révolution tranquille*. Quebec City: Presses de l'Université Laval, 2012.

Barros, José D'Assunção. "Francisco Mignone e sua obra orquestral nacionalista." *Revista Música e Linguagem – Vitória/eS* 1, no. 3 (2013): 38–56.

Beaunoyer, Jean. *Fleur d'Alys*. Montreal: Leméac, 1994.

Beezley, William H. "The Rise of Cultural Nationalism and Its Musical Expressions." In *Cultural Nationalism and Ethnic Music in Latin America*, edited by William H. Beezley, 1–27. Albuquerque: University of New Mexico Press, 2018.

Béhague, Gerard. *The Beginnings of Musical Nationalism in Brazil*. Detroit: Information Coordinators/Detroit Monographs in Musicology, 1977.

– *Heitor Villa-Lobos: The Search for Brazil's Musical Soul*. Austin: Institute of Latin American Studies/University of Texas, 1994.

Belchior Rodrigues, Pedro Henrique. "O maestro do mundo: Heitor Villa-Lobos (1887–1959) e a diplomacia cultural brasileira." PhD dissertation, Universidade Federal Fluminense, 2019.

Berg, Jerome S. *Broadcasting for the Short Waves, 1945 to Today*. Jefferson, NC: McFarland and Company, 2008.

– *On the Short Waves, 1923–1945: Broadcast Listening in the Pioneer Days of Radio*. Jefferson, NC: McFarland and Company, 2007.

Berg, William J. *Literature and Painting in Quebec: From Imagery to Identity*. Toronto: University of Toronto Press, 2017.

Bergère, Marc. *Vichy au Canada: L'exil québécois de collaborateurs français*. Montreal: Les Presses de l'Université de Montréal, 2016.

Betcherman, Lita-Rose. *Ernest Lapointe: Mackenzie King's Great Quebec Lieutenant*. Toronto: University of Toronto Press, 2002.

Bethell, Leslie. "Brazil." In *Latin America between the Second World War and the Cold War, 1944–1948*, edited by Leslie Bethell and Ian Roxborough, 33–65. Cambridge: Cambridge University Press, 1992.

Bhabha, Homi K. *The Location of Culture*. London: Routledge, 1994.

Boise, Sam de. *Men, Masculinity, Music, and Emotions*. New York: Palgrave Macmillan, 2015.

Bomeny, Helena M.B. "Três decretos e um ministério: A propósito da educação no Estado Novo." In *Repensando o Estado Novo*, edited by Dulce Pandolfi, 137–66. Rio de Janeiro: Editora FGV, 1999.

Born, Georgina. "After Relational Aesthetics: Improvised Music, the Social, and (Re)Theorizing the Aesthetic." In *Improvisation and Social Aesthetics*, edited by Georgina Born, Eric Lewis, and Will Straw, 33–58. Durham, NC: Duke University Press, 2017.

– "Music and the Materialization of Identities." *Journal of Material Culture* 16, no. 4 (2011): 376–88.

– "The Social and the Aesthetic: For a Post-Bourdieuian Theory of Cultural Production." *Cultural Sociology* 4, no. 2 (2010): 171–208.

Born, Georgina, and David Hesmondhalgh, eds. "Introduction." In *Western Music and Its Others: Difference, Representation, and Appropriation in Music*, edited by Georgina Born and David Hesmondhalgh, 1–58. Berkeley: University of California Press, 2000.

Bothwell, Robert. *Alliance and Illusion: Canada and the World, 1945–1984*. Vancouver: UBC Press, 2007.

Brebner, John Bartlet. *North Atlantic Triangle: The Interplay of Canada, the United States, and Great Britain*. New York: Columbia University Press, 1945.

Brison, Jeffrey D. *Rockefeller, Carnegie & Canada: American Philanthropy and the Arts & Letters in Canada*. Montreal and Kingston: McGill-Queen's University Press, 2005.

Brumana, Fernando Giobellina. "Mario de Andrade y la missão de pesquisas folclóricas (1938): Une etnografía que no nue." *Revista de Indias* 63, no. 237 (2006): 545–72.

Buckner, Phillip, ed. *Canada and the End of Empire*. Vancouver: UBC Press, 2005.

Buckner, Phillip, and R. Douglas Francis, eds. *Canada and the British World: Culture, Migration, and Identity*. Vancouver: UBC Press, 2006.

– eds. *Rediscovering the British World*. Calgary: University of Calgary Press, 2005.

Burges, Sean. "Mistaking Brazil for a Middle Power." *Journal of Iberian and Latin American Research* 19, no. 2 (2013): 286–302.

Burns, Patricia. *Life on the Home Front: Montreal, 1939–1945*. Montreal: Véhicule Press, 2012.

Burril, Fred, and Catherine C. LeGrand. "Progressive Catholicism at Home and Abroad: The 'Double Solidarité' of Quebec Missionaries in Honduras, 1955–1975." In *Within and Without the Nation: Canadian History as Transnational History*, edited by Karen Dubinsky, Adele Perry, and Henry Yu, 311–40. Toronto: University of Toronto Press, 2015.

Burtch, Andrew. "The Sword and the Mind: Canada's Psychological Warfare at Home and Abroad, 1945–1960." Unpublished paper presented at the 87th Annual Meeting of the Canadian Historical Association, Vancouver, July 2008.

Calabre, Lia. *Políticas culturais no Brasil: Dos anos 1930 ao século XXI*. Rio de Janeiro: Editora FGV, 2009.

– "Políticas públicas culturais de 1924 a 1945: O rádio em destaque." *Estudos históricos* 31 (2003): 161–81.

Campbell, Jennifer L. "Creating Something Out of Nothing: The Office of Inter-American Affairs Music Committee (1940–1941) and the Inception of a Policy for Musical Diplomacy." *Diplomatic History* 36, no. 1 (2012): 29–39.

– "Shaping Solidarity: Music, Diplomacy, and Inter-American Relations, 1936–1946." PhD dissertation, University of Connecticut, 2010.

Carleton, Sean, and Andrew Woolford. "Ignore Debaters and Denialists, Canada's Treatment of Indigenous Peoples Fits the Definition of Genocide." *The Conversation*, 25 October 2021. https://theconversation.com/ignore-debaters-and-denialists-canadas-treatment-of-indigenous-peoples-fits-the-definition-of-genocide-170242.

Carney, Lora Senechal. "Modern Art, the Local, and the Global, c. 1930–50." In *The Visual Arts in Canada: The Twentieth Century*, edited by Anne Whitelaw, Brian Foss, and Sandra Paikowsky, 99–119. Don Mills, ON: Oxford University Press, 2012.

Carr, Graham. "Diplomatic Notes: American Musicians and Cold War Politics in the Near and Middle East, 1954–60." *Popular Music History* 1, no. 1 (2004): 37–63.

– "'No Political Significance of Any Kind': Glenn Gould's Tour of the Soviet Union and the Culture of the Cold War." *Canadian Historical Review* 95, no. 1 (2014): 1–29.

– "Visualizing 'The Sound of Genius': Glenn Gould and the Culture of Celebrity in the 1950s." *Journal of Canadian Studies* 40, no. 3 (2006): 5–42.

Castro, Flávio Mendes de Oliveira. *1808–2008 – Itamaraty: Dois séculos de história. Volume 1, 1808–1979*. Brasília: Fundação Alexandre de Gusmão, 2009.

Caute, David. *The Dancer Defects: The Struggle for Cultural Supremacy during the Cold War*. New York: Oxford University Press, 2005.

Cavell, Janice. "Canadiana Abroad: The Department of External Affairs' Book Presentation Programmes, 1949–1963." *American Review of Canadian Studies* 39, no. 2 (2009): 81–93.

Cellard, Karine. "Avant *Refus global*: L'essai personnaliste sur l'art moderne." *Voix et images* 41, no. 2 (2016): 83–93.

Cervo, Amado Luiz, and Clodoaldo Bueno. *História da política exterior do Brasil*. Brasília: Instituto Brasileiro de Relações Internacionais/Editora da Universidade de Brasília, 2002.

Chapnick, Adam. "The Canadian Middle Power Myth." *International Journal* 55, no. 2 (2000): 188–206.

– "Middle Power No More? Canada in World Affairs since 2006." *Seton Hall Journal of Diplomacy and International Relations* 14, no. 2 (2013): 101–10.

– *The Middle Power Project: Canada and the Founding of the United Nations*. Vancouver: UBC Press, 2005.

Clendinning, Anne. "Exhibiting a Nation: Canada at the British Empire Exhibition, 1924–1925." *Social History* 39, no. 77 (2006): 79–107.

Coelho, Patrícia. *Educadores no rádio: Programas para ouvir e aprender, 1935–1950*. Rio de Janeiro: Editora PUC, 2016.

Cohen, Ronald D. *Rainbow Quest: The Folk Music Revival & American Society, 1940–1970*. Amherst: University of Massachusetts Press, 2002.

Comeau, Paul-André. *Le Bloc populaire, 1942–1948*. Montreal: Québec/Amérique, 1982.

Cooper, Andrew Fenton. "Canadian Cultural Diplomacy: An Introduction." In *Canadian Culture: International Dimension*, edited by Andrew Fenton

Cooper, 3–26. Toronto: Centre on Foreign Policy and Federalism, University of Waterloo/Canadian Institute of International Affairs, 1985.

Copeland, Daryl. "Is Canada 'Back?' Engineering a Diplomatic and International Policy Renaissance." In *Canada's Public Diplomacy*, edited by Nicholas J. Cull and Michael K. Hawes, 29–54. Cham, CH: Palgrave Macmillan, 2021.

Corsi, Francisco Luiz. *Estado Novo: Política externa e projeto nacional.* São Paulo: Editora UNESP, 1999.

Crespo, Flavia Ribeiro. "O Itamaraty e a cultura brasileira: 1945–1964." In *A quarta dimensão das relações internacionais: A dimensão cultural*, edited by Hugo Rogelio Suppo and Mônica Leite Lessa, 111–38. Rio de Janeiro: Contra Capa, 2012.

Cressman, Darryl Mark. "The Concert Hall as a Medium of Musical Culture: The Technical Mediation of Listening in the 19th Century." PhD dissertation, Simon Fraser University, 2012.

Cull, Nicholas J. *The Cold War and the United States Information Agency: American Propaganda and Public Diplomacy, 1945–1989.* New York: Cambridge University Press, 2008.

– "Public Diplomacy: Taxonomies and Histories." *The annals of the American Academy of Political and Social Science* 616, no. 1 (2008): 31–54.

Cull, Nicholas J., and Michael K. Hawes. *Canada's Public Diplomacy.* Cham, CH: Palgrave Macmillan, 2021.

Dalio, Danilo José. *O segundo governo Vargas: Política externa e diplomacia econômica (1951–1954).* Curitiba, BR: Editora CRV, 2017.

Davenport, Lisa E. *Jazz Diplomacy: Promoting America in the Cold War Era.* Jackson: University Press of Mississippi, 2009.

Davis, Darién J. *Avoiding the Dark: Race and the Forging of a National Culture in Modern Brazil.* Aldershot, UK: Ashgate, 1999.

– *White Face, Black Mask: Africaneity and the Early Social History of Popular Music in Brazil.* East Lansing: Michigan State University Press, 2008.

Dawn, Leslie. *National Visions, National Blindness: Canadian Art and Identities in the 1920s.* Vancouver: UBC Press, 2014.

Dawson, Michael, Catherine Anne Gidney, and Donald A. Wright, eds. *Symbols of Canada.* Toronto: Between the Lines, 2018.

Degler, Carl. *Neither Black nor White: Slavery and Race Relations in Brazil and the United States.* Madison: University of Wisconsin Press, 1971.

Demers, Maurice. *Connected Struggles: Catholics, Nationalists, and Transnational Relations between Mexico and Quebec, 1917–1945*. Montreal and Kingston: McGill-Queen's University Press, 2014.

– "De l'exotisme à l'effet miroir: La représentation de l'histoire latino-américaine au Canada français." *Mens: Revue d'histoire intellectuelle et culturelle* 13, no. 1 (2012): 19–54.

– "Réimaginer les rapports nord-sud. Le CIDOC de Cuernavaca et la promotion de relations plus égalitaires." In *L'Amérique du Nord: Une histoire des identités et des solidarités*, edited by Maurice Demers and Catherine Vézina, 55–72. Quebec City: Presses de l'Université Laval, 2020.

Denning, Michael. *Noise Uprising: The Audiopolitics of a World Musical Revolution*. New York: Verso, 2015.

DeNora, Tia. "Musical Patronage and Social Change in Beethoven's Vienna." *American Journal of Sociology* 97, no. 2 (1991): 310–46.

Desautels, Andrée. "Quadrilha brasileira (1942)." Liner notes for *Anthologie de la musique canadienne*, by Claude Champagne. Radio-Canada International, ACM-30, 1982, 4 x 33⅓ rpm LPs.

Desautels, Éric. "La représentation sociale de l'Afrique dans le discours missionnaire canadien-français (1900–1968)." *Mens: Revue d'histoire intellectuelle et culturelle* 13, no. 1 (2012): 81–107.

Desmarais, Marcel-Marie. *La magie du passé*. Ottawa: Éditions Leméac, 1985.

– *Mon voyage au Japon*. Montreal: Éditions du lévrier, 1956.

Désy, Jean. *Les sentiers de la culture*. Montreal: Fides, 1954.

Dickinson, John Alexander, and Brian J. Young. *A Short History of Quebec*. Montreal and Kingston: McGill-Queen's University Press, 2003.

Donaghy, Greg, and Michael K. Carroll, eds. *In the National Interest: Canadian Foreign Policy and the Department of Foreign Affairs and International Trade, 1909–2009*. Calgary: University of Calgary Press, 2011.

– "Introduction." In *In the National Interest: Canadian Foreign Policy and the Department of Foreign Affairs and International Trade, 1909–2009*, edited by Greg Donaghy and Michael K. Carroll, 1–9. Calgary: University of Calgary Press, 2011.

Druick, Zoë. *Projecting Canada: Government Policy and Documentary Film at the National Film Board*. Montreal and Kingston: McGill-Queen's University Press, 2014.

Dubinsky, Karen, and Marc Epprecht. "Canadian Businesses and the Business of Development in the 'Third World.'" In *Canada and the Third World: Overlapping Histories*, edited by Karen Dubinsky, Sean Mills, and Scott Rutherford, 60–87. Toronto: University of Toronto Press, 2016.

Dubinsky, Karen, Adele Perry, and Henry Yu, eds. *Within and Without the Nation: Canadian History as Transnational History*. Toronto: University of Toronto Press, 2015.

Dumont, Juliette. "De la coopération intellectuelle à la diplomatie culturelle: Le parcours du Brésil dans l'entre-deux-guerres." *Caravelle* 99 (2012): 217–38.

– *L'Institut international de coopération intellectuelle et le Brésil (1924–1946): Le pari de la diplomatie culturelle*. Paris: Éditions de l'IHEAL, 2008.

Dumont, Juliette, and Anaïs Fléchet. "Brazilian Cultural Diplomacy in the Twentieth Century." *Revista Brasileira de História* 34, no. 67 (2014): 1–19.

Dunn, Christopher. *Brutality Garden: Tropicália and the Emergence of a Brazilian Counterculture*. Chapel Hill: University of North Carolina Press, 2001.

Durflinger, Serge Marc. *Fighting from Home: The Second World War in Verdun, Quebec*. Vancouver: UBC Press, 2006.

Edmonton Art Gallery. *The Contemporary Arts Society: Montreal, 1939–1948*. Edmonton: Edmonton Art Gallery, 1980.

Edwardson, Ryan. *Canadian Content: Culture and the Quest for Nationhood*. Toronto: University of Toronto Press, 2008.

Enloe, Cynthia. *Bananas, Beaches, and Bases: Making Feminist Sense of International Politics*. Berkeley: University of California Press, 2014.

Eschen, Penny M. Von. *Satchmo Blows Up the World: Jazz Ambassadors Play the Cold War*. Cambridge, MA: Harvard University Press, 2004.

Evans, Gary. *In the National Interest: A Chronicle of the National Film Board of Canada from 1949 to 1989*. Toronto: University of Toronto Press, 1991.

Fabre, Gérard. "Un arc transatlantique et sa tangente ou comment se dessine un réseau intellectuel franco-québécois?" *Globe: Revue internationale d'études québécoises* 7, no. 1 (2004): 43–78.

Fahrni, Magda. "Reflections on the Place of Quebec in Historical Writing on Canada." In *Contesting Clio's Craft: New Directions and Debates in Canadian History*, edited by Christopher Dummitt and Michael Dawson, 1–20. London: Institute for the Study of the Americas, 2009.

– "The Second World War: Wartime Production and War Efforts." In *Montreal: The History of a North American City*, vol. 2, edited by Dany

Fougères and Roderick MacLeod, 37–73. Montreal and Kingston: McGill-Queen's University Press, 2017.

Falk, Andrew J. *Upstaging the Cold War: American Dissent and Cultural Diplomacy, 1940–1960*. Amherst: University of Massachusetts Press, 2010.

Fejes, Fred. *Imperialism, Media, and the Good Neighbor: New Deal Foreign Policy and United States Shortwave Broadcasting to Latin America*. Norwood, NJ: Ablex Publishing, 1986.

Felix, Regina R., and Scott D. Juall, eds. *Cultural Exchanges between Brazil and France*. West Lafayette, IN: Purdue University Press, 2016.

Ferguson, Barry. *Remaking Liberalism: The Intellectual Legacy of Adam Shortt, O.D. Skelton, W.C. Clark, and W.A. Mackintosh, 1890–1925*. Montreal and Kingston: McGill-Queen's University Press, 1993.

Fernández Tabío, Luis René, Cynthia Wright, and Lana Wylie, eds. *Other Diplomacies, Other Ties: Cuba and Canada in the Shadow of the US*. Toronto: University of Toronto Press, 2018.

Ferreira, Roberta Lima. "Difusão cultural e projeção internacional: O Brasil na América Latina (1937–45)." In *A quarta dimensão das relações internacionais: A dimensão cultural*, edited by Hugo Rogelio Suppo and Mônica Leite Lessa, 65–88. Rio de Janeiro: Contra Capa, 2012.

Fillion, Eric. "P.K. Page and the Art of Diplomacy: An Ambassadorial Wife in Brazil." In *Breaking Barriers, Shaping Worlds: Canadian Women and the Search for Global Order*, edited by Greg Donaghy, Jill Campbell-Miller, and Stacey Barker, 229–65. Vancouver: UBC Press, 2021.

Fléchet, Anaïs. "As partituras da identidade: O Itamaraty e a música brasileira no século XX." In *A quarta dimensão das relações internacionais: A dimensão cultural*, edited by Hugo Rogelio Suppo and Mônica Leite Lessa, 139–68. Rio de Janeiro: Contra Capa, 2012.

– *Villa-Lobos à Paris: Un écho musical du Brésil*. Paris: L'Harmattan, 2004.

Foisy, Catherine. *Au risque de la conversion: L'expérience québécoise de la mission au XXe siècle (1945–1980)*. Montreal and Kingston: McGill-Queen's University Press, 2017.

– "Relire le catholicisme québécois au XXe siècle à partir des 'remarquables oubliés' que sont devenus les missionnaires." *Québec français* 172 (2014): 36–8.

Folch-Ribas, Jacques E. *Jacques de Tonnancour: Le signe et le temps*. Montreal: Presses de l'Université du Québec, 1971.

Fosler-Lussier, Danielle. *Music in America's Cold War Diplomacy*. Berkeley: University of California Press, 2015.

Fournier, Marcel. "Édouard Montpetit et l'université moderne, ou l'échec d'une génération." *Revue d'histoire de l'Amérique française* 36, no. 1 (1982): 3–29.

– *L'entrée dans la modernité: Science, culture et société au Québec.* Montreal: Éditions Saint-Martin, 1986.

Fox, Annette Baker. *The Politics of Attraction: Four Middle Powers and the United States*. New York: Columbia University Press, 1977.

Fox, Elizabeth. *Latin American Broadcasting: From Tango to Telenovela.* Luton, UK: University of Luton Press, 1997.

Freyre, Gilberto. *Casa-grande & senzala: Formação da familia brasileira sob o regime de economia patriarcal.* Rio de Janeiro: Livraria José Olympio, 1954.

Gagnon, Ernest. *Chansons populaires du Canada*. Quebec City: Bureaux du Foyer canadien, 1865.

Gagnon, Maurice. *Pellan*. Montreal: Éditions art global, 1983.

Gallo, Guy. "Dansereau, Jean." In *Encyclopédie de la musique au Canada*, edited by Helmut Kallmann, Gilles Potvin, and Kenneth Winters, 259. Montreal: Fides, 1983.

Garcia, Thomas George Caracas. "Music and the Brazilian Estado Novo: Getúlio Vargas, Heitor Villa-Lobos, and a National Music Education System." In *Music and Dictatorship in Europe and Latin America*, edited by Roberto Illiano and Massimiliano Sala, 613–40. Turnhout, BE: Brepols, 2009.

Gaudry, Adam, and Darryl Leroux. "White Settler Revisionism and Making Métis Everywhere: The Evocation of Métissage in Quebec and Nova Scotia." *Critical Ethnic Studies* 3, no. 1 (2017): 116–42.

Gauvreau, Michael. *The Catholic Origins of Quebec's Quiet Revolution, 1931–1970*. Montreal and Kingston: McGill-Queen's University Press, 2005.

Gendron, Robin S. *Towards a Francophone Community: Canada's Relations with France and French Africa, 1945–1968*. Montreal and Kingston: McGill-Queen's University Press, 2006.

Gienow-Hecht, Jessica C.E., ed. *Decentering America*. Oxford: Berghahn Books, 2007.

– "Introduction: Decentering American History." In *Decentering America*, edited by Jessica C.E. Gienow-Hecht, 1–20. Oxford: Berghahn Books, 2007.

– "On the Diversity of Knowledge and the Community of Thought: Culture and International History." In *Culture and International*

*History*, edited by Jessica C.E. Gienow-Hecht and Frank Schumacher, 3–26. Oxford: Berghahn Books, 2003.

– *Sound Diplomacy: Music and Emotions in Transatlantic Relations, 1850–1920*. Chicago: University of Chicago Press, 2009.

– "The World Is Ready to Listen: Symphony Orchestras and the Global Performance of America." *Diplomatic History* 36, no. 1 (2012): 17–28.

Gienow-Hecht, Jessica C.E., and Mark C. Donfried, eds. *Searching for a Cultural Diplomacy*. Oxford: Berghahn Books, 2010.

Gienow-Hecht, Jessica C.E., and Frank Schumacher, eds. *Culture and International History*. Oxford: Berghahn Books, 2003.

Gil-Montero, Martha. *Brazilian Bombshell: The Biography of Carmen Miranda*. New York: Donald I. Fine, 1989.

Giumbelli, Emerson. *Símbolos religiosos em controvérsia*. São Paulo: Editora Terceiro Nome, 2014.

Giumbelli, Emerson, and Izabella Bosisio. "A política de um monumento: As muitas imagens do Critso Redentor." *Debates do Ner* 2, no. 18 (2010): 193–210.

Glass Joseph B. "Connections between Canada and Brazil before World War One." *Interfaces Brasil/Canadá* 11, no. 2 (2011): 22–52.

Gossage, Peter, and J.I. Little. *An Illustrated History of Quebec: Tradition & Modernity*. Don Mills, ON: Oxford University Press, 2012.

Goudreault, Henri. "Les missionnaires canadiens à l'étranger au XXe siècle." *Sessions d'étude – Société canadienne d'histoire de l'Église catholique* 50, no. 1 (1983): 361–80.

Gronberg, Tag. "Sonia Delaunay's Simultaneous Fashions and the Modern Woman." In *The Modern Woman Revisited: Paris between the Wars*, edited by Whitney Chadwick and Tirza True Latimer, 109–23. New Brunswick, NJ: Rutgers University Press, 2003.

Groulx, Lionel. *Le Canada français missionnaire*. Montreal: Fides, 1962.

Haglund, David G. "And the Beat Goes On: 'Identity' and Canadian Foreign Policy." In *Canada among Nations, 2008: 100 Years of Canadian Foreign Policy*, edited by Robert Bothwell and Jean Daudelin, 343–67. Montreal and Kingston: McGill-Queen's University Press, 2009.

Haines, John. "Marius Barbeau et le Moyen-Âge." In *Around and About Marius Barbeau: Modelling Twentieth-Century Culture*, edited by Lynda Jessup, Andrew Nurse, and Gordon E. Smith, 185–98. Gatineau, QC: Canadian Museum of Civilization, 2008.

Hall, James L. *Radio Canada International: Voice of a Middle Power*. East Lansing: Michigan State University Press, 1997.

Hall, Stuart. "Cultural Studies: Two Paradigms." *Culture/Power/History: A Reader in Contemporary Social Theory*, edited by Nicholas Dirks, Geoff Eley, and Sherry B. Ortner, 520–38. Princeton, NJ: Princeton University Press, 1994.

Hansson, Kailey. "Dancing into Hearts and Minds: Canadian Ballet Exchanges with the Communist World, 1956–76." In *Undiplomatic History: The New Study of Canada in the World*, edited by Asa McKercher and Philip Van Huizen, 233–52. Montreal and Kingston: McGill-Queen's University Press, 2019.

Hantel-Fraser, Christine. *No Fixed Address: Life in the Foreign Service*. Toronto: University of Toronto Press, 1993.

Hart, Justin. *Empire of Ideas: The Origins of Public Diplomacy and the Transformation of U.S. Foreign Policy*. New York: Oxford University Press, 2013.

Harvey, Fernand. "Les relations culturelles entre la France et le Canada (1760–1960)." In *France-Canada-Québec: 400 ans de relations d'exception*, edited by Paul-André Linteau and Serge Joyal, 95–126. Montreal: Presses de l'Université de Montréal, 2008.

Hastings, Paula. "The Limits of 'Brotherly Love': Rethinking Canada-Caribbean Relations in the Early Twentieth Century." In *Dominion of Race: Rethinking Canada's International History*, edited by Laura Madokoro, Francine McKenzie, and David Meren, 38–53. Vancouver: UBC Press, 2017.

– "Rounding Off Confederation: Geopolitics, Tropicality, and Canada's 'Destiny' in the West Indies in the Early Twentieth Century." *Journal of Colonialism and Colonial History* 14, no. 2 (2013). https://muse.jhu.edu/article/513260.

Hawes, Michael K. "'We're Back': Re-imagining Public Diplomacy in Canada." In *Canada's Public Diplomacy*, edited by Nicholas J. Cull and Michael K. Hawes, 13–28. Cham, CH: Palgrave Macmillan, 2021.

Hawker, Ronald W. *Tales of Ghosts: First Nations Art in British Columbia, 1922–61*. Vancouver: UBC Press, 2003.

Hazan, Marcelo Campos. "Religious Music and Church-State Relations in Brazil during the Vargas Era (1930–1945)." *Review: Literature and Arts of the Americas* 44, no. 2 (2011): 303–7.

Helmer, Paul. *Growing with Canada: The Émigré Tradition in Canadian Music*. Montreal and Kingston: McGill-Queen's University Press, 2009.

Henderson, T. Stephens. "Angus L. Macdonald and the Conscription Crisis of 1944." *Acadiensis* 27, no. 1 (1997): 85–104.

Hentchke, Jens R., ed. *Vargas and Brazil: New Perspectives*. New York: Palgrave Macmillan, 2006.

Hertzman, Marc A. *Making Samba: A New History of Race and Music in Brazil*. Durham, NC: Duke University Press, 2013.

Hess, Carol A. *Representing the Good Neighbor: Music, Difference, and the Pan American Dream*. New York: Oxford University Press, 2013.

Hibbitts, Bernard J. "The CBC International Service as a Psychological Instrument of Canadian Foreign Policy in the Cold War, 1948–1963." MA thesis, Carleton University, 1981.

High, Steven. "Recognizing Genocide in Canada." *Canadian Historical Association*, 20 August 2021. https://cha-shc.ca/news/recognizing-genocide-in-canada-2021-08-20.

Hilliker, John. *Canada's Department of External Affairs*, vol. 1, *The Early Years, 1909–1946*. Montreal and Kingston: McGill-Queen's University Press, 1990.

Hillmer, Norman. "National Independence and the National Interest: O.D. Skelton's Department of External Affairs in the 1920s." In *In the National Interest: Canadian Foreign Policy and the Department of Foreign Affairs and International Trade, 1909–2009*, edited by Greg Donaghy and Michael K. Carroll, 11–26. Calgary: University of Calgary Press, 2011.

– *O.D. Skelton: A Portrait of Canadian Ambition*. Toronto: University of Toronto Press, 2015.

– "O.D. Skelton: Innovating for Independence." In *Architects and Innovators: Building the Department of Foreign Affairs and International Trade, 1909–2009*, edited by Greg Donaghy and Kim Richard Nossal, 59–73. Montreal and Kingston: McGill-Queen's University Press, 2009.

Hilton, Stanley E. *Brazil and the Soviet Challenge, 1917–1947*. Austin: University of Texas Press, 1991.

Hixson, Water L. *Parting the Curtain: Propaganda, Culture, and the Cold War, 1945–1961*. New York: St Martin's Griffin, 1997.

Holmes, John W. *Canada: A Middle-Aged Power*. Toronto: McClelland and Stewart, 1976.

Hopkins, Antony G. "Rethinking Decolonization." *Past and Present* 200, no. 1 (2008): 211–47.

Houle, Alain. "La galerie Dominion: Éléments d'histoire." *Vie des Arts* 37, no. 149 (1992–93): 54–60.

Hudson, Peter James. "Imperial Designs: The Royal Bank of Canada in the Caribbean." *Race & Class* 52, no. 1 (2010): 33–48.

Igartua, José E. *The Other Quiet Revolution: National Identities in English Canada, 1945–71*. Vancouver: UBC Press, 2008.

Ion, Hamish. "Soul Searchers and Soft Power: The Canadian Protestant Missionary Movements in Japan, 1873–1951." In *Contradictory Impulses: Canada and Japan in the Twentieth Century*, edited by Greg Donaghy and Patricia E. Roy, 10–28. Vancouver: UBC Press, 2008.

Iriye, Akira. "Culture and International History." In *Explaining the History of American Foreign Relations*, 2nd ed., edited by Michael J. Hogan and Thomas G. Patterson, 241–56. Cambridge: Cambridge University Press, 2004.

Jambeiro, Othon. *Tempos de Vargas: O rádio e o controle da informação*. Salvador, BR: Editora da UFBA, 2003.

Jeffrey, Brooke. *Dismantling Canada: Stephen Harper's New Conservative Agenda*. Montreal and Kingston: McGill-Queen's University Press, 2015.

Jessup, Lynda, and Sarah E.K. Smith. "Introduction: Curating Cultural Diplomacy." *Journal of Curatorial Studies* 5, no. 3 (2016): 283–4.

Kallberg, Jeffrey. *Chopin at the Boundaries: Sex, History, and Musical Genre*. Cambridge, MA: Harvard University Press, 1998.

Keillor, Elaine. "Marius Barbeau as a Promoter of Folk Music Performance and Composition." In *Around and About Marius Barbeau: Modelling Twentieth-Century Culture*, edited by Lynda Jessup, Andrew Nurse, and Gordon E. Smith, 141–9. Gatineau, QC: Canadian Museum of Civilization, 2008.

– *Music in Canada: Capturing Landscape and Diversity*. Montreal and Kingston: McGill-Queen's University Press, 2006.

Kelly, Brendan. *The Good Fight: Marcel Cadieux and Canadian Diplomacy*. Vancouver: UBC Press, 2019.

King, Hayden. "The Erasure of Indigenous Thought in Foreign Policy." *Open Canada*, 13 July 2017. https://opencanada.org/erasure-indigenous-thought-foreign-policy/.

King, Ross. *Defiant Spirits: The Modernist Revolution of the Group of Seven*. Vancouver: Douglas and McIntyre, 2010.

Krenn, Michael L. *Fall-Out Shelters for the Human Spirit: American Art and the Cold War*. Chapel Hill: University of North Carolina Press, 2005.

Kuisel, Richard F. "Coca-Cola and the Cold War: The French Face Americanization, 1948–1953." *French Historical Studies* 17, no. 1 (1991): 96–116.

Lackenbauer, P. Whitney. "Race, Gender, and International 'Relations': African Americans and Aboriginal People on the Margins in Canada's

North, 1942–48." In *Dominion of Race: Rethinking Canada's International History*, edited by Laura Madokoro, Francine McKenzie, and David Meren, 112–38. Vancouver: UBC Press, 2017.

Lacroix, Michel. "'Il faudrait que nous sachions être aussi cela': Les 'modèles' québécois en France, 1919–1939." In *Culture québécoise et valeurs universelles*, edited by Yvan Lamonde and Jonathan Livernois, 111–21. Quebec City: Presses de l'Université Laval, 2010.

– *L'invention du retour d'Europe: Réseaux transatlantiques et transferts culturels au début du XXe siècle*. Quebec City: Presses de l'Université Laval, 2014.

– "Lien social, idéologie et cercles d'appartenance: Le réseau 'latin' des Québécois en France, 1923–1939." *Études littéraires* 36, no. 2 (2004): 51–70.

Lafer, Celso. "Brazilian International Identity and Foreign Policy: Past, Present, and Future." *Daedalus* 129, no. 2 (2000): 207–38.

Lake, Marilyn, and Henry Reynolds. *Drawing the Global Colour Line: White Men's Countries and the International Challenge of Racial Equality*. Cambridge: Cambridge University Press, 2011.

Lalande, Gilles. *The Department of External Affairs and Biculturalism: Diplomatic Personnel (1945–1965) and Language Use (1964–1965)*. Ottawa: Queen's Printer, 1969.

Lamonde, Yvan, and Esther Trépanier. *L'avènement de la modernité culturelle au Québec*. Quebec City: Institut québécois de recherche sur la culture, 1986.

Laurendeau, Jean. *Cent ans de Prix d'Europe*. Montreal: Académie de musique du Québec, 2011.

Leary, John Patrick. *A Cultural History of Underdevelopment: Latin America in the U.S. Imagination*. Charlottesville: University of Virginia Press, 2016.

Leclerc, Richard. "God's Envoys: Canadian Catholic Missionaries in Japan, 1898–2000." In *Contradictory Impulses: Canada and Japan in the Twentieth Century*, edited by Greg Donaghy and Patricia E. Roy, 29–45. Vancouver: UBC Press, 2008.

Lefebvre, Marie-Thérèse. "Le milieu musical québécois et ses réseaux: Le cas des bourses du gouvernement attribuées aux compositeurs (1919–1929)." *Globe: Revue internationale d'études québécoises* 7, no. 1 (2004): 107–45.

LeGrand, Catherine C. "L'axe missionnaire catholique entre le Québec et l'Amérique latine: Une exploration préliminaire." *Globe: Revue internationale d'études québécoises* 12, no. 1 (2009): 43–66.

Lerner, Loren. "Marius Barbeau and Sam Borenstein." In *Around and About Marius Barbeau: Modelling Twentieth-Century Culture*, edited by Lynda Jessup, Andrew Nurse, and Gordon E. Smith, 119–36. Gatineau, QC: Canadian Museum of Civilization, 2008.

Leroux, Darryl. *Distorted Descent: White Claims to Indigenous Identity*. Winnipeg: University of Manitoba Press, 2019.

Lessa, Mônica Leite. "L'influence intellectuelle française au Brésil: Contribution à l'étude d'une politique culturelle (1886–1930)." PhD dissertation, Université de Nanterre, 1997.

– "A política cultural brasileira e a Sociedade das Nações." *Sociedade Brasileira de Pesquisa Historica*, anais da XXII reuniao (2002): 89–97.

Levine, Lawrence W. *Highbrow/Lowbrow: The Emergence of Cultural Hierarchy in America*. Cambridge, MA: Harvard University Press, 1988.

Levine, Robert M. *Father of the Poor? Vargas and His Era*. Cambridge: Cambridge University Press, 1998.

Litt, Paul. *The Muses, the Masses, and the Massey Commission*. Toronto: University of Toronto Press, 1992.

Lochery, Neill. *Brazil: The Fortunes of War. World War II and the Making of Modern Brazil*. New York: Basic Books, 2014.

MacFarlane, John. *Ernest Lapointe and Quebec's Influence on Canadian Foreign Policy*. Toronto: University of Toronto Press, 1999.

MacLennan, Hugh. *Two Solitudes*. Toronto: Macmillan of Canada, 1945.

MacMillan, Ernest. "Problems of Music in Canada." In *MacMillan on Music: Essays on Music by Sir Ernest MacMillan*, edited by Carl Morey, 77–92. Toronto: Dundurn Press, 1997.

Madokoro, Laura, and Francine McKenzie. "Writing Race into Canada's International History." In *Dominion of Race: Rethinking Canada's International History*, edited by Laura Madokoro, Francine McKenzie, and David Meren, 3–24. Vancouver: UBC Press, 2017.

Madokoro, Laura, Francine McKenzie, and David Meren, eds. *Dominion of Race: Rethinking Canada's International History*. Vancouver: UBC Press, 2017.

Magaldi, Cristina. *Music in Imperial Rio de Janeiro: European Culture in a Tropical Milieu*. Lanham, MD: Scarecrow Press, 2004.

– "Two Musical Representations of Brazil: Carlos Gomes and Villa-Lobos." In *Brazil in the Making: Facets of National Identity*, edited by Carmen Nava and Ludwig Lauerhass Jr, 205–27. Lanham, MD: Rowman and Littlefield, 2006.

Mahiet, Damien, Mark Ferraguto, and Rebekah Ahrendt. "Introduction." In *Music and Diplomacy from the Early Modern Era to the Present*, edited by Damien Mahiet, Mark Ferraguto, and Rebekah Ahrendt, 1–16. New York: Palgrave Macmillan, 2014.

Mariz, Vasco. *Vida musical (1946–1950)*. Porto, PT: Lello and Irmão Editores, 1950.

Martins, José Eduardo. "A pianística multifacetada de Francisco Mignone." *Revista música* 2 (1990): 89–113.

Marx, Anthony W. *Making Race and Nation: A Comparison of South Africa, the United States, and Brazil*. Cambridge: Cambridge University Press, 1998.

McCann, Bryan. *Hello, Hello Brazil: Popular Music in the Making of Modern Brazil*. Durham, NC: Duke University Press, 2004.

McCulloch, Tony. "The North Atlantic Triangle: A Canadian Myth?" *International Journal* 66, no. 1 (2010–11): 197–207.

McDowall, Duncan. *The Light: Brazilian Traction, Light, and Power Company Limited, 1899–1945*. Toronto: University of Toronto Press, 1988.

McKay, Ian. *The Quest of the Folk: Antimodernism and Cultural Selection in Twentieth-Century Nova Scotia*. Montreal and Kingston: McGill-Queen's University Press, 1994.

McKay, Ian, and Jamie Swift. *Warrior Nation: Rebranding Canada in an Age of Anxiety*. Toronto: Between the Lines, 2012.

McKenna, Peter. *Canada and the OAS: From Dilettante to Full Partner*. Ottawa: Carleton University Press, 1995.

McKercher, Asa. "Southern Exposure: Diefenbaker, Latin America, and the Organization of American States." *Canadian Historical Review* 93, no. 1 (2012): 57–80.

– "'Ultimate Destiny' Delayed: The Liberals, the Organization of American States, and Canadian Foreign Policy, 1963–1968." *Diplomacy & Statecraft* 25 (2014): 472–91.

McKercher, Asa, and Philip Van Huizen, eds. *Undiplomatic History: The New Study of Canada and the World*. Montreal and Kingston: McGill-Queen's University Press, 2019.

Melnyk, George. *One Hundred Years of Canadian Cinema*. Toronto: University of Toronto Press, 2004.

Meren, David. "The Tragedies of Canadian International History." *Canadian Historical Review* 96, no. 4 (2015): 534–66.

– *With Friends Like These: Entangled Nationalisms and the Canada-Quebec-France Triangle, 1944–1970*. Vancouver: UBC Press, 2012.

Mesli, Samy, and Ivan Carel, eds. *50 ans d'échanges culturels France-Québec, 1910–1960*. Montreal: AQHP/VLB éditeur, 2011.

Michon, Jacques. *Les éditeurs québécois et l'effort de guerre (1940–1948)*. Quebec City: Presses de l'Université Laval, 2009.
– ed. *Histoire de l'édition littéraire au Québec au XXe siècle*. Montreal: Fides, 2004.
Miller, Jim. "Petitioning the Great White Mother: First Nations' Organizations and Lobbying in London." In *Canada and the End of Empire*, edited by Phillip Buckner, 299–318. Vancouver: UBC Press, 2005.
Miller, Kailey. "'An Ancillary Weapon': Cultural Diplomacy and Nation-Building in Cold War Canada, 1945–1967." PhD dissertation, Queen's University, 2015.
Mills, Sean. "Democracy in Music: Louis Metcalf and Montreal's Jazz History." *Canadian Historical Review* 100, no. 3 (2019): 351–72.
– "The End of Empire? Third World Decolonization and Canadian History." In *Within and Without the Nation: Canadian History as Transnational History*, edited by Karen Dubinsky, Adele Perry, and Henry Yu, 341–63. Toronto: University of Toronto Press, 2015.
– *A Place in the Sun: Haiti, Haitians, and the Remaking of Quebec*. Montreal and Kingston: McGill-Queen's University Press, 2016.
Mitchell, Gillian. *The North American Folk Music Revival: Nation and Identity in the United States and Canada, 1945–1980*. Burlington, VT: Ashgate, 2007.
Moraes, Julio Lucchesi. *São Paulo, capital artística: A cafeicultural e as artes na belle époque (1906–1922)*. Rio de Janeiro: Beco do Azougue, 2014.
Morey, Carl. "Introduction." In *MacMillan on Music: Essays on Music by Sir Ernest MacMillan*, edited by Carl Morey, 9–13. Toronto: Dundurn Press, 1997.
Mosquin, Alexandra Marie. "Advertising Canada Abroad: Canada on Display at International Exhibitions, 1920–1940." PhD dissertation, York University, 2003.
Moura, Gerson. *Autonomia na dependência*. Rio de Janeiro: Editora Nova Fronteira, 1980.
– *Sucessos e ilusões: Relações internacionais do Brasil durante e após a Segunda Guerra Mundial*. Rio de Janeiro: Editora FGV, 1991.
Murray, D.R. "Canada's First Diplomatic Missions in Latin America." *Journal of Interamerican Studies and World Affairs* 16, no. 2 (1974): 153–72.
Naves, Santuza Cambraia. "O Brasil em uníssono." In *O Brasil em uníssono: E leituras sobre música e modernismo*, edited by Eduardo Jardim, 21–75. Rio de Janeiro: Editora PUC/Casa da Palavra, 2013.

– "Os regentes do Brasil no período Vargas." In *O Brasil em uníssono: E leituras sobre música e modernismo*, edited by Eduardo Jardim, 122–42. Rio de Janeiro: Editora PUC/Casa da Palavra, 2013.

– *O violão azul: Modernismo e música popular*. Rio de Janeiro: Editora FGV, 1998.

Needell, Jeffrey D.A. *Tropical Belle Époque: Elite Culture and Society in Turn-of-the-Century Rio de Janeiro*. Cambridge: Cambridge University Press, 1987.

Nelson, Michael. *War of the Black Heavens: The Battles of Western Broadcasting in the Cold War*. Syracuse, NY: Syracuse University Press, 1997.

Nilsen, Sarah. *Projecting America, 1958: Films and Cultural Diplomacy at the Brussels World's Fair*. Jefferson, NC: McFarland and Company, 2011.

Ninkovich, Frank A. *The Diplomacy of Ideas: U.S. Foreign Policy and Cultural Relations, 1938–1950*. Cambridge: Cambridge University Press, 1981.

Nye, Joseph S. *Soft Power: The Means to Success in World Politics*. New York: Public Affairs, 2005.

Ogelsby, J.C.M. *Gringos from the Far North: Essays in the History of Canadian-Latin American Relations, 1866–1969*. Toronto: Maclean-Hunter Press, 1976.

Olechowska, Elzbieta. *The Age of International Radio: Radio Canada International (1945–2007)*. Oakville, ON: Mosaic Press, 2007.

Oliveira, Lucia Lippi. "Vargas, os intelectuais e as raizes da ordem." In *As instituções brasileiras da era Vargas*, edited by Maria Celina D'Araujo, 83–93. Rio de Janeiro: Editora FGV, 1999.

Ord, Douglas. *The National Gallery of Canada: Ideas, Art, Architecture*. Montreal and Kingston: McGill-Queen's University Press, 2003.

Osgood, Kenneth. *Total Cold War: Eisenhower's Secret Propaganda Battle at Home and Abroad*. Lawrence: University Press of Kansas, 2006.

Palmer, Steven, Dominichi Miranda de Sá, and Magali Romero Sá. "Ecology, International Cooperation, and the Biogeographic Configuration of Brazil: Pierre Dansereau and the Brazil-Canada Scientific Agreement in the 1940s." *Varia Historia* 33, no. 63 (2017): 745–77.

Palomino, Pablo. "Nationalist, Hemispheric, and Global: 'Latin American Music' and the Music Division of the Pan American Union, 1939–47." *Nuevo Mundo, Mundos Nuevos* (2015). https://doi.org/10.4000/nuevomundo.68062.

Paquin, Stéphane, ed. *Histoire des relations internationales du Québec.* Montreal: VLB éditeur, 2006.

Peers, Frank W. *The Politics of Canadian Broadcasting, 1920–1951.* Toronto: University of Toronto Press, 1969.

Pelletier, Wilfrid. *Une symphonie inachevée.* Montreal: Leméac, 1972.

Peronne, Charles A., and Christopher Dunn. "'Chiclete com Banana': Internationalization in Brazilian Popular Music." In *Brazilian Popular Music & Globalization*, edited by Charles A. Peronne and Christopher Dunn, 1 38. Gainesville: University Press of Florida, 2001.

Poiger, Uta G. *Jazz, Rock, and Rebels: Cold War Politics and American Culture in a Divided Germany.* Berkeley: University of California Press, 2000.

Pope, Maurice, ed. *Public Servant: The Memoirs of Sir Joseph Pope.* Toronto: Oxford University Press, 1960.

Potter, Evan H. *Branding Canada: Projecting Canada's Soft Power through Public Diplomacy.* Montreal and Kingston: McGill-Queen's University Press, 2009.

Price, John. *Orienting Canada: Race, Empire, and the Transpacific.* Vancouver: UBC Press, 2011.

Proctor, George A. *Canadian Music of the Twentieth Century.* Toronto: University of Toronto Press, 1980.

Raibmon, Paige. "Theatres of Contact: The Kwakwaka'wakw Meet Colonialism in British Columbia and at the Chicago World's Fair." *Canadian Historical Review* 81, no. 2 (2000): 157–90.

Rawnsley, Gary D. "Introduction to International Broadcasting and Public Diplomacy in the 21st Century." *Media and Communication* 4, no. 2 (2016): 42–5.

– *Radio Diplomacy and Propaganda: The BBC and VOA in International Politics, 1956–64.* New York: St Martin's Press, 1996.

Razack, Sherene H. *Dark Threats & White Knights: The Somalia Affair, Peacekeeping, and the New Imperialism.* Toronto: University of Toronto Press, 2004.

Rempel, Roy. *Counterweights: The Failure of Canada's German and European Policy, 1955–1995.* Montreal and Kingston: McGill-Queen's University Press, 1997.

Renda, Mary A. *Taking Haiti: Military Occupation and the Culture of U.S. Imperialism, 1915–1940.* Chapel Hill: University of North Carolina Press, 2001.

Reus-Smit, Christian. *On Cultural Diversity: International Theory in a World of Difference.* New York: Cambridge University Press, 2018.

Riley, Matthew, and Anthony D. Smith. *Nation and Classical Music: From Handel to Copland*. Woodbridge, UK: Boydell Press, 2016.

Robert, Guy. *Pellan: His Life and His Art*. Montreal: Éditions du Centre de psychologie et de pédagogie, 1963.

Robertson, Kirsty, Stephanie C. Anderson, Elizabeth Diggon, Ahlia Moussa, and Sarah E.K. Smith. "'More a Diplomatic Than an Esthetic Event': Canada, Brazil, and Cultural Brokering in the São Paulo Biennial and 'Isumavut.'" *Journal of Canadian Studies* 47, no. 2 (2013): 60–88.

Robinson, Dylan. *Hungry Listening: Resonant Theory for Indigenous Sound Studies*. Minneapolis: University of Minnesota Press, 2020.

Rochlin, James. *Discovering the Americas: The Evolution of Canadian Foreign Policy towards Latin America*. Vancouver: UBC Press, 1994.

Rolland, Denis. "A instrumentalização das culturas estrangeiras no Estado Novo: Entre o Brasil e os Estados Unidos, o espaço da França durante a Segunda Guerra Mundial." In *Relações internacionais: Visões do Brasil e da América Latina*, edited by Estevão Chaves de Rezende Martins, 223–48. Brasília: Instituto Brasileiro de Relações Internacionais, 2003.

Rosenberg, Emily S. *Spreading the American Dream: American Economic and Cultural Expansion, 1890–1945*. New York: Hill and Wang, 1982.

Roussin, Marcel. "Le Canada, fils et héritier de la coutume." PhD dissertation, Université d'Ottawa, 1945.

– "Nos voisins latins: Des raisons historiques et géographiques qui associent nos économies respectives." MA thesis, Université d'Ottawa, 1942.

Rudin, Ronald. *Making History in Twentieth-Century Quebec*. Toronto: University of Toronto Press, 1997.

Rudy, Jarrett. *The Freedom to Smoke: Tobacco Consumption and Identity*. Montreal and Kingston: McGill-Queen's University Press, 2014.

Rumilly, Robert. *Histoire de la Société Saint-Jean-Baptiste de Montréal: Des patriotes au fleurdelisé, 1834–1948*. Montreal: L'Aurore, 1975.

Rushton, Sean. "The Origins and Development of Canada's Public Diplomacy." In *Branding Canada: Projecting Canada's Soft Power through Public Diplomacy*, edited by Evan H. Potter, 75–93. Montreal and Kingston: McGill-Queen's University Press, 2009.

Rutherdale, Myra, and Jim Miller. "'It's Our Country': First Nations' Participation in the Indian Pavilion at Expo 67." *Journal of the Canadian Historical Association* 17, no. 2 (2006): 148–73.

Sadlier, Darlene J. *Americans All: Good Neighbor Cultural Diplomacy in World War II*. Austin: University of Texas Press, 2012.

– *Brazil Imagined: 1500 to the Present*. Austin: University of Texas Press, 2008.

Said, Edward W. *Culture and Imperialism*. New York: Vintage Books, 1994.

Santomauro, Fernando. "De Brésil to Brazil. A política cultural como instrumento de poder: Os casos de França e Estados Unidos no Brasil na primeira metade do século XX." In *A quarta dimensão das relações internacionais: A dimensão cultural*, edited by Hugo Rogelio Suppo and Mônica Leite Lessa, 211–40. Rio de Janeiro: Contra Capa, 2012.

Santos, Raquel Paz dos. *Um novo olhar sobre o país vizinho: A cooperação cultural como crítica ao paradigma da rivalidade no contexto das relações Brasil-Argentina (1930–1954)*. Rio de Janeiro: Editora Multifoco, 2012.

Saunders, Frances Stonor. *Who Paid the Piper? The CIA and the Cultural Cold War*. London: Granta, 1999.

Savard, Pierre. "Pax Romana, 1935–1962. Une fenêtre étudiante sur le monde." *Les cahiers des dix* 47 (1992): 279–323.

Schabas, Ezra. *Sir Ernest MacMillan: The Importance of Being Canadian*. Toronto: University of Toronto Press, 1994.

Schoultz, Lars. *Beneath the United States: A History of U.S. Policy toward Latin America*. Cambridge: Harvard University Press, 1998.

Scott-Smith, Giles, and Hans Krabbendam, eds. *The Cultural Cold War in Western Europe, 1945–1960*. New York: Routledge, 2003.

Seigel, Micol. *Uneven Encounters: Making Race and Nation in Brazil and the United States*. Durham, NJ: Duke University Press, 2009.

Seitenfus, Ricardo. *A entrada do Brasil na Segunda Guerra mundial*. Porto Alegre, BR: EDIPUCRS, 2000.

Seul, Stephanie, and Nelson Ribeiro. "Revisiting Transnational Broadcasting: The BBC's Foreign-Language Services during the Second World War." *Media History* 21, no. 4 (2015): 365–77.

Sévigny, Jean-Pierre. "The Influence of Latin Music on the French-Canadian Popular Song and Dance Scene, Especially as Reflected in the Career of Alys Robi and the Pedagogy of Maurice Lacasse-Morenoff." Paper presented at the 1994 meeting of the International Association for the Study of Popular Music. Montreal: Productions Juke-Box, 1994.

Sevin, Efe, Emily T. Metzgar, and Craig Hayden. "The Scholarship of Public Diplomacy: Analysis of a Growing Field." *International Journal of Communication* 13 (2019): 4814–37.

Shaw, Lisa. *Tropical Travels: Brazilian Popular Performance, Transnational Encounters, and the Construction of Race*. Austin: University of Texas Press, 2018.

Shuker, Roy. *Popular Music: The Key Concepts*. 3rd ed. London: Routledge, 2002.

Siegel, Arthur. *Radio Canada International: History and Development*. Oakville, ON: Mosaic Press, 1996.

Skidmore, Thomas E. *Black Into White: Race and Nationality in Brazilian Thought*. Durham, NC: Duke University Press, 1993.

– *Brazil: Five Centuries of Change*. New York: Oxford University Press, 1999.

Smith, Allan. "From Guthrie to Greenberg: Canadian High Culture and the End of Empire." In *Canada and the End of Empire*, edited by Phillip Buckner, 206–15. Vancouver: UBC Press, 2005.

Smith, Andrew, and Kirsten Greer, "Monarchism, an Emerging Canadian Identity, and the 1866 British North American Trade Mission to the West Indies and Brazil." *Journal of Imperial and Commonwealth History* 44, no. 2 (2016): 214–40.

Smith, Joseph. *Brazil and the United States: Convergence and Divergence*. Athens: University of Georgia Press, 2010.

– *A History of Brazil, 1500–2000: Politics, Economy, Society, Diplomacy*. London: Pearson Education, 2002.

– *The United States and Latin America: A History of American Diplomacy, 1776–2000*. New York: Routledge, 2005.

Smith, Sarah E.K. "Art and the Invention of North America, 1985–2012." PhD dissertation, Queen's University, 2013.

Sousa, Marquilandes Borges de. *Rádio e propaganda política: Brasil e México sob a mira norte-americana durante a Segunda Guerra*. São Paulo: Annablume Editora, 2004.

Spooner, Kevin A. "'Awakening Africa': Race and Canadian Views of Decolonizing Africa." In *Dominion of Race: Rethinking Canada's International History*, edited by Laura Madokoro, Francine McKenzie, and David Meren, 206–27. Vancouver: UBC Press, 2017.

Stacey, C.P. *Canada and the Age of Conflict*, vol. 2, *1921–1948: The Mackenzie King Era*. Toronto: University of Toronto Press, 1982.

Stam, Robert, and Ella Shohat. *Race in Translation: Culture Wars around the Colonial Atlantic*. New York: New York University Press, 2012.

Steblin, Rita. "The Gender Stereotyping of Musical Instruments in the Western Tradition." *Canadian University Music Review* 16, no. 1 (1995): 128–44.

Stephens, L.A.D. *Information and Press Activities of the Department of External Affairs at Home and Abroad: A Study*. Ottawa: Department of External Affairs, 1967.

– *Study of Canadian Government Information Abroad, 1942–1972: The Development of the Information, Cultural and Academic Divisions, and their Policies*. Ottawa: Department of External Affairs, 1977.

Suppo, Hugo Rogélio. "La politique culturelle française au Brésil entre les années 1920–1950." PhD dissertation, Université Paris III – Sorbonne, 1992.

Surmont, Jean-Nicolas de. "Genèse de l'enquête ethnomusicologique collective au Canada français." In *Around and About Marius Barbeau: Modelling Twentieth-Century Culture*, edited by Lynda Jessup, Andrew Nurse, and Gordon E. Smith, 199–212. Gatineau, QC: Canadian Museum of Civilization, 2008.

Szczepanik, Petr. "On the Ethnography of Media Production: An Interview with Georgina Born." *Iluminace* 25, no. 3 (2013): 99–119.

Taylor, Timothy D. *Beyond Exoticism: Western Music and the World*. Durham, NC: Duke University Press, 2007.

Teigrob, Robert. *Warming Up to the Cold War: Canada and the United States' Coalition of the Willing, from Hiroshima to Korea*. Toronto: University of Toronto Press, 2009.

Tinhorão, José Ramos. *História social da música popular brasileira*. São Paulo: Editora 34, 1998.

Tippett, Maria. *Making Culture: English-Canadian Institutions and the Arts before the Massey Commission*. Toronto: University of Toronto Press, 1990.

Tota, Antonio Pedro. *O imperialismo sedutor: A americanização do Brasil na época da Segunda Guerra*. São Paulo: Companhia das Letras, 2000.

Touhey, Ryan M. *Conflicting Visions: Canada and India in the Cold War World, 1946–76*. Vancouver: UBC Press, 2015.

Trépanier, Esther. "Les paramètres épistémologiques et idéologiques d'un premier discours sur la modernité." In *Des lieux de mémoire: Identité et culture modernes au Québec, 1930–1960*, edited by Marie Carani, 29–41. Ottawa: Presses de l'Université d'Ottawa, 1995.

– *Peinture et modernité au Québec, 1919–1939*. Montreal: Éditions Nota bene, 1998.

Turino, Thomas. "Nationalism and Latin American Music: Selected Case Studies and Theoretical Considerations." *Latin American Music Review* 24, no. 2 (2003): 169–209.

– *Nationalists, Cosmopolitans, and Popular Music in Zimbabwe*. Chicago: University of Chicago Press, 2000.

Valiani, Salimah. "The Articulation of an Independent Foreign Policy: Canada and Latin America in the Early Twentieth Century." *Latin American Perspectives* 39, no. 6 (2012): 165–80.

Velloso, Mônica Pimenta. *Os intelectuais e a política cultural do Estado Novo*. Rio de Janeiro: Editora FGV, 1987.

Vianna, Hermano. *The Mystery of Samba: Popular Music and National Identity in Brazil*. Translated by John Charles Chasteen. Chapel Hill: University of North Carolina Press, 1999.

Viau, Guy. *Modern Painting in French Canada*. Quebec City: Department of Cultural Affairs, 1967.

Vidal, Laurent, and Tania Regina de Luca. "Les Français au Brésil: Enjeux historiographiques d'une présence oubliée." In *Les Français au Brésil*, edited by Laurent Vida and Tania Regina de Luca, 7–22. Paris: Les Indes savantes, 2016.

Vilela, Marie-Thérèse. "Les relations culturelles entre la France et le Brésil (1889–1930): Échange ou transfert?" In *Les échanges culturels internationaux: France, Brésil, Canada-Québec*, edited by Guy Martinière and Éric Monteiro, 95–122. Paris: Les Indes savantes, 2013.

Villanueva Rivas, César. "Theorizing Cultural Diplomacy All the Way Down: A Cosmopolitan Constructivist Discourse from an Ibero-American Perspective." *International Journal of Cultural Policy* 24, no. 5 (2018): 681–94.

Vipond, Mary. *Listening In: The First Decade of Canadian Broadcasting, 1922–1932*. Montreal and Kingston: McGill-Queen's University Press, 1992.

– "The Royal Tour of 1939 as a Media Event." *Canadian Journal of Communication* 35 (2010): 149–72.

Vizentini, Paulo Fagundes. *Relações exteriores do Brasil (1945–1964): O nacionalismo e a política externa independente*. Petrópolis, BR: Editora Vozes, 2004.

– *Relações internacioais do Brasil: De Vargas a Lula*. São Paulo: Editora Fundação Perseu Abramo, 2003.

Vorano, Norman. "Inuit Art: Canada's Soft Power Resource to Fight Communism." *Journal of Curatorial Studies* 5, no. 3 (2016): 313–38.

Vucetic, Srdjan. *The Anglosphere: A Genealogy of a Racialized Identity in International Relations*. Stanford, CA: Stanford University Press, 2011.

Wade, Peter. *Race and Ethnicity in Latin America*. London: Pluto Press, 1997.

Wagnleitner, Reinhold. *Coca-Colonization and the Cold War: The Cultural Mission of the United States in Austria after the Second World War*. Chapel Hill: University of North Carolina Press, 1994.

Waligorska, Magdalena. "Music and Imagined Communities. Articulations of the Self and the Other in the Musical Realm." *H-Net Reviews*, February 2012. http://www.h-net.org/reviews/showrev.php?id=35409.

Walker, Barrington, ed. *The African Canadian Legal Odyssey: Historical Essays*. Toronto: University of Toronto Press, 2017.

Warren, Jean-Philippe. *L'art vivant: Autour de Paul-Émile Borduas*. Montreal: Boréal, 2011.

Webb, Brandon. "'How to Raise a Curtain': Security, Surveillance, and Mobility in Canada's Cold War–Era Exchanges, 1955–65." *Cold War History* 21, no. 2 (2021): 215–33.

Webster, David. "'Red Indians' in Geneva, 'Papuan Headhunters' in New York: Race, Mental Maps, and Two Global Appeals in the 1920s and 1960s." In *Dominion of Race: Rethinking Canada's International History*, edited by Laura Madokoro, Francine McKenzie, and David Meren, 254–83. Vancouver: UBC Press, 2017.

– "Rethinking Religion's Role in Canadian Transnational Relations." In *Undiplomatic History: The New Study of Canada and the World*, edited by Asa McKercher and Philip Van Huizen, 76–103. Montreal and Kingston: McGill-Queen's University Press, 2019.

Weinstein, Barbara. *The Color of Modernity: São Paulo and the Making of Race and Nation in Brazil*. Durham, NC: Duke University Press, 2015.

Whitaker, Reg, Gregory S. Kealey, and Andrew Parnaby. *Secret Service: Political Policing in Canada from the Fenians to Fortress America*. Toronto: University of Toronto Press, 2012.

Whitaker, Reg, and Gary Marcuse. *Cold War Canada: The Making of a National Insecurity State, 1945–1957*. Toronto: University of Toronto Press, 1994.

Williams, Daryle. *Culture Wars in Brazil: The First Vargas Regime, 1930–1945*. Durham, NC: Duke University Press, 2001.

Williams, Margaret Todaro. "Church and State in Vargas's Brazil: The Politics of Cooperation." *Journal of Church and State* 18, no. 3 (1976): 443–62.

Wolfe, Patrick. "Settler Colonialism and the Elimination of the Native." *Journal of Genocide Research* 8, no. 4 (2006): 387–409.

– *Traces of History: Elementary Structures of Race*. New York: Verso, 2016.

Wright, Simon. *Villa-Lobos*. Oxford: Oxford University Press, 1992.

Wylie, Lana. *Perception of Cuba: Canadian and America Policies in Comparative Perspective*. Toronto: University of Toronto Press, 2010.

Young, Robert J.C. *Colonial Desire: Hybridity in Theory, Culture, and Race*. London: Routledge, 1995.

Zimmermann, Eduardo. "Intellectual Elites." In *The Palgrave Dictionary of Transnational History*, edited by Akira Iriye and Pierre-Ives Saunier, 547–50. New York: Palgrave Macmillan, 2009.

Zorbas, Jason. *Diefenbaker and Latin America: The Pursuit of Canadian Autonomy*. Newcastle upon Tyne, UK: Cambridge Scholars Publishing, 2011.

Zucchi, John. *Mad Flight? The Quebec Emigration to the Coffee Plantations of Brazil*. Montreal and Kingston: McGill-Queen's University Press, 2018.

# Index